Investing for Generations

Investing
for Generations
A History of Alliance Trust

Charles W. Munn

Dundee
University
Press

First published in
Great Britain in 2012 by
Dundee University Press
University of Dundee
Dundee DD1 4HN

http://www.dup.dundee.ac.uk/

ISBN: 978 1 84586 143 8

British Library Cataloguing-in-Publication Data
A catalogue record for this book is available
on request from the British Library

Typeset by Mark Blackadder

Printed and bound by TJ International Ltd, Padstow, Cornwall

Contents

Foreword

Over the 125 year history of Alliance Trust, it has survived wars, the great depression and other more recent financial crises through a combination of prudence and foresight born out of its roots in Dundee, where it remains firmly headquartered today. It would be wrong, however, to dismiss Alliance Trust as insular – from its earliest days it has searched the globe for opportunities to invest its shareholders' funds and this book records in detail the courage and determination of its employees over the years.

Today Alliance Trust retains these qualities and I have been struck by the commitment of everyone connected with the company. This is also true of our shareholders, whose close interest in our progress is welcome in an era of increasing intermediation and loss of contact between companies and their owners.

When we commissioned this history in 2008, we decided that the book should be both accurate and balanced, and for this reason Professor Charles Munn was given full access to our own extensive records. He also took full advantage of the opportunity to speak to current and past directors and employees. The outcome of his painstaking work is a book that truly captures the personalities of those who have shaped our company over the last 125 years and how they successfully overcame the many challenges that were faced along the way, as well as setting out the bare facts and figures. I commend this book to you.

Karin Forseke
Chairman
Alliance Trust PLC

Preface

In 1888 Dundee was a thriving city. Those who set Alliance Trust going were amongst its leading citizens. Investment in the jute business and in other industries continued at a high level, notwithstanding increased competition from other parts of the world. Profits were accumulating at a growing rate. The modest returns that investors could achieve from domestic investments or bank deposits encouraged many to seek outlets for their savings overseas in hopes of making a higher return. It was a risky endeavour and, for many, highly successful.

Alliance Trust was part of that wider movement of savers pooling their funds into trusts that could be managed as collective investments. The Scots played a disproportionately large role in this movement. From the outset, Alliance was one of the largest trusts and remains so today.

In writing its history I have drawn very largely on the company's own archives which have now been vested for cataloguing and safe keeping in the archives of the University of Dundee. In the interests of future historians I have also provided the University with a copy of all the notes that I made in preparing this volume. As there was no catalogue when I researched and wrote the book I have kept footnotes to a minimum, but hopefully have been sufficiently clear in the text as to where source material originated.

Charles Munn

Acknowledgements

In writing this book I have benefited from conversations and correspondence with a wide range of people.

I am especially grateful to W. Grant Lindsay, formerly Head of Equities, whose knowledge of the company, its people and its archives knows no rival. Not only did Grant guide my path, he also read and commented upon the text at various stages.

Professor Christopher Whatley, Vice-Principal of the University of Dundee and Professor of Scottish History read and commented upon the whole text. I have much cause to be grateful to him not just for his knowledge of Scottish history but for saving me from many infelicities of style.

Donald McPherson, Company Secretary, read and commented upon the more recent chapters. He has also been most helpful in guiding the project from its inception.

I have also incurred debts of gratitude to many members of the current board and staff of the company, including Richard Bowman, Sara Clark, Chris Dudek, Katherine Garrett-Cox, Evan Bruce-Gardyne, Iain Smith, Matthew Strachan and Neil Tong. I have also benefited from conversations, usually at the coffee machine, with many members of the investment department.

Similarly, many former members of the board and staff gave freely of their time to share their experiences and knowledge with me. These include Iris Black, Lyndon Bolton, Rob Burgess, Alan Harden, Alan Hunter, Lesley Knox, Sheila Ruckley, Sir Robert Smith, Gavin Suggett, Jenny Thorpe and Alan Young.

I have cause of be grateful to several others outside the company who were prepared to share their knowledge and insights with me. These include Ivor Guild, John Newlands, George Peden, Claire Swan and Ron Weir. I have drawn heavily on John Newlands' books on the history of other investment trusts.

To all of them I am grateful for giving so generously of their time and experience.

Charles W. Munn, May 2012

Chapter 1
Setting the Scene

The Alliance Trust was established in Dundee in 1888. It was created by local businessmen to invest their surplus earnings in American mortgages. It was to absorb the Dundee Mortgage and Trust Investment Co. Ltd and the Dundee Investment Co. Ltd. These companies had, themselves, taken over other investment companies, all of them Dundee-based, and all involved in lending money on mortgages in the western United States and in Canada. The first of these companies was the Oregon and Washington Trust Investment Co. Ltd, established in 1873.

From its inception, the Alliance Trust was one of the biggest investment companies in the United Kingdom. It remains so today.

The history of investment trusts in the United Kingdom began with the formation of the Foreign and Colonial in London in 1868, but the model for their future good governance emerged from the Scottish American Investment Trusts established by Robert Fleming in Dundee in 1873.

These events marked the beginnings of a great surge of investment, much of it directed overseas, which enabled savers to pool their resources and take advantage of the wealth of expertise in investment that had been building up over many years. Yet there was little that was new in the idea of investing surplus monies in overseas enterprises. As a maritime and trading nation the British had contacts and business connections in every part of the world. These were growing quickly as colonial ambitions during Queen Victoria's reign knew no bounds. The industrial revolution and urbanisation had made Britain the 'Workshop of the World' and, in the process, the migration of capital overseas had been a distinctive feature of these processes throughout the nineteenth century.

By the end of the Napoleonic Wars in 1815, Britain had become the world's major creditor nation and it remained so for the rest of the century. Capital was needed in the developing regions of the world for investment in the land and in capital-intensive industries like the railways. A major influencing factor in the flow of funds overseas was the fact that higher returns could be obtained than were achievable on most types of investment in the UK. Indeed between 1830 and 1914 the yield on consols (government stock) only rose above 3.5% on two occasions.[1] There is an abundance of evidence from contemporary comments that the UK had created a surplus of funds and that investors found it increasingly difficult to find high-earning outlets for their savings at home. Scotland, in particular, had experienced an enormous growth of wealth in the second and third quarters of the century and would become the locus for a large part of the UK's life assurance and investment trust industries. Deposits in Scottish commercial banks increased from £63m in 1870 to £92m in 1890, and £132m by 1914.[2] In 1879 the Scottish *Banking and Insurance Magazine* was able to write: 'It is well known that there is a superfluity of working capital in Scotland, or in other words that the public is in possession of more capital than can be safely and profitably employed . . . within the country.'[3]

The impression of Scotland as a wealthy country seems to be confirmed by a comparison of probate returns in the different parts of the United Kingdom (see Table 1.1).

Some years later the *North British Economist* took the view that 'bankers cannot now employ their money so profitably as was the case 10 years ago . . . Scotland has more money by far than is required within her own borders by

Table 1.1 The wealth of Scotland (from Probate records)[4]

Country	Millions sterling		£s per inhabitant	
	1840	1877	1840	1877
England	3,320	6,552	210	262
Scotland	196	970	81	277
Ireland	308	438	38	83
UK	3,824	7,960	147	239

1 J. Newlands, *Put Not Your Trust in Money*, London, 1997, p. 9.
2 S.G. Checkland, *Scottish Banking: A History 1695–1973*, Glasgow, 1975, Table 44, pp. 744–5.
3 *Scottish Banking and Insurance Magazine*, vol. 1, 1879, p. 282.
4 *North British Economist*. vol. 4, March 1882.

her own industries and trade, and her "savings" – fruit of her proverbial thrift – go on increasing year by year."[5]

By the mid nineteenth century the country's financial institutions were sufficiently mature as to make overseas investment a relatively simple matter. The banks, through their system of correspondents, were able to move money to any part of the world and, just as importantly, to move it back again. And there were other factors that helped to facilitate the international movement of money. Changes to UK company law made possible the creation of joint-stock limited liability companies in what was regarded as the most liberal company law in Europe. In Scotland the law was even more liberal than in the rest of the UK, as business organisations were recognised under common law. This made it straightforward for companies to be promoted that would bring savers together to pool their resources into joint investment activities. It was this pooling of the resources of ordinary savers in investment trusts which created a new dimension in overseas investment. Until then overseas investment had been conducted by institutions and by very wealthy individuals.

The major focus of British investment was the Americas – both North and South – and by the time that the first transcontinental railroad was opened to Sacramento, California in 1869 it was reckoned that foreign investment in the US, mostly British, amounted to £300m. The Civil War in the United States, which raged between 1861 and 1865, had interrupted the normal flow of investment but it had also focused attention on the country – especially as the demand for munitions and other necessities of war brought business opportunities to European suppliers. Producers of jute in Dundee were particularly well placed to profit from the war, as there was an enormous demand for sandbags, tents and wagon covers. With these opportunities came profits, a new range of business connections and an enhanced understanding of the country's need for capital investment. Wartime damage in the east, where much of the civil war had been fought, had to be repaired, but it was not long before the focus for investment turned west.

The shift of focus was helped by a wide range of pamphleteers and article writers who wrote glowing reports of the potential of the American West. Some of these people had actually been on the train to Sacramento, or had even been on the Oregon Trail in a covered wagon (covered, that is, with jute

---

5 *North British Economist*, vol. 12, 1890, p. 33.

from Dundee), while others happily copied what they had read elsewhere. One of the pamphleteers was William Reid, a Dundee lawyer who was also US vice-consul in Dundee. Whether he had ever been to the United States is uncertain, but he was certainly highly influential in setting up the Oregon and Washington Trust Investment Co. Ltd in Dundee in 1873 and, in the process, persuading leading Dundee businessmen to become involved – notwithstanding the fact that Robert Fleming was also busy establishing his investment trusts in the city at the same time.

There were two main sources of these funds. First were the savings of local people built up over generations. Second were the profits from economic activity that had grown substantially in the nineteenth century. The bulk of Dundee's wealth came from the jute industry that had grown from, and all but replaced, flax-spinning and weaving. Dundee was also a major world centre of the whaling industry and had a substantial shipbuilding and engineering capability. All four industries were dependent on international connections for their very being, and with that came knowledge and resources that were essential to the development of the investment trusts.

William J. Menzies, a solicitor who was also law agent for the Church of Scotland, established similar ventures to the Dundee trusts in Edinburgh in 1873 – notably the Scottish American Investment Co. Ltd. Menzies had made three trips to the United States. In 1872 bankers in New York and Chicago persuaded him that handsome profits were to be made by establishing an investment company to channel savings to the United States. He secured the commitment of several leading businessmen who became directors of his new company. It was the appearance of such names on the publicity for the new company that encouraged ordinary investors to commit their savings.

Robert Fleming in Dundee and William Menzies in Edinburgh had similar approaches to the nature, purpose and governance of their companies. They formed trusts whose sole purpose was to invest in securities – mostly railroad securities. During his visits to North America, Menzies had noted that 'the land under cultivation in America is almost wholly in the possession of small farmers, who are themselves the proprietors and to lend money to this class of subjects involves dealing in small amounts, delay in payment of interest and considerable trouble in collection'.[6] William Reid's approach to overseas investment was rather different. Despite its name, and despite what Menzies

---

6 Quoted in Newlands, *Put Not Your Trust*, p. 80.

thought, the Oregon and Washington Trust Investment Co. Ltd, the first forerunner of the Alliance Trust, was not an investment company at all, but a mortgage company.

America as a Field for Investment

The journey along the Oregon Trail from east to west of the United States took many months. But when the transcontinental railway opened in 1869 the journey time was reduced to several days. Yet few of the British travellers who ventured west in the early 1870s made the journey in one train. Their purpose was to see, and experience, the country, and the growing number of branch lines and feeder routes enabled them to do just that.

However, many of them recorded some disappointment at what they found. Nearly all '... were surprised to find a society quite different from that which they had expected and in almost every report there is the comment that Western America was something of a disappointment in that the bawdiness and rawness they had come to expect were missing'.[7]

In Denver, Colorado, for example, travellers commented on the broad streets, the fine public buildings and the number of sidewalks. They were duly impressed by the fact that the average male was likely to be dressed in black broadcloth rather than in the rough woollen pants and miners' boots which might have been the standard in earlier years.

Isabella Lucy Bird, who travelled there in 1873, commented that it had 'good shops, some factories, fair hotels and the usual deformities and refinements of civilisation'.[8]

Denver had become an entrepôt and distribution centre for a large mining and agricultural area and was described by one traveller as the 'most English City in America'.

John Leng, Dundee newspaperman and one of the founders of the Oregon and Washington Trust, travelled through North America in Centennial year, 1876. Along the way he visited Virginia City in Nevada and described it as a representative mining town where he saw nothing but 'the most perfect order

---

7 R.G. Athearn, *Westward the Briton: The Far West 1865–1900,* Lincoln, Nebraska, 1973, p. 7.
8 Quoted in Athearn, *Westward,* p. 41.

and decorum'.[9] He then travelled on to Sacramento and San Francisco where, rather than take the coach to Portland Oregon, he boarded a boat one Saturday morning and sailed to Astoria on the Columbia River, arriving on Monday afternoon.[10]

It seems clear that a desire for good order and social conformity had made great strides in the American West. This was undoubtedly healthy for business, and in 1883 when General W.T. Sherman made his final report to the secretary for war, he wrote that the West was now 'completely open in regions where a few years ago no single man could go with safety'.[11] He attributed this progress to three things: the presence of the army, the large number of settlers and the coming of the railway.

Travellers, mostly British, wrote accounts of great opportunities in many areas of business, but mainly in farming and mining and in their concomitant – land speculation. There was, however, a need for caution. Isabella Bird railed against the avariciousness she encountered in the Plains States. West of the Mississippi, she said, there was no other god than the almighty dollar. 'Sharp dealing was simply classified as "smartness" and a smart man was held up as an example to be imitated.'[12] Residents of the west usually had scant regard for the economic morals of easterners, but Edith Nicoll Bowyer, who lived in New Mexico for 20 years, wrote: 'The West railing against the East as the idolater of wealth, kneels in truth far nearer to the god's footstool, worshipping more blindly and ignorantly.'[13] Anyone travelling in the west would be asked on several occasions whether they were an investor or merely a traveller. If the answer was that they were an investor then they would be besieged by promoters of all kinds.

In 1892 William J. Menzies, WS, founder of the Scottish American Investment Co. Ltd, gave a lecture to the Chartered Accountants' Student Society in Edinburgh. By that time he had been involved in the investment business for 20 years and was widely acknowledged as an expert. The advice that he dispensed to the young accountants was both cautious and encouraging. His watchwords were care and scepticism. Investors should not believe

9 Athearn, *Westward*, pp. 42, 60.
10 J. Leng, *America in 1876 and Aspects of American Life*, Dundee, 1877.
11 Athearn, *Westward*, p. 11.
12 Quoted in Athearn, *Westward*, p. 93.
13 E.N. Bowyer, *Observations of a Ranchwoman in New Mexico*, London, 1898, p. 183

much of what they were told by vendors of investment opportunities. 'You may take it for granted . . . that if a security is offered in this country to pay a large rate of interest, there is some reason to be urged against it.' America, like all developing nations, he went on, suffers from a low moral code and 'there are temptations to haste to be rich'. And 'the temptation of amassing money by means which here would not be considered legitimate often prove greater than could be borne'.[14]

Having issued his warnings, Menzies moved on to a more positive and hopeful view of North America. He provided the students with statistics about the prodigious growth of American cities and about the output of its industry and agriculture. He took the view that states such as Texas, California and Oregon, and cities such as Portland were capable of considerable expansion and development. He believed that the land needed to be better managed and that wheat yields equivalent to those produced in the UK were possible in North America. This was where opportunity lay. America needed good farmers and hard workers and these men needed good financiers to back them.[15]

It was certainly a land of great promise, and many of those who wrote about it probably exaggerated its attractiveness. In 1883 James Aitken told his fellow Scots that their hope of a brighter future and redemption from a life of profitless toil 'lies in the fair and fertile fields of the West . . . as yet untouched by the industry of man'.[16] Blandishments such as these proved to be enormously popular, and there was much speculation about just how many people could be absorbed by the United States.

Nor was it was just the British and other Europeans who went to the United States in search of a better life. Large numbers of Canadians, estimated at two million, went south between 1867 and 1896, and it was not until the closing years of the nineteenth century that the population of Canada finally began to expand again.[17] It then did so at a prodigious rate – largely as a result of migration from Europe.

North America needed people and capital, and northern Europe, especially the UK, supplied much of the demand. The outpourings from numerous British writers created a largely positive picture that encouraged

---

14 W.J. Menzies, *America as a Field for Investment*, Edinburgh, 1892, pp. 18–21.

15 Menzies, *America*, 1892, p. 10.

16 J. Aitken, *From the Clyde to California with Jottings by the Way*, Greenock, 1882, p. 152.

17 R. Bothwell, *The Penguin History of Canada*, Toronto, 2006, p. 218.

people to contemplate investing their money in the United States and Canada. High interest rates were an additional factor in their calculations. It only remained to find a vehicle through which their savings could be channelled. The investment trusts were the answer, and there were plenty of organisations in North America and elsewhere that were proactive in seeking savings from the UK and in forging business partnerships with the trusts. Scotland was ripe for this purpose. As the *North British Economist* observed in 1890, 'Our own advertising columns and those of the whole Scottish press, proclaim Scotland a happy hunting ground for money.'[18]

Foremost amongst the American companies that advertised for money in Scotland were Underwood, Clark and Co. in Kansas City and Smith and Hannaman in Indianapolis. Both were to become associated with the Alliance Trust.

---

18 *North British Economist*, vol. 12, 1990, p. 33.

Chapter 2
Before the Alliance: 1873–1889

The years between 1873 and 1889 were years of experimentation. These were the times when the businessmen who established the Alliance Trust discovered how to run their new businesses. Through years of economic difficulty they toiled to stick to their original business model but had the flexibility of mind to adjust it when local circumstances deemed it prudent. It was a period of great change in the economies of many parts of the world. The United States, with the Civil War behind it and the Indian wars almost concluded, was ripe for development and badly in need of capital. Much of money that was required came from the United Kingdom and was channelled through the financial centres of London and Edinburgh. But there was a third source – the small Scottish east coast city of Dundee.

The Oregon and Washington Trust Investment Company Ltd

The inaugural meeting of subscribers to the Oregon and Washington Trust Investment Company Ltd took place in Dundee on 7 October 1873. Eighteen men attended, including leading Dundee businessmen William Lowson and Thomas Cox. Also in attendance were the newspaperman, John Leng, and the lawyers James Pattullo and Thomas Thornton. The purpose for which the company was founded was to lend money on mortgages on which interest of between 10% and 12% would be charged. This was a normal rate for loans in the western United States at that time and would not have been thought of as excessive. Interest rates in the east and midwest were only a little lower.

It is clear from the speed at which matters moved forward from this date that a great deal of preparatory work had already been undertaken. A draft memorandum and articles of association had been prepared. The documents were gone over, adjusted and approved. William Lowson, who chaired the meeting, then ordered that the company should be registered 'with all despatch'. At the same meeting a draft of an agreement with Alonzo Cook was agreed, subject to the discretion of the directors. He was present at the meeting. An American by birth, Cook had trained as a lawyer in Ohio. He was to be the company's agent in Portland, Oregon.

The meeting went on to appoint the following men as the first board of directors:

Rt Hon. the Earl of Airlie
William Lowson
Thomas Bell
James Neish
Thomas Cox
John Leng
Thomas Couper

The 8th Earl of Airlie was well connected in the business world and had travelled widely in North America. He was also the current Lord High Commissioner to the General Assembly of the Church of Scotland. Lowson, Bell, Neish and Cox were all jute magnates, while John Leng was chairman and Thomas Couper was manager of the Dundee, Perth and London Shipping Company. Leng was also editor and publisher of the *Dundee Advertiser*. Local lawyers, Messrs Pattullo and Thornton, were appointed to be solicitors to the company. All that remained to be done before the company could commence business was to have it registered, appoint a secretary and establish a registered office. These matters were left in the hands of the directors.

The legal process of registering the company under the Companies Acts of 1862 and 1867 was completed on 16 October, and the directors met the following day to attend to business. Airlie was elected chairman of the company. The man appointed to be company secretary was William Reid. He was a law graduate of Glasgow University but his family roots were firmly in the east of Scotland. He was practising as a solicitor in Dundee and he also held the post of vice-consul for the United States of America. He was to be extremely influential in the development of the company, but ultimately he fell out of favour. Reid's office was at 81 Murraygate, and this became the registered office of the company. He was instructed to purchase a seal for the company, the first use for which was to formalise the contract given to Alonzo Cook who had, by this time, returned to the United States.

The next stage was to deal with the detail. A subcommittee of Cox, Lowson and Bell was appointed with instructions to make 'financial arrangements for the transmission to Portland, and the payment and receipt of money there, insurances, a local board and all other matters of detail'. It was also agreed that, of the authorised capital of £150,000, the subscribed capital was to be £50,000 and the solicitors and secretary were instructed to receive applications for shares up to that amount.

The subcommittee set to work, assisted by Thornton and Reid. Their priority was to devise methods of working which would make it easy both to do business and protect the assets of the company. They met on 23 October and agreed that all money should be remitted to Portland by the Royal Bank of Scotland using bills of exchange drawn on its London office. These bills were to be payable to the Bank of British North America, a London registered bank, which was to be the company's banker in the United States. (They were much less explicit about how money was to be remitted home. The matter was left for future consideration by the directors.) They also decided that cheques could only be drawn on the Portland account for sums equivalent to the mortgages that they had approved.

A local board was to be appointed in Portland. Ex-governor of Oregon, Addison Gibbs and local merchant John McCracken were asked to serve. They were authorised to approve applications for loans up to $1,000 and, in aggregate, not more than $5,000 without permission from Dundee. They would work closely with Alonzo Cook, whose appointment was confirmed. Cook was told to submit a monthly report and accounts. He was not to keep cash on hand but to pay it all into the bank account. The Bank of British North America was also expected to submit a monthly account to Dundee, and the comparison of the two reports would enable the directors to check the accuracy of the book-keeping and the safety of their funds.

Before a new mortgage could be approved by the board of directors in Dundee, it had to have both the recommendation of the local board and a dossier with full information about the land that was to be mortgaged, including a proper valuation of the property. Two local valuers were to undertake the valuations. Cook, who had been resident in the city of Vancouver, Washington Territory (just across the state line from Portland, Oregon) would not be paid a salary, but he would receive all legal and profes-sional charges plus two-thirds of the commission payable by the borrowers on receipt of the loans (such commission was never to exceed 2%). He would also receive $50 for rent of an office and 0.5% on all the interest collected. He was expected to go and inspect the lands that were to be mortgaged and also ensure that the mortgagee had a good legal title. In all Cook was given 25 instructions about what he was to do and the standards by which he was to conduct business. All this reflected the directors' understanding of the business into which they were entering and their realisation of the pitfalls into which they might stumble.

Cook was told that the directors preferred mortgages on prairie land in the Willamette Valley. These were 'the most saleable and reproductive lands'. No application would be entertained on places beyond Seattle, on Puget Sound nor further east than Cascade City, nor further south than Roseburg. Lands offered should be within ten miles of a railway or navigable river or within ten miles of a town of at least 800 inhabitants.

Applications for mortgages over property in towns were less favoured and were only to be entertained from Portland, Salem, Albany, Vancouver, Olympia, Tacoma, Walla-Walla, Astoria and Seattle. No applications for loans were to be considered if the security offered was wharfs, grain stores, factories, sawmills, woollen mills, flouring mills, tanneries, oil works, sash and door factories, 'being hazardous risks and fluctuating in value'. Mineral values were not to be considered. No loans were to be made on land that was only timber. Loans on 'improving' lands were only to be made if the land was at least one-third cleared, under cultivation or ready for the plough.

Mortgages were to be recorded with the county recorder, the clerk of the district court and the county treasurer. Insurance was to be taken out, preferably with the Imperial Fire Insurance Company Ltd. British insurance companies were to be preferred to American. All mortgages were to be taken out in the name of the directors in Dundee rather than in the name of the company. This last point was a caution, as it was by no means clear what the legal position was in relation to a British company doing business in the United States. This was a situation which was to bedevil British investment and mortgage companies for many years to come as individual states passed laws which placed legal requirements or inhibitions on the activities of 'foreign corporations' and then Congress passed a similar law to cover those territories, such as Washington, which had not yet gained statehood. These were the so called Alien Acts. The solution, untidy as it was, was to register the mortgages in the names of two or more of the directors of the company.

With all of that in place the company was ready to commence business. But despite the initial haste to get the company registered there was now no pressure for it to commence operations. A serious commercial crisis, which began in the United States, and was caused by over-speculation in railways and a sharp decline in the demand for silver, had percolated to the United Kingdom, bringing uncertainty and heightened caution. Moreover a fire had destroyed much of the city centre in Portland, creating confusion. It also created opportunities for a mortgage company, like Oregon and Washington, as the city was rebuilt over the next few years.

The first annual meeting of shareholders took place in Dundee on 14 January 1874; only 18 shareholders bothered to attend. They were told that the commercial crisis had prevented the company from starting business, but as order had now been restored in the foreign exchange markets it was likely that the first call on shareholders would soon be made. Meanwhile Cook had sent reports from Portland saying that demand for loans was high and that he could easily place £25,000 at 12–13% interest.

Business at the meeting was formal. The shareholders received a report from the directors. Robert Moody Stewart, CA, was appointed auditor and the directors were given powers to borrow under article 72 of the memorandum and articles of association.

The directors met immediately after the annual meeting. Their first act was to confirm Airlie as chairman. He became the kind of chairman who took a deep interest in the affairs of the company, but he was a man of many interests who spent a great deal of time travelling, especially in North America. So Lowson was called to the chair at the 4 February meeting and he was formally appointed to be deputy chairman later that month.

The first call on shareholders was £2 10s (£2.50) and it was payable at the Royal Bank on 2 March. A cash account (overdraft) was to be negotiated with the bank which would allow borrowing up to £10,000, and debentures were to be issued to the public which would raise up to £12,500. These were to be issued to pay 5% interest on 2-year loans, 5.5% for 3–4 years and 6% for 5–7 years.

In late February 1874 the directors were sufficiently confident of the prospects for the company that they decided to issue more capital. Only £50,000 of the authorised capital of £150,000 had been subscribed, and it was now decided to issue a further £100,000 on the understanding that only one third of the total would be called up – 'the uncalled up balance to remain as security to the Company's bankers and Debenture holders for the purpose of strengthening the Company's credit'. This was an important point, as the people who lent money to the company – the bankers and debenture holders – considered that the liability of shareholders for the payment of the uncalled capital was their primary security for their loans to the company. In times of difficulty the uncalled capital could be called up and the money thus raised would be used to pay the company's creditors, i.e. the debenture holders and the bank.

The Royal Bank cavilled at the cash account terms as they did not have a guarantee that the directors would not call up the uncalled capital. The directors offered the assurance that they would not. The bank was not satisfied and insisted on the personal guarantees of the directors who, in turn, declined to give it, as money was coming in from the new share issue and the borrowings from the bank were no longer necessary.

The new share issue was highly successful. Existing shareholders were given preference in subscribing, and by early March 1874 all but £3,000 had been subscribed and this was taken up the following month.

Debenture issuing was equally successful. Debentures were essentially bonds of the company and could be issued at any time. The primary source of this money was local solicitors who were investing on behalf of their clients. An advertisement was sent around their offices before being published in the *Dundee Advertiser, Dundee Courier* and the *Perthshire Advertiser*. Almost £6,000 was raised by March 1874, and money came in steadily thereafter. Such was the confidence in the new venture that Leng persuaded his fellow directors to apply for a listing of their shares on the London Stock Exchange.

By then Reid had bought office furniture and mounted a brass plate on the door at 81 Murraygate. They were ready to commence business. The first loan was to Henry Edward Ankeny who had arrived in Oregon in a wagon train as a six-year-old boy in 1850. He had become a wealthy farmer with many other business interests. He applied for a loan of $12,000 over two years at 12% interest. The duration of this loan and the interest rate charged became the standard.

As time went on it was debentures, rather than share capital, that became the major source of company funds. And as most of these were taken up for periods ranging from two to three years there was a good match with the loans that were for similar periods of time. Reid was authorised to transfer £3,000 to Portland to meet Ankeny's loan and to provide the local board with its discretionary money of $5,000.

Lowson, Cox, Bell and Reid had been appointed as a finance committee, and it fell to them to review all lending applications. They were busy, and it was clear that the company was off to a good start. Five applications were approved in April 1874 and it was agreed that, as soon as approval was given, Reid would send a telegram to Portland. Otherwise correspondence went in the mail, which could take in excess of two weeks to arrive. The local board was discouraged from undertaking too much advertising as the Dundee board had 'no doubt that the advantages offered by the company will be fully appreciated now that they have been announced'.

The directors continued to give careful thought to how to manage the business. Safety and security were their prime concerns. Caution was required, and the company was no more than a few months old when it became evident that the original instructions about loan proposals were not being observed. As a result some loans were restricted to smaller amounts than had been requested. Lending principles were restated to Cook and the local board. Reid was told what book-keeping was required. The Bank of British Columbia, which had superseded the Bank of British North America in the company's favour, was given instructions about cheques and other documents passing through their hands. They declined to accept the responsibility required by Dundee, and Airlie's solution was to have documents in transit insured. The bank had been helpful in other ways and had offered to remit money to Portland from its London office at a more favourable rate than that offered by the Royal Bank – an offer that was accepted.

Airlie's view was that, now the company was underway, someone from Dundee should visit Portland to view the business close up and to gather commercially useful information. None of the directors were likely to be able to go so he had asked Reid, who had agreed. This may have been the chance that Reid was waiting for. As United States vice-consul in Dundee he clearly had a great interest in the country. He had also written a pamphlet about the virtues of investing in Portland, apparently without ever having been there. And, as events unfolded, his latent entrepreneurial talents were put to full use in Oregon.

Reid was given very broad instructions about what he was to do in Portland and Washington. There was still uncertainty about the rights of foreign corporations to do business there, and Reid was instructed to find out what he could and to report to Dundee. He was expected to meet state officials and representatives of other companies, including the Bank of British Columbia, that were doing business there. He was also to acquire maps and other printed information.

While in Portland Reid became a member of the local board with his own telegraphic address. This suggests that the directors in Dundee saw him in the role of an inspector and not just as a gatherer of market information. With his own telegraphic address he would be able to report to Dundee in confidence.

There were signs, in the loan applications coming from Portland, that Reid's mission was well timed. Despite the board having restated its original lending instructions, applications were still being made which were outwith the lending limits.

Cook's letter to Dundee, dated 30 March, gave the first indication that Reid's appointment in Portland might be permanent. Cook was not happy. Meanwhile arrangements had been made for John McCracken, a member of the local board, to visit Dundee, and his visit was eagerly anticipated. The directors wanted to talk to him about the relationship between Cook and Reid. By the time he arrived in August, Cook was off work due to ill health. He resigned that same month. It seems likely that this may have been a diplomatic illness, as he had purchased a tract of land in California on which he was to found the settlement of Garden Grove. Reid was later appointed to be manager of the Portland office in his place.

Meanwhile he had been busy. He had rented offices for the company in H.E. Ankeny's office building. He had secured legal opinion from Chief Justice Shattock about the legality of the company's operations and had been assured that all was well. He had also persuaded Shattock to act as an adviser to the local board. Somewhat to the directors' surprise he had announced that mortgages could be repaid in instalments. This proved to be very popular with borrowers, but the fact that he had acted independently of his board was a harbinger of troubles ahead. He had strong expansionist instincts and was keen to open a savings bank. His directors told him that the time was not right as the Hibernian Savings and Loan Company had recently established an office in Portland, and this would serve the need for a savings institution in the city.

McCracken greatly impressed the board during his visit to Dundee in the summer of 1874, and they learned a great deal from him about local business conditions in Oregon. They also had a visit from Thomas Macleay, originally from the Scottish Highlands, of Macleay and Corbett, shipowners in Portland. The ability to gain information from people like these was critical to an organisation doing business so far from home. To this end they had also taken out subscriptions to the Oregon newspapers.

Lending had already reached $112,000, but in what seems to have been a clear breach of instructions, a loan had been made on the security of the Salem Opera House. Getting adequate insurance over the property and its contents created a major headache. There followed a restatement of the operating principles. Lending was to be 'safe, unchallengeable and reasonably remunerative'. The valuers of property were to be men of virtue and not friends of the borrowers. Above all, the directors wanted to avoid having 'to put the law in operation against defaulting borrowers'. Nor did they want to finance land speculators, who were a major problem in Oregon. They wanted to assist 'honest and industrious settlers'. They were shy of lending to sawmills and other manufactories 'but by our lending on first class farm lands and town lots we shall cause more local money to be available for such works under local guidance and knowledge'. In effect their lending on good security released the personal resources of local people for riskier projects where local knowledge was at a premium.

The directors seemed glad to have Reid in Oregon. Their correspondence with him was extensive and positive. When he was appointed manager it was realised that his duties would not take up his whole time. Consequently he was told that he was free to take up other responsibilities provided that they did not interfere with his primary duties to the company. He was also told that, notwithstanding he had rented offices that the company would occupy, he was to be personally responsible for the rent and other costs. Cook's departure and Reid's appointment was also an opportunity to change the local board. Gibbs resigned to become the company's law agent, and Bernard Goldsmith and Judge Shattock became local directors. Goldsmith was a former mayor of Portland. Shattock's term was short-lived as he became a Supreme Court judge in Oregon and had to resign.

Before the end of the year the tone had changed. The directors were not entirely happy about Reid's introduction of mortgage repayment by instalments. The nature of their correspondence with him became much less friendly and more directional. There were also concerns about Reid's paperwork, as some of the application forms that reached Dundee were incomplete. Perhaps the board had been too hasty in advising him that he was at liberty to become involved in other activities.

It was now evident that Reid would remain in Portland, and this created a gap in Dundee. Walter Baxter, who had deputised for him, was thanked for his services, and the job of secretary was given to William Mackenzie, a local stockbroker. It was also necessary to get a new office and, as Mackenzie already occupied offices at 6 Panmure Street, Dundee, that is where the company went.

Relations between Mackenzie and Reid were always polite but never very friendly. Although Reid was praised for his diligence in getting payment for the interest notes on mortgages, he was also criticised for his sloppy administration. Moreover there was a worry for the board that Reid had been party to an article in the local Portland paper in which he had said that loans by instalments were available at 10%. He was told that he had been 'hasty and precipitate' and that he should have talked to his local board about this, who should then have communicated their thoughts to Dundee. More fundamentally they were worried that Reid's actions could upset their business model. 'The calculation of working profit on which the shareholders were induced to invest their money may be found only to have led them astray.' They did not really believe Reid when he said that loans at 12% were impossible to make and that Oregon money was being moved to California. They decided to make loans at 11% until such times as they discovered that there was no demand at this rate. In February 1875 Reid was given a warning about not exceeding his powers.

There was also a problem with the duration of loans. Reid had been giving the impression that it might be possible to borrow for periods up to 12 years. The view of the directors was that this was far too risky as it was not possible to see so far into the future. Nor was it possible for them to issue debentures for such a lengthy period to cover the advances. Normal practice was to match the duration of the loans with debentures of a similar number of years. Nevertheless, within months, Reid's view of the business had proved to be correct. Interest rates were moving downwards and a trial of his scheme for making a few longer-term loans at 10% was begun.

The directors in Dundee also took a strong line with the local board, and when it was learned that McCracken had refused to take up the shares he had been allotted in the company because he could use the money more profitably in his own company, he was asked to resign. Donald Macleay, a Scot who hailed originally from Ross-shire, soon took his place. Macleay was a leading businessman in Portland with interests in a wide variety of businesses. Macleay and Reid became close collaborators in a number of ventures. The local board was then issued with instructions about how often it should meet – monthly – and what kind of records it should keep.

Despite the name of the company, the directors had always been somewhat cautious about lending money in Washington Territory. Goldsmith had warned them against it. Reid went ahead and appointed John Wheat as agent in the Territory. The directors told him that he had no authority for doing so but went on to homologate his action.

At the half-yearly meeting of shareholders in Lamb's Temperance Hotel, Reform Street, Dundee, which took place on 25 September 1874, the board gained powers to invest in securities other than mortgages. This was uncontroversial as it was necessary to keep any surplus capital in interest-earning securities that could be sold as lending opportunities arose or when cash was needed. Shareholders also learned that mortgages amounted to $111,827 (about £22,900) based on capital of £23,604 and debentures of £6,200.

In March 1875 Reid was paid £339 10s (£339.50) for his services to the company since its inception. But there were mounting concerns about his efficiency and his activities. He was discovered to have been lending without authority and failing to keep his records up to date. At one stage the directors placed a hold on new lending until he caught up. He was told to write weekly, and his letters had to coincide with the arrival of the Oregon newspapers in Dundee.

From time to time the directors referred to their 'anxiety' at Reid's actions and, occasionally, they felt the need to clarify or deny his statements. At one point he was found not to have been inspecting some of the properties on which loans were to be made – even those close to Portland. At another time it was necessary to clarify to borrowers in Washington that instalments on loans could not be repaid at the borrowers' option but could only be made in accordance with the terms of the mortgage. An article by Reid in the local press had given the opposite impression. Despite this he was given permission to become involved in setting up the Portland Board of Trade, and he served as its secretary for several years. Doubtless the prospect of business opportunities that could come from such a connection outweighed more general concerns about Reid's book-keeping. Nevertheless the board was sufficiently concerned about him to insist that he sign a bond of fidelity for £3,000. However, when they learned that the premium to be charged by the Guarantee Association of Scotland was quite high they hastily reduced the amount of the required bond to £2,000.

Nor were matters going well with the local board. The increasing strictures placed on Reid by the directors in Dundee sometimes impacted on them, and in June 1875 they telegraphed Dundee to say: 'Directors respectfully intimate unless greater confidence exhibited in ourselves prefer resigning.' They had gained the impression that they were being expected to supervise Reid on a routine basis and were assured that that had never been the intention. Perhaps it should have been. They were also upset about changes to the banking arrangements that had been made in Portland without their having been consulted. They were soon placated – perhaps by the revelation that they were to be paid $150–$200 per annum. Some months later their lending powers were extended when they were advised that they could lend up to $7,000 without reference to Dundee.

Nevertheless many of these early problems can be ascribed to teething troubles and the difficulties involved in establishing such a unique business with modest communication channels stretching over 6,000 miles. At the annual meeting in March 1875 the directors felt sufficiently confident of performance and prospects to declare a dividend of 6%. This was despite the fact that the price of wheat had fallen and farmers in Oregon were under pressure. The mortgage book had grown to $157,000 and all interest due in December had been collected. The average sum advanced was 35% of the appraised value of the land so there was an ample margin of security. Indeed the stability of the company was further strengthened the following month when Airlie wrote to say that the surplus funds should be invested in first-class American railroad securities which could be sold quickly should the need arise. The directors acted quickly and had soon invested over £4,000 in mortgage bonds of the Philadelphia and Reading Railroad Company, Central New Jersey Railroad Company, Central Pacific Railroad Company and several others.

At the half-yearly meeting in September a further dividend of 6% was declared. The mortgage book had almost doubled in six months and now stood at $316,613. The shareholders were told that borrowers had been paying their interest and instalments with 'promptitude' despite the low price of wheat. They learned that the state of Oregon 'has probably been tested in the last year as severely as it will be for some time to come'. They were further encouraged in the knowledge that migration to Oregon was increasing and there was a good prospect of getting a direct rail connection with the east. The shareholders were sufficiently impressed that they voted £250 in remuneration to the directors. The division of this money was made at Airlie's suggestion. He wrote to propose that Lowson should get one quarter and the others should share the rest equally. This was agreed.

Reid continued his erratic ways. In December 1875 his administrative work was falling behind and he was told to get it up to date. But in the same communication he was given permission to become manager in a new savings bank that was to be established in Portland. This seems to have been a paradoxical decision given the tremendous growth that was taking place in the company's business at that time. Reid must have been under considerable pressure. However, this does not seem to have deterred him from writing lengthy letters. In a telegram headed 'Prolix communications' they wrote: 'The Directors earnestly urge Mr Reid to condense his communications to them so far as can be done consistently with conveying briefly and clearly the information which it is necessary to submit.' Perhaps he was trying to conceal his intentions and actions behind a torrent of words.

His intentions were perfectly clear when Gibbs resigned as the company's attorney in Portland and Reid proposed that the role of manager and attorney should be combined in himself. He was given an emphatic rejection, and the role of attorney eventually fell to Ellis T. Hughes, who had been Gibbs' partner in his law firm.

All this kept the directors in Dundee very busy. The board meetings were taken up with listing the communications received, authorising cheque payments, accepting and issuing debentures. There was also a certain amount of vetting of new shareholders. The directors understood that if the uncalled part of the ordinary share capital was to stand as security for debenture holders then the shareholders had to be people who were likely to be able to pay the calls if required to do so. A few were rejected, but there was no doubt about Robert Fleming when he purchased shares in September 1875. Fleming was the Dundee-based founder of the Scottish American Investment Trusts. He would become a good friend to the company and a source of sound advice over many years. Two months after he first acquired shares he advised the purchase of bonds of the Union Pacific Railroad. The purchase was authorised and made through his firm.

The original directors were still in place, although in September 1875, John Leng intimated his intention to resign due to pressure of business. He was persuaded to withdraw his resignation. Perhaps the real pressure came from a trip that he proposed to make to the United States in 1876 – Centennial year. As the railway system in North America expanded, travel became much easier. Spurred by their senses of adventure and curiosity, the number of businessmen and travellers who ventured there grew substantially. Airlie had made many trips, and he wrote to Lowson in February 1876 to propose that a new company should be formed to invest in parts of North America from which the Oregon and Washington Trust was precluded. The proposal was considered but no decision was made. It was a proposal that would be considered again. They did not wait for long.

The third annual meeting took place in Lamb's Temperance Hotel, Reform Street, Dundee on 7 March 1876. There were 28 gentlemen present. Most of the business was formal. Minor amendments to the memorandum and articles of association were approved, and the shareholders learned that the directors, having paid off all the foundation expenses, were recommending a final dividend of 7%. They also learned that the directors were planning some expansion. They felt that the company could do more in Oregon and Washington, but 'At the same time and on the ground that on general principles a division of risk is always prudent they think it well worthy of consideration whether fields not as yet occupied by this company should not be opened up.'

The proposal was to set up a new company under the same management. For the time being it would not replace the Oregon and WashingtonTrust Investment Company Ltd. The lawyer, Thomas Thornton, was invited to a subsequent meeting of the board and asked to prepare a prospectus for the new company that would be called the Dundee Mortgage and Trust Investment Company Ltd.

Meanwhile the business of the Oregon and Washington Trust Investment Company continued as before. Reid again provided unwelcome news when it was discovered that he had been issuing mortgages with an option to repay on giving four months' notice. This was a surprise to the directors, and they were aware that if interest rates fell then existing borrowers would exercise their right to repay and then negotiate loans at lower rates. Faced with this situation they could do nothing but re-state Reid's duties, which they did in April 1876. At the same time they made it clear that 'it is from no distrust of his perfect integrity that they resolve as above but simply because it is absolutely necessary that the company's business should in all respects be conducted formally and systematically'. Clearly some trust remained, and there was certainly an appreciation that Reid had put a great deal of effort into getting the company off to such a good start. Moreover it would have been difficult to find a suitable replacement.

Nevertheless the blandishments of the directors made little difference to Reid, whose relationship with Mackenzie in Dundee remained strained. Reid had to be reminded that Mackenzie's letters 'convey the wishes of the Directors and are to be accepted . . . as reflecting their voice'. Increasingly the letters assumed an instructive, even a pedantic, tone. Reid believed that the directors were hostile to his involvement in setting up the savings bank. He was assured that this was not the case but told that he was to have no other business involvements. When he asked for a pay rise it was given without hesitation.

The local board continued to perform well and was complimented on its good work. At one stage Goldsmith indicated that he wished to resign, but a personal intervention from Leng during his visit to Portland persuaded him to remain. Macleay came up with the idea that a full-time inspector and valuer should be appointed, such was the growth in applications for loans. There was frustration, too, that some potential borrowers withdrew their applications after considerable expense had been incurred in valuing the property. The local board wrestled with the idea that they should charge an application fee but decided not to for fear that they might fall foul of local usury laws.

Applications for loans continued to come in at a healthy rate. At a board meeting on 15 August 1876 loans were approved at rates of interest varying between 10 and 12%. There is nothing in the minutes to suggest that the differing rates reflected the relative risks in the lending, although there is a hint that rates for loans in Washington Territory were slightly higher than in Oregon State. It seems more likely that they were simply charging what their rather dispersed markets would bear.

When Leng was in Oregon in the summer and autumn of 1876 he carried with him a power of attorney that authorised him to act on behalf of the Dundee board. His powers were quite draconian and authorised him to take 'prompt and authoritative action'. He was extremely diligent and wrote home once or twice per day. But his letters were 'satisfactory and encouraging', so his more extreme powers were left in abeyance. In exercising his lending authority he approved new loans totalling $100,000 so that by November of that year the total lent by the Portland office was $585,620. Overdue interest amounted to only $1,925. Notwithstanding that some of the early loans were maturing and being repaid, the demand for money was growing fast, and a further call on shareholders was made in the summer of 1876. There was also quite an active market in the shares with many being taken up by the directors themselves.

It was clear that the company was off to a good start. Despite Reid's erratic ways the business was growing well. Indeed there can be no doubt that he had the company's interests, as well as his own, at heart. A further interim dividend of 8% was declared in August 1876 and there was confidence that better was to follow. Thought had also been given to the need for more space for the Dundee office, and in April 1876 Lowson, Cox and Leng were appointed as a committee to find new premises. They looked across the road and moved into two front-room offices at 13 Panmure Street in the summer. A five-year lease was taken at £65 per annum.

Leng was welcomed back from America in November 1876 and his report prompted action. The local board were complimented on their diligence, and their lending powers were further extended. Reid was given a pay rise to $200 per month and a bonus, but he was told very clearly that he was to confine himself to the work of 'this company and the savings bank'. His salary was later restricted to $180, apparently at his own request, but he was also to receive a commission on new loans.

Early in 1877 Reid was thinking very seriously about the need for a building in Portland. His special concern was for the savings bank that he had set up and was now running, but it was faultless logic to think that the Trust would share the building and the building costs. At first this logic was shared by everyone, and Thornton even gave his approval, but Mackenzie believed that it was outwith the powers of the Trust to become involved in building projects. Eventually Reid agreed that the bank would bear the whole cost of building. Before that happened, however, things got quite heated and Macleay threatened to resign from the local board. Littlejohn, who was the Dundee-based secretary of the bank weighed in. Feelings were running high, and it was eventually agreed that the Trust would put up its half share of the money required but ownership would have to be registered in the names of the directors – Lowson, Leng and Cox.

No sooner had that furore died down than another arose. Reid had pursued a debtor in the courts and lost. He had acted entirely without instructions from Dundee. When the directors discovered what had happened they sent clear orders that he was not to proceed against anyone in the courts without their permission. Moreover he was to do all in his power to keep the Trust out of the courts, even in bankruptcy cases where the directors in Dundee were happy to accept a voluntary settlement. The directors feared that involvement in court cases was bad for the Trust's image and might cause the public to distrust it. Reid was further instructed not to lend to religious or charitable organisations, as the damage to the Trust's reputation would be enormous if foreclosure proved to be necessary.

Most lending, however, was achieved without difficulty, and by the time of the annual meeting in March 1877 there were 263 mortgages outstanding at $654,299. The local board valued the security for these at $1,886,690. Later that year lending was authorised in Washington Territory in a town called Puyallup – a newly established community thirty miles south of Seattle, set up by Ezra Meeker, who went on to gain fame as the historian and champion of the Oregon Trail.

To help finance this expansion of lending a new issue of shares was announced at the annual meeting in 1877. There was also a continuing emphasis on debentures which, by this stage, totalled £108,656 (About $530,000). The new shares were launched as a rights issue and were immediately taken up. Because of the fixed relationship between debentures and shares it was necessary to increase the share capital before new debentures could be raised. Good progress was also made in adding to the reserve, but at the beginning of 1878 it was decided to sell US government securities and purchase Royal Bank of Scotland stock. It was not a good year to be buying bank stock of any kind, as the failure of the City of Glasgow Bank in October created a commercial crisis and a serious reduction in the price of all bank shares.

A final dividend of 10% was paid, making 20% in all for the 1877 business year. The shareholders were sufficiently impressed to vote £500 to be shared amongst the directors. It had been a good year in Oregon. The harvest was much better than in the preceding year and the directors also noted that, 'The canning of preserved salmon on the Columbia River has also developed into a large and profitable business.' Rising fast to prominence amongst the canners was John West, originally from Linlithgow, who had established his first canning factory in 1868.

Yet just as things were going well the Oregon legislature passed an act which allowed local borrowers to deduct their indebtedness from the gross value of their property for tax purposes, but only if the lender was a locally owned company. This proved to be a major disincentive for the Oregon and Washington Trust. Enthusiasm for lending in the state waned. In truth, Dundee energies and money were already being diverted elsewhere and the Trust would soon be taken over by the Dundee Mortgage and Trust Investment Co. Ltd, but not before the directors had one more attempt to bring some discipline to Reid's management of their affairs.

Early in 1878 the directors in Dundee decided to appoint Robert Connel to be joint manager in Portland with Reid. Whether this was motivated by a desire to assist Reid or control him was not made clear. Connel was a university graduate and had worked in the Clydesdale Bank. His appointment was the occasion for a complete rewrite of all the powers of attorney, the responsibilities of the local board and the rules for doing business. There were also instructions about which books of account were to be kept. It was stated very clearly that if Reid refused his new appointment then Connel would be appointed as sole manager. To cater for this possibility Connel was issued with a power of attorney that would enable him to act alone but this was only to be used if Reid rejected the new arrangements.

Sensing trouble, the directors asked L.B. Sidway, a leading Chicago banker, to accompany Connel to Portland. Reid tried to get the directors to appoint Connel as his assistant but this was rejected. He tried to press his case by writing directly to Lowson but was told that all correspondence should be via the secretary.

Mackenzie was then sent to Portland in the summer of 1878. Reid took the opportunity of Mackenzie's visit to absent himself and make a tour of Oregon. His report is a very detailed analysis of business activity and opportunity in Oregon. Mackenzie was sufficiently impressed to include an abridged version in the subsequent annual report to shareholders. Thereafter relations with Reid took a somewhat calmer course. Connel did not last and resigned, due to ill health, in June 1879.

Meanwhile the commercial crisis associated with the failure of the City of Glasgow Bank had erupted in October 1878. More than £5,000 of debenture money was withdrawn during the crisis and the company was forced to borrow from the Dundee Mortgage and Trust. Some cash was recalled from Portland and the Royal Bank stock was sold. But the crisis did not last long, and by January 1879 the loan had been repaid and the reserve fund money was invested in consols and in a loan to the Dundee Police Commissioners. The company's own stock was still selling at a healthy premium over the issue price and an annual dividend for 1878 of 20% was declared at the following annual meeting. Lending of interest collections in Portland recommenced in February 1879, and new money was sent out the following month.

Reid continued to receive new money for investment through-out the remainder of 1879. At the board meeting in September, however, the possibility of merging with the Dundee Mortgage and Trust Company was placed on the agenda. Apparently it had been discussed before but nothing had been recorded in the minutes. An extraordinary general meeting of shareholders in Lamb's Hotel on 21 October 1879 gave its approval to the proposed merger, and thereafter the minutes were primarily concerned with what had to be done to make the merger work. When Reid submitted a new report on investment opportunities in eastern Oregon the directors simply passed it over to Dundee Mortgage and Trust, but not before Reid was thanked for his 'able and interesting report'.

The merger was referred to as an amalgamation but was, in effect, a takeover. It is doubtful if this diplomatic language was necessary. Given that the people involved in both companies were largely the same, there would be no sensitivities to concern them. The date of vesting was 30 January 1880, and shareholders in the Oregon and Washington Trust received shares in the Dundee Mortgage and Trust. For every six shares of the old company in which £2 10s (£2.50) per share had been paid they received six shares of the new company (£2 paid). They also received a 10% closing dividend.

The Oregon and Washington Trust Investment Co. Ltd had enjoyed a relatively short life but it had been successful and had met the shareholders expectations for healthy dividends. Just as important, if not more so, were the lessons that had been learned about how to conduct a business of this nature. Lengthy lines of communication and fairly tempestuous economic circumstances had produced many challenges for the directors in Dundee and Portland. Reid's wilful, but often helpful, behaviour had tested their patience. Important lessons had been learned and these would be put to good use in the next stage of their enterprise.

The Dundee Mortgage and Trust Investment Company Ltd

Quite early in the life of the Oregon and Washington Trust Investment Co. Ltd the directors came to the view that there were other and better lending and investment opportunities to be had in North America. Encouraged by their early success in Oregon they decided to set up another company with much wider powers. They had big plans. The Dundee Mortgage and Trust Investment Company Ltd had powers to operate in 'any of the Unites States or Territories of America, and also to the Dominions of Canada, Australia and New Zealand and any other Dominions and Territories of her Majesty'. Given the rate at which Her Majesty's territories were expanding at that time this was a very ambitious project. It was not long, however, before they decided to confine their activities to North America. They were clear, too, that it would not just be a mortgage company but would have powers to invest in railways, utilities and government stocks.

In many respects the new company was simply the old company writ large. They shared the same office, the people were the same and the business model was virtually identical.

The company was registered on 2 May 1876, two months before the Oregon and Washington Mortgage Savings Bank. The organisers were

William Lowson
James Neish
Thomas Cox
Thomas Bell
John Leng

At the first general meeting, held nine days later, they were appointed as directors with the addition of the 8th Earl of Airlie, who became chairman, with Lowson as deputy chairman. William Mackenzie was appointed to be company secretary.

The shareholders in the Oregon and Washington Trust were given priority in the allocation of shares. They were also allowed to buy shares at par while others had to pay a premium of 2s 6d (12.5p). This premium became the basis for the reserve fund. When it became clear that the Oregon-based shareholders had little interest in the new company the directors took up the shares themselves, as they were empowered to do. The list of shareholders included the directors and almost all of the other major names in the Dundee business community including Robert Fleming, William Smith, Alex Gourlay, Thomas Gilroy and G.W. Boase.

One of the first shareholders was the New York banking firm of Jesup, Paton and Co. which purchased 250 shares. This firm was to play a central role in the company's North American enterprise. John Paton hailed originally from Ancrum in Roxburghshire in the Scottish Borders. His career had started with a merchant in Liverpool before he joined the Bank of British North America, whose agent he became in Kingston, Canada and then New York. He entered into partnership with Morris Jesup in 1872, one of the founders of the YMCA. Paton involved himself in many of New York's philanthropic activities and served for some years as president of the St Andrew's Society. He was a frequent visitor to the UK and was present at some of the directors' meetings.

The nominal capital of the new company was £500,000 divided into 50,000 shares of £10. Only 30,000 shares were issued and 10 shillings (50p) per share was paid up on application, although shareholders were told that a further £1 10s (£1.50) would be called in equal instalments at six, twelve and eighteen months. In the event, a call of 10s per share was made in November 1876 but a third call, due to be made in the spring of 1877, was delayed because the company was in abundant funds. A quotation was secured on the Edinburgh Stock Exchange within months of the company being registered.

The reason for the delay in making the call on shares was the success of the company in raising money on debentures. At the time of the second shareholders meeting in July 1877 more than £140,000 had been raised in this way. At the same meeting the shareholders were told that share capital amounted to £37,425. There were also temporary loans of £25,132. These monies had been invested in mortgages amounting to £177,711 and 'temporary investments' amounted to £33,387.

No time had been lost in moving the company forward but nothing could happen before agents were appointed in various places in North America. The first was John Maule Machar, who was a barrister in Kingston, Ontario. His father, a Presbyterian minister, had been principal of Queen's University and his sister, Agnes, was a well-known social reformer and critic. Machar, who was in Scotland at the time when the company was being established, wrote to offer his services and to suggest Manitoba as a suitable field for investment. He was first invited to meet Thornton, the company solicitor, who was impressed by the proposal. A meeting with the board of directors followed. There was a long discussion, after which it was decided that further enquiries would be made and, if the board then approved, Lowson would write to Machar to tell him what was expected of him.

Manitoba had become the fifth province of Canada in 1870 and Winnipeg had been incorporated as a city in 1873. A railway from Lake Superior to the city was commenced in 1875. Machar was not alone in seeing the possibilities but the directors were a little disappointed when they had to reject Machar's first two loan applications, which were for a factory and a water power project, because they did not meet the investment criteria. In response to a letter from Airlie the Manitoba project was dropped but Machar was encouraged to find lending opportunities in Ontario.

Almost as quick as Machar to approach the new company were Messrs Balfour, Williamson and Co. of Liverpool, one of the largest general trading companies. They offered their services of their firm in San Francisco, Messrs Balfour, Guthrie and Co., to be the California agents. Dundee Mortgage and Trust was delighted to accept such an offer from a high-ranking firm. They were immediately authorised to draw £5,000 and place it in one of the California savings banks until it was required for lending. A further £5,000 was sent the following month. Leng visited them during his trip to the United States in the summer of 1876 and agreed their remuneration. They were to be paid a commission of 1% on loans made and ½% on temporary loans and investments. In addition they were to receive 2½% commission on collections. This was the model for the remuneration of other agents. Nevertheless, despite the blue chip nature of Balfour Guthrie, the relationship did not work particularly well. Robert Forman, one of the partners in San Francisco, called on the directors in Dundee in the summer of 1877 to renegotiate his firm's remuneration. Although some good, high-interest loans were made, they found it difficult, at times, to lend at the rate of interest that could be obtained in the other agencies. In August 1877 the directors decided that if Balfour Guthrie could not get 8.5% or better on their loans then the money would be sent to other agencies. It could certainly be put to better use than to lie in the three

Californian savings banks in which Balfour Guthrie had deposited it.

Paton in New York was given various credits amounting to over $50,000 for lending on mortgages. He was also given discretion to invest in bonds. The Illinois Trust and Savings Bank was given a similar commission and a similar amount of money. The state of Illinois and its capital city of Chicago were fast expanding places and were the epicentre of the United States' meat trade. L.B. Sidway wrote from Chicago to say that his borrowers wished to repay by instalments and that an extra 1% could be charged if this was allowed. This was similar to the suggestion that Reid had made in Portland. The directors in Dundee were warm to this idea as it improved their security and cash flow. Sidway and his Illinois bank were not confined to lending in the state and in November 1876 he was given a credit of $25,000 for lending in Iowa. By the end of that year total credits for Illinois and Iowa were $330,000 (about £66,000).

When Leng visited the US in 1876 he met the Corbin Banking Company in New York and, on his return, recommended that they receive a credit of $30,000. Corbin were active in several states but it seems clear that they never achieved the scale that was reached by some of the other agencies.

Leng also recommended that an agency be established in Indianapolis and that Francis Smith and William Hannaman be appointed agents, with a local board comprising of Robert McOuat and James C. Ferguson. No sooner was this agency established than Paton went to visit. He was impressed, and recommended further lending which was soon forthcoming. In the summer of 1877 Smith and Hannaman exceeded their lending limits but the directors approved their actions. It became a very successful agency. The only problem with it was the Indiana state legislation that required foreign corporations to be registered with the circuit courts in each county of the state in which they did business. This required 14 registrations.

The agents were assiduous in their attention to business. Paton in New York and Smith in Indianapolis wrote almost daily to Dundee. This placed quite a strain on Mackenzie's office there. In June 1876 he was given permission to appoint a full-time accountant and book-keeper at £120 per annum. This appointment was to be shared with the Oregon and Washington Trust. D. Kippen from Crieff was appointed but he was dismissed within the month. There are other signs, too, that the administration was under some pressure, as when the minute writer wrote that these were the minutes of the Oregon and Washington Trust rather than the Dundee Mortgage and Trust Investment Company. In every other respect the company had got off to a good start.

Leng's visit to the United States had been particularly useful. His letters home had been informative, he had made many new contacts and he brought back a large supply of books, pamphlets, maps and business forms which he passed over to Mackenzie. At the board meeting on 14 September 1877 it was recorded that total lending was $1,163,899. The sterling equivalent of this was £230,121 and the loans were secured over land valued at $2,649,767.

In the background to this development was a political problem that would bedevil businesses for many years. There was a move afoot to monetise silver and give the United States a bimetallic monetary standard based upon both gold and silver. It was a highly controversial proposal that polarised political opinion for decades. Each time it moved up the political agenda businesses took a deep breath and pondered what the consequences might be. In the summer of 1876 it looked as if those who favoured the monetisation of silver might get their way. The directors in Dundee took note and asked for comments from Paton and Leng. The fear was that if silver was monetised then this would lead to a depreciation in the value of the US currency. This would have serious consequences for companies like Dundee Mortgage which had large sums invested in the United States. The House of Representatives favoured the idea and, when this became known, the directors paused the allocation of further credits to their agencies. They then considered inserting a clause in their mortgage contracts that would allow them to refuse payments in silver. They were already averse to taking payments in paper money, which was still suffering the after-effects of the Civil War, and most contracts insisted in payments in gold coin. Sidway wrote from Chicago to say that there was no need to change the form of mortgage contracts until such times as the federal government had passed legislation. In the end the threat diminished, but it did not disappear entirely and would reappear from time to time over the next 20 years.

Thereafter the business settled down to a period of steady expansion. Sidway and his Illinois Trust and Savings Bank announced that they were about to expand into Missouri and were given an initial credit of $50,000. Smith and Hannaman decided that they were about to commence business in another six counties in Indianapolis and required to register there. They were also given a credit for $50,000. Balfour Guthrie in San Francisco were told that they could lend at 8%.

Further calls were made on shareholders to finance this expansion and, occasionally, money was borrowed from the Oregon and Washington Trust on a temporary basis to cover commitments before call money on shares was received. Early in 1878 John Paton advised that he was sitting on surplus funds and Mackenzie authorised the purchase of bonds of the Central Pacific Railroad and the Union Pacific Railroad. He also authorised the purchase of gold bonds as a defence against the proposed monetisation of silver, but when Paton advised that Smith and Hannaman could lend the money profitably that order was rescinded and the money went to Indianapolis.

The challenge in running this kind of business was twofold. The primary concern was always to have good, reliable information on which sound business decisions could be made. The second was to have systems that enabled the accuracy and veracity of book-keeping to be checked. Neither of these was easily attainable when such vast distances in a developing country were involved. Correspondence from the agents has already been mentioned as a source of information. But who would check that the agents were doing what they said they were doing? At first the answer to this question was the other agents, and in March 1878 Sidway was en route to Portland to help install Reid's new, but unwanted, joint manager. As there was then no railway to Portland he had no option but to go via San Francisco. Whilst there he was asked to go and inspect the securities in Balfour Guthrie's hands.

The second option was to send someone from Dundee to inspect the agencies. Leng's visit in 1876 had certainly proved useful but it was more of a holiday and fact-finding trip than an inspection. The directors decided that Mackenzie was the person best placed for, and most in need of, a tour of the agencies. The number of agencies had been further expanded by the appointment of Andrew Drummond of Drummond Brothers in Montreal, so Mackenzie's trip would be to Canada as well as the United States. Machar's initial appointment in Canada had not been successful and the Drummond appointment was effectively a replacement for him.

Mackenzie was given his commission (instructions) in August 1878 and he was to be accompanied on his trip by William Smith, farmer in Stone o'Morphie near Montrose. He was told to check everything in the agencies and, at the same time, look for new opportunities. The failure of the City of Glasgow Bank occurred in October 1878 while Mackenzie was still in the United States. He did not hasten home. Indeed the failure seems to have had little impact on the business. In late October the agency in Indianapolis asked for more money to lend and was refused. In mid November one of the Chicago loans was repaid early and the agency asked for instructions. They were told to remit the money to Dundee. Other monies were repatriated from Montreal. Some of the investments of the reserve fund money were sold and the money deposited in a deposit receipt.

These efforts to enhance the liquidity of the company are perfectly under-standable in the circumstances. But the crisis did not last for very long. Lending in the agencies was resumed in January 1879 and the California agents were told to 'abstain from urging repayments' now that the company was in 'sufficient funds to meet its obligations'. By March 1879 the agencies were provided with substantial sums for lending and were authorised to relend monies that they had collected in repayments. Defaults were infrequent, and the agents were given discretion in dealing with slow payers. Foreclosures were rare.

The City of Glasgow Bank failure did, however, make the directors think about how they ran their business. They decided that they were rather encum-bered by administration, and Mackenzie, who had now returned from North America, was asked to prepare a weekly statement, 'with a view to disencum-bering the company's record of sundry details'. The statement was circulated to the directors and initialled by the chairman.

Most of the business at the regular meetings of directors was formal. They dealt with debenture issuing, cheque signing, share transfers and communi-cations. The meetings themselves were irregular. There was no set pattern. But they were frequent. It was unusual for there to be more than ten days between board meetings and they were often more frequent.

In the summer of 1879 the company had surplus cash. Applications for debentures were turned away and agents were given permission to lend in ways and on securities that were innovative. Indianapolis asked if they could lend on brick buildings in small towns and were given some leeway. Until then almost all of the lending had been on agricultural land.

The opportunity was also taken to expand the investment portfolio beyond what was needed for the reserve fund. The advice was sought of Robert Fleming who recommended investment in various railroad companies. These included Lehigh Valley, Canada Southern, Baltimore and Ohio, Chicago and Alton, Albany and Susquehanna and Central Pacific. John Paton contributed to the investment decisions by recommending investment in the Toledo, Peoria and Warsaw Railroad.

In a quiet moment at their meeting on 1 August 1879 the directors thought about the nature of their relationship with the Oregon and Washington Investment Company and decided to amalgamate with it. Mackenzie was asked to prepare the relevant documents. It seemed a sensible move. The two companies had almost everything in common and frequently lent money to one another to smooth out cash flows.

But before finally deciding to merge the two companies the directors took stock of what they had achieved since the inception of Dundee Mortgage and Trust just three years earlier. With a paid up capital of £70,000 and debentures of £285,381 they had issued mortgages for £285,341 and made investments of £10,126. A reserve fund of £15,000 had been built up and shareholders had received regular dividends. It was a strong performance.

Their objective was to make it stronger. By December 1879 the merger agreement was ready and the opportunity was taken to strengthen the capital of the company. They also made it rather complex by issuing three different types of shares. Some 10,000 unissued shares of the original capital were now to be issued and made use of in settling with the shareholders of the Oregon and Washington Trust.

There were now to be 14,000 shares of £10 each to be considered the original capital of the company. They also issued 16,000 'A' shares of £2 each that were to be fully called up within two years. These shares were to rank equally with the original capital. They also issued 16,000 'B' shares of £8 each that would bear a dividend of 5.5%. These, in effect, were preference shares, although that term was not used to describe them. Holders of these shares would be entitled to their dividend before the ordinary and 'A' shareholders received anything. They were also redeemable after 1890 upon six months' notice being given. The issuing of A and B shares was really a reaction to the City of Glasgow Bank failure. None of the shareholders had unlimited liability, as had been the case with the Glasgow Bank, but the existence of limited liability shares with a large margin of uncalled capital was increasingly unpopular with shareholders who feared that, despite what directors might say, they might easily be called upon to pay the balance of their shares in times of difficulty. Many of the Glasgow Bank shareholders had been sequestrated, as they could not pay the numerous calls that were made on their shares – calls that were far in excess of the nominal value of their shareholdings.

The merger had the effect of requiring an agency in Portland, Oregon, and William Reid was appointed to be agent. He was soon suggesting new lending opportunities in eastern Oregon and Washington. Drummond Brothers in Montreal had been pressing the case for lending in Manitoba and the decision was made to start lending there. As interest rates were falling in some parts of the United States through 1879 surplus funds were moved to Canada where higher rates of interest could be obtained. Drummond Brothers, the agents there, were expected to lend at 10%.

Apart from this lending in Canada there was little attempt to live up to the company's stated objective of lending in Her Majesty's other territories. In January 1880 Airlie received a letter from W.W. Billyard in Sydney, Australia, as a result of which he was appointed agent there with a lending limit of £5,000. He lent the whole amount to Joseph Aarons of Montefiores in New South Wales for three years at 8%. This was rich agricultural land just beyond the Blue Mountains where the railway had just arrived. He was immediately offered another £5,000. It was a promising start but it seems that no more lending was undertaken in Australia.

In addition to adding the agencies in Portland and Manitoba the increased scale of the company gave it the opportunity to participate in bigger loans and in some of the syndicated lending which was becoming popular. Balfour, Williamson and Co. in Liverpool was the source of lending opportunities. They facilitated a loan of $75,000 in Butte and Tehema Counties in California. Dundee Mortgage put up one third of this sum and Edinburgh-based Scottish American Mortgage put in a similar sum.

A proposed loan of $400,000 to Dr Hugh Glen on the Jacinto Land Grant, in which a number of Edinburgh and Dundee lenders were involved, fell through when it was discovered that there was a problem over the title to the land. This problem of title to large land grants, some of them of great age, was a recurring problem, as were the questions of borders and measurements.

The other problem, although relatively rare at this time, was when a borrower failed to pay and the agent had to foreclose. The margins between land value and loan were usually sufficiently wide to avoid ultimate loss but, in the interim, there was the problem for the agent about finding a new purchaser who would pay a reasonable price. The related problem was how to maintain the property in good order until a new purchaser could be found. On one occasion the company paid for some drainage work on a piece of land that had been foreclosed in Illinois. The work made the land more saleable.

Before foreclosure happened there is evidence to show that the directors were prepared to exercise a good degree of tolerance in the case of borrowers who had fallen behind with their payments. In September 1879 Sidway wrote from Chicago about a loan which was in arrears and which a local lawyer was prepared to take off their hands. However, Sidway suspected that the lawyer would then seek to ruin the borrower. The directors replied that 'They do not wish to be the means of bringing ruin to an industrious man and that they were agreeable that he should be shown as much leniency as possible with respect of his arrears as is consistent in the interests of the Company.'

One month later Sidway reported that arrears in his agency were $587.

This did not create any alarms in Dundee, and Sidway was given permission to expand his lending activities.

It was evident to the directors that if the quality of lending and administration at the agencies was to be maintained at a high level then there had to be a mechanism for measuring that quality. William Smith from Stone O'Morphie had fulfilled that role in 1878 when he accompanied MacKenzie on a tour of the agencies. That role now fell to another Scot, J. McCulloch, a farmer from Denbie Mains farm in Dumfriesshire. He was appointed to be superintendent of agencies and inspector of loans at a salary of £700 plus travelling expenses. He was given a five-year contract. He spent one week in Dundee before leaving for the United States.

His first task was to inspect the loan book and mortgages of the New England Loan Company that the Corbin Banking Company had advised was being wound up. Corbin had suggested that Dundee Mortgage might take up $50,000 of the loans but $100,000 was offered, although not before McCulloch had the opportunity to make his inspection. In the end, $75,000 of loans were acquired. McCulloch was then sent to Kansas City where Messrs Underwood, Clark and Co. had offered loans up to $100,000. In June 1880 he sent telegrams in code to Dundee to approve the lending in Kansas City that would yield 8%. The money was remitted via the Bank of Montreal in New York. Two months later Underwood, Clark proposed lending in Nebraska and again the money was sent via New York.

McCulloch also recommended I.C. Easton of Lanesboro, Minnesota, who could make loans to yield 8%. Later that month he advised the directors that it would be expedient to start lending in Manitoba. It was a remarkable start to his career as an inspector. A prodigious amount of travelling and work had been accomplished in a very short space of time.

McCulloch's appointment was shared with the Dundee Land Investment Co. Indeed there were many points at which the two companies touched. Dundee Land sometimes borrowed relatively small sums from Dundee Mortgage and, on occasion, their acceptances were cashed in London before repayment was made in Dundee. There were times, too, when the borrowing was in the other direction, usually just before a call on shareholders was due and the company was running short of cash.

There were additional alliances with other companies. In October 1880 I. Duncan Smith, managing director of the Edinburgh-based Scottish American Mortgage Co. wrote to Lowson to suggest south-eastern Dakota as a safe place for investment. He recommended the firm of Easton, McKinney and Scougal, who operated in Sioux Falls and Yorkton, as suitable agents, and they were duly appointed as joint agents.

It is tempting to suggest that these friendly working relationships with what were, in effect, rival companies must have caused conflicts of interest for the agents but there is very little evidence of this being a frequent problem. And the model of agents such as Underwood, Clark and Co. in Kansas City and Smith and Hannaman in Indianapolis acting as agents for several companies, as well as acting in their own right, did not throw up many problems. When, in November 1881, Smith was with McCulloch in the southern states in an effort to develop new business, the directors in Dundee simply recorded that they would pay Smith's expenses on the understanding they were to have preference over his other clients. It was simply a matter of trust.

What is certainly clear is that information gathering continued to be a vital part of the company's activities. It was also increased. Letters and telegrams were the main source of business intelligence. All the agents wrote very regularly, and McCulloch was assiduous in his duties in this respect. But there was sometimes no substitute for a face-to-face meeting. Mackenzie and some of the directors made regular trips to North America and many of the personnel there made frequent trips to Dundee. McCulloch was home in January 1881 and was given a list of instructions so lengthy that Mackenzie was told to provide him with a document that would serve as an 'aide memoire' and action plan. Drummond from Montreal and Winnipeg was in Dundee in the same month. He was followed by John Paton, the New York banker.

Top of the list for discussions at these meetings were new lending opportunities. The United States was growing at a prodigious rate and needing capital for infrastructure as well as for land developments. Canada was growing less quickly and was, in fact, haemorrhaging population to the United States. Many municipalities had started to issue bonds to fund their local developments. The quality of these bonds, and the risk attaching to them, were the subject of frequent discussions. American local government was not known for its stability.

Paton seemed keen to buy municipal bonds from Colorado. Knowing that this would come up for discussion, Mackenzie had written to James Barclay, chairman of the Colorado Land Co. for his opinion. Barclay then declined to offer an opinion on them, which the directors took to be a negative view. They were right to be cautious, as it transpired that there were legal problems connected with these investments. In July 1881 Messrs Rollins and Young were about to be appointed agents in Denver. They specialised in municipal bonds.

Yet again the solution to the problem was to have local men with local knowledge feeding information back to Dundee, with McCulloch acting both as an inspector and as a filter. His report about Rollins and Young was not favourable and they were not appointed.

The directors' attentions were also focused, more than usual, on Portland, where Reid had been engaged in some speculative ventures, not the least of which was the Oregonian Railway Company. In this he was associated with some of the leading figures in Dundee, including Lowson. This led, in a very short space of time, to Dundee Mortgage absorbing the Oregon and Washington Mortgage Savings Bank, but by that time savings activity had ceased and no one had the appetite for raising money in that way.

The challenge for the directors in Dundee was to decide which opportunities to pursue and which to decline. Established links were favoured, and when Mr Corbin said that he had been looking at opportunities in Georgia, Alabama and Arkansas he was promptly authorised to do business in these states for Dundee Mortgage. However, he soon discovered that he could not obtain better than 7% for loans and his credit was cancelled. This may have been a bit precipitate as the amount of money pouring into the United States coupled with the amount being generated there was driving down interest rates across the country.

The big opportunity in the early years of the 1880s was cattle and ranch companies. Large amounts of British money were poured into these ventures, with very mixed results. Three were run from Dundee. They were

The Texas Land and Cattle Co. (1881)
The Matador Land and Cattle Co. (1882)
The Hanford Land and Cattle Co. (1883)

In the summer of 1881 Morris K. Jesup, John Paton's banking partner in New York, offered shares to Mackenzie when he was visiting the city, in a cattle company that he had established in Texas. Thornton, when he heard about this, was immediately doubtful that the company had the legal powers to acquire shares in other companies. Nevertheless, Mackenzie was keen on the idea and went to Texas to have a look. This only strengthened his enthusiasm but he was eventually overruled by his directors.

He was also keen on the Colorado Company's plans for a canal and reservoir enterprise. Again he was overruled by his board. When he returned to Dundee he made the mistake of expressing his regret at their decision. The directors told him that he had made an error of judgement 'and they instructed that their disapproval should be recorded accordingly'.

While Mackenzie was still in America the company suffered a double blow. Hannaman, the joint agent in Indianapolis, died in September 1881. Lord Airlie, the company chairman, died of pneumonia in Denver a few days later. Lowson replaced Airlie as chairman and Robert Fleming filled the vacant seat on the board. He was joined soon afterwards by John Guild who had been chairman of Fleming's own Trusts – the three Scottish American Mortgage Trusts.

The early part of the 1880s was a boom time in the United States. The ranch and cattle companies led the way but the United States was fast becoming an advanced industrial nation. Dundee Mortgage was not at all interested in industrial developments, other than by investing in railroads, although most of that investment was for the reserve fund. The addition of Robert Fleming and John Guild to the board added enormous strength to the organisation and ensured that there would be a ready source of good recommendations about investments.

The opportunity was taken to expand the company's horizons into new and, it was hoped, fertile areas for lending. Peter MacMaster of Fergus Falls, Minnesota was appointed agent there with a remit to lend in north-western Minnesota and a portion of north-east Dakota. W.J. Balentine Paterson was given an agency in San Antonio, Texas. Alex Guthrie of Balfour Guthrie in Liverpool provided a reference for him. Francis Smith expanded into the southern states, especially Alabama. Underwood, Clark expanded into Nebraska and formed the Muscatine Mortgage Company through which to conduct the business.

It was a great expansionary phase, even if it did put some pressure on Dundee to fund it. At one stage Corbin, of the eponymous banking firm, wrote to criticise some of the loans made by Francis Smith in the southern states. (A new lender will always be the target for unscrupulous borrowers.) The directors put this down to business rivalry as Corbin was also trying to expand in this region. Nevertheless they despatched McCulloch to inspect the loans and, meanwhile, sent Smith a letter in which he was told to suspend lending. They said that their funds were temporarily exhausted, which was true, but they were probably more concerned about the question mark over the quality of his lending.

If the funds were under pressure so too was McCulloch. He was busier than ever and took the opportunity to ask for a raise. His salary was duly increased from £700 per annum to £900 but there were signs that the directors were worried that he might resign. A clause was duly entered into his new contract that required him to give three months' notice. His discomfiture might simply be explained by the fact that his co-employer, Dundee Land, was in some difficulty and was undergoing a transformation that would see it re-emerge as the Dundee Investment Co. Ltd.

The pressure of work was also reflected in the bill for telegrams. In a normal year the charge, as revealed in the annual accounts, would be in the region of £100. But in the 1881 it was £273.

At the annual general meeting on 26 April 1882 the directors assured the 44 shareholders who attended that business was going well: 'There has been on the whole a satisfactory promptitude shown in collections and while there are some arrears and defaults, these are necessarily incidental to a mortgage business and do not, in the aggregate, exceed what may be expected.'

Mortgages totalled £728,000 that was funded by capital of £288,000, debentures amounting to £505,000 and an overdraft at the British Linen Bank of £23,000. Arrangements were well advanced for the absorption of the Oregon and Washington Mortgage Savings Bank, but although this was soon settled, it also led to a very lengthy correspondence with William Reid about the terms of his remuneration. In one typically prolix letter he offered four different options. The situation was not helped by the fact that Reid was in dispute with Ellis Hughes, the attorney who had done the legal work in Portland.

Matters with Reid were moving to a climax. He was something of a paradox. He had been enormously hard-working, ambitious and imaginative. He had also been stubborn, difficult to deal with and vague. He had become involved on his own account, and on behalf of his employers, with a wide variety of business and public service activities in Oregon. His own project, in which were involved several leading Dundee businessmen, including Lowson, was the Oregonian Railway Company. Like all railway companies there were speculative activities in land and buildings that, although separate from the railway, were nevertheless dependent upon it. Reid had a hand in most of it.

In September 1882 Mr Lowe, who had been accountant in the Portland office, resigned. The directors moved quickly and appointed Hugh Roger, until then working in Edinburgh for a firm of chartered accountants, to be accountant and assistant manager. Lowe's resignation had raised the directors' suspicions, and when they discovered that a senior London solicitor was about to go to Portland to investigate the affairs of the Oregonian Railway Company they moved quickly to secure his services.

Professor Edmund Robertson, barrister-at-law in London and Professor of Roman Law, was provided with a wide-ranging power of attorney that gave him authority to investigate all matters relating to the business done in the Portland office. On his arrival there he established an office in the Bank of British North America and set to work. Within a couple of weeks he was sufficiently confident of what he had discovered to write to Dundee to express his dissatisfaction with various aspects of the way in which the Portland office had been managed.

The directors, after full and careful discussion, had no doubt about what had to be done. They sent the following telegram to Robertson: 'The Dundee Mortgage Co, the Dundee Land Investment Co, Oregon and Washington Mortgage Savings Bank. Directors authorise you dismiss William Reid replace Ellis G Hughes if you think well of it. Suggest keeping Lowe associated with Roger if former dissevers all connection with William Reid both acting meantime under guidance you and new attorney.'

Various other instructions were given about gaining control over assets and securing titles to property.

There was much to be done. William Macmaster, who had worked for Dundee Land, was recruited and sent to Portland to assist Robertson and Roger, especially in 'visiting delinquent borrowers, collecting arrears and otherwise'. Robertson discovered that Reid had been charging commissions on collections made by him when he was a salaried employee. He should not have done so. Reid was also claiming to have permission to purchase lands on which there had been foreclosure. Dundee advised Robertson that this was not the case. Some months later Effinger, the new attorney, wanted to raise a suit against Reid for trafficking in foreclosed mortgages but the directors declined to become involved. There was also a row over Reid's attempt to sell his shares. The directors took legal advice to prevent him from doing so.

Early in December 1882 the company took out advertisements in the local papers advising the public that Reid was no longer an employee. Thornton, ever the cautious adviser, told the directors to 'Take care . . . to prevent him (Mr Roger) drifting into the position of a general agent, which has given you so much plague with Reid.'

It took a long time to sort out what Reid had done, and the dealings with Hughes were almost as vexatious and included appeals to the Supreme Court.

Meanwhile the other agencies were doing well although there were some signs of difficulties ahead. Francis Smith was busy extending further into the southern states but the directors were displeased to learn about a worryingly upward trend in the number of foreclosures. Underwood, Clark were given a further credit of $100,000 for lending on the security of buildings in Kansas City. McCulloch continued his extensive tours of the agencies. He professed himself less that content with the mounting arrears in the Canadian agency.

On one of his regular visits to Dundee, John Paton recommended South Carolina as a suitable place in which to do business. He suggested Colonel J.B. Palmer for the agency. Palmer was, at that time, in London, and was duly invited to Dundee. He was present for the board meeting on 18 January 1883 and, after a fruitful exchange of views, he was despatched to meet Thornton and Lowson. He was formally appointed at the next board meeting.

Despite the foreclosures in Indianapolis and Winnipeg, the shareholders at the annual general meeting in April 1883 were informed that defaults were less than last year and that foreclosures were a very small portion of the total. The directors averred 'the present and general prosperity of America has doubtless contributed to the result now reported'. It was not to last. A year later the shareholders were told that 'The past year has been one of great and general depression in Canada and the United States and prices of agricultural produce have reached a low level.'

The company headed into this difficult period without the services of McCulloch, whose contract had not been renewed after a very detailed examination of his expenses.

The first signs of difficulties came from Kansas where it was discovered that Underwood, Clark had made some 'injudicious investments' that had to be foreclosed immediately. There were doubts about the legality of the loans. Andrew Drummond was present at the June 1883 meeting of the board to explain the foreclosures in his agency in Winnipeg. William Macmaster, from Portland, stepped temporarily into McCulloch's shoes and was sent to Indianapolis to inspect Smith's agency. He was assisted by T. Lyon White, who recommended that lending be stopped. It was. He went on to discover irregularities in Palmer's new agency in South Carolina. White then assumed the role of inspector although he was never formally appointed to this role.

In August 1883 the Indiana Banking Company, which was used by Smith, closed its doors. There followed a great period of uncertainty with the rating agency R.G. Dun saying that it would resume payments and just about everyone else saying that it was 'bust'. A poor harvest set the seal on what would appear, when the books were balanced, to have been a bad year. Inspections were stepped up but there was little sign that lending was being restricted. Greater emphasis was placed on treasury management, and whenever it appeared that an agency was sitting on uninvested funds, instructions were issued for their remittance to New York, from where they would be redeployed.

There were still positive signs, and progress was being made in a number of areas. New agents were appointed in Texas, including William Sommerville in Fort Worth. Lending was restored in Oregon despite difficulties with new local taxation. William Birrell, a Dundonian, was appointed to be accountant in Oregon. Until then he had been working for the Arizona Copper Company.

Fleming was in the United States in the closing months of 1883 and saw opportunity in the deteriorating economic conditions. The Roanoke Improvement Company and the Norfolk and Western Railway were only two of his many buy recommendations – most of which were followed up. He was also making recommendations for Dundee Investment and, presumably, his own trusts. Whilst in the United States Fleming was approached by a variety of people who wanted to establish agencies for the two Dundee companies. It seemed that many of the indigenous lenders were withdrawing facilities. In Oregon, even the long established private bank of Ladd and Tilton called in many of its loans. The consequence was that borrowers were finding it increasingly difficult to secure credit while others saw the opportunity of plugging the gap by opening agencies with companies that still had funds to lend. A decision about new agencies was delayed until Fleming returned home.

Fleming had wanted Mackenzie to join him in the United States but Mackenzie declined the invitation and said that Professor Robertson, who was again in North America, would be able to help sort out any difficulties. At that stage Mackenzie was still a part-time employee and ran his own stockbroking business, so it would have been difficult for him to go to the United States at short notice. He realised that this situation could not continue indefinitely, and in February 1884 he proposed to his directors that he should give up the stockbroking business and concentrate full time on his role as company secretary to Dundee Mortgage and Dundee Investment. The directors readily agreed, and his salary was set at £800 per annum.

Mackenzie's appointment as full-time secretary was an important milestone for him and for the company, but it was only part of a much bigger shift in company politics. At the annual general meeting in April 1884 both Lowson and Cox retired from the board, leaving effective control in the hands of Fleming and Guild. They nominated Henry Gourlay, engineer in Dundee, and Alexander Henderson, a local merchant, to replace the two retirees. This left John Leng as the only one of the original directors. He was duly elected to be chairman but he made it clear that, in view of his other commitments and the state of his health, his appointment could only be viewed as temporary. He retired in October that same year, claiming that he could not sleep and did not have 'the physical strength for the incessant strain upon me and I am compelled, however, reluctantly, to forego engagements which overtax my powers'. Nevertheless he recovered to go on to be Member of Parliament for Dundee and to lead an active life.

Alex Gourlay also retired to be replaced by his brother Henry. These changes had the effect of placing a great deal of power in the hands of Fleming and Guild. In addition to their control over the Scottish American Investment Trusts they now had control of Dundee Mortgage and Dundee Investment.

Mackenzie, in his new full-time role, had more time to devote to company affairs and set about enhancing some aspects of the administration. He was dissatisfied that there were so many different styles of mortgages in the United States and blamed the attorneys for the confusion. He set about designing a series of forms where blanks could be filled in with applicants' names, amount borrowed and the security offered. He then asked Professor Robertson to visit the agencies and to have this and related matters placed on a more standardised footing.

Mackenzie was also concerned that there was no replacement for McCulloch. Although Macmaster was filling the gap, he had the Portland agency to run and would find it difficult to do both jobs. In April 1884 James Haggart was appointed to the vacant role of inspector. He was given a six-month contract and paid $100 per month. It was an inauspicious beginning for a man who was to become a legend in the company. The inspection function was further strengthened by the appointment of T. Lyon White to be agent at Fargo. He was also prepared to act as an inspector when required. William Macmaster in Portland could also be called upon.

Given the difficult economic conditions into which the American economy was moving, it was a sensible time to be strengthening the administration and management of the company. Various problems emerged which needed the attention of senior people. There was a suspicion that Francis Smith had been engaging in usurious lending and he had to be temporarily suspended; the Illinois Trust and Savings Bank continued to delay sending its accounts; the issuers of the defaulted Lake County Bonds in Colorado had to be pursued because they had paid local holders of bonds but not those from further away; and various legal processes had to be pursued against Reid and Hughes in Oregon. The directors were convinced that Reid had been guilty of 'gross and culpable negligence'. The Drummond brothers in Winnipeg fell out and a decision had to be made about which one should continue the agency. There were many problems loans in Manitoba. Indeed such were the problems there that Haggart's contract was renewed for a year on the condition that he based himself in Winnipeg. It was a vexatious time for Mackenzie and the directors.

Lending did continue but agents were told that the company preferred 'good securities' to 'full rates'. At the annual general meeting in April 1885 the shareholders were advised about the 'financial crisis and disaster' in the United States which was described as being similar to 1873. The directors conceded that there had been depreciation in the investments but expressed the view that this would be a temporary phenomenon. Nevertheless, in the same month, several of the agents were given fresh credits for lending. Further extensions were granted in the summer.

Mackenzie was busy preparing for an extended trip to North America and was given a power of attorney with wide-ranging powers, including the option to authorise new credits for the agents. Meanwhile the board was further strengthened with the appointment of Andrew Whitton, a local businessman.

Commodity prices had fallen and a major consequence was that land prices were also depressed. But that did not prevent the company from becoming involved in a syndicate formed by Lord George Campbell to lend £70,000 for five years at 10% to Charles Goodnight on the security of his Paloduro Ranche on the Texas Panhandle. Goodnight was one of the big names of the ranching industry. The security was 500,000 acres of freehold land and 75,000 head of cattle and various other animals and equipment. Dundee Mortgage agreed to participate to the extent of £5,000 although the directors were otherwise not well disposed to the ranching industry.

Various people continued to arrive in Dundee, some as supplicants, others as information providers, and some as both. A.S. Caldwell of the firm of Francis Smith and Co. arrived in September 1885 to discuss matters in Indianapolis. He received a new credit of $200,000. Soon afterwards Caldwell became Smith's partner. Underwood, Clark in Kansas City also underwent a restructuring by establishing the Kansas City Investment Company through which they conducted their agency business. John Paton arrived from New York the following month for general discussions.

The company emerged from the recession in good shape. When the annual general meeting took place in April 1886 Alex Henderson was in the chair. He reported that stocks and shares had recovered well but the expected agricultural recovery had not yet happened. The company owned real estate, as a result of foreclosures, valued at £36,638. But there was Bank of England and other stocks in the reserve fund of £90,000. Bank deposits in New York were about £12,000 each but the bank account in Dundee contained the princely sum of £19.

The directors were in the habit of sharing £1,000 as a reward for their efforts, but one shareholder proposed that, in the light of recent events, this should be reduced. He failed to find a seconder. Of greater importance was the resignation of Robert Fleming from the board. An effort was made to retain him but he felt strongly that his frequent absences in the US and London made it impossible for him to serve conscientiously as a director in Dundee. His services, however, were not lost to the company and Mackenzie continued to use him as a source of investment advice and for effecting investment transactions.

Thereafter the business built up steadily once more. But federal and state legislation continued to throw up problems. The difficulties associated with the various Alien Acts continued to create problems, especially in the territories for which Congress passed a new Alien Act in 1887. But a number of states were now flexing their muscles with tax-raising powers. When opportunity arose the company tackled these robustly, usually on the grounds that they affected companies in different ways and were therefore unconstitutional. On one occasion, in Alabama, Smith, Caldwell and Co. wrote to say that they had turned up at the court house for a hearing but 'no progress was made because the judge had gone fishing'.

Early in 1887 some new legislation in Texas cast doubt as to whether the company was operating legally in that state. The doubt arose as the law required foreign companies to conduct the same business in their own countries as they did in Texas. At least that is what they thought it meant. The law was by no means clear. Thorntons were consulted and adopted their traditional cautious approach. But it was Thornton himself who came up with the idea that the company should merge with Dundee Investment because that company's wider investment powers would make the argument irrelevant.

Before that could happen the possibility of establishing some new agencies was being actively considered, and Alex Henderson's visit to the United States was to be a fact-finding trip with this in mind. Some of the existing agencies continued to give occasional trouble. Andrew Drummond eventually resigned from Winnipeg and was replaced by John L. Morris from Montreal. Macmaster wrote to say that he thought Sommerville in Fort Worth had been overvaluing the properties on which he lent the company's money. Underwood, Clark in Kansas City were financially embarrassed and were struggling to pay their debts.

Most of these problems were soon resolved but not before Mackenzie made another trip to North America and gave them his personal attention. Whilst there he extended credits for the agencies in Fort Worth, Kansas and Indianapolis. He also established a new agency under Messrs Cochrane and Walsh in St Paul, Minnesota. That particular firm were recommended by the German American National Bank and given a good rating by R.G. Dun and Co. Mackenzie also extended the credit of the Muscatine Mortgage and Trust Co. but, as the secretary of that organisation was his brother, he first asked approval from his board. These are the actions of a self-confident operator. Mackenzie was now sure of his ground in North America and, while there may have been some comfort for him in having Fleming in the background, he was perfectly capable of working on his own initiative.

Perhaps with a possible merger with Dundee Investment in mind Mackenzie set about a capital issue and restructuring which had the effect of making the eventual merger easier to accomplish. The capital restructuring was accomplished in June 1886 but even then it was being said that the time was not right for an amalgamation with Dundee Investment. Nevertheless there does not seem to have been any doubt in anyone's mind that a merger would eventually happen and, to anticipate a planned increase in stamp duty, the new company – The Alliance Trust Company Ltd – was registered on 21 April 1888. For the time being it would lay dormant.

The directors' thinking was recorded in the minute book:

> Whereas an amalgamation with the Dundee Investment Company has been suggested, but said proposal is not yet ripe for discussion, and whereas it will be necessary to incorporate a new company to carry the same into effect and if the same be not immediately incorporated there will have to be paid on registration thereof the new duty of £1 per £1,000 proposed by the Chancellor of the Exchequer in the budget bill now before the House of Commons instead of the present maximum of £50, it was resolved to register a new company forthwith and a remit with the full powers was made to the company's solicitors accordingly.

The eight promoters of the new company, each of whom subscribed for ten shares of £10, were

Alex Henderson	Dundee
John Smith	Alyth
Geo. Carmichael	Broughty Ferry
Robert Duke	Brechin
W.O. Dalgleish	Errol
Robert Lamb	Broughty Ferry
Alex Gilroy	Dundee
John Guild	Broughty Ferry

All were major names in the Dundee business community.

Despite the creation of the new company, it was business as usual for Dundee Mortgage. Consolation was taken from the fact that the market value of reserve fund investments was well ahead of the book price. But one shareholder was unhappy about the expenses. He was told that other companies reported differently and Dundee Mortgage provided fuller figures so that expenses might seem higher than those incurred by other companies. He was not satisfied, and raised a motion to reduce the remuneration paid to the directors. He eventually withdrew his motion. Another shareholder proposed that the number of directors should be increased to six. The meeting then degenerated for a time into the motion- and counter-motion scenario that has company secretaries reaching for the rule book. The person proposed to be the new director solved the problem by saying that he did not really wish to be a director.

A proposal to establish a new agency in Minnesota was declined because of a shortage of funds. The Palmer agency in South Carolina was inspected because there was an unacceptably high number of overdue loans. In the west the cattle company loans were proving to be a little restrictive because they required borrowers to ask permission before they sold any cattle. The terms were then adjusted to remove this restriction. The new terms required there to be a minimum head count at any one time with Dundee Mortgage reserving the right of inspection without giving prior notice. This was a wise precaution, as erroneous head counts were a major cause of loss in the ranching business.

As the economy of North America continued to recover, the company took the time to assess the damage done by the depression years. All the agents were asked to provide reports on arrears, and reports were duly received from

San Antonio
Western Securities Co. (Fort Worth)

Montreal
Winnipeg
Corbin Banking Co.
J.B. Palmer and Son (South Carolina)
Kansas City Investment Co.
Smith, Caldwell and Co.
MacMaster, Burnham and Co.
Muscatine Mortgage Co.

No further comments were made on the arrears, but the inspection of agencies was stepped up and Mackenzie was again in North America in the early months of 1889. Patterson and Scudder, the agents in San Antonio, had fallen out, and Mackenzie did not wish to appoint either to act alone. Smith, Caldwell and Co. wanted the agency but Mackenzie thought that they already had a sufficiently large portion of the company's business. He favoured appointing H.P. Drought who hailed originally from Ireland. As soon as he was appointed Mr Patterson left town.

At the annual meeting in April 1889 there was a less than wholehearted reference to the proposed merger with Dundee Investment: '. . . if the proposed combination can be arranged on satisfactory terms, it is in the interests of the mortgage company that the same should be carried out'. However, the legal problem in Texas was not resolved and legal opinion was, for once, of a single mind that to continue lending would be 'unsafe'. Paradoxically Minnesota had just passed legislation to make it easier for foreign corporations to lend money there. But there were not the same lending opportunities in Minnesota as there were in Texas.

Nevertheless the decision was made that the merger would go ahead; both companies would disappear to be replaced by The Alliance Trust Company Ltd.

Oregon and Washington Mortgage Savings Bank Ltd

William Reid had become familiar with, and impressed by, the savings banks in California. He would also have been familiar with savings banks in his native Scotland, but the model for the projected Oregon and Washington Mortgage Savings Bank would be American rather than Scottish. The 26 Californian savings banks that had been established had been very successful and had raised $70m in deposits. These were not mutual organisations, as savings banks were in many other countries, but commercial banks that had share capital and which lent money on first mortgages. The minimum interest paid to depositors was 7.5% and the maximum 9%. Reid was aware that the constitution and laws of the state of Oregon, unlike California, did not permit the establishment of savings banks unless they were established by foreign companies.

He had first raised the possibility of setting up a savings bank in Portland in the summer of 1874 but had failed to gain support from Dundee. He returned to the subject two years later. His ambition was 'to supply a want hitherto felt viz: an Institution where the working, farming and other classes, both in Scotland and Oregon may deposit their various savings at remunerative rates of interest to be invested in the safest of all American securities, – First Mortgages, secured over Real Estate in Oregon and Washington Territory, Bonds of the United States, state of Oregon and Territory of Washington (if thought advisable) and counties therein.'

In truth there was very little difference between the proposed Mortgage Savings Bank and the Investment Trust. The differentiating factor was that deposits would be raised in Oregon. The local board was to be Donald Macleay, B. Goldsmith and William Reid, with Ellis Hughes as Attorney. This was the same group of people who served the Oregon and Washington Investment Trust. The board in Dundee, however, was an entirely different group of men from the Trust's board.

The directors were

Alex Gourlay, Chairman
William Robertson, Iron Merchant
George Gilroy, Manufacturer
Alex Thomson, Shipowner
DS Littlejohn, Solicitor

The British Linen Company Bank was to be the banker and Thomas Littlejohn was to be the secretary. The offices were to be in his office at 27 Bank Street, Dundee.

The memorandum and articles of association, containing 121 articles, gave the company three main powers. It was to be a savings bank, an investment company and a financial commission company. It also had wide general powers that included property dealing but it is unlikely that there was ever any intention to do this kind of business. Indeed the commission business was soon set aside so that the company could concentrate on banking and investing.

The company was registered in Scotland on 28 July 1876 and an initial call of £2 per share was made on the subscribed capital. The amount of authorised capital was £60,000 divided into 3,000 shares of £20 each. All the shares were issued and two-thirds of them were taken up by the Scottish and American directors and their immediate circle of friends. Indeed John Leng, who had been in Oregon when the company was formed, applied for 50 shares immediately upon his return to Scotland. He had been sufficiently impressed by what he had seen and heard whilst in Oregon that he turned up at the first ordinary meeting, held on 20 November 1876, and told the shareholders about Oregon and about the members of the local board. He was clearly impressed by the prospects but he was also cautious and 'recommended the shareholders to allow the business quietly and gradually to develop itself and the directors to follow a safe and cautious policy and especially not to offer too high rates of interest or aim at paying too high dividends'.

A telegram had been received from Portland that morning to say that the bank had opened for business. And, despite Leng's warning words, the directors continued to extol the virtues of similar organisations in California, some of which were paying dividends of 12% besides laying up large reserves. They should have listened to Leng, as it was not long before the Californian banks began to show signs of weakness and a banking commissioner had to be appointed to sort out the 'rotten banks'. One cutting from a Californian newspaper contained the memorable lines: 'Every once in a while the people in all communities seem to get "looney" and lose control of their balance wheels to a remarkable extent. Many persons in this city are in just that kind of mood at the present time. They jump from excitement to excitement without a particle of cool reflection, and when it is all over wonder how they could possibly have been so thoughtless.'

Scottish investors, on the other hand, whilst not averse to risk, were more wary. They readily agreed to a request from the American shareholders that the Hon. J.T. Brown, registrar of the US Land Office at Olympia be appointed to the local board. They were also wise enough to decline a suggestion that Scottish savers should be allowed to deposit money in the bank at the same rates as were to be paid to American depositors. Moreover there were different rates for different maturities. Short-term deposits received 5% while rates for 18 months' money were 8%.

It was not long before William Reid was up to his old tricks. As early as January 1877 the directors in Dundee had to tell him to get the local shareholders register up to date. The following month Dundee demanded explanations about some of the loans being made. They also insisted that the accounts be audited by the state auditor of Oregon.

Reid was clear in his mind that a savings bank needed a building, and that the offices that he had rented from H.E. Ankeny would not suffice in the long run. The directors of the Oregon and Washington Trust rejected his suggestion that the two companies should share a building but he proceeded to acquire land. He purchased lot 6 of block 27 on First Street for $7,500 and had a sizeable building erected on the site. The Trust changed its mind and agreed to take offices in the new building, but before doing so Mackenzie had another look at the Trust's memorandum and articles and declared that it was outwith its powers to own a building. This did not deter Reid who took the view that it was better to buy than to rent, and that good tenants could be found for the building that would deliver a return of 10% on the capital investment. The US Signal Service Bureau was an early tenant. The problem was solved when William Lowson, John Leng and Thomas Cox purchased a half share in their own names which was then let to the Trust, although this still leaves open the possibility that the Trust put up the money. The other major tenant was the Bank of British North America. There was general agreement that the building was 'a handsome structure and reflects well on Mr Reid'.

Mindful of the Portland fire of 1873, Reid acquired a large fire-and-burglar-proof safe. For even greater security he insisted that, when the vault was being built, the stones should be bolted together. A time lock was a later addition. Reid actually put some of his own money into the fitting out of the bank, which was described as being in walnut and glass. He also declined, perhaps in an effort to ingratiate himself with his directors, to accept any salary for the first year and asked for only $70 per month thereafter – a figure that the local directors thought to be 'far beneath the value of his services to the bank'.

Meanwhile the business had been growing well, and by mid February 1877 $20,000 had been lent on mortgages. In effect the bank's business was basically the same as the Trust's – the only difference being that the bank accepted deposits from the public in Portland. The bank was going so well that the Dundee board proposed an increase in capital, but this was rejected by the local board who argued that to increase the capital might depress interest rates and increase competition. This merely pushed the bank into a position where the Dundee board had to borrow money from the British Linen Bank. That bank was unhappy with the US securities that were offered as security for the advance and insisted on the personal guarantees of the directors. Some months were to pass before the local board saw the wisdom and necessity of a further call on the capital of the bank.

A minor panic occurred in November 1877 when articles appeared in the local press in Portland that questioned the security of depositors' money and suggested that local taxes had not been paid. The local board was told to frame a reply and submit it to Dundee for approval. The anxiety that this caused soon passed, and when the first annual general meeting took place in May 1878 the shareholders learned that they were to receive a dividend of 6% and that all preliminary expenses incurred in setting up the bank had been paid and £100 had been transferred into a reserve fund. They were also told that the bank building had been completed and it was expected to yield 11% on the cost. There were 149 depositors whose savings totalled £10,856, and £9,853 had been lent on 61 mortgages.

Plans were afoot to send the company secretary, Thomas Littlejohn, on a tour of inspection. He was given a number of specific instructions that included the appointment of a neutral auditor and accountant. He was also expected to enquire into the bank's prospects, investigate other local organisations and appoint a local valuer, as well as to make arrangements for the call that was to be made on share capital.

It seems that no one in Dundee was appointed to act as company secretary while he was in America as there is a four-and-a-half-month period when no meetings are recorded in the minute book. When he returned to Dundee in October Littlejohn commented favourably on the bank's lending. He had inspected the properties in Portland and some of the country districts and found the loans to be very safe. Doubtless influenced by Reid he took the view that there was no need for a new accountant or an independent auditor. The original accountant had blundered, and some of his mistakes had not been uncovered until he had left, but there was a new man in place now and he was doing well. Similarly he advised that he had not appointed a valuer as there were none to be had and the job was being done well by Mr Dunbar, who was Reid's father-in-law.

Whilst in Oregon Littlejohn had learned that the Pacific Loan and Investment Company, an offshoot of Messrs Balfour and Williamson in Liverpool, a large trading company, was planning to open an office in Portland. It was decided that the bank's chairman and secretary should go to Liverpool for discussions, but the City of Glasgow Bank failure in October 1878 caused a commercial crisis and the visit never took place.

The crisis also caused the bank to suspend its advertising, which was thought likely to be 'fruitless' in the current climate. However it was soon restored. Financial companies everywhere were prompted by the crisis to review their governance structures and their financial arrangements. The Dundee board took the view that the shares were held in too few hands, especially in Portland, and this was prejudicing the raising of debentures in Scotland. The local board took a contrary view. Nevertheless Reid and Hughes were eventually prevailed upon to sell some of their shares.

It was also fortuitous that Thomas Macleay, a member of the local board, was in Dundee when the crisis broke. He was persuaded to arrange for the appointment of 'a properly qualified and neutral auditor on his return to Portland'. The matter was still being discussed a year later. But in reality this crisis seems to have had very little effect on the bank. The beneficial effect was that a supply of well-trained bankers became available, some of whom were prepared to travel to North America for a new job. The bank received several applications. By May of 1879 the situation had sufficiently recovered for the chairman and secretary to travel to several Scottish towns to appoint solicitors as agents for the bank. In effect, their role was to raise debentures, for which they received a commission.

Throughout 1879 there were discussions about the Trust acting as agent for the bank. The details were never specified, and Reid blew hot and cold on the idea. Yet this was the first indication of what was to follow – the gradual assimilation of the bank by the Trust. The Trust itself had undergone changes. In 1879 the Oregon and Washington Trust Investment Co. Ltd became the Dundee Mortgage and Trust Investment Co. Ltd. The matter of an independent auditor was settled when Robert Bell, lately secretary of the Trades Lane Calendering Company in Dundee and then accountant to the Trust in Portland, was appointed to the role. Quite how independent he could be is a moot point. He was later entrusted with the task of cementing the agency agreement between the two companies.

Yet if there were still doubts about the independence of the auditor in Portland the same could not be said about the auditor in Dundee. In March 1880 they qualified the accounts. They were concerned about arrears in the accounting records and about arrears in payments of interest. The latter only amounted to $500 and was probably not the major concern. At the subsequent annual meeting several of the directors of the Trust were present – Lowson, Leng, Cox and Neish. Some of the shareholders claimed that the meeting had not been properly constituted and the chairman adjourned the meeting. When it was reconvened in May, both Lowson and Cox were elected to the board. The faction, led by Gourlay, resigned but stood for re-election and was duly reappointed. An extensive revision of the memorandum and articles of association then ensued with the powers of the local board much diminished.

Meanwhile Reid was asked to explain why he had lent $35,000 on the security of steamers owned by the Oregon Navigation Company. On the day that the new rules were approved – 11 October 1880 – the board met immediately after the extraordinary general meeting, and after 'full and anxious discussion' declared themselves unhappy with Reid's behaviour. The loan to the Navigation Company represented more than half of the bank's paid-up capital and it was not on the security of real estate. Moreover it was made to a company that was composed of members of the local board. The loan had been made on the full-price value of the boats, so there was no margin for security, and it had been made at 9% which was less than was currently being obtained for mortgages. The board decided that a schedule should be set for early repayment, insurance should be taken out and personal obligations should be sought from the local board.

The steamers in question were needed to link elements of the Oregonian Railway Company across the Willamette valley. Both Lowson and Reid had stakes in this company, although Reid claimed to have only one share. The loan was transferred to the books of the Dundee Mortgage and Trust Investment Company Ltd. Lowson eventually agreed that the Railway Company would take over the steamers and repay the loan.

The general run of lending business was going well, with mortgages reaching $244,000 in February 1881 although the deposit side was doing much less well at only $79,000. At the annual general meeting the next month a dividend of 8% was declared against profits of £1,485, and the reserve was now £500. Gourlay chose this time to resign and was replaced by Lord Airlie and Peter M. Cochrane. The takeover by the Trust was all but complete. New auditors, Messrs Moody, Stuart and Robertson, were appointed, and when it was announced that the company office would move to the Trust's office at 13 Panmure Street, Thomas Littlejohn resigned as secretary to be replaced by William Mackenzie.

Tensions between Dundee and Portland remained. The Bank of British North America was getting worried about Reid's intromissions and said that unless he was issued with a letter of credit they would cease to honour his drafts. And when Reid, together with Hughes, the lawyer, and Bell, the accountant, came up with new plans for the running of the bank, the board did not agree. In effect, the bank was now the agent in Oregon and Washington for the Trust.

The position was not helped by legislation in Oregon that was prejudicial to the position of the bank. Oregon had passed an Aliens Act that made it more difficult for foreign corporations to operate in the state. Reid's solution was that the bank's business should be transacted through a native American bank that Bell was in process of establishing. Alternatively the directors in Dundee should arrange for the local incorporation of a new bank. Neither solution was acceptable to the directors, who told Reid that if the bank could not be operated profitably then they would simply take their money away. They thought that this would not happen and that the legislature in Oregon would soon see the error of its ways and the dangers that would be done to the development of Oregon by the withdrawal of foreign capital. Reid was duly instructed to remit surplus funds to the Illinois Trust and Savings Bank in Chicago.

In January 1882 the decision was made to stop taking deposits in Oregon and to pay off all existing deposits 'as soon as possible'. The agency agreement was suspended, and when the annual general meeting took place in April a proposal was put before the shareholders that the bank should be merged with the Dundee Mortgage and Trust Investment Company Ltd. The proposal was unanimously approved at a subsequent extraordinary general meeting.

Meantime Reid was making progress with the setting up of his own bank in Portland. His powers to act for Dundee Mortgage and Dundee Land were formally recalled in June 1883, but he was told that he would be paid commission for any business that he brought to these companies.

Dundee Land Investment Company Ltd

The Dundee Land Investment Company Ltd was an altogether more speculative venture than many of the other companies and trusts that were being established at this time. Its declared strategy was to

1. Buy land which can be rented out so as to provide a dividend of 3–4%.
2. Buy land which can be subdivided and sold to Scottish migrants either for ready money or in instalments –'the company giving facilities for building houses and breaking the ground'.

3. Acquire a few lots in the neighbourhood of expanding towns.
4. Maybe acquire lands in intermediate sections between
   railway grants.

The prime mover behind this new venture was William Lowson but he was soon joined by his close circle of friends Viscount Airlie, John Leng, Andrew Whitton and Thomas Couper.

Registration of the new company was completed on 7 September 1878 when it was declared that the company's registered office would be at 13 Panmure Street and the company secretary would be William Mackenzie, although as he was in the United States at the time, his assistant, David Stewart, was appointed pro tem. Airlie was to be the chairman and Lowson the deputy chairman.

There were 131 applications for the 10,000 shares. The offer was over-subscribed, and Mackenzie had the task of allotting the shares. Messrs Pattullo and Thornton, who were to be solicitors to the company, got 300 shares and Jesup, Paton and Co., bankers in New York, were allotted 250 shares. Most of the subscribers were from Dundee and the surrounding area.

A business such as this needed someone to be 'on the ground' and looking out for investment opportunities and appointing appropriate people to be the agents. The directors did not have far to look. The man they appointed to the task was William Smith, a farmer from Stone O'Morphie near Montrose. Quite what qualifications he had for the role is unclear, but the directors were clearly impressed when they interviewed him. Doubtless Smith was attracted to the role and to the somewhat generous daily allowance of 4 guineas (£4.20). At the same time he was appointed to a similar role for Dundee Mortgage.

But before the company could get started the banking crisis broke in October and, for a time, the directors were reluctant to make any call on the shareholders. This stance was confirmed at the first ordinary general meeting of the company that took place on 3 January 1879. Only the directors and six other shareholders attended the meeting. There was no sign therefore that the shareholders were unduly worried by the turn of events in Glasgow.

Nevertheless some funds had been raised on debentures and the company was able to make a modest start. As with so many of the other investment companies, a great deal of preparatory work was undertaken before the company was formed. Moreover the directors were well connected in North America and were able to draw on these connections to make contacts and raise business deals for the new company.

The first agent appointed was John Maule Machar from Kingston, Ontario, who, like Smith, was also appointed to work for Dundee Mortgage. Maule's first task was to give an opinion on Winnipeg as a field for investment.

Meanwhile Smith was dispatched to the United States with letters of introduction to many of the friends and acquaintances of the directors in Dundee. Foremost amongst these was L.B. Sidway in Chicago. Mackenzie was already in Chicago when Smith arrived. Letters from Smith to Dundee were sent on 4, 13 and 16 November. From there he went to Denver, Kansas and Indianapolis.

It was not long, however, before doubts began to surface about Smith's real intent. Mackenzie wrote home from Texas on 6 December to say that Smith had purchased 35 sections of land (about 22,400 acres) in Swister County in the Texas Panhandle for 40 cents an acre. It was good grassland but Smith's idea was that he would keep half for himself and offer the other half to the company. The response of the directors was to say, more than once, that they were happy to take a half share but only if all the land was held jointly. Smith had returned from America and was present at the board meeting, but it was only a short visit and he was soon back in America.

Mackenzie had also been busy making his own connections and contacts. While in New York he had met Austin Corbin of the Corbin Banking Company. Corbin had been heavily involved in the development of Coney Island as a recreation area for New Yorkers but he was now keen to invest in other parts of the United States and had a particular interest in the Pacific North West. A deal was done which involved Dundee Land investing $15,000 while Corbin put in $10,000. Any lands purchased were to be held in the name of one of John Paton's staff in Jesup, Paton and Co. in New York. It was said that the lands could not be held in Paton's own name as he was Scottish and had never become a naturalised American citizen. This was not the first sign that life would become more complicated for foreigners trying to do business in the United States.

Paton was given discretionary powers of investment up to $25,000 as it was recognised that there was often a need for speed in these transactions and, given the distances involved, speed was not always possible. He was highly conscientious, and in a two-week period in April 1879 he wrote six letters to Dundee. His brief was wide and he was authorised to invest money in lands in Wisconsin, Minnesota, Iowa and Missouri. But this was the root of the problem. Well connected as he was, it was not really possible for Paton to be well versed in the value of land in such a wide, geographically diverse and underdeveloped area. Inevitably a lot of the deals available were with railroad companies, and many of them were highly speculative.

One such deal was with the Milwaukee Lake Shore and Western Railroad Company. The intention was that Dundee Land should purchase property upon which the Railroad planned to build an extension the following year. It was not long, however, before Dundee Land was insisting that the Railroad had to get its plans 'into proper business shape at once'. Meanwhile in Minnesota plans were well advanced for two town sites through which another railroad company was to build a line. The towns were to be called Airlie and Dundee. A further deal was being done with Balfour Guthrie in San Francisco to purchase land in California.

There is a real sense of the risks being spread but there is also a sense of the net being cast too wide. The fact that Dundee Land was in business soon got around and attracted investors, developers and promoters. Sometimes it was difficult to tell the difference. One such visitor to Dundee was J.W. Barclay, MP for Forfar and chairman of the Colorado Mortgage and Investment Company, which, despite its name, was a London-based organisation. Barclay had lengthy discussions with the directors over the possibility of joint ventures.

Hard on Barclay's heels in the summer of 1878 John Paton came for a visit. He recommended no more investment in Iowa and counselled that investment in agricultural lands in Texas and Kansas should be avoided. He was much keener on town properties. It was left to him to select which properties might be acquired in Kansas City but the directors insisted that Paton send one of his men on a reconnaissance visit.

Mackenzie's brother Robert was then working for William Reid in Portland and he wrote in July 1879 with a proposal for land acquisition in Oregon. The directors were favourable to this idea.

In August Barclay was back with a new proposal which involved acquiring a cattle ranch and its stock. Further consideration was given to investments in Manitoba in view of the building of the Canadian Pacific Railway. By the end of the summer the directors took stock. They concluded that they had probably spent enough on acquiring property that would take time to mature and acquire value. They now turned their thinking to investments which would give a more immediate return. The shareholders, after all, would expect a dividend.

They were disappointed. When the annual general meeting took place on 30 December 1879, 27 shareholders turned up. They listened to the directors' report and were told that interest on investments was only £299. They would have to be patient, but they might not have to wait long. Some of the town properties that had been acquired in Kansas were letting well, and houses and shops were being built on other sites that had been purchased. Messrs Underwood and Clark rented one of the Kansas properties at $1,400 per annum.

Barclay kept coming back with new ideas and proposals, and although Airlie was quite keen on some of them, the other directors were, at best, lukewarm. They came close to participating in one of his ranching ventures but when Thornton told them that it was *ultra vires* for Dundee Land to own shares in other companies the idea died.

By this stage at least two calls had been made on the shareholders for capital, and £15,000 had been paid up. A further £5,000 had been raised on debentures.

No more was heard of William Smith, and his place as inspector was taken, in March 1880, by John McCulloch of Denbie Mains in Dumfries. As we have seen, this was a joint appointment with Dundee Mortgage and there was to be greater co-operation between the two companies as opportunities presented themselves.

McCulloch was off to North America within the month. The summer was much preferred for travelling. His first stop was Minnesota, where John Paton was selling land and McCulloch was asked to take a look. He was then sent to Canada from where he wrote to say that he preferred city investment to farming lands although he subsequently recommended timber lands.

William Reid in Portland got involved by recommending city-centre land investment in Portland in connection with his railway company. He also advised that he was building himself a new house and recommended that Dundee Land should join him in the project and build in the neighbourhood. He had other plans to build a hotel at one of the stations on his railway line. The directors delayed a decision until Airlie and McCulloch arrived to take a look.

Further lending and building opportunities came from Underwood and Clark in Kansas who became close collaborators with Dundee Land. And, eventually, a deal was done with Mr Barclay of the Colorado Mortgage and Investment Company. Airlie had proposed a number of land purchases in Denver, and Barclay agreed that his company would build artisans dwellings on the properties. By the end of 1880 the company was building houses on some of the lots it owned in Winnipeg.

It was soon time to raise more capital. In November 1880 the decision was made to issue 10,000 shares of the authorised capital. Despite the fact that no dividend had yet been paid and local investors would know very little about the company, demand was brisk, and at their meeting on 17 December 1880 the directors were told that all the shares had been issued. This gave them the confidence to bring forward a special resolution that would enlarge the company's powers. The plan was to acquire powers to engage in agricultural activities, especially on Iowa lands, and to raise cattle, undertake agricultural activities and cut timber. The age of the cattle company had well and truly begun.

At the annual general meeting held in Lamb's Hotel on 30 December 1880 the 28 shareholders learned that they were to be paid a dividend of 5% and that the company was now concentrating on revenue-producing investments. Shareholders were invited to anticipate a larger dividend next year. Meanwhile the directors were awarded £300 by the shareholders.

This meeting was immediately followed by an extraordinary general meeting at which the memorandum and articles of the company were altered to give it the extra powers that were necessary to undertake the agricultural business. William Macmaster was present and he was given a three-year contract to run the contemplated cattle company in Lyon County, Iowa although McCulloch was also involved. Macmaster was given powers to purchase 800–1,000 head of cattle. He was also to acquire bulls, hire servants and build buildings. A credit was opened in McCulloch's name with the Bank of Montreal in New York and there was to be a subsidiary account with the Illinois Trust and Savings Bank in Chicago. McCulloch was also empowered to break and crop other lands in Iowa.

W.J. Menzies of Scottish American Land in Edinburgh tried to get the directors interested in a joint ranching operation in Kansas on the recommendation of Underwood, Clark and Co. but the feeling was that the project was too big. Size did not deter them in other projects, and at the same meeting in which they declined the Menzies project they learned that they had been successful in acquiring 60,000 acres in Campbell and Claiborne Counties in Tennessee, 5,000 acres in Scott County, Tennessee and four parcels of land in Whitley County, Kentucky amounting to over 100,000 acres. These lands were described as being valuable timber, grazing and mineral-yielding lands with some farming acreage.

Reid, meanwhile, was still pressing the directors to fund his planned hotel in Oregon. But while the directors were happy to work with him in building villas in Portland they were less sanguine about the hotel. True to form, Reid exceeded his spending powers and the directors responded by curbing his credit.

Agreement was eventually reached with the ever-persistent Barclay and 720 acres of Colorado coal lands were purchased. These were also said to be good agricultural lands with access to water. James Duff was the Denver-based manager of the Colorado Company and he was given powers to manage Dundee Land's interests.

In May 1881 Duff was authorised to purchase a half share, with Colorado Land, in a large parcel of land in New Mexico. This was the Chaves Grant that was to become an important, if difficult, part of the company's story.

All of these purchases were rapidly diminishing the company's bank balances, but some extra effort was put into raising debenture money in Dundee. This was so successful that the directors decided to postpone a planned call on the shareholders for extra money. The debenture money was raised at 4.25% for three-year money and 4.5% for five years.

The company also pursued the acquisition of town lots in Winnipeg, Portland and Kansas. There was soon an active market in the houses that were built on these lands. The directors confessed themselves disappointed at the prices available in Portland but were much more satisfied with the surpluses they made in Winnipeg and Kansas.

The advantage of town lots was, of course, that there was a ready market as the population of the United States and Canada grew and became more prosperous. The other advantage was that good legal title was easily secured. This was certainly not the case with the large purchases of other lands. The title to the Chaves Grant in New Mexico took many years, and much legal activity, before the directors were convinced that they had a good title. There was also the question of what to do with the land. In November 1881 the directors, in agreement with Barclay, appointed two men to live on the land, supervise the fencing and try to keep squatters at bay. Two months later Barclay wrote to propose that Mr Shirres, from Aberdeen, who was returning home to his sheep farm in New Zealand via San Francisco, should detour and inspect the land. This was agreed.

There were similar difficulties in Kentucky and Tennessee but fortunately these were uncovered before the purchases were finalised and the company was able to back out of some of them. The Tennessee problem was only resolved after being referred to the State Supreme Court. Eventually T. Lyon White of Tennessee agreed to purchase a 25% interest in the Tennessee and Kentucky lands. He would also devote his whole time and attention to their development. He eventually claimed that the lands purchased were a good deal smaller than the selling agents had suggested. He even went so far as to accuse the agent, Francis Smith of Indianapolis, of knowingly misrepresenting the acreage. The directors were highly sceptical about this claim and Smith eventually became a highly trusted agent of several of the Dundee companies.

This was a recurring problem. The directors became increasingly dependent on McCulloch and his good judgement, but even he was not able to assess the ultimate accuracy of acreage claims made in land documents. Another problem encountered from time to time with land and financial agents was the problem of deals being done with other people before the directors in Dundee had a chance to respond to an offer. This was a particular issue with Underwood, Clark and Co. in Kansas who were inclined to take the first offer that came along.

Occasionally the directors got into what can only be described as a fankle. In May 1881 John Paton in New York forwarded deeds for the purchase of 720 acres in Minnehaha and Moody Counties in Dakota. The directors immediately instructed McCulloch to inspect the land, as they were not at all clear about what they had actually purchased.

They were very clear about Winnipeg. Charles Drummond, the agent there, had visited Dundee in the summer of 1881 and had his credits increased to $100,000. He was authorised to proceed with building houses on several lots in Winnipeg. The company doubled its money on the Edmonton Street lots.

While in Scotland Mackenzie had introduced Drummond to W.J. Menzies in Edinburgh and the three men had come up with a plan for a new company that had the prospect of acquiring 100,000 acres of land from the Canadian Pacific Railway. The new company, the Scottish Canadian Company, was to be managed from Edinburgh with three directors from Dundee Land and three from Menzies' company, Scottish American Land. There was a slight problem in that Dundee Land still did not have powers to acquire shares in other companies but the problem was easily overcome by the legal nicety of having Dundee Land's interest in the new company as a 'pro indiviso' share. John Clay, who became a leading US cattleman, was to manage the company and would spend the summers in Manitoba and his winters in Scotland, promoting emigration. In the event, this company was soon wound up and another, the North West Canada Company, with wider powers, replaced it.

There was suddenly some excitement in the housing market in Portland and the opportunity was taken to sell some units at a good profit. Some of the

Colorado land was sold at a profit of $4,000. Elsewhere the directors purchased 140,000 acres in Arkansas that they advertised as being available 'rent free for five years to Negroes, and others', on condition that they cleared the land to make it available for agriculture.

The directors in Dundee were certainly kept very busy and some of them made visits to north America. Mackenzie made several visits, as did Airlie. It was during one of these trips that Airlie died suddenly of pneumonia in Denver in September 1881. It was a great loss to the company as he was the director who was best acquainted with matters in North America. It was not long, however, before the most suitable of all replacements was found. Robert Fleming, who had pioneered investment trusts in Dundee in 1873, became a director in February 1882. At the same time William Lowson was appointed as chairman.

The general tone of comments in the minute books at that time suggests that business, notwithstanding some difficulties, was going well, and at the annual general meeting on 31 January 1882 the directors were able to report that net revenue was £4,304. The shareholders could therefore expect a dividend of 5% but they were doubtless delighted to learn that, in addition to the dividend, they would be paid a bonus of another 5%. They were assured that only profits actually realised had been taken into the accounts.

Accepting this assurance that they were not being paid out of capital, the shareholders felt sufficiently confident to think about bigger things, and they met again in March 1882 for an extraordinary general meeting at which it was decided to form a new company with wider powers. Thornton, who by this time had severed his partnership with Pattullo, was asked to draft a memorandum and articles of association for a new company.

Notwithstanding this development, the directors of Dundee Land did not soft-pedal. In the spring of 1882 they participated in a city development company that Underwood and Clark had established to build houses, shops and offices in Kansas, they sold assets in Winnipeg because prices were high, they established a new agency under Peter Macmaster at Fergus Falls and, at Fleming's prompting, they purchased railway bonds. They met again in extraordinary meeting on May 1882 and agreed to transfer the assets and liabilities of the company to the new enterprise, the Dundee Investment Company Ltd. Mackenzie was appointed as liquidator of Dundee Land.

Doubtless some of the assets that were transferred to the new company were of questionable value, and some were well short of what their documentation said they were. But the bulk of business was generally sound.

Hawaii Investment and Agency Company Ltd and the Western and Hawaiian Investment Company Ltd

As with the other investment trusts and mortgage companies which were set up in Dundee at this time a great deal of preparatory work had been done before anything was recorded in the minutes of the Hawaii Investment and Agency Company Ltd. A provisional committee comprising

Alex Gilroy, Jnr, Chair
Alex Gourlay
Thomas Bell, Jnr
George Macfarlane
Alexander Thomson
John W. Shepherd

met on 1 October 1880 where they learned that Mr McCrindell, a lawyer in Honolulu, had secured the agreement of four leading men to serve on the local board in Hawaii.

The four who had agreed to serve were:

Hon. W.L. Green, ex-Minister of Foreign Affairs,
Hon. H.P. Carter, ex-Minister of Foreign Affairs,
I.S. Walker, Merchant and late Minister of Finance
W.W. Hall, Merchant in Honolulu

Clearly these were men of power and influence. A fifth man, S.M. Castle, who was a missionary, had declined to serve. Links between Dundee and Honolulu had been growing for some time, as both cities were major centres of the whaling industry. There was already a Hawaiian consul in Dundee. There were also sugar industry links between Glasgow and Honolulu.

By that time the prospectus had been prepared and orders were given for 2,000 to be printed. The memorandum and articles of association had also been drafted and 500 were to be printed. The company was then incorporated on 6 October when it was declared that the registered office would be at 6 Panmure Street. Instructions were given to John Shepherd, who became the company secretary, to seek private sales for as many of the shares as he could. He was apparently quite successful, and when the provisional committee met at the end of October to effect an allocation of shares it was discovered that they were oversubscribed in the ratio of 3:1. McCrindell was to get 2,500 shares for allocation in Hawaii. Various other business matters were dealt with including local taxation in Hawaii. McCrindell was asked to provide information about this and to provide maps and a copy of the *Hawaiian Almanac,* a guide to the institutions on the islands.

One of the Hawaii shareholders was none other than King David Kalakaua, the reigning monarch in Hawaii, who purchased 200 shares. (Hawaii was an independent kingdom but the monarchy was strongly influenced by British, and subsequently American, commercial interests.)

There were 42 subscribers at the first general meeting on 5 November. The directors elected were

> Alexander Gourlay, Merchant
> Alexander Gilroy, Merchant
> George Halley, Manufacturer and President of the Chamber
>   of Commerce
> William Ritchie, Merchant
> D.S. Littlejohn, Solicitor

The directors, the first four of whom were leading figures in the jute industry, met immediately after the general meeting and dealt with largely practical matters such as the company seal and the signing authority for cheques. But they also took time to elect Halley as chairman and to appoint Shepherd as company secretary. Some time was devoted to a discussion regarding the Protectorate of the Hawaiian Islands, and further clarification was sought from McCrindell.

November's meetings dealt largely with administrative matters and it was not until the end of the month that there was any real discussion of the lending on mortgages which was the company's purpose in life. It was then that McCrindell was authorised to draw down £3,000 and the same again if he was convinced that good lending opportunities were available.

All looked as if it was going quite smoothly until the Glasgow firm of George Gray Macfarlane and Co. submitted a claim for £500 in respect of the assistance they had provided in getting the company established. The preliminary expenses of setting up the company were £262 and these had already been paid, so the Glasgow firm's claim was, to say the least, unwelcome. It was also stoutly resisted. A great deal of correspondence ensued. A meeting was duly convened at which it was alleged that McCrindell was unhappy and wished to be relieved of his duties in Honolulu.

It looked as if a battle royal might ensue but cooler heads prevailed and at the general meeting on 10 February 1881 Macfarlane produced a statement of various outlays that he had incurred and then withdrew his claim. The directors agreed to give him their best consideration 'on the success of the company being assured'. He, in turn, made every effort to get McCrindell to remain in post. In the interim he received £14 7s 1d (£14.35).

The business seemed to be growing well and there was an active market in the shares. One of the early loans was $20,000 to the Moanii Sugar Plantation on Molokai. The possibility of advertising for debenture money in Glasgow was given serious consideration, and active planning was devoted to promoting another company to do similar business in Fiji. The directors actually decided to go ahead with the Fiji idea and even decided how much capital to raise – £250,000 in 50,000 shares of £5. In the end the idea came to nothing as a company was being promoted in London to engage in the same business. The Dundee men were offered a seat on that company's board but decided not to accept, and by the summer of 1881 they had given up the idea.

The directors were certainly being kept busy on the Hawaiian front. McCrindell was ordered to return home at the 'earliest opportunity' for discussions, and the Hon. W.L. Green assumed responsibility for the Hawaiian operation. Lending continued at a brisk pace and included $7,500 to Macfarlane and Co. on the security of sugar held in a warehouse and ready for shipment.

McCrindell was in Dundee when the board met on 18 August. He made a lengthy report but Shepherd was not sufficiently zealous as a company secretary to record anything that was said. What is clear was that the matter of his remuneration had not been settled and that Macfarlane was still sniping around and claiming money. Between them they claimed over £400, but before the matter went to arbitration they settled, at Lowson's instigation, for half that amount.

When the half-yearly general meeting took place in Lamb's Hotel on 14 February 1882 the 26 shareholders present learned that the company had got off to a slow start because a smallpox outbreak had restricted inter-island travel. However, the company was then moving forward, and total lending had risen to £47,440 which included loans to some of the most successful sugar plantations, including the Honokaa Sugar Plantation of F.A. Schafer and Co. and the Honomu Plantation. The shareholders were not told that the company had been involved in shipping gold sovereigns from Sydney to Honolulu. They were, however, reassured that the directors in Dundee and the local board in

Honolulu had 'acted all along with great caution'.

The lending reflected the ethnic and national melting pot that Hawaii had become. Amongst the borrowers were Americans, Chinese and Germans. Many of the loans were for relatively small amounts, but none of this seems to have created any difficulties, except for the auditors in Dundee who sought guidance in April 1882 as to how they were to verify the Honolulu books. The reply, if any, is not recorded.

In truth the Dundee board had little to do. Lending decisions were largely made in Honolulu where the local board had the company established and moving forward. There was no shortage of loan applications. Having little to do, the Dundee directors did nothing. There is no recorded meeting of the board between the annual general meeting in early September 1882 and 21 November 1882. No meetings were held in January or February 1883. But when they met in March 1883 they were in an expansive mood.

Although they recommended that no dividend should be paid they 'carefully considered the propriety of extending the powers of the company'. Littlejohn's legal firm was commissioned to prepare a draft constitution. William Grant submitted notes on land and finance in Egypt and suggested that a lending operation could be conducted there, but this was immediately rejected because of 'the unsettled state of affairs in Egypt'.

There was no doubt in anyone else's mind that, if the firm was to expand, it would best do so by looking to North America. At the annual meeting in August 1883 it was decided that the new company should be called the American and Hawaiian Investment Company Ltd but the directors were authorised to change this if they felt it wise to do so. In the event they settled for the Western and Hawaiian Investment Company Ltd.

Thereafter it was a relatively simple matter to get the new company established, close the old one and issue the new shares to the old shareholders. It was a very straightforward share swap and, for the time being, no new capital was called up.

The Western and Hawaiian Investment Company Ltd

The new company was incorporated on 3 October 1883. The promoters

George Halley, Chairman
William Ritchie

D.S. Littlejohn
Alex Gourlay
Alex Gilroy

with John W Shepherd in attendance as secretary, met in the Union Bank Building at 6 Panmure Street, Dundee on 8 October to start the new company. They agreed the formalities and stated that the transfer date from old company to new would be 30 November. In Hawaii W.L. Green was granted powers to settle the affairs of the old company.

The company's first target for expansion was Texas, where they appointed William Sommerville as agent. Sommerville needed no introduction in Dundee as it was he who had organised the transfer of the Matador Land and Cattle Company into Dundee hands in 1882. He was also active in investment matters for some of the other Dundee and Edinburgh interests.

His initial endeavours involved lending on the security of vendors' lien notes for which rates of interest varied between 10 and 15%. He was also instructed to lend on mortgages and, such was the worry about the right of foreign companies to do business in Texas that the lending was done in the names of Halley and Gilroy. It was not long before Sommerville had exhausted his initial credit of $25,000. He asked for more and was given $15,000

In the meantime Green continued lending in Hawaii but the rate of interest there was falling gradually. His letters usually reached Dundee within a month of leaving Hawaii so the directors were kept reasonably well up to date with what was going on. Sommerville's letters from Fort Worth reached Dundee in less than three weeks.

Such was Sommerville's success that it created some embarrassment when the directors had to go to the British Linen Bank to ask for an overdraft and were required to provide personal guarantees. The solution to this temporary shortage of funds was to send Shepherd on a tour of towns in the North-east of Scotland to speak to solicitors and to raise further debenture monies. The other solution was to begin to withdraw money from Honolulu where lending opportunities were smaller and where the political situation was becoming very unstable.

By the summer of 1884 the new company was well established. The annual meeting took place in Lamb's Hotel on 5 September and the shareholders were satisfied to hear that they would receive a final dividend of 3% to add to the interim of 3% which they had already been paid. A year later the full year dividend was increased to 8%. There can have been no doubt that the increased dividend was due to the success that Sommerville was making of the Fort Worth agency, and this merely accelerated the withdrawal of funds from Honolulu. Early in 1887 Sommerville was asked to write to Portland and Kansas to ascertain what investment conditions were like in those places.

This seems a little strange, as there were a number of people around in Dundee who could have answered that question. Perhaps there were some commercial confidences that prevented the question being asked. When advice was sought about how to invest the gradually increasing reserve fund, they called upon the man whose knowledge of these matters was without parallel – Robert Fleming who, by that time, had withdrawn from his directorships in rival Dundee investment companies.

The Dundee Investment Company and the Dundee Mortgage and Trust Investment Company were by then well advanced with their plans to create a large general-purpose investment and mortgage company. The new company had been registered and named as The Alliance Trust but would not commence business until 1889. Nowhere is there any hint that the Western and Hawaiian Investment Company was invited to join in. If it had become part of the new company it would have made very little difference, as the scale of the Alliance Trust quite simply dwarfed the Western and Hawaiian.

The Western and Hawaiian Investment Company soldiered on for many years to come but it never grew to threaten the progress of the Alliance Trust, in whose shadow it remained until the 1920s when it became the Second Alliance Trust.

Dundee Investment Company

The Dundee Investment Company Ltd was incorporated on 18 April 1882 and the first board meeting was held three days later. William Lowson, John Leng and Andrew Whitton met at 13 Panmure Street. William Mackenzie was also there, and he was appointed to be the company secretary. The four men now had a great deal of experience in the formation of new companies and their actions were confident and decisive. They were soon joined by Robert Fleming.

Within weeks they had held an extraordinary general meeting to agree the takeover of the Dundee Land Investment Company. They had also raised money on debentures and made their first loan. This was a joint loan with the Dundee Mortgage and Investment Company Ltd to the Coleman Fulton Pasture Company. Loans made jointly with Dundee Mortgage became a common feature of the activities of the new company.

Most of the well-known names in the Dundee business community became shareholders in Dundee Investment. Thomas Cox, Henry Gourlay, Alexander Gilroy, Jnr, Robert Fleming, Thomas Thornton and Peter Cochrane were amongst the 145 shareholders and all had sizeable shareholdings. The largest shareholding outside Dundee was the 625 shares held by Thomas Nelson, the Edinburgh publisher who was closely involved with a number of investment companies. Jesup, Paton and Co., the New York bankers, held 625 shares.

In some respects Dundee Investment was simply Dundee Land writ large, albeit with a more conservative lending policy. But it was more than just a mortgage company and had clear intentions to be an investment company as well. The new company assumed all the agents and obligations of the old company and there was no attempt to renegotiate contracts. The major challenge was to divest the new company of some of the less liquid assets that had been acquired by Dundee Land. The least worrisome assets were in growth towns like Kansas City where Underwood, Clark were able to sell several buildings. The directors in Dundee approved but said, in return, that they would be quite happy if about 60% of the purchase price was to remain on mortgages at a fair rate. One of the Kansas properties was leased to the Smith American Organ Company for five years at $2,400 per annum. Clearly these were premium properties. The practice of selling properties for part payment in cash and with a mortgage for the balance became very common.

Of much more doubtful value were the lands which had been acquired in Kentucky and Tennessee. Indeed there was still some doubt about what had actually been purchased, and McCulloch, the inspector, was sent to survey the lands. The directors' fears were confirmed some time later when the survey revealed that they had paid for more land than they had received. All but 400 acres of the Iowa land was sold at a loss. Yet McCulloch was keen for the company to purchase the 'big bayou' lands in Arkansas despite there being a problem with the title caused by the fact the county records had been burned. He was told to proceed with caution. The directors must have thought that the matter was settled by the acquisition of 2,500 shares in the Arkansas Valley Land and Cattle Company. Dundee Investment was more interested in share acquisitions rather than land purchases. But McCulloch was not to be thwarted and he took an option to purchase 60,000 acres of the Harris and Atkins property that he would exercise if an arrangement could be reached with the Arkansas Land and Lumber Co., an Edinburgh-based company in process of incorporation, to acquire the timber lands. This company's incorporation was never concluded and it was too late for the Dundee Investment to pull out of the land deal. It seemed that the new company had got itself into the kind of deal that it was trying to avoid. It may have cost McCulloch his job, as his contract was not renewed. His situation was not helped by the fact that there were irregularities in his expenses.

The investment side of the business got off to a slow start. Robert Fleming was the main source of investment advice. He recommended shares in the Roanoke Land and Improvement Company and in various cattle companies. The Dominion government in Canada had granted a township to Dundee Land. This was sold to the Montreal and Western Land Company in exchange for shares in that organisation. This deal eventually fell apart when Montreal and Western decided to stop purchasing townships.

Underwood, Clark and Co. recommended the purchase of shares in the Kansas City Cattle Company, which had just sold 5,000 head of cattle for $40 per head. This recommendation was accepted but a similar invitation to acquire shares in the Muscatine Cattle Co. was rejected.

The first annual general meeting took place in 13 Panmure Street on 28 July 1882. It was attended by five people. Lowson, as chairman, read the notice calling the meeting. He said that the amalgamation with Dundee Land was proceeding smoothly. There were no questions and no other business, and the meeting was brought to a close. By the end of the following month the amalgamation was complete, and all obligations of Dundee Land had been assumed by Dundee Investment.

Thereafter company policy made progress on two fronts – the disposal of non-earning assets acquired from Dundee Land and investment in many of the new opportunities that were available.

Foremost amongst the new opportunities was investment in cattle companies. This was the great age of the large ranches and the cattle drives. Improvements in rail transport, refrigerated trucks and ships and meat packing ensured an enormous growth in the meat business both in the US economy and for export. Many new cattle companies were formed in the early years of the 1880s. Mr Frewen, promoter of the Powder River Cattle Company made the trip to Dundee and persuaded the directors to subscribe for 2,000 shares of the preferred stock in his new company. Frewen went on to borrow McCulloch's services to inspect the property that his new company had acquired. Several cattle companies were promoted from Dundee but the directors acquired shares, at this time, only in the Texas Land and Cattle

Company. Hansford Cattle Co. shares were acquired later, although these were sold before the market in cattle tuned downwards in the middle years of the decade.

The mining of minerals was already big business in the United States and was growing quickly. The company participated with the Colorado Land Company, though not very successfully, in prospecting for coal in Boulder County. It also acquired options to purchase shares in the Arizona Copper Company.

Elsewhere Miller and Macmaster acquired 160 town lots in Fergus Falls and proceeded to sell them. However in Winnipeg, Manitoba it was a different story. The property market there was extremely sluggish and it took years before any serious progress was made in disposing of property. Other disposals were made when the Edinburgh-based North West Canada Company was wound up in 1882 to be replaced by the London-based Canada North West Land Company. Dundee Investment sold its interest to the new company and agreed to receive half its investment in cash and half in shares. In view of the deteriorating cash position, however, they then decided to take the whole payment in cash.

Similarly when the Canadian River Cattle Company was taken over by the Dundee-based Hansford Cattle Company the shareholding was sold for cash rather than the shares that were on offer.

An opportunity also presented itself to dispose of the Chaves Grant. Interested parties acquired an option to purchase it in six months for $150,000 but they declined to make a forfeitable deposit if they did not subsequently take up the option. Mackenzie, in Dundee, was happy to leave the matter to the discretion of the Colorado Land Company, who were the joint owners and who had people in Colorado who could manage the situation. Anticipating the sale, James Barclay, M.P., who was chairman of the Colorado Company, wanted to make purchases of further coal lands, but Dundee Investment declined as money was running short and there were already borrowings from the bank.

Part of the solution to the cash flow problem was to increase payments to solicitors who acted as agents for the raising of debenture money. This had the desired effect. Another part of the answer was to try and turn non-earning assets into revenue earners. Some of the Kentucky lands were put to productive use by T. Lyon White, who experimented with cutting staves on the land that were then sold for fencing. This, however, was only a temporary solution. The preferred option was to sell the land.

At the annual meeting in March 1883, attended by 29 shareholders in Lamb's Hotel, the company's policy was restated. Shareholders were told that investments were in 'carefully selected railroad bonds, first mortgages and other securities yielding a regular revenue, and the bulk of their investments are now in this position. It is believed that in this way a steadiness will be imparted to the course of the company's business which would be more satisfactory to all concerned than to have carried out without change the original policy of the company [i.e. the policy of Dundee Land]. To have done so might ultimately have proved more profitable, but it certainly would have been more speculative.'

They were also told that most of the unsold real estate held by the company was in the rising cities of Portland, Winnipeg and Kansas. This may have been intended to reassure the shareholders, but a brief reading of the annual report would have revealed that real estate holdings were £99,283 – almost half of the company's assets.

The big problems were in Kentucky, Tennessee and Arkansas. Time, effort and lawyers' bills were expended in pursuing Dr Allen, who had sold the lands in Kentucky and Tennessee and some of the lands with poor title in Arkansas. Allen seemed amenable to a settlement but this was a smokescreen for a more intransigent attitude. Squatters were a problem everywhere, and there was a worry that they might acquire title to the lands they occupied through the operation of the laws of prescription. The negotiations with Allen went on for quite some time – they did not reach an agreement until December 1883 – and left the company still holding a substantial amount of unproductive land. It took much longer to convert the agreement into a settlement. In the meantime the hope was expressed that government efforts to build levees on the Mississippi to control flooding would have the desired effect and enhance the value of the land.

Concerns also arose in Kansas City when Mackenzie discovered that Underwood had vested the land belonging to his property company in his own name rather than in the names of shareholders acting as trustees. Dundee Investment was a shareholder. Mackenzie became even more concerned when Underwood's reply to his letter on the subject came from Long Beach, California. Underwood's partner, Clark, was in Edinburgh soon afterwards and Mackenzie went to see him. Clark then cabled Underwood who proposed that he would sign a trust deed in favour of his creditors. There was much delay, and in September 1883 both Fleming and Whitton were in the United States. By December they had the matter settled in their favour, although another year passed before Underwood's property company had made sufficient sales to repay the shareholders. Dundee Investment was content to receive part of its repayment in mortgages over properties in the appropriately named Dundee Place, Kansas City.

Nevertheless, the problem with Underwood, Clark and Co, did not disappear. Towards the end of 1884 Dundee Mortgage reported that the firm had not been able to pay cash for a payment due to them. 'Some discussion took place as to the ability of a firm in such a position . . . to represent the company satisfactorily, and the propriety of making a change was discussed.' Clark had again been in Scotland for discussions, and the mortgages that had been discussed a year earlier were examined in great detail.

At the annual meeting in 1884 shareholders received both good and bad news. There was net revenue of £6,057, and £2,500 was transferred to the reserve making it £5,000. But it was also announced that the directors anticipated a loss of £3,500 on an investment. They declined to accept their annual remuneration. The source of this loss was not revealed but it is likely to have been connected with the assets acquired from Dundee Land. Although sales had been made, there were still £61,000 of these unproductive assets on the books.

Lowson took the opportunity to bow out and was replaced by Henry Gourlay, who was the largest shareholder. The decision was also made to increase the number of directors and George Halley was appointed to the board. Quite why Halley accepted the appointment is something of a mystery as he never attended a meeting and resigned in the summer. Henry Gourlay lasted only a few weeks more before being replaced by his brother Alexander. Halley was replaced by James Guthrie. John Leng also took the opportunity to bow out. The old guard was rapidly being replaced by the new.

The United States was fast plunging into a depression, and despite net revenue of £5,358 the annual meeting of shareholders in April 1885 was told that there would be no dividend. 'The past year has been one of severe and general depression in America and little progress has been made in realising the company's real estate investments.' It also revealed that £55,000 of unproductive assets remained on the company's books: '. . . the bulk may require to be retained until the return of better times'.

Stocks and bonds purchased by the company were standing at a book loss of £2,000. But much of the real estate was yielding a good return. One shareholder moved that a dividend of 3% should be paid but there was no seconder for his motion. Another motion from the floor proposed that the directors should share £200 as reward for their efforts, and this was approved.

Mackenzie went off to the United States on a tour of inspection in May 1885 and was told to visit as many of the agencies as possible. His primary task was to settle the problems with the agency in Kansas City and he managed to do this. Underwood, Clark and Co. were given a new contract.

The primary objective of company policy at this time was to liquidate assets; Fleming was busy selling railway bonds, but land sales were much more problematic. Efforts to sell timber lands in Wisconsin broke down. Plans to lease the Chaves Grant were drawn up yet again, and Barclay came to Dundee for discussions. The legal suit to establish good title over the grant had been successful but there was now some doubt about the exact acreage and the boundaries. Colorado Land was authorised to lease the land at a minimum rent of 4 cents per acre. But there were other problems ahead and a long time was to pass before the company received an economic return from this particular investment. Early in 1888 there was a threat that the US government would declare Chaves, and similar land grants, to be illegal and the land would be thrown open for settlers. Other holders of land grants were getting themselves organised to defend their holdings in Washington, DC, and the Colorado Land Co. was asked to represent Dundee Investment's interests in the negotiations.

The challenges at that time were to sell real estate, enhance security and find new investments. Fortunately there were still good investments to be found. Notwithstanding the problems faced by the cattle industry, the directors were well disposed to a communication received from Lord George Campbell as a result of which they participated in a loan to Charles Goodnight, a leading cattleman.

Business had shown little signs of improvement when the shareholders met for their annual meeting in April 1886. 'Some of the Real Estate investments inherited from the old Company continued to be a burden upon the more valuable and satisfactory business of this company.' But the shareholders were assured that, 'The Company is under no necessity to sell and can afford to wait the return of better times, when it is hoped that satisfactory realizations can be made.'

Signs of better times were already visible. Stock markets were showing some recovery, and the company's holdings of shares and bonds were reckoned to be worth their book value. When Fleming resigned from the board there were expressions of regret from the other directors but his advice and services continued to be available and he remained a good friend to the company.

Mackenzie went back to North America in 1886. He had learned that, in times of commercial pressure, people would take greater risks than in ordinary times and that it was when times were tough that shortcuts were most likely to be exposed. If the problems were to be identified then there was a need to have someone there to do it. Underwood, Clark were finally removed as agents in Kansas City when it was discovered that they had been over charging on commissions. They were replaced by the Kansas City Investment Company. There were problems, too, in Montreal where it was suspected that the agent, Andrew Drummond, had been appropriating business for himself rather than passing it on to the company. His brother, Charles, was the agent in Winnipeg but the only problem there was to decide which kind of heating system to put into the houses that were being built on the company's lots. Elsewhere, efforts were being made to sell the Arkansas lands to investors in Germany and Holland.

The annual meeting in April 1887 received better news. The net revenue was £13,835 and a dividend of 5% was proposed with a sizeable sum being paid to the reserve fund. A profit of more than £3,000 had been made on sales of lands taken over from the old company. New debentures were being raised at 4% and the directors were confident that better times were ahead.

One shareholder, Rev. Dr Grant, doubtless breathing a sigh of relief at the return of better times, but still fearful that difficult times might return, took the opportunity to propose that this would be a good time to merge the interests of the company with Dundee Mortgage. The proposal must have seemed eminently sensible, especially since the meeting had just been told that the main business of the company was, once again, mortgages on real estate. He was firmly told that his suggestion was 'inexpedient'. Nevertheless, it was an idea that was in the minds of many people.

It would not be long before the merger of the two companies became highly expedient, especially since a growing proportion of the lending was done jointly. In August 1887 Dundee Mortgage had decided that Smith, Caldwell, the agents in Memphis, were to receive credits of $300,000 for the forthcoming lending season. Dundee Land would provide an unspecified portion of this.

Although none of the old land assets were sold in 1887 the company had a good trading year. It did not develop new business but mortgages were again in demand at satisfactory rates of interest. 'This class of business continues to yield your Directors more satisfaction than any other. Some defaults have necessarily been experienced but they do not occasion anxiety, and the securities held are believed to be ample for the company's protection.'

Nothing more was said in public about a merger with Dundee Mortgage but the prospect was apparently under active consideration. The minutes record that the Alliance Trust Company Ltd was registered in April 1888. But business, for Dundee Investment, went on as before. The major preoccupation was land sales but there were continuing worries that legislation passed by the various states would interfere with business. The agents were charged with regular reporting on what was happening in their state legislatures. In the spring of 1888 Caldwell wrote from Mississippi: 'The Mississippi Legislature has adjourned and no bad bills were passed. The laws stand exactly as they did before the beginning of the session. All the redemption bills were killed, so also all bills interfering with trust sales, and all bills making local attorneys the agents of the foreign corporations for whom they acted. We breathe free for another two years.'

As we have seen the real legislative pressure came from Texas. In February 1889 Thomas Thornton expressed the view that new legislation in Texas made it unsafe to lend there as the legislation said that companies could not lend money in Texas if they could not also lend in their home country. His view was that Dundee Investment was better placed than Dundee Mortgage but he considered it generally unsafe for both companies to lend. Lawyers on both sides of the Atlantic were consulted. The stop-gap solution was to provide a new credit to Sommerville in Fort Worth but for him to do the lending as an individual rather than do it through his company, Western Securities.

It was only a temporary solution, and in April 1889 a committee of share-holders was appointed to confer with Dundee Mortgage regarding a merger. 'The Union will be brought about by merging both companies in The Alliance Trust Coy which will give the Mortgage Coy share for share.' The merger agreement was signed in September 1899, and an extraordinary general meeting the following month voted in favour of the merger.

Mackenzie, who by this time had an assistant, had been busy and the papers were ready. However it was not until 1912 that Dundee Investment was finally wound up.

The Alliance Trust Ltd, which had been registered the previous year, was about to be brought to life. The experience of Dundee investors that had been gained in the years since the formation of the Oregon and Washington Trust Investment Company was invaluable. Important lessons had been learned about how to conduct mortgage and investment business in the United States and in Canada. Mistakes had been made, but for the most part these were not expensive mistakes as the various balance sheet figures in the appendices and dividend payments reveal. In Mackenzie and others there was both experience and confidence. He and his colleagues were then ready to move onto a bigger stage.

Chapter 3
The Early Years: 1888–1892

The troubles experienced by the American economy in the middle years of the 1880s dampened the enthusiasm of British investors for American securities. The creation of new investment trusts, mortgage companies and cattle companies slowed to a trickle after 1883. Leading investors, however, were well aware that the trade cycle would eventually turn upwards. The challenges were to be watchful for when that happened and to be ready to take advantage of new opportunities when they arose. Investors were hungry for higher returns especially after Chancellor George Goschen rescheduled the national debt in 1888 and, in the process, reduced real returns for investors. People with money to invest were ready for new investment opportunities despite worries, expressed in *The Economist*, that they were being incautious.[19]

It was clear that the investment business in Dundee was moving towards consolidation, and that came with the creation of the Alliance Trust in 1888. The immediate pressure for the creation of a new company came from Texas, where the directors of the Dundee Mortgage and Trust faced a threat from state legislators who proposed enacting a law that would make it impossible for foreign companies to operate in Texas. The solution proposed by the company's solicitor, Thomas Thornton, was to merge the Dundee Mortgage and Trust with the Dundee Investment Company, the constitution of which was sufficiently open to intrepretation as to accommodate the terms of the proposed Texas act. It made further sense then to create a new company that would enable the directors to strengthen the capital base and take advantage of improving business conditions in the United States.

Although the new company was registered on 21 April 1888 it did not commence business until the following year. The directors knew that it would not be required until then but they thought it prudent to get the Alliance Trust

---

19 Newlands, op. cit, p. 131.

registered as a company before the impending increase in stamp duty. In so doing they saved £850.

From the outset the Alliance Trust was a large company. Its ordinary share capital was £950,000, of which £222,000 was paid up. In addition there was preference stock of £160,000. Debentures amounted to £700,000. In all this totalled £1,082,000.

Getting started

The first meeting of the board of the Alliance Trust took place on 15 June 1888. There were only seven people at the meeting:

> John Guild, who was appointed as Chairman
> Andrew Whitton
> Alexander Henderson
> Alex Gourlay
> James Guthrie

These five were appointed to be the directors and William Mackenzie was appointed to be the company secretary. His assistant, James A.H. MacNair, was the seventh man in the room.

These men were also the directors of the Dundee Mortgage and Trust. This meeting and several that followed were held to comply with the requirements of the Companies Acts. The new company had done no business and so there was nothing to report. The first general meeting took place on 20 August. Only Guild and three shareholders were present.

Almost a year went by before the next meeting took place in July 1889. Its purpose was to allot further shares than those that had been allotted to get the company started. The directors were each allotted 200 shares. Thereafter matters moved forward swiftly. It was agreed that the offices at 13 Panmure Street would be the registered office and that the seal of the company would contain the griffin and lilies that were part of the Dundee city coat of arms. It does not seem that the city's permission was sought. Nor was the Lord Lyon King of Arms consulted. Dundee had gained city status that very year.

The second annual general meeting took place in Panmure Street on 16 August 1889. There were only eight people in attendance. The directors were re-elected with the addition of John Leadbetter. The only other piece of business was to decide on the remuneration of directors. The sum of £1,200 would be divided amongst them. The legal niceties of UK company law had been complied with and the Alliance Trust was ready to start business, but it could not do so until it had also complied with company law in Canada and the United States.

A board meeting followed on immediately from the AGM. Thomas Thornton, the company solicitor, was present to give his advice about compliance with US federal and state laws regarding foreign corporations. His recommendation was that the company should comply with the legal require-ments of Oregon, Alabama, Louisiana and Arkansas. He outlined what had to be done to comply in each state. In most cases the need was to register the name of someone on whom writs could be served. Consequently the need was to have a legally qualified person to deal with writs.

The men appointed were

Henry Hall Northup, Portland, Oregon
Talliaferro Alexander, Shreveport, Louisiana
Eben W. Kimball, Little Rock, Arkansas
Horace Stringfellow, Montgomery, Alabama

What was happening, in effect, was that the agents and legal representatives who had worked with Dundee Mortgage and Dundee Investment were taking up their responsibilities with Alliance Trust. Almost nothing is recorded about the agents themselves, suggesting that it was very much business as usual.

Legal matters were less clear in California, where it was decided that the Alliance Trust would operate through its agents Balfour, Forman and Guthrie. There was still a lack of clarity about Texas law, and it was decided that Drought or Sommerville would be asked to file the memorandum and articles and apply for the required licence to operate.

In Canada, Drummond Brothers and Moffat were to be agents in Manitoba and Charles Sinclair Drummond was to apply for a licence.

Some states required to know who was president of the company. This term had no place in British company law and it became company practice to nominate one or other of the directors whose name would serve the purpose. Guild was appointed to be president to meet the requirements of Alabama and Arkansas while Henderson was appointed to meet Canadian requirements.

Thornton was certainly kept busy. There were still the legal issues of the merger with Dundee Mortgage and Dundee Investment to be dealt with, and these were soon on the agenda. An extraordinary general meeting was held on 8 October 1889, when the arrangements for the mergers were ratified.

A further extraordinary general meeting was held later that month to give force to a major rethink on how the capital of the new company would be structured. It had originally been decided that the new shares that were to be issued would comprise 20,000 ordinary shares of £10. These were now to be cancelled and replaced with 20,000 'A' shares and 20,000 preference shares bearing interest at 4.25%. This was a major change from the model followed by the earlier companies such as the Oregon and Washington Trust, where debenture holders saw ordinary shares with a large uncalled element as their security if things went wrong. In deciding upon this new model the directors were undoubtedly reflecting concerns revealed after the failure of the City of Glasgow Bank in 1878 when ordinary shareholders with unlimited liability had been driven to bankruptcy. There were very few companies still with unlimited liability but investors would see a large uncalled liability on ordinary shares as almost as risky. Consequently partly paid ordinary shares were not very popular with investors. The corollary of this was that debenture holders could no longer look to this source for relief in times of trouble. Their security lay in the fact that if a company to which they had lent money was wound up then they would be paid ahead of the preference and ordinary shareholders. They would also derive comfort from lending their money to a company with a healthy reserve fund.

The final minute for 1889 contains a list 59 pages long of the shareholders in Dundee Mortgage and Dundee Investment who were to become shareholders in the new company. Although there were shareholders in various parts of the United Kingdom the vast majority were from East Central Scotland. Many years were to pass before much change was to be seen in this aspect of the shareholders register.

At the second annual general meeting held on 28 April 1890 there were 40 shareholders in attendance. The Alliance had formally taken over Dundee Mortgage and Dundee Investment on 1 November 1889. The shareholders were pleased to hear that a dividend of 10% was to be declared. They were told that the forthcoming final call on the ordinary shareholders would effect 'a considerable reduction of the company's debt thus improving the already exceptionally strong security offered to Debenture holders'. It was left unsaid that the other outcome of a debt reduction might be an increase in the dividend for ordinary shareholders. A minor shareholder's attempt to get the dividend increased in 1891 was unsuccessful but the directors agreed to increase it to 12.5% in 1892.

Debentures were a large part of the company's funding and there was always an important decision to be made about the best rate to offer. In 1890 the rate was reduced from 4% to 3.75% – doubtless after due consideration had been given to what other companies were offering and what could be obtained by investing in government securities. Small savers did not complain, but when some of the large insurance companies and the British Linen Bank Widows' Fund discovered that their rate was to be reduced they endeavoured, without success, to hold the rate at 4%. That the Alliance was able to resist pressure from large investors is a clear measure of the success of its strategies and of its early standing in the investment world.

The debt referred to was monies borrowed from Messrs Cox and Henderson and from the British Linen Bank with which the dividend was paid. These loans were repaid when the final call was paid on the new shares that had been issued.

The numbers attending the meeting in 1890 had obviously been a tight squeeze for the offices in Panmure Street, and subsequent meetings were held in Lamb's Temperance Hotel, 64 Reform Street, Dundee – a building which, in the course of time, would become the company's own office. It was a wise move, as there were 52 shareholders at the meeting in 1891.

The Secretariat

Thereafter matters moved smoothly, although MacNair, who was a chartered accountant, resigned. He had been officially appointed assistant secretary only a month earlier. He went to take up a position in London as manager of the Equitable Mortgage Company. This in itself is a measure of the growing reputation of the Dundee investment business. He was thanked fulsomely for the role that he had played as Mackenzie's assistant.

There was apparently no hurry to appoint someone else to the role of assistant secretary despite the prodigious amount of work that fell on the secretary's shoulders. Not only did Mackenzie have to attend to the business of issuing new shares and debentures for Alliance Trust, he also had to transfer all the mortgages, bonds and other securities of Dundee Mortgage and Dundee Investment into the name of the Alliance Trust. He did have some assistance, and when he announced that he was going to Carlsbad for six weeks' holiday in the summer of 1890, George Spence and William Findlay, who were appointed joint secretaries *ad interim*, took his place. It appears that there was some strength in the staff of the Trust – people who could be relied upon when the need arose.

The need arose often as Mackenzie's role evolved. It was clear that, from time to time, he was expected to visit the agencies in the United States and Canada. He had been doing this for a number of years. He visited the agencies in 1891, and Spence and Findlay deputised once more. But his role was expanding in other directions as the Alliance Trust entered a number of agreements with other companies.

In July 1891 the directors learned that a new mortgage company was to be established in Edinburgh, of which John Guild was to be the chairman. The prospectus said that it would act in 'close and friendly association with the Alliance Trust Company'. Mackenzie had been giving 'considerable assistance' in setting up this United States Mortgage Company Ltd. The Alliance directors confirmed that they were comfortable with the arrival of the new company that would share some of its agents. Guild's death in January 1892 was a blow to all concerned, and his seat on the United States Mortgage Board, although not the chairmanship, was offered to Mackenzie. He accepted, but not before consulting with Thornton and the Alliance directors in Dundee.

Also in 1892 the Alliance found that good lending opportunities were harder to find, and surplus funds were building up in New York. The exchange rate was against returning the money to the UK, and Mackenzie was asked to go to London to consult with Fleming with a view to investing the money in railroad or other bonds in the US. By this stage Mackenzie had been involved in the investment business for almost 20 years, and it is clear that his role was more than the routine business of a company secretary. He was playing a major role in the investment decision-making process and his presence on the investment scene did much to enhance the reputation of the Alliance Trust. He clearly enjoyed the trust of his directors.

Guild's death in February 1892 removed from the scene a man who was held in great esteem by his peers. The tribute that the directors recorded in the minutes went far beyond what was normal practice. They referred to his constant attention to business matters and praised 'the fidelity and assiduity of his services, the weight and wisdom of his counsels and also the courtesy, fairness and quiet dignity which characterised his chairmanship'. They also recorded their personal grief. No man was more experienced in investment matters. He had been chairman of Fleming's trusts since their inception in 1873 and had joined the board of Dundee Mortgage and Dundee Investment in 1882.

Lending and Investing

Although Fleming never became a director of Alliance Trust, his influence was nevertheless strong and went far beyond his role as a major shareholder. His advice was often sought on investment matters as when, in February 1891 there was $75,000 to be invested and it was left to Guild and Fleming to advise on suitable bonds. It became company practice to invest the reserve in US bonds, mostly railroads, which were Fleming's specialism.

Perhaps it is just as well that Fleming never became a director of Alliance, as he was never very keen on American mortgages. His contemporary, William J. Menzies, who had established the Scottish American Investment Company in Edinburgh in 1873, was equally sceptical. In a speech to young chartered accountants in Edinburgh in 1894 he gave a very frank and instructive talk about the dangers and difficulties in lending on mortgages. Given the prevalence of such views the presence of either man on the Alliance Trust board would have made them very uncomfortable colleagues. Nevertheless Fleming was, and remained, a very faithful friend to the company. As his own business evolved into underwriting new issues in the London market he always offered a participation to Alliance Trust. One of the earliest issues was in 1890 when a $40m subscription for the Missouri, Kansas and Texas Railroad was offered and in which the Alliance participated to the extent of $50,000.

Fleming was certainly not the only source of investment advice available to Alliance Trust. The directors had their own range of contacts. Several of them made regular visits to the United States and Canada where they built up a range of confidants and advisers. Andrew Whitton, in particular, was a regular trans-atlantic traveller. He was also a director of the Scottish American Mortgage Company. A visit to the United States on behalf of that Company in 1891 was put to good use by the Alliance when he was able to visit the Ashly estate in the Mississippi valley, which had been one of Dundee Land's less judicious investments. The practice of directors sitting on the boards of several, ostensibly competing, investment companies became common and continued for many years.

The main concern for the Alliance Trust was to ensure the quality of its lending on the mortgages which were its primary asset. The early success of the pre-Alliance Trust companies was, in large measure, due to the fact that they had employed an inspector to provide assurance that the quality of land on which it was proposed to lend was high, that the appropriate legal processes were followed and that the borrower was likely to repay the loan. The first men appointed to this role were people with a strong farming background, but George Haggart, who had worked for Dundee Mortgage was, first and foremost, a lawyer. He was employed as inspector of agencies although he was sometimes assisted in this by William Macmaster, the agent at Portland, another lawyer. G.M. Foreman of Sioux City was appointed Haggart's assistant at $10 per day plus expenses in 1893, although it was made clear that this was not to be thought of as a permanent appointment. Haggart was initially based in Winnipeg and his journeys on behalf of the company became the stuff of legend. In September 1890, for example, he was asked to visit the new agency in Carolina. Although the railroad network was improving all the time this was nevertheless a very lengthy journey.

Although the Alliance Trust was essentially a mortgage company it also engaged in investment activities. Primarily these investments were selected to provide a safe repository for the company's reserve fund. The preferred investments were the bonds of well-established US railway companies. The Atcheson, Topeka and Santa Fe Railroad was a particular favourite, and $50,000 of its 4% bonds were purchased in 1889. Fleming, from his London base, was increasingly involved in the new issue markets, especially for US railroads. He was the major source of investment opportunities for Alliance Trust. The Missouri, Kansas and Texas Railroad, and the Norfolk and Western Railroad were early examples of these issues. Some of these were sold soon after the issue had been made, but others such as the New Orleans North Eastern Railway Company and the Rio Grande Junction Railroad were purchased for the reserve fund and retained for many years. Although Fleming was the main conduit for the Trust's investment funds, some purchases were also made via Messrs A. Ogilvie and Co., stockbrokers in Dundee.

Bonds of county authorities were less popular, although Alliance Trust found itself holding a quantity of Lake County bonds from Colorado that had been purchased by Dundee Investment and on which there had been a default. The story of these bonds became a saga but the directors refused to give up and eventually received a repayment after many years.

Government bonds were somewhat more popular than local authority bonds, and in 1892 Mackenzie was authorised to apply to Rothschilds for £10,000 of a new issue of South African Republic (Transvaal) 5% government loan. This particular issue was oversubscribed and Alliance received only £600, although it was subsequently able to purchase more in the market.

Nevertheless investment was not a major part of the Trust's activities in these early years and was only done if new reserve funds were available, or if the company found itself with surplus funds on hand and needed a safe repository for a short time.

The Agencies

Although very little is said about the agents in the first minute book it is clear that they were simply given extended contracts following upon their employment with Dundee Mortgage and Dundee Investment. Mackenzie or one of the directors might visit them but they were also expected to visit Dundee from time to time.

Although Portland, Oregon was the first focus for Dundee investments its importance seems to have diminished and to have been replaced by Texas (Fort Worth and San Antonio), Kansas City and Memphis. Macmaster and Birrell continued as agents in Portland but they were rarely mentioned. In October 1891 they agreed to indemnify the company against claims of usury. The Usury Act in Oregon was both strict and complicated. The following year, after legal opinion had been taken from Thornton in Dundee and Drought in Texas, permission was given to the Oregon agents to lend in Washington State. Washington had achieved its statehood in 1889 and it was thought that the strict federal law inhibiting foreign corporations in territories no longer applied in Washington now that it was a state. The extent of the lending that was done there was not revealed but is unlikely to have amounted to very much. Some of Macmaster's time was taken up with his role as assistant to Haggart, the inspector of agencies. In the summer of 1892 he was with Haggart in Kansas City and was asked to inspect Fort Worth on his way back to Portland.

The agent in Fort Worth was William Sommerville, who had been instrumental in securing the Matador Ranch for Dundee interests in 1882. He seems to have been a man of integrity who took personal responsibility for two of his loans that were getting into difficulty. This may not have been wise, as some months later he found himself paying the interest on one of the loans and declaring the other a complete loss. He placed himself in the hands of the directors as to 'whether he should make this loss good to the company'. The directors declined his offer. Nevertheless it seems that his reputation in Fort Worth may have been damaged by these events. During a visit to Dundee in August 1890 he revealed to the directors his plans to leave Texas and set up in London. His intention was to leave his Texas business, the Western Securities

Company, in the hands of his assistants Thomas Ross, attorney and George C. Burton who had worked for Lord Airlie. He would visit once a year.

References were duly taken up for Ross and Burton and they proved to be satisfactory. But the directors were cautious and a further request for a new lending credit was rejected. They were sufficiently concerned by November 1890 to send Macmaster to Fort Worth to inspect the agency. Before Macmaster got there Sommerville fell from a ladder whilst repairing his barn, and died. The settlement of his estate was a lengthy and complicated matter but it does not appear that there was anything untoward in his affairs – merely that his various business interests were extensive and complicated. The matter was made more difficult because one of the loans on which Sommerville had given his personal guarantee turned out not to be a first charge on the property. Despite a search of the public records the official who conducted the search, the 'abstractor', had failed to reveal that there was a prior charge on one of the loans. It was decided to sue him and it was not anticipated that the case would be defended.

The Fort Worth agency was then continued, with Ross and Burton acting initially as the Western Securities Company. Some time was to elapse before they were given more money for lending, despite their requests. The delay was caused not by any lingering doubts about the agency but because of confusion over the operation of the Texas Alien Act as it impacted on foreign corporations. It was eventually declared to be unconstitutional but it was immediately followed by a new piece of legislation and the task of ascertaining the legal position had to be repeated. Fortunately the new legislation proved much less threatening to foreign companies.

Henry P. Drought was the agent in San Antonio. Originally from County Clare in Ireland, he was qualified as an attorney. In 1889 he joined the firm of Francis Smith, Caldwell and Company which retained the Alliance agency. Both Smith and Caldwell had long-established relationships with Dundee investment interests. In May 1890 the firm of Smith, Caldwell and Co. was dissolved and it was agreed that a new firm of Smith and Drought would run the San Antonio agency. Meanwhile Caldwell took John Judah into partnership to run the Memphis office, from where the Alliance Trust's business in Louisiana, Arkansas, Mississippi and Alabama would be conducted.

Albert Caldwell was keen to make progress and felt sufficiently secure in his position to tell the directors in Dundee that he could easily do more business and that the company needed to issue more capital to enable him to expand. Notwithstanding the competition that Alliance faced from existing and new mortgage companies, the directors put Mr Caldwell firmly in his place and told him that the present disturbed state of the money markets rendered his suggestion inadvisable.

In Memphis Caldwell and Judah were equally ambitious. Early in 1891 it was discovered that they had overextended their credit and were immediately given a further $45,000 to cover the difference. It is clear from this that the nature of the relationship between Dundee and the agencies had changed from the days of the Oregon and Washington Trust. The agents made the lending decisions without reference to Dundee. They were remunerated largely by a commission on the collections of principal and interest, so their income was tied to the quality of their lending activities. There was always the discipline of a visit from Haggart or Macmaster that acted as a further control on the temptation to over-lend. The only occasions on which Dundee's permission would be sought were when some unusual or innovative opportunity presented itself.

On one such occasion Caldwell and Judah reported to Dundee on a loan to a recently deceased borrower. It now transpired that the borrower was insolvent and Caldwell and Judah asked permission to take over the property themselves. This was agreed, as was a loan of $15,000 'to make next year's crop'. Other borrowers in this agency, in addition to their mortgages, borrowed to finance the crop.

Many of the Mississippi Valley plantations operated on a large scale. One such was a British company, the Ashly Co. Ltd. Early in 1891 it got into difficulties thanks to a profligate manager. It had no funds and was indebted to the extent of $140,000 in addition to its mortgage of $375,000, which was shared amongst several mortgage lenders, including Alliance Trust. Its remaining assets would be 'distrained by the outside creditors'. Caldwell thought that the company was worth saving, and travelled to London for a meeting of the mortgage bondholders where he met up with Mackenzie. The two then returned to Dundee for a meeting with the Alliance directors when they decided that every effort should be made to save the Ashly Co. They then endeavoured to mobilise the Scottish investment trust industry. A visit to the offices of Holmes, Ivory in Edinburgh secured support from the United States Mortgage Co., the Scottish Investment Trust Co. and the Second Scottish Investment Trust Co. John Guild promised to get the British Investment Trust onside. Meanwhile the manager of the Ashly Company had been trying, and failing, to raise capital for a rival scheme in Chicago.

The Scottish deal was wrapped up in a few weeks. The result was that the

Scottish investors now held the capital stock of the company. The Alliance Trust was the largest shareholder. The whole episode had been an impressive mobilisation of enterprise and capital to save the Ashly Company but it was an investment that was probably more trouble than it was worth. In the summer of 1892 a disastrous overflow left 3,000 acres of the Ashly lands under water. Caldwell returned to Dundee for further discussions with the investors. A committee was established, with Whitton and Mackenzie representing the Alliance's interests. Within months Caldwell announced that he wished to retire from the management of the Ashly Company. Perhaps he realised the difficult situation he was in. The American economy was entering a serious downturn with agricultural prices severely depressed. Caldwell was prevailed upon to stay, but it was not long before he wrote to say that more money would be needed if the Ashly lands were to be managed properly. The Dundee response was to ask for more facts.

The agency in Kansas City got off to a shaky start – perhaps surprisingly because it was well placed geographically to serve the cattle trade, and new killing and curing establishments were being built. The city was well served by railways, and Whitton thought that it would grow to rival Chicago. Consequently there was a lot of speculative activity that could catch out the unwary lender. The Kansas City Investment Company, which held the agency, got into financial difficulties and, late in 1891, was endeavouring to raise new capital. Haggart was sent immediately and managed to have the agency transferred to Mr Holmes. But he was also disturbed at the state of general business and recommended that all lending should be stopped. The directors in Dundee were surprised to learn that one of the loans made via the Kansas City Investment Co., and which had now been foreclosed, was not as it seemed. The loan had originally been made for a block on which 12 houses were to be built. The plan had been amended to build 36 apartments, but more money was needed for extra plumbing work, municipal requirements and sanitary matters. Even the name of the development had been changed – a fact that the directors only learned from a photograph that had been sent.

Matters were further complicated in Kansas City when the state of Missouri passed its own Aliens Act in 1891. This went further than much of the legislation that had been passed by other states or by the federal government, in that, in addition to demanding the usual registration documents, it required foreign companies to say what portion of their capital was connected with their business in the state.

In November 1889 the liquidation of Messrs Jessup, Paton and Co., bankers in New York was announced. This firm had been bankers to various Dundee interests since 1873 but Jessup was retiring. The business continued for a time as John Paton and Co., but in 1890 the directors thought that this firm had too much of the company's funds. They decided to split the New York business between Paton and the branch of the Bank of Montreal.

In deciding who to use as bankers and agents, extensive use was made of the credit reference agencies to provide reports on their credit worthiness. This was done, not just at the outset of a business relationship, but on an ongoing basis. In 1891 Dun and Co. (subsequently Dun and Bradstreet) reported that John Paton and Co. was 'regarded as a very respectable house doing a careful and conservative banking business and amply safe for their engagements'. Paton retired soon afterwards and two of the junior partners, Cuyler and Morgan, continued the business, although it was widely known that both Paton and Jessup, although technically retired, were still 'special partners'.

Shareholders and the Annual General Meetings

The early annual general meetings in Dundee were often lively affairs. The Companies Acts did not require companies to reveal very much about themselves to shareholders who, given their investments and the risks that they took, were curious about what was happening and why.

In making his speech to the annual general meeting in April 1890 John Guild, as chairman, said: 'We had a good deal of work to do getting the amalgamation through all the legal difficulties, but with perseverance, these were overcome, and the shares of the old Companies have been exchanged for those of the new. There is a great deal of detail in the management of such a business as this, which requires very close attention. You may have some idea of it when I tell you we have about 2,245 different loans. There are 1,316 debenture holders, and including the different classes of shares we have 948 shareholders.'

This was more information than he was required to divulge but it did not entirely satisfy the shareholders. One investor wanted to know how much was in the reserve fund and was told. There were concerns, too, about the amount of real estate that the company held – much of it as the result of foreclosures. The meeting was also informed that surpluses made on the sale of real estate had been used to write down the value of other real estate in the company's books. Consequently Guild was able to assure shareholders that the company had value for the £90,000 of real estate that remained. The reserve fund was a topic for discussion at the following annual general meeting when share-holders were advised that a large reserve was necessary to encourage debenture holders to keep their money with the company. As has been explained, this was doubly so now that there was a decreasing amount of uncalled liability on the ordinary shares – liability which debenture holders had traditionally looked to as security for the money that they placed with the company.

Shareholders could also get exercised about the management expenses incurred. At the annual general meeting in 1892 the shareholders were informed that the expenses had risen because Mackenzie had been to visit the agents in North America. They were also told that the directors considered the money well spent: '. . . for we all know that agents, however good, are none the worse for a visit'.

At the same meeting R.A. Miller rose to propose the adoption of the annual report and, in a speech full of classical allusions that greatly entertained the shareholders, he congratulated the directors on their sound management of the Trust's affairs. He was particularly impressed that, 'No gold mining pyrotechnic exhibitions, displaying Yankee smartness, disguised in gilt-edged deception, have been bequeathed by our late sagacious shaggy-eyebrowed Chairman (Guild) to allure and deceive the shareholders, to paralyse and mar the cheerful record of Alliance Trust Company – no, not one.'

The Rev. Dr Grant then rose to spoil the party by demanding to know by how much the real estate, acquired as a result of foreclosures, had increased during the year. Without waiting for an answer he insisted that bad lending was the cause of this non-revenue earning burden on the balance sheet. Mackenzie and the chairman then tried to persuade him that most of this had been inherited from the Dundee Investment Co. and that was why a contingency fund had been established. Grant was not to be pacified and went on to request more detail about expenses, salaries of the executive and remuneration of the directors. The reply was that this information had never been provided in the past. He then promised that he would bring a motion to the next general meeting on the subject of expenses.

At the annual meeting the following year Grant was first on his feet to object to the minutes, as his notice of motion had not been recorded. Attempts by Mackenzie and the chairman to mollify him were to no avail. He found support from Thornton who said that the notice should have been recorded in the minutes. He put his case succinctly, if bluntly, when he said, 'I presume we are invited to attend this meeting, not for the purpose of going through the dumb show of blindly acquiescing in whatever the directors may choose to say to us, but of expressing our deliberate and independent opinion as to their annual report and relative accounts.'

Grant went on, 'If these details were printed, as I maintain they ought to be, it would be seen at a glance that some of the items are of so exorbitant a character that we need not marvel at the prudent reserve of the directors in studiously withholding them from publication.' The directors responded by saying that they had withheld the details because they did not want them getting into the hands of the press, and that any shareholder who wished to have more information could visit the office and receive it. Grant took the view that that this was not good enough. But his motion to have shareholders determine the remuneration of the directors was not seconded. As befitted his profession, he was sufficiently generous of spirit to propose the vote of thanks to the chairman at the end of the meeting.

By 1892 the company was well established. The people in charge were well versed in their business but their talents would be severely tested in the economic downturn that was to follow.

Chapter 4
Globalisation and Depression: 1893–1914

The years between 1893 and 1914 were a time of great upheaval in world affairs. Countries with imperial ambitions and with interests to protect, such as the UK, France, Germany and the US, continued to expand their spheres of influence. Consequently investors had to keep a wary eye on current events. Wars between the US and Spain over Cuban interests in 1898 and between Russia and Japan in 1904–5 over Korea did little to disrupt the flow of foreign investment. But the Boer Wars were a serious distraction – at least for British investors. The building of the first Dreadnought in 1906 signalled the beginning of the arms race that would culminate in the First World War in 1914.

Moreover, growing labour unrest in many parts of the world, especially after 1900, caused investors to fear that change was afoot, as indeed it was. Revolution in the Russian Empire in 1905 did substantial damage to investments in the nascent oil industry.

However, the American economy, in which the Alliance Trust was primarily interested, continued to grow, although the trajectory was certainly not smooth. Major problems in agriculture in the middle years of the 1890s and a worldwide commercial crisis in 1907–8 created serious problems for investors. Nevertheless the long-term trends were positive.

Ellis Island, the reception centre for migrants to the US in New York, opened in 1892. By 1905 more than a million people a year were migrating to the US, whose population rose to 92 million by 1912. Many of these people made their way west, and a large portion of them made their living in agriculture. The US and Canada were fast becoming major exporters of foodstuffs. Consequently, demand for mortgages remained buoyant, although there were pronounced regional differences. Others found employment in the new industries. The advent of electricity and the motor car quite simply changed the world. Production of the Model T Ford commenced in 1908 and there were many other motor manufacturers all over the US and Europe, including Duryea, Bailey, Olds, Riker, Benz and Lambert. This, in turn, gave an enormous stimulus to a wide variety of industries.

Demand for rubber for tyres grew dramatically, creating opportunities for planters and a need for capital. The Straits Mortgage and Trust Company was established in Edinburgh in 1909. It was one of a number of companies established to provide funds for rubber planters in the Malay Peninsula, Ceylon and elsewhere. It subsequently became Baillie Gifford.

The oil industry was not new but the motor car created a huge increase in demand and in the need to refine crude oil in ways that would meet the needs of internal combustion engines. It, too, created a demand for capital. The Sherman Anti-Trust Act of 1890 led to the enforced break-up of Rocke-feller's industry-dominant Standard Oil Company in 1911, and thereafter new producers were better able to enter the American oil market. But the US was not the only producer. Canada and Russia were fast emerging as oil-producing regions, as were the Middle East and Burma. Oil companies such as Anglo Persian Oil (subsequently BP) and the Glasgow-based Burmah Oil Company came into existence with growing needs for capital.

The electricity industry, too, made new methods of production a practical possibility in many businesses. It also helped to transform the transport industry with the advent of electrically propelled tram cars. Again, major investments of capital were required.

Developments in the last quarter of the nineteenth century created enormous demands for new capital and demonstrated how mobile capital could be. But, by the outbreak of war in 1914, the railways, which had been the great consumers of capital, had lost their dominant position and were gradually giving way to newer industries.

This was the environment into which the Alliance Trust began its transition from being purely a mortgage company to becoming an investment trust. Over these years the company made tremendous strides, but its progress was not without its hesitations and interruptions. Nor did it have a clear field. By 1900 there were 82 investment trusts in the UK, of which 11 were in Scotland. And over the next decade two major new players were added to the list – Baillie Gifford and Murray Johnstone. It was becoming a very crowded industry. Between 1909 and 1914 a further 17 investment companies were established in Scotland, mostly in Edinburgh.

Annual General Meetings

The purpose of the Alliance Trust annual general meetings was twofold. It was to meet the requirements of the Companies Acts and to inform investors about what was happening in their company. In truth, the amount of information that the shareholders received was very modest. A summary balance sheet with a brief receipts and payments account and some modest chairman's remarks were all that they were given.

Whilst Alliance Trust was no different from other companies in this regard, the shareholders were, nevertheless, largely kept in the dark about the inner workings of the company in which they had invested their savings. The directors justified this by saying that the holding of real estate by foreign corporations was difficult in some US states. They were therefore reluctant to publish the information requested by the shareholders in case it fell into the wrong hands and created difficulties for the company. Strangely the shareholders were more likely to be vociferous about the dearth of information in the good times than when times were tough. But the interventions of the kind by the Rev. Dr Grant, described in the last chapter, mostly became a thing of the past as the US economy slid into a deep depression in the middle years of the 1890s.

As the economy worsened, shareholders' main concern was with the amount of real estate lying on the company's books. In 1897 a motion was passed to the effect that no credit should be taken in the revenue account for accrued interest until it had actually been collected. This was relatively uncontroversial, but the shareholders also wanted to know what portion of real estate had been obtained by foreclosure. At the next annual meeting the chairman merely stated that all the agents in North America had advised against any publication that showed how much real estate was held. This seemed like a rather self-serving argument, as to reveal this figure would also reveal how risky their lending had been. Nevertheless the status quo prevailed when Sir Thomas Thornton, the company's solicitor, declared himself against publication.

At subsequent annual meetings the use of proxy votes was introduced for shareholders who were not able to attend. As proxies would normally be cast in support of the directors, this had the effect of enhancing the power of the board. The main task for the directors was always to maintain confidence in the company, and they did this by declaring that their stated strategy was to build up a strong reserve fund. They also revealed that the company possessed a healthy contingency fund without ever revealing how much it held. In 1895 a shareholder raised an objection to the fact that money was being taken out of the contingency fund. He went so far as to suggest that the directors were using this fund to pay dividends out of capital. The chairman was quick to point out that the contingency fund was not capital but was nothing more than accumulated revenue.

The directors maintained that a healthy reserve would 'add to the stability and credit of the company. It enables us to get our Debenture money on the most advantageous terms, and comes in between the shareholders and any chance of a call on the shares, besides giving such an addition to the annual revenue as to offset to some extent the probable fall in the rates of interest to be obtained on mortgages.'

The point being made here was that the reserve was an earning asset on which no interest or dividend had to be paid.

At the AGM in 1895 the directors referred explicitly to the depression in the US and said that shareholders should be 'prepared to find its influences reflected in the accounts', but that they

> will no doubt consider them satisfactory. The company has also been affected by the low prices of agricultural products, and especially by the unprecedented fall in the price of cotton, the staple in the production of which many of its clients are engaged, and by the fact that all over the American Continent the market for real estate has been remarkably dull and limited. In consequence, there has been an increase of those cases in which the company has found it necessary or expedient to assume the temporary ownership of properties mortgaged to it. After deducting realizations, the amount of real estate acquired in this way has been increased by £29,359. Re-sale without loss as speedily as possible, and not speculative profit, is the company's uniform policy in dealing with such properties, but in order to accomplish this, some expenditure is often necessary or advisable, it being obvious that a property which is in good order can be sold more advantageously and promptly than one which has been allowed to suffer dilapidation . . . The directors expect these properties to be gradually realized without any material loss, and are in possession of advices and valuations which confirm this expectation.

The directors found support for their position from no less a source than the *Financial Times* which reported that: 'Trust companies got into rather bad odour of late years owing to the discoveries of very black sheep, which had got mixed up in what was popularly supposed to be a milk-white flock. But they are not all tarred with the same black brush, and the Alliance Trust Company has just issued a report which ought to be satisfactory to the shareholders . . . Considering the conditions that prevailed during 1894, the Alliance Trust may be said to have done very well.'

There were other factors affecting the state of business. Although prices began to rise again in 1895 recovery was a slow process. The currency question over the monetisation of silver, which had been discussed since the 1870s, was thought to be inhibiting economic growth. This was most often an issue in presidential election years. At the AGM in 1897 the directors reported that the presidential election in 1896 had produced 'a practical paralysis of business throughout the country'.

There had also been a war scare in 1895 when there had been a danger that the United Kingdom and the United States might go to war over a boundary dispute between British Guiana and Venezuela in which President Cleveland supported the Venezuelan position. Common sense prevailed, but given that the two countries were major trading partners, the mere threat of war caused some disruption to business.

Some of the difficulties affected Alliance Trust directly, as when flooding in the Mississippi Delta in 1894 badly affected the company's real estate and added to a year of 'trouble and disaster on every quarter'.

It was not until 1899 that the directors felt secure enough in the recovery of the US economy to say that prosperity had returned. Guthrie, who was in the chair, claimed: 'The increase of wealth is going on rapidly in America at present; and it is the general rule that the population is making money and is paying off old debts.' Developing his optimistic theme, he told the shareholders that bond and share prices had improved and that 'progress has also been made in other directions, it has not been on the same general and substantial scale; but this is only in accordance with a well known economic law, that real estate and advances based upon it, do not respond so quickly as investments of a more elastic character to the appreciating influence of restored prosperity.'

But Guthrie and his fellow directors were sufficiently well versed in the turns of the trade cycle to speculate on when the next downturn might occur. When it did, in 1907–8, it passed without comment at the annual meetings.

As the First World War approached, the amount of information given to the shareholders in print was probably less than it had been in the early years of the company. Figures for reserve investments and mortgage lending were no longer given separately but included under the general heading of 'investments'. But this was counterbalanced by the fact that there was often one of the American agents present at the annual meeting to report on his sphere of activity and to answer questions. It was also counterbalanced by the fact that the annual dividend to ordinary shareholders had climbed steadily upwards. It had started this period at 12.5% before falling to 8% in 1896, where it remained until 1905. Thereafter it rose steadily until 1914, when it was 18%.

Strategy

The economic difficulties that struck the United States in the early 1890s were deep and long lasting, and forced the directors in Dundee to rethink their strategy. In November 1892 they decided to rationalise the business. The agencies in Memphis, San Antonio and Portland were told to remit all interest collected to Dundee but were allowed to reinvest all repayments collected. They were also allowed to use their discretion to renew maturing loans. The rating agency, Dun and Co., were asked for an opinion on Edward Holmes and his new partner Myers in Kansas City. The reply was less than encouraging. 'So far as local authorities have knowledge they are not worth anything the law could reach.' Nevertheless they were retained in post although not given new lending credits.

Small agencies and subagencies in Columbia, Montreal, Fergus Falls, Indianapolis, Fargo, Chicago, Muscatine and the agency with the Corbin Banking Company were to be liquidated as rapidly and expeditiously as possible. Fort Worth was to experience a gradual and judicious liquidation. No special instructions were given for San Francisco, St Paul and Red Oak. Winnipeg, which was Haggart's own agency, escaped the cuts. Haggart had been given the agency in 1891 when it was discovered that the previous agents had claimed commissions on profits made on foreclosures.

Liquidating some of these arrangements proved more difficult than might be imagined. Calling in loans was not an option, as the mortgages made no provision for such an event. Efforts to sell the loans to other organisations produced only limited success. Selling real estate that had been foreclosed proved difficult in a depressed market. So, in some cases, several years went by before effect could be given to all of these instructions. However, conditions in Fort Worth improved to the extent that the agency was reprieved.

A major preoccupation of Alliance Trust was to divest itself of the real estate that it had inherited as a result of the activities of Dundee Land and Dundee Investment. Principal amongst these problems was the Chaves Grant. This piece of real estate in New Mexico had been purchased jointly with the

Colorado Mortgage Company, whose chairman was the MP for Forfar, James W. Barclay. In the early months of 1890 relationships with the Colorado Company had soured to the extent that 'further correspondence of a friendly character . . . is useless'. The Colorado Company had attempted to charge Alliance Trust £759 for its 'management' of the land. As nothing had been done and there was no revenue, the Alliance directors decided to invite Mr Barclay to Dundee for 'friendly discussions'. The word 'friendly' was used often when the going was tough, which suggests that the directors were always anxious to reach amicable and negotiated settlements rather than pursue problems by legal means. They were often successful in doing so. On this occasion the matter went to arbitration and the Lord Advocate greatly reduced the claim. Other lands, jointly held, near Boulder Colorado, were slightly more productive and were found to have coal deposits, although early lessees of these lands took some time to find it. Early test bores produced mixed results.

There were further difficulties with the Colorado Co. in 1905 when it decided that it would no longer manage the Alliance Trust interests. That particular difficulty was smoothed over and some of the Boulder county lands were sold later that year. Alliance had to press for its share of the money and there were concerns that the Colorado Co.'s Denver office was not being well run. A year later Alliance decided to buy the Colorado Co.'s share of the Chaves Grant, for which it paid just $15,000. At the same time it wrote off its own share of the Grant – $16,000. There were also difficulties when Haggart died and it was discovered that the title to the land had been registered in his name. There were tenants on the land so it was producing some income, but squatters were a perennial problem. Nevertheless the directors maintained high hopes that further coal deposits would be found, and in 1913 they were approached for a lease that would allow oil exploration. Before granting the lease they consulted at a high level, including J.T. Cargill, chairman of Burmah Oil, and Sir Boverton Redwood, a leading chemical engineer and oil specialist.

Alliance Trust would gladly have sold its interest in the Chaves Grant, and made several efforts to do so, but in the absence of a willing buyer, it had no alternative but to make the best of a bad deal. Part of the problem with the grant was that it had been made when Spain controlled the land in question and the United States took many years to make its mind up about whether or not it would recognise these types of land grant. Until that happened the title was regarded as being defective. In 1891 the US government established a special commission for settling matters regarding Spanish land grants.

Property matters, in particular the Chaves Grant and the Ashly Company in Mississippi, occupied a great deal of the board's time and energies but they were not the core of the business. The core was in the routine of mortgage business, and by the fourth annual general meeting in April 1892 mortgages exceeded £1m. But the company had moved far beyond the simple agricultural mortgage that had been the basis of the business of the Oregon and Washington Investment Trust in 1873. It was almost as likely now that the mortgages would be on town properties. This was certainly the case in Portland, Winnipeg and Kansas City.

In Winnipeg, for example, the company found itself the owner of a block of houses called the Dundee Block. A sales agreement was reached in 1890 but Haggart advised that the houses had been sold too cheaply and wanted to back out of the transaction. The directors replied that they were honour bound to respect the deal. They did, but the purchaser did not. Early the following year Alex Gourlay, one of the directors, was in Manitoba and wrote to Dundee to say that the Dundee Block was in the middle of the main street in Winnipeg, and population expansion was expected to happen soon. Consequently prices were expected to rise. Although the directors in Dundee were always keen to divest themselves of real estate, they were conscious of the commercial opportunities presented by a potential rise in property prices. There was also a decision to be made about whether to sell properties or to let them at good rents.

The Trust owned properties in Lowson Terrace, Winnipeg, but the central heating system that had been installed to serve all the houses had been a failure and the Trust found itself in the position of having to install a new system. The matter was left in Haggart's hands. He eventually proposed a 'slump sale' of the Winnipeg properties, from which it was confidently predicted that the company's outlays would be recovered.

The People

The matter of the chairmanship of the board was never really resolved. Following Guild's death early in 1892, Alex Henderson was the senior director and occupied the chair at most of the subsequent meetings that year. At the 1892 annual general meeting the shareholders were asked to leave it to the directors to 'make a nomination which they feel to be consistent with the interests of the company'. They never did, and even at the annual general meetings any one of the directors could be nominated to be the chairman for that day. By 1893 Andrew Whitton assumed the lead role and became the de facto chairman of the company. Ill health forced him to relinquish this role in 1905 when it was assumed by James Guthrie, but it was not until 1913 that Guthrie was formally appointed as chairman. Whitton remained a board member until 1914, but by that time he had been absent for a year.

There was a great deal of stability in the make-up of the board in these years. James Cunningham, Jnr, merchant in Dundee, was elected in 1893 to fill the place made vacant by Guild's death. He resigned in 1894, as did Alex Henderson. Only one replacement was made. William L. Boase was a member of a family long established in the business affairs of Dundee. One of his family members, Charles Boase, had run the Dundee Banking Company until it was taken over by the Royal Bank in 1864. John Ogilvy, who was the largest single holder of ordinary shares, became a director in 1899 and sometimes stood in for Whitton, but he was not a well man and died in 1903. The board was ageing. Alex Gourlay, a local shipbuilder who had been involved from the outset, died in 1899. Early in 1906 Whitton and Boase were on extended sick leave. This left only Guthrie, Leadbetter and Maitland to run the company but they were in no hurry to add to their numbers. William Thomson, shipowner in Dundee, joined the board in 1908, and it was not until 1911 that further strength was added when Frederick B. Sharp, jute manufacturer in Dundee, was appointed. This did little to enhance the numbers, as John Leadbetter died the following month.

Most of the board business was routine and dealt with loans, permissions to sell real estate and agents' commissions, although very little detail was recorded. Occasionally the agenda was quite full. In January 1901 the directors had to deal with share transfers, debenture purchases, bond acquisitions, the sale of American railroad and other securities, a legal case dealing with defaulted bonds, problems on a Texas ranch, legal issues regarding the Chaves Grant and the status and salaries of officers in the American branches. When a matter which was exceptional or of an unusual nature arose, then the directors were spurred into action. In September 1893, 'The directors, after consideration instructed the Secretary to call the friendly notice of Sir John Leng, to an article which appeared in the *Dundee Advertiser* . . . in which the Hawaiian Investment Company and mortgage companies generally are subject to criticism which the directors consider irrelevant and calculated to excite unnecessary and prejudicial alarm.'

Leng, in addition to being the local newspaper proprietor, was also the local MP. His response is not recorded.

The reason the directors seem to have had relatively little to do was that Mackenzie was shouldering an increasing amount of the work. This was despite his connections with two Edinburgh investment companies who were paying his rail season ticket from his home in Broughty Ferry to Edinburgh. One of those companies, the Investors' Mortgage Security Company, contributed a share of Mackenzie's expenses for his visit to the United States in 1891. They had been asked to pay 75 guineas but offered £50, which the Dundee men thought 'rather narrow and shabby' but accepted so as to avoid controversy.

By this time Mackenzie had been involved in the mortgage business for 20 years and was at the height of his powers. He was sent again to the United States in 1894 and was accompanied by Haggart on his tour. He took ship at Liverpool, but before doing so, he purchased cotton futures there from Joseph Thorburn in respect of the company's actual holding of cotton. This cotton was the product of the real estate that the company held in the Mississippi valley, including the Ashly lands.

A well-earned holiday in 1896 gave him time to go to Europe for a few weeks, during which time the minutes of the company record very little. He was back in the United States in 1897, and again in 1898 and 1899. Some of these trips were made in the winter months, reflecting the improvements that had been made in modes of transport in the United States. The main purpose of these visits was to gather information about economic conditions and investment opportunities and to impress upon the agents the need for extra efforts to be made to dispose of real estate. When he returned to the United States during the crisis of 1907–8 the power of attorney that he was given was couched in the widest terms. It gave him powers to buy and sell; appoint and dismiss; establish local boards or disband them; and to open bank accounts.

Mackenzie was clearly increasingly valuable to the company as an investment manager rather than as a company secretary, and he gradually relinquished the secretary's duties. In 1901 he was relieved of the duty of signing dividend warrants which, in future, would be signed by his assistant, W. Finlay. Yet more than a decade passed before he was finally relieved of all his secretarial duties. In June 1912 he was appointed to be a director of the company (in effect, managing director). His place as secretary was taken by a local solicitor William D. MacDougall. Mackenzie's elevation to the board spurred him on to clear up loose ends, and the various companies that had merged to form Alliance Trust were finally liquidated.

Also key to the success of the organisation was the inspector of agencies.

Haggart had been in the role for some years, and was also the agent in Winnipeg. In 1895 he was granted a new assistant, George Murray, a man of Scottish origins but who had been in the United States for many years. This was also a joint appointment with United States Investment and Investors Mortgage Security, although Alliance Trust was the senior partner in the arrangement and paid 55% of the costs. The various parties, not least Haggart, were seriously impressed by the young man and made his appointment permanent a year later. This enabled Haggart to make plans for a visit home to Scotland. During an extended trip he attended several board meetings in Dundee and had extensive conversations with Mackenzie about agency remuneration and inspections. He was awarded a pay rise to $4,500 per annum, subject to the agreement of the other two companies.

The relationship between Haggart and Murray was very fruitful. A close bond of trust developed between them, and in 1900 Haggart's job title was recast as superintendent of agencies, with Murray assuming the title of inspector of agencies The following year Haggart was unwell and asked for four months' sick leave and an allowance of £200. The directors acquiesced. He returned to Scotland and to his home in Blairgowrie. The directors were worried about him and told him that he could have whatever leave he might need. They also increased his allowance. Fortunately he recovered and was back at work early in 1902. This allowed Murray to visit Scotland, where he insisted to the directors that Texas was best placed to deliver the investment returns that were required. Murray was rewarded with a bonus and a holiday.

The accuracy and security of company documents were a constant source of concern to the directors and, notwithstanding that Haggart and Murray were in place, advantage was taken of a visit to America in 1902 by J.C. Robertson, CA, the company auditor. He was asked to check the books in the agencies. This was not to suggest that the agents and inspectors were not trusted. It was simply a matter of good business to take every opportunity to check on the accuracy of company records. Robertson did what he was asked and found everything to be in good order, for which he was rewarded with 50 guineas.

By the end of 1902 Haggart was unwell again and planned to go to San Antonio to recover. Mackenzie, who was in America at the time, gave him $500 to meet his expenses. It was too late. Haggart died in Kansas City on 20 December. He had served Alliance Trust and Dundee Mortgage for 18 years and the tribute to him was fulsome. Fleming was in America and helped to sort out Haggart's extensive affairs. Alliance put up some money to help finish a building project in which he had been involved.

There was never any doubt but that Murray would succeed Haggart. He was appointed in May 1903 at a salary of $4,000 in year one. This was to rise to $5,000 in year three. The chief clerk in what was now described as the 'American office' in Kansas City was Miss Minnie B. Secrist, whose salary was $100 per month. Her assistant was Miss Jessie Landes, who earned $70 per month.

These appointments were also the time for a rethink about how the American business would be run. Robertson's audit of the agencies' books suggested to the directors that, notwithstanding Murray's appointment, it would be a good idea to have a formal audit on a regular basis. A.P. Spence, a Scottish chartered accountant based in New York, was given the task.

The existence of the American office and the appointment of Spence was an attractive package, and it was not long before the United States Mortgage Co. asked to join the arrangement. This was agreed. The cost-sharing arrangement between the four companies was reviewed and Minnie Secrist was given a pay rise. Within weeks of this new arrangement Henry Jones was appointed as Murray's assistant. This gave Murray the space to expand his remit, and in November 1905 he was making plans to visit Cuba to investigate a large loan that Fleming was organising and in which the four companies might take an interest.

Early in 1909 Murray suddenly died. Jones was appointed to the post several months later. It is evident that both Macmaster from Portland and Nares from Winnipeg would occasionally assist Jones with inspection duties. The new appointment was clearly successful, and there was some worry that another company might poach him. So his salary was regularly increased until, by 1912, he was earning $7,500 per annum. The following year Mackenzie appointed Leighton Myles to be his assistant.

There can be no doubt that the role of the inspectors was central to the success of the Alliance Trust's American investments. The lending of money on another continent was always going to be a pursuit fraught with difficulties, and to lend in a frontier society made the venture even more risky. There was always the danger that things would go wrong or that dishonest borrowers and corrupt officials might compromise the integrity of the operation. The inspector's role was to make sure that did not happen, and when difficulties did arise his role was to protect the interests of his employers and minimise any losses. In this regard Haggart, Murray and Jones served their employers well.

Investments

Robert Fleming continued to play a major part in the investment strategy of the company, despite the fact that he was not a director. His special interest was in the purchase of railway bonds and these remained his primary interest for many years. His recommendations for purchase were followed without exception. But the directors were always especially keen on railways that were being developed or extended in areas where they were active on the mortgage front. They well understood that the coming of a railroad would have a beneficial impact on the value of land that would make existing mortgages safer and create a demand for new mortgages as population increased.

One of Fleming's particular strengths was to pursue interests in railway companies that had got into difficulty and which had to be restructured. He even managed to recover monies from the Oregonian Railway that had created such difficulties for Dundee interests in the early years of the 1880s. In 1896 Alliance Trust received consolidated gold bonds and non-cumulative preferred stock in the company. Clearly Fleming was prepared to play the long game.

Many of the railway reconstructions in which Fleming was involved were syndicated loans, as the amounts of money involved could be substantial. One of the larger ones was for the Baltimore and Ohio Railroad, which was reorganised in 1898. Alliance Trust applied for $250,000 (about £50,000) of the new share issue but it was so popular that they received only half of that amount.

Nor was Fleming solely interested in the United States. His interests spread to other parts of the world – especially to South America. Argentina had long been a focus for British overseas investors, and in 1897 Fleming was busy raising £200,000 for the Primativa Gas Company in Buenos Aires. Alliance Trust offered to buy £5,000 of the shares. Whitton and Mackenzie also applied for these shares and, when they were issued, offered them to Alliance Trust. This suggests that the Trust wanted more shares than it was likely to get when they were allotted. This event was followed by an investment in the Mexican Central Railroad gold bonds. There was also a short-dated loan to the Electricity Supply Company of Spain.

By the turn of the century Alliance Trust was purchasing bonds and preference shares in a wide range of companies. Purchases in 1899 included Consolidated Gold Fields of South Africa, Baku Russian Petroleum Company, Waring and Gillow Ltd and the Nobel Dynamite Trust. It seems clear from these purchases that the risk of investment was being spread both geographically and by industrial sector.

Holmes, the agent in Kansas City, had business interests in Mexico and made several attempts to persuade the directors to invest there. J.H. Meyer visited Dundee in 1901. He was the Mexico City manager of the United States and Mexican Trust, of which Holmes was a director. Mexican National Railway bonds were purchased in 1901 but Holmes' and Meyer's entreaties were resisted.

Many purchases of securities were made as long-term investments and were designated as being for the reserve fund, whilst others were more short-term investments which would be held until mortgage-lending opportunities presented themselves. There was something of an annual rhythm to this, as investments were often sold in August or September and the money raised was used to meet mortgage borrowers' requirement for funds to finance crop sowing. Occasionally some of these investments were re-designated for the reserve fund, and although this was only a book-keeping entry it does suggest that the company was conducting regular reviews of its investments and its strategy.

Alliance Trust was not solely dependent on Fleming for investment advice; Mackenzie was more than capable of making his own judgements. His frequent visits to the United States had a dual purpose. He went to check on the agents but he also went in search of investment opportunities. Some simply turned up. For instance, on his way back to New York in 1897, he was offered gold car trust bonds of the Bangor and Aroostook Railroad Company, which he duly purchased.

Nor was the Trust dependent on Fleming to effect purchases. In 1898 they bought debentures and preference stock in the American Thread Company via W.D. Fisher, stockbroker in Dundee. Another local stockbroker, John M. Watson, offered 207 shares in the Dundee-run Matador Land and Cattle Co. at £5 per share, and these were duly purchased.

The Alliance Trust and its predecessors had had very little interest in ranches and cattle companies despite these being highly popular with Scottish investors, especially in their heyday in the early 1880s. But in the late 1890s there was a renewed interest after the American economy began to drag itself out of the difficulties of the mid 1890s. The sum of £67,650 was lent to the Cresswell Land and Ranche Co. to pay off its debentures. The security offered was the company's assets, and the interest rate was 6% paid half yearly. This was an unusual transaction. The company was not keen on ranches simply because of the difficulties they could present if things went wrong. The company had earlier foreclosed on the Morris ranch in Texas, which was then leased. In 1899 it was originally decided not to renew the lease but to leave the land empty in the expectation that the grass would improve and this would make it more attractive to prospective purchasers. However, advice from the San Antonio agents was averse to this idea, as they believed that adjoining ranchers would cut the fences and allow their cattle to graze on the land. Henry Drought acquired 498 cows and 151 calves for $9,376 and drove them onto the ranch. The directors in Dundee approved. Two years later the rigs arrived at the Morris ranch to drill for oil. Regrettably nothing came of this, and in 1904 Drought was being pressed to sell the ranch, even at a small loss.

It is clear that the range of investment opportunities was expanding. The new industries of electric power and the motor car would change the face of all stock exchanges and create an insatiable demand for capital. Moreover many more countries were trying to raise loans on the London market, although some of these appeared a little too risky to the directors. In 1899 they were considering a participation in a loan to the Japanese government that was being raised in London. Participation was declined. Towards the end of 1898 there was a discussion at the board in which it was noted that requests for mortgages were in short supply and interest rates were likely to fall. The question was raised as to whether or not the Alliance Trust should extend into a more general investment business. Thereafter there was almost as much discussion at board meetings regarding investments as there was about mortgages. Nevertheless, despite a marked growth in its investment business, the Alliance Trust remained, for the time being, primarily a mortgage company.

In the years leading up to the First World War little changed in the company's investment strategy. Trends that were noticeable in the final decade of the nineteenth century continued into the early years of the twentieth.

Railroads continued to be a key element in the portfolio but they were almost as likely to be in Brazil, Cuba, Mexico or Guatemala as in the United States. Some of the new investment was in urban railway systems such as the Chicago Elevated Railway and the New York Metropolitan Street Railway. But if urban railways were popular so too were tramways, and investments were made in London, Montevideo, Kirkcaldy and Dundee. In the latter case £10,000 in debentures and £2,500 in preference shares were purchased in the Dundee and Broughty Ferry Tramway.

Risks were spread with a highly diversified portfolio. In August 1905 the directors decided to invest $25,000 in a loan being raised by Balfour, William- son for a large land-reclamation project in the Sacramento valley in California. Two months later a meeting of the board recorded purchases in a railway in

Buenos Aires, a railroad in Cuba, an Egyptian supply store, California oilfields and a Manila electric light company.

By that time news was being received of revolutionary activity in the Russian Empire. Disturbances in Azerbaijan rendered the investments in the European Petroleum Co. and the Baku Russian Petroleum Co. of doubtful value. There were other, less well known, but still profitable investments in companies such as Gath and Chaves, a Harrods-style store in Buenos Aires. But the strategy of diversifying risk paid off and the company invested in some stocks that became staples of most investment companies' portfolios. These included International Harvester, Otis Elevator Co., Liggett and Myers and P. Lorillard and Co. (The last two were acquired as a result of the enforced break-up of American Tobacco under the American anti-trust legislation.) In various states, including Texas, Alliance was required to demonstrate that it complied with this legislation by submitting an annual affidavit attesting that it was not a member of any pool, trust, combination or other business-sharing arrangement.

There had been a small number of investments in British firms and this trend continued. Companies such as Imperial Tobacco, British Aluminium, Burmah Oil, Anglo Persian Oil and British Westinghouse began to appear in the portfolio, although the purchases were nearly always preference shares, reflecting the company's interest in regular dividends rather than capital appreciation. The move into equities was still some way in the future. There was also a start to what would become a longer-term strategy of purchasing shares in other investment trusts, beginning with an investment in the Edinburgh-based Scottish American Investment Co. Ltd.

The move into a structured investment policy imposed on the directors the need to review their investments on a regular basis. On one occasion when this was being done the directors did not approve of the revenue account of the Consolidated Tea Company. This company was run by the Glasgow firm of James Finlay and Co. A letter was duly dispatched to James Finlay and Co. to express the Alliance's dissatisfaction, but the directors did not consider the matter sufficiently serious to warrant selling the shares. They probably came to wish that they had.

Two years later the company failed to pay the dividend on its preference shares and the Alliance board decided that Messrs Mackenzie and Guthrie should attend the company's annual general meeting. But before this happened they met the senior directors from Finlay's, Sir John Muir and R.H. Sinclair, who agreed to make a call on the ordinary shareholders and not to expand the company beyond its existing commitments. A not dissimilar situation arose with the investment in United Collieries, and Mackenzie was a member of the committee of debenture holders which was set up to protect investor's interests. Both incidents demonstrate the growing power of institutional investors such as Alliance to influence policy in companies in which they had made investments.

This power could also work across the Atlantic. In 1909 Brown Brothers in New York wrote to express their dissatisfaction with the management of Newport News and Old Point Comfort Electric Traction Co. They proposed to do something about it and Mackenzie agreed to lend his weight to a bondholders' action group. Brown Brothers wrote a few months later to say that they had achieved their objectives.

Throughout these years Alliance Trust had kept abreast of the new investment opportunities available to it. In doing so it had made extensive use of Fleming's advice and services but they have also received advice and suggestions from local brokers in Dundee and Edinburgh, as well as from their bankers and brokers in New York. The world was moving fast towards the disaster that would be the First World War. It is somewhat surprising, therefore, that apart from the investment in Nobel Dynamite and an underwriting participation in Cammell Laird there were no investments in the armaments industry.

The Agencies

As noted earlier the directors in Dundee would receive, each year, a visit from at least one of the North American agents. Francis Smith from San Antonio was the most frequent visitor to Scotland. Such visits, together with the directors' own excursions to the United States and Canada, and Mackenzie's trips, ensured that there was a good flow of information and opinion moving in both directions. They also helped establish trust, and on that basis firm friendships developed.

The contracts with the agents were designed to give them a certain amount of freedom to assess lending propositions, but they were also designed to ensure fair play and gave the agents no room for manoeuvre in their dealings with clients. Section 'G' of the contract with Caldwell and Judah in 1896 stated:

> The Firm must not make any charges against, or exact any fees or
> commissions from, borrowers, except such moderate charges, fees, or

commissions, if any, as can be properly and legally charged against them: But declaring always and emphatically that no charges, fees, or commissions shall be made, received, or exacted which could directly or indirectly imperil or affect the legality of any of the company's loans or transactions, or be taken into account as an illegal or improper addition to interest or otherwise in any question under usury or other laws, and that the company shall be informed fully with reference to such charges, fees, or commissions should it so desire at any time or in any case.

In other respects the contracts were quite similar to those entered into when the Oregon and Washington Trust started out in 1873. No loans were to be made without proper inspection of the property, and loans were to be no more than 40% of the assessed value of the property.

Although there might be a great deal of very forthright discussion about the minutiae of how the agents were to be managed and rewarded for their endeavours, there was never any long-running dispute. The above contract with Caldwell and Judah, which is very similar to the contracts with other agents, was designed to ensure that the company acted legally and that customers were treated fairly.

It was not just the customers who were treated fairly. In the depression of the mid 1890s Caldwell, in Memphis, found himself in financial difficulty, with assets somewhat less than his liabilities. He had wide-ranging business interests in addition to his agency for Alliance Trust. There had been signs of trouble early in 1893 when he had written some intemperate letters to Dundee. This was out of character, and Haggart was sent to investigate. His view was that Caldwell was suffering from stress through overwork. When the directors in Dundee learned of this their response was to lend him enough money to cover his positions until such times as the economy recovered and he was able to trade out of his difficulties, which he duly did. The extent of this support also extended to offering him friendly advice from time to time about keeping his commitments to manageable levels.

With his money worries receding, Caldwell, whose firm, Caldwell and Smith described themselves as attorneys, loan brokers and financial agents, was soon back at work attracting German settlers to the Delta and working on the reconstruction of the Ashly Company. He was also the man who came up with the idea of buying cotton futures as a way of dealing with price fluctuations – a policy which was duly adopted and which, in the course of time, proved to be highly profitable. As noted earlier, within weeks of receiving this suggestion, Mackenzie, en route for the US, was in Liverpool buying futures from Joseph Thorburn and Co. Five hundred bales of cotton were subject to these contracts, and £600 profit was made within five months. Given the amount of land that was being acquired by foreclosures in the cotton-producing areas of America, these contracts became an important and regular feature of Alliance policy and practice.

Cotton farming in the Mississippi Delta was often a precarious business. A good crop could depress prices, weather was unpredictable and labour was in short supply. Flooding could be a mixed blessing. It could deposit material that helped growth or it could sweep away topsoil. In these circumstances it was vital that the directors in Dundee were kept up to date with what was happening, and Caldwell and Judah (later Caldwell and Smith), were assiduous in providing information to the board.

The company's big investment in the region was in the Ashly Company – a large plantation which had got into difficulties, and, as has been said, thanks largely to Alliance Trust, had been refinanced. Caldwell looked after the investment but Haggart lent a hand and, in July 1893, recommended a loan of $12,000 to get the crop finished. He also recommended that a private levee should be erected, and this was done after the other companies involved had been consulted. The Willow Bayou levee was duly built.

In 1894 the Ashly Company was reconstructed as the Deltic Investment Company, with Alliance as the main shareholder. Caldwell's responsibility was to manage the investment, not just for Alliance but also for the other Scottish and English trusts that had a stake. He saw clearly what needed to be done, and on one occasion had a tramway built to assist the movement of crops. A steamboat pier was his next investment. Ventures such as these were the only way to make a large estate a profitable and saleable investment. By the end of 1895 Alliance's loan to Deltic was almost $200,000. Notwithstanding the enthusiasm and support of everyone who visited the estate, including Alliance's auditor, Caldwell's renewed energy and determination were no match for the Delta weather, and it was not until the interwar years that the loan was repaid, with a further period of time before the investment was sold. Between 1892 and 1917 the net loss on Deltic was $330,945 but it is not possible to say what portion Alliance had to bear.

Indeed there was a catalogue of difficulties to overcome in managing this particular investment. An outbreak of charbon disease, a type of anthrax, amongst the mules in Memphis caused inconvenience and expense. It was not until 1897 that it was reported that the cotton crop was going well, although that news simply served to depress prices. In 1898 the directors, in briefing Mackenzie prior to his US visit, declared themselves to be happy with the Memphis agents but still worried about the Deltic/Ashly investment. They were right to be worried. Relations with the other investors were sometimes fractious. A dividend to preferred creditors was paid in 1905 when Alliance received £1,901 but the following year they told the Deltic directors that they were dissatisfied with progress. Their expectations for a sale of all or part of the land was based on the fact that there was a large quantity of good quality timber. The Singer Sewing Machine Company made an offer for 19,100 acres of the timber lands in 1912 but their offer of $16 per acre was thought inadequate. The offer was raised to $17 but the Deltic directors refused and thought that they could get a better price 'through patience'. In other respects there was a shortage of labour to farm the plantations. In 1907 the Deltic directors sent Mr Gino Pierotti to Italy to recruit settlers for the Ashly land. Mackenzie was sent to lend a hand 'as far as possible'. Subsequent events may have made them wish that they had accepted the Singer offer, as an outbreak of boll weevil attacked the cotton crop in 1913 and, as a consequence, revenues were severely depressed.

In other ways the Memphis agency went well. In 1899 Alliance owned six plantations in the Delta, the net profit from which was $18,261. The directors were particularly pleased with the work that Caldwell's partner, Bolton Smith, had performed in selling off real estate, and when Caldwell visited Dundee that year he was given a gold watch to take to Smith and a ring for Mrs Smith. The watch was inscribed, 'Pro meritis bene merenti – omnium horarum amico.'

In 1902 Caldwell was hard at work trying to recover some of the land that had been abandoned because of defective title deeds. The directors made it clear that he would be well rewarded if he was successful. By late summer the agency was able to report that they had sold 8,537 acres of Arkansas land at $7 per acre and a further 1,347 acres of the 'suspensory lands (i.e. the lands with defective title) at the same price. This was a major coup, as much of this land had been acquired many years earlier at $2 per acre.

Caldwell was in Dundee in 1906 to report that more land had been sold and that the company had made a profit of $200,000. He was also hopeful that he would eventually be able to sell the Ashly lands. He was however less sanguine about an experiment in growing alfalfa. His agency was also suffering from competition from other lenders, especially American insurance companies, and in 1909 he reported that he was not able to lend the credits he had been sent. He suggested lending at a lower rate of interest but the directors deferred a decision.

In July 1910 it was known that Caldwell's partner, Bolton Smith, was to be in Rotterdam, and Mackenzie was sent to speak to him there about the lack of lending in the Memphis agency. Smith then called at Dundee and suggested lending in Tennessee but it transpired that legal difficulties made this impossible, whereupon Smith proposed lending in Mississippi and Louisiana. Both Caldwell and Smith were in Dundee in 1911 to discuss their remuneration. Proposals were made but before agreement had been reached Caldwell and Smith had left for home. Mackenzie was sent to Paris to meet them before they embarked for home at Boulogne. What was agreed must have provided the necessary incentives. In 1912 they were earnestly soliciting extra funds for lending.

In the summer of 1914 the Mercantile Bank of Memphis, in which Caldwell was a director, failed as a result of cotton speculation by the president, who lost $780,000 and went to jail. Both Alliance and Deltic had deposits in the bank, which was duly liquidated. Caldwell had been off ill when the defalcations took place. The liquidator paid out 75c in the $. Caldwell then paid the remaining balances due to Alliance and Deltic from his own pocket. It cost him $5,000. 'It was pointed out that Mr Caldwell took this action spontaneously and without any obligation on his part but simply in a spirit of loyalty and regard for the interests of the companies. The directors recorded their 'high appreciation' of this action.

The other agencies were making progress, although each had its own particular set of issues. In places like Kansas City where there were numerous loans on urban property the challenge was always to keep abreast of a rising tide of municipal requirements for improved pavements, street lighting and sanitation, all of which were the responsibility of local proprietors rather than the authority itself. In some of the buildings over which the company held mortgages the wooden stairs rotted and had to be replaced at a cost of $1,300. A further $440 was to be spent putting in a pavement and kerbstone.

Early in 1893 it was clear that all was not well with this agency, which was described as being subject to 'some conversation'. The result was that Myers retired and the agency was carried on by Holmes, who had engaged his brothers to assist him in the business. There were worries about the number of loans that had been foreclosed and, for the first time, the directors were provided with photographs of the properties involved. Haggart, the inspector, who had been based, somewhat inconveniently, in Winnipeg, moved to Kansas City in 1894 and became joint agent with Holmes, whilst still retaining his role as inspector of agencies. The company paid his removal expenses, and despite his $3,000 per annum salary, he was also allowed to become the Kansas City agent for the Canadian and American Mortgage Trust Co. and the United Trust of Liverpool. He was also to retain his existing role as inspector for the United States Investment Corporation and the Investors Security Company Ltd. The directors were less keen on Holmes and Haggart running a rental agency business but approved of Haggart running an insurance agency. It seems likely that his role and standing with Alliance Trust made him a magnet for many offers.

The threat of war between the United States and Spain in 1898 made the directors in Dundee cautious about long-term investments in North America, and when they were invited to participate in raising capital for the Roanoke extension to Kansas City they declined but they did declare themselves willing to listen to enquiries about mortgages on the new properties.

Haggart's old agency in Winnipeg was left in the hands of a Mr Nares, who had been Haggart's colleague there. Like his old boss he also had agencies with other companies. These organisations were involved in the Ashly/Deltic arrangement in Memphis, and Nares was appointed to be the Deltic auditor. To assist him in the agency he took Mr Nicholls as a partner. Nares and Nicholls must have known what they were getting into, for the problems in some of the housing terraces continued unabated. The heating problem in Lowson Terrace rumbled on and tenants were allowed a reduction in their rents to help pay their coal bills. In 1896 Nares had gone to San Francisco and was told to return to Winnipeg to get the needed repairs to the Whitton villas carried out. He then fell out with Nicholls, and it took a visit from Mackenzie in 1896 to restore some order to the troubled agency. Nares eventually became a partner in the firm of Robinson and Black, which then assumed the agency.

Matters were less problematical, although still difficult, in the west. T. de Will Cuyler, a scion of the New York banking family, was the agent in Fort Worth. The mortgage business there rolled on almost without comment. The problems arose in some of the bigger loans and it was the extractive industry rather than agriculture that provided the problems. In 1893 a loan to the Texas Copper Company was under discussion. R G Dun, the rating agency, gave the opinion that R. Duncan Harris, one of the directors, was as solid as a rock. The loan was extended but personal guarantees were required from Harris and his partner.

Early in 1896 there were plans to foreclose on property in the, as yet, under-developed Arlington Heights area. Having done so they then proposed to give 100 acres to the Grand Lodge of Masons of Texas on condition that they built their state home for widows and orphans on it. It was hoped that if this was done then the value of the surrounding land would be enhanced. However, this gift was declined because of a defect in the title. The records are then silent but the home was opened there in 1899 and it may be assumed that the legal problem was resolved.

In San Antonio Francis Smith and Henry Drought ran the agency and represented upwards of 15 firms in their lending business. The loan to the Falfurrias Ranch in Southern Texas was sometimes a matter of concern, not because there was any doubt about the Lassater family who owned it, but simply because the ranch was thought to be vulnerable to drought. Francis Smith was present in Dundee for discussions on this loan in September 1895, as was J.C. Robertson, CA, the Trust's auditor, who had recently returned from Texas. The loan was renewed.

Smith was looking for $65,000 of new money to lend. He was given $25,000 and told that he would get more if he managed to sell off some of the real estate on which the company had foreclosed. He was back in the UK in 1897 trying to raise money to buy the cattle companies on which many mortgage companies had foreclosed. He forecast, correctly, that the depression was coming to an end and that there was likely to be a rise in values. However he found his London friends 'so discouraged at present about American matters' that they would not agree to raise money for his new venture.

By this time Smith was getting old and was not attending to business full time. The directors in Dundee advised him to appoint an assistant to Mr Drought, on whose shoulders the bulk of the work of the agency was falling. He was eventually prevailed upon to retire and the agency continued as H.P. Drought and Co.

In Portland Messrs Macmaster and Birrell had been busy selling off real estate and, from all accounts, making a better job of it than their counterparts in the other agencies. They had been particularly successful in selling off the remainder of the property that had once belonged to the Ankeny family. However, by the end of the decade they had lost their edge, and George Murray, the assistant inspector, was sent there to encourage them to redouble their efforts. It was not a happy excursion for Murray, who contracted pleurisy and had to be nursed by Macmaster. His recovery was aided by a holiday in 1900 and the gift of £100.

Oregon was fast emerging as a major exporter of wheat and other foodstuffs. It does not appear to have suffered to anything like the same extent from the depression as other parts of the United States. In the summer of 1895 the agents sent very positive reports about the year's crop to Dundee. Their reply was not a word of congratulation but a warning about the need to lend on good security. Nevertheless they were soon busy extending lending into the eastern part of the state, towards the Cascade Mountains. They had some enthusiasm, too, for going further east, into Idaho, but Dundee would not countenance such a move at this time. To the north they were also stopped in their tracks when, in 1897, the Washington State legislature passed a law making it impossible to do business there. Ameliorating legislation was passed the following year, but this was not considered sufficient to allow the company to do profitable business and further legislation was sought.

In the late 1890s the American economy recovered from the recession and business began to pick up. At the AGM in 1899 Guthrie was in the chair. In his report he said: 'The increase of wealth is going on rapidly in America at present; and it is the general rule that the population is making money and is paying off old debts.' Interest rates were being pushed downwards as competition increased. In 1900 Macmaster's partner, Birrell, was in Dundee and given permission to lend at the 'low rate' of 6.5% in Oregon and 7% in Washington. As the economy improved Alliance Trust received several offers from people wishing to establish agencies for the company. But the business cases put forward usually suggested a rate of interest of 5% and the directors thought that this was inadequate. The offers were rejected. In 1900 an American company, Fidelity Security, was being wound up and was trying to sell loans in Iowa, Minnesota and South Dakota. Haggart was sent to investigate but his recommendation was not to invest.

The mortgage business was then still very much the core of the Alliance business and Table 4.1 shows the extent of the company's commitments and the commissions paid to the agents.

The Kansas agent's commission is not recorded because that was the main US office and the agent was paid by salary rather than commission. The total cost of running the Kansas agency, including the expenses of inspection, was £2,907 (c. $14,535).

Overall it seems to have been a well-run business. In 1912 it was recorded that total arrears were only 0.3% of total loans. It was also profitable. The percentage returns by agency varied between 6.18% in Portland and 7.07% in Fort Worth.

Table 4.1 Agency accounts, 1911

Agency	Investment in agency in agency ($)	Commission paid to agent ($)
Portland	2,345,244	20,141 (0.92%)
Memphis	754,982	11,300 (1.18%)
Kansas City	1,461,246	
San Antonio	1,638,241	15,815 (1.01%)
Fort Worth	1,187,345	13,032 (1.18%)
Winnipeg	601,350	3,064 (0.65%)
Total	$7,988,408	$63,352

Performance

In the years between 1893 and 1914 the Alliance Trust more than doubled in size. Ordinary and preference share capital increased from £525,000 to £1.4m. The consequences for ordinary shareholders of the failure of the City of Glasgow Bank in 1878 had been severe and other investors, taking note of this, had begun to favour other forms of investment especially when there was a large uncalled element to their shares. There was a general move in business, which the Alliance followed, of allowing ordinary shareholders to pay up the uncalled element of their ordinary shares and then convert part of their holding into preference shares.

Revenues earned from all sources in 1893 were almost £76,000, and by 1914 this had grown to £237,000. Dividends on ordinary shares, which had been 12.5% in 1893, were 18% in 1914.

In the same period debentures had grown from £600,000 to £1.8m. Interest paid to debenture holders in 1914 was £73,000. True to their strategy the directors had also built up a large reserve fund that grew from £195,000 in 1893 to £780,000 in 1914. There was also a contingency fund that was to be used 'as occasion may require'. The balance was not revealed but in 1903 and 1904 the view was taken that the money in this fund was in excess of the likely need for it, and sums of £10,000 and £36,000 were transferred to the main reserve fund.

By 1914 total investments, including mortgages, exceeded £4m. Alliance Trust had also begun to demonstrate something for which it later became famous – modest management expenses. In 1914 they were only £12,752.

Changes were afoot. By this time the Scottish mortgage companies were beginning to experience competition from US insurance companies, banks and government agencies. The economics of raising money in the UK to lend on mortgages in the US was changing and the model would soon become unsustainable. On the eve of the First World War the mortgage business was yielding a return on capital of 6.43% but the bond business was returning 8.5% and this, of course, made the switch from being a mortgage company to an investment trust all the more likely. But before the logic of this development could be pursued the war changed everything.

Chapter 5
The First World War: 1914–1918

On the eve of the First World War the investment trust industry was still relatively small, despite a substantial growth in the number of trusts that had been established between 1900 and 1914. By that year there were 32 trusts in Scotland and 58 in England. Nevertheless they accounted for less than 1% of the total nominal value of the stocks that were traded on the London Stock Exchange. However this relatively small size belied their importance to the British economy, as they contributed £180m in foreign earnings to the balance of payments.

The experience of the trusts during the war was quite mixed. All were under pressure to purchase government-issued war bonds and, in so doing, to contribute to the war effort. Many trusts managed to maintain, and some to increase, their dividends to ordinary shareholders, while others suffered grievously from falling stock prices. Many witnessed a substantial diminution of their reserves. Moreover, rising rates of interest made borrowing, whether on debentures or from banks, more expensive.

The imminence of war in August 1914 caused stock exchanges to close all over Europe. Paris and London were the last to close (on 30 July) and, while it was said that this was purely a temporary measure to prevent a panic, the London market did not reopen until January 1915.

The United States was a non-combatant at this stage of the war but the New York Stock Exchange also closed and did not reopen for nine months. The special problem in New York was that much of the foreign investment in its market was from the very nations that were now at war. They, of course, wanted their money back and preferred to have it in gold. The market for gold was severely traumatised when, in August 1914, Britain, where many countries held their reserves, left the gold standard.

Part of the problem for the United States was that there was a serious run on the banks as depositors queued to withdraw their deposits. Gold left the United States, heading for Europe, in vast quantities, but it was not long before it was heading back again to pay for war supplies and foodstuffs. The United States emerged from the war no longer a debtor but a creditor nation.

The British government's requirement for money to finance the war was paramount. Huge war loans were successfully raised in increasing amounts. There was even a new loan when the war was over. During the hostilities several trusts sold or lent their securities in American companies to the government. They had been 'invited' to do so and this invitation remained just that until January 1917 when the Treasury acquired powers to requisition securities.

Companies, like Alliance Trust, whose business was still largely in mortgages, found themselves in an awkward position. They were perfectly at liberty to continue lending in Canada, but when a loan matured in the United States, the proceeds had to be handed over to the government and new loans declined. American farmers took a dim view of this as they considered themselves as allies of the British whose efforts in growing food were essential to feed the troops. But it was not until several months after the United States entered the war in 1917 that this anomaly was removed.

Alliance Trust in Wartime

There was nothing recorded in the Alliance Trust board minutes to suggest that war was imminent. In the summer of 1914 plans were being laid to extend lending activities into Arkansas. Investments continued to be made in US, and in a few UK securities. There was also an involvement in a loan to the city of Buenos Aires. The only security sold in the run up to the war was an investment in the Cordoba Central Railway Company. New capital had been issued, two-thirds of which was immediately converted into 4% fixed cumulative preference shares. The vast majority of the purchasers of the new shares were still predominantly from Dundee and its environs. Women were beginning to figure more often in the shareholders' registers.

There was no meeting of the board in August 1914, and when the directors met again in September no mention of the war was recorded in the minutes, although there can be little doubt that it was a major topic of discussion. The first written mention of the war came at the October meeting. Alliance held £3,000 of a £60,000 loan to the Utilities and General Trust. Balfour Beatty, who were fast becoming a major construction and civil engineering company, had proposed that, in view of the outbreak of war, the loan should be extended for a year. This was agreed. (Balfour had served his engineering apprenticeship in Dundee and may well have been known personally to the directors.)

The first government war loan was issued in November, and Alliance purchased £20,000 of the 3.5% stock at £95. The loan was repayable in 1928. Thereafter it was very much business as usual. New credits amounting to $105,000 were extended to the American agencies early in December, with a further $100,000 later in the month.

Jones, the inspector of agencies, and his assistant Myles were busy. In December Jones reported on the possibilities of Georgia as a field for investment and in January 1915 Myles reported on opportunities in the relatively new state of Oklahoma.

Further credits were approved for the agencies in the early months of 1915 but when the Treasury placed restrictions on the ability of companies to raise fresh issues of capital the Alliance board took the view that this did not apply to debentures and that new credits for the agencies could be financed in that way. Whilst this may have been perfectly legal it was hardly in the spirit of wartime finance.

A further tranche of the first war loan was purchased in July 1915 and an application was made for £75,000 of the new 4.5% war loan. Money was brought back from the Bank of Montreal in New York to pay for it.

By that time the Treasury had issued several notices and guidelines about the conduct of investment business. Inevitably these could not be all-encompassing, and Treasury clerks were kept busy corresponding with those who had questions about the strict meaning of the notices. Alliance Trust was among the letter writers, and MacDougall sought guidance about a Treasury circular in relation to mortgage business in the United States. The Treasury reply was that an exact interpretation of the circular in question 'must be left to the loyalty and discretion of the Companies'. The directors concluded that it was not necessary to withdraw any loans from the US or do anything else that 'would be hurtful to the Company's business or impair its machinery or goodwill'.

As the United States was a major source of food for the United Kingdom, it would have been unwise to do anything to disrupt the mortgage business. Moreover, from a purely business perspective, the directors were well aware that war brought higher food and land prices and this could only be good for mortgage lenders.

By the end of 1915 more money was being brought back from North America, although the agencies continued to receive small credits for lending from time to time.

Early in 1916, 12 investments – of which 11 were in US companies – were sold. The money was repatriated and most of it used to purchase Treasury bills. But by the summer of that year the directors were still agonising over what they should do regarding the Treasury's 'invitation' to sell or lend stocks to the government. They decided to do so, and by July the process of selling stocks, mostly US securities, to the Treasury had begun. Later that year they lent 20 stocks to the Treasury. Most were railroad bonds but the list also included investments in light and power companies.

The process of selling and lending stocks to the Treasury continued through 1917. Nor was the Alliance Trust's support for the war effort confined to the United Kingdom. In the autumn of 1916 France raised a loan of Fr 1m and Alliance Trust participated in the underwriting. At that point they were also holding £31,000 of French treasury bills. Early in 1917 £20,000 of Russian government treasury bills were acquired. Quite what the motivation for lending to the Russian government might have been can only be guessed at. The first Russian revolution of 1917 was only weeks away.

In March 1917 the British Treasury decided that it could no longer leave the matter to the discretion of investment companies and began to requisition securities. Ten investments were handed over, with a further fifteen in May of that year. Inevitably this activity began to impinge on the US mortgage business, and Ross in Fort Worth was asked how much of his credit he could relinquish without doing damage to his business. The answer was $25,000, and this was duly returned to the UK via the New York bankers. A further brake was put on mortgage lending in the autumn when it was learned that the US authorities had proposed providing money to the UK if mortgage companies would transfer their loans to US federal land banks. The effect of this proposal, if it had been enacted, would have been to put many of the mortgage companies out of business and to create serious problems for the others.

In October 1917 Mackenzie and MacDougall reported to the board that they had been at a meeting with the Treasury at which Stanley Baldwin had presided. Also present were a large number of mortgage company officials from various parts of the UK. There was a long discussion but no definite decision. The mortgage companies, led by Mackenzie, took legal advice and then sought another meeting with Baldwin. By this stage the US authorities had withdrawn their proposal, leaving the mortgage companies free to conduct their business, with the UK Treasury proviso that they were not to increase their business or to remit funds from the UK for that purpose.

This outcome was immediately conveyed to Jones and the agents, and the board 'expressed great satisfaction with this happy turn of events'. A.R. Shattuck was the US representative of the British and American Mortgage Company. He had been at the Washington end of the negotiations over the discontinuation of UK mortgage business in the US. In doing so he had incurred expenditure of £600. Mackenzie took this matter up with the other mortgage companies and secured remittances of £458. Alliance Trust paid the remainder. Mackenzie's initiative in this matter and the amount paid by Alliance Trust are, doubtless, some measures of the leadership position that the company had assumed amongst its peer group.

Just as there had been no mention in the minute book of the start of the war in 1914 so there was no mention of the armistice in 1918.

Annual General Meetings

The outbreak of the war caused dislocation in every market. The financial markets were certainly no exception. They had been particularly badly affected by the closure, albeit temporary, of stock exchanges in many parts of the world. There was uncertainty in many markets caused, inter alia, by government restrictions, not all of which were well understood. And there was further disruption and dislocation caused by company failures brought about by the war itself as supply lines were closed off and payment systems curtailed.

At the Alliance Trust annual general meeting in April 1915 the shareholders were told that, 'In common with other investors the Company has suffered prejudice from the conditions of default and depreciation now existing throughout the world. While the directors are in agreement with the general expectation that much of this will prove to be temporary, they are prepared for some eventual loss.'

A year later the shareholders were told that large remittances had been made to the UK and that substantial sums had been invested in British and French government securities. In order to make these purchases it had been necessary to borrow funds from the New York banks and, at the time of the annual report (31 January 1916), £52,000 was outstanding.

In 1917 the chairman's report made it clear what contribution the company had made to the war effort:

> The duties and exigencies of national service have imposed large sacrifices upon the Company, and have occasioned many difficulties.

Its natural growth has been arrested, and instead its business has accepted important limitations and has suffered diminution. In common with similar Companies considerable depreciation exists, some of which is expected to prove permanent. Happily the revenue has been fully maintained, and the directors might have made an addition to the reserve fund out of the surplus now available. In view, however, of the uncertainties which must prevail as long as the war continues they have thought it better to carry £40,000 to the company's inner reserve or Contingent Fund which is considered more than sufficient to cover all probable demands upon it even if no recovery in present prices takes place.

Alliance Trust then (31 January 1917) had £1.076m invested in government stocks and in stocks issued by the Allies. In 1916 alone sales and deposits made in deference to the wishes of the Treasury amounted to £828,000. As the war drew to a close in 1918 there was concern that hostilities had driven up taxes and had made it more expensive to borrow money. The rate at which the company could borrow money on debentures was then 5¼%.

It was perhaps in the nature of investment managers to adhere to a cautious approach in everything that they said and, in 1919, the chairman advised shareholders that the consequences of the war 'still bear heavily on the company's business. Taxation in the UK and US has increased and the higher rates of interest has [sic] diminished revenue'.

However, it had not diminished it sufficiently to do damage to the dividend, as had happened in many other trusts. The ordinary share dividend, which began the war at 18%, rose to 19% in 1915 and remained at that level for the duration of hostilities.

Management and Control

Alliance Trust had no legally appointed chairman of the board from 1892 until 1913 when James Guthrie was officially appointed as chairman. Whether Mackenzie's enhanced role as a director had anything to do with this appointment is unclear. The board met monthly, or more often as required, but there were also many informal meetings where no minutes were kept.

MacDougall's appointment as company secretary in 1912 added a new dimension to the management of the company, but before he could prove his worth, it was necessary for him to undergo a period of induction. In July 1913 it was decided that he should go to North America to visit the agencies. He embarked on the SS *Megantic* (a White Star liner built in 1908) at Liverpool on 30 July and sailed to Quebec. From there he made his way to Montreal, Winnipeg and Portland. Thereafter he was asked to visit the other agencies 'at his convenience'. He was accompanied on the first part of the trip by one of the auditors, R.C. Thomson. Bearing in mind that there had been some adverse criticism about Mackenzie's expenses on an earlier trip, it was decided that 'the whole expense of this trip should be charged to the Company on a liberal scale but without any addition by way of personal remuneration'.

Whilst he was away Mackenzie made progress with a new share issue and an issue of terminable debentures with a fixed repayment date. On his return MacDougall took full control of the functions of company secretary. By early 1914 the board minutes had assumed a very standard style. They recorded the monies that had been borrowed on debentures or from the banks; they listed the investments that had been purchased and sold; they dealt with any matters relating to the agencies and with any other relevant business. In 1915 the minutes also began to record that the directors had examined the loan abstract. This is the first mention of such a document but, as this was recorded as abstract no. 477, it may be assumed that this had been a regular activity at board meetings. Nor is it clear from the minutes who made the investment decisions. It is most likely that they emerged as collective decisions after due consideration.

Mackenzie and MacDougall seem to have worked well together. There is no sign or suggestion that they had difficulties in their relationship. Mackenzie seems to have been able to relinquish the secretarial role that he had held for nearly 40 years. There is every sign that he came to appreciate the talents and abilities of MacDougall, whose particular strength was in dealing with matters of taxation. He did this with equal aplomb on both sides of the Atlantic. Towards the end of 1915 he was deep in negotiations in the US and the UK. The Internal Revenue service in Kansas City had been pressing for payment of taxes but MacDougall took the case to the US Treasury in Washington where he was invited for a personal interview. This particular invitation was declined, but correspondence on the subject was continued until September 1916 when the company paid a much reduced tax bill.

MacDougall enjoyed similar success in 1915 with the Inland Revenue in the UK. On this occasion he did present himself to the UK tax commissioners, who acknowledged the rightness of his claims. No sooner had that victory

been won than the commissioners denied the company's claim against tax for
the costs of issuing new debentures. King's Counsel was consulted and again
the tax commissioners backed down, but they were immediately back on the
case and raised a new assessment against Alliance Trust for surpluses made on
foreign exchange transactions that the company had carried to its contingency
fund. In 1918 there was yet another appeal because the Inland Revenue refused
to allow losses incurred in the reorganisation of companies in which the
company had an interest. These cases say much about MacDougall's determination and his preparedness to back his claims to the highest authorities.

Other taxation issues were less controversial. Both Canada and the United
States introduced special war taxes and the company made its returns as and
when requested.

Agencies and Investments

The traditional role of the agents was to lend on mortgages and to do all the
administrative work, including collections, which were part of the day-to-day
activities of this kind of business. They were also responsible for keeping the
directors in Dundee appraised of legislative and tax changes that might be
threatened. But just as the nature of the business being done in Dundee was
changing from that of a mortgage company to that of an investment trust, the
agents found that their role was expanding.

Some of the projects that they were being asked to provide funds for were
large ventures that required sums of money far beyond the normal farm or
city block mortgage. In these cases permission from Dundee was required
before money could be advanced but, equally, the directors were dependent
on the agent for information and judgement about the risks involved in these
projects. In 1913 Macmaster, in Portland, had lent $25,000 to the Columbia
Agricultural Company for a dykeland project. When a further $95,000 was
requested, permission had to be sought from Dundee but in doing so
Macmaster was required to provide a detailed report. The money was duly
lent and remitted to him via Maitland, Coppell and Co. in New York.

Macmaster was busy again early in 1914 when the state of Oregon passed
a law banning the selling of bonds. The company was required to submit an
affidavit declaring that it did 'not engage in the kind of business attempted to
be prevented'. He visited Dundee in April 1914 for discussions about his agency.

But the outbreak of war put a halt to ideas about expanding the business in North America. The inspectors, Jones and Myles, made various recommendations but these were never acted upon – at least during the war years. The agencies received reasonably sized credits at the beginning of the war, but as hostilities in Europe intensified and government restrictions made it more and more difficult to send money to America, the amount of these credits diminished to the point where they were only sufficient to pay local costs and taxes. The North American business was ticking over, but only just. When the opportunity arose money was brought back from the United States. The situation was not helped when two veterans of the business died within days of one another in 1917. E.M. Robinson had been joint agent in Winnipeg for 21 years, and H.P. Drought had been agent in San Antonio for 28 years.

And if the agencies fared poorly during the war, the general investment business did little better. As has been said, substantial sums were invested in British and Allied war loans but the general investment business was greatly diminished. The virtually worldwide investment strategy described in the last chapter was severely curtailed, as wartime conditions and necessities took precedence.

Curiously, Fleming raised a loan for the Holy Synod of Russia in 1916. Alliance applied for £10,000 at 7%. The loan was to be repayable one year after the war. It was eventually written off. Such new issues as were made were mostly directed at the war effort, and in 1917 Fleming organised a share issue for Anglo Persian Oil, in which Alliance participated. Early in 1918 the British Metal Corporation was established to develop the non-ferrous metal industry in the Empire and amongst the Allies. Alliance subscribed £15,000.

The Alliance Trust emerged from the war in relatively good shape. A few British investment trusts, of which Alliance was one, had managed to maintain their dividends. The Alliance dividend had actually increased by 1% despite an overall reduction in net revenue. This reduction was mostly explained by the increase in debenture interest. In other respects the balance sheet and revenue account were in good order. The reserve had not increased but the company was well placed to meet the demands of the peacetime economy. It could not have known that the difficulties ahead were to be far greater than those they had faced during the war.

Chapter 6

From Mortgage Company
to Investment Trust: 1918–1939

The end of the First World War in November 1918 brought peace but it did not bring stability. The Russian Revolution in 1917 had traumatised the business and political communities and induced a defensive mind-set in industrial relations. Most of the investments which Alliance Trust had made in Russia were eventually written off.

In the UK the heavy industries had received massive investment to support the war effort. The return to peacetime conditions was a painful process that led to a great deal of industrial unrest, culminating in the General Strike in 1926. Yet, whilst there was this difficult readjustment, there were also good growth points in the economy that were apparent on both sides of the Atlantic. Standards of living for most people in employment were increasing, and this was reflected in house building and car ownership. Both industries, of course, created demand in other sectors of the economy; people bought new furniture and fittings for their houses, and the car industry gave a boost to tourism. There was also substantial growth in the leisure industries, with spending on cinema admissions and radios and gramophones benefiting from the increase in disposable incomes.

But if manufacturing and service industries were making good progress the same could not be said for agriculture. War-inflated prices for agricultural land and commodities in the United States soon gave way to lower prices. Overcapacity in some crops, poor weather, droughts and political wrangling created enormous problems. Alliance Trust and other lenders eventually made the decision to quit mortgage lending to concentrate on investments in securities where there were fewer problems and higher returns. Those trusts that failed to make this move suffered grievously. The ordinary shareholders of the Glasgow American Trust and the West of Scotland Investment Trust lost everything.

The generally upward trend of people's incomes in this period is also reflected in the growth of bank deposits and in the increase in the number of investment trusts, which grew strongly in the 1920s. Between 1926 and 1929, 78 new trusts were established in the UK. Nevertheless the Depression in the years 1929–32 was a dramatic shock to the world economy, and if new business and investment opportunities in the US had been greater than in the UK, so the Depression made its mark much more severely in North America. It took the controversial policies of the New Deal to help bring the United States out of the Depression.

In the UK, recovery was faster than in the US, but until rearmament began, the rate of growth was quite modest. Consequently activity in the investment trusts reflected these trends. The figures for capital and investments in the Alliance Trust show very strong growth in the 1920s and very little growth in the 1930s.

The Association of Investment Trust Companies was established in 1932 and Alliance Trust became a member. This organisation arose out of an idea that when companies in distress were being wound up or reconstructed there was a tendency to seek the help of big investors e.g. investment trusts. It made sense therefore to have an organisation to co-ordinate this activity on behalf of all.[20] Its launch appeared in the *Daily Express* under the headline 'Campaign for clean finance: Solid front against the defaulters.' Nevertheless much of its early work was in sorting out problems over taxation.

Performance and Growth

Despite the enormous difficulties of the interwar period these were years of good growth for the Alliance Trust, at least in the 1920s. Those trusts that had been salting away reserves for many years were better placed to withstand the pressures. There seems little doubt that the decision to divest itself of the mortgage business and concentrate on investments was the correct decision to make.

Table 6.1 (a) reveals that all the key figures at least doubled in the interwar years, although most of the progress was made in the 1920s. Opportunities were taken, in the light of heightened demand for the shares of investment trusts, to increase the share capital and debentures where possible. The performance figures in Table 6.1 (b) reveal a similar trend.

———

20 J Newlands, *Put Not Your Trust in Money*, London, 1997, p. 195.

Table 6.1 (a) The Alliance Trust key figures, 1918–1939

Year	Ordinary share capital (£)	Ordinary share dividend (%)	Preference share capital (£)	Debenture debt (£)	Reserves (£)	Total (£)
1918	400,000	19	1,100,000	1,927,368	800,000	4,227,368
1919	400,000	19	1,100,000	2,146,389	800,000	4,446,389
1920	400,000	19	1,100,000	2,277,635	825,000	4,602,635
1921	400,000	20	1,100,000	2,140,072	862,500	4,502,572
1922	500,000	21	1,200,000	2,567,345	1,000,000	5,267,345
1923	500,000	21	1,200,000	2,717,175	1,040,000	5,457,175
1924	550,000	22	1,250,000	2,776,695	1,171,250	5,747,945
1925	625,752	23	1,325,752	2,872,020	1,440,000	6,263,524
1926	650,000	24	1,350,000	3,151,738	1,440,000	6,591,738
1927	750,000	25	1,500,000	3,513,535	1,765,000	7,528,535
1928	825,000	25	1,500,000	4,127,305	2,000,000	8,452,305
1929	907,500	25	2,000,000	4,236,495	2,000,000	9,143,995
1930	1,000,000	25	2,100,000	4,518,705	2,200,000	9,818,705
1931	1,000,000	25	2,100,000	5,168,760	2,100,000	10,368,760
1932	1,000,000	25	2,100,000	5,316,740	2,100,000	10,516,740
1933	1,050,000	25	2,100,000	5,563,075	2,100,000	10,813,075
1934	1,050,000	25	2,200,000	5,638,820	2,100,000	10,988,820
1935	1,050,000	22	2,200,000	5,450,055	2,100,000	10,800,055
1936	1,050,000	22	2,200,000	5,417,840	2,100,000	10,767,840
1937	1,050,000	23	2,200,000	5,533,030	2,100,000	10,883,030
1938	1,050,000	25	2,200,000	5,769,665	2,100,000	11,119,665
1939	1,050,000	25	2,200,000	5,880,975	2,100,000	11,230,975

Of particular note in these figures is the low ratio of management expenses to total investments, which was maintained at about 0.25% throughout the period. This ratio was one for which the Alliance Trust became well known throughout the investment trust industry, and one which competitors looked upon with some envy. It was a source of some pride within the organisation.

Table 6.1 (b) The Alliance Trust key figures (continued)

Year	Investments including mortgages (£)	Gross revenue (£)	Net revenue (£)	Debenture interest paid (£)	Management expenses (£)
1918	4,279,376	270,948	126,718	66,105	11,330
1919	4,458,338	276,768	117,484	70,555	11,230
1920	4,617,191	297,668	142,744	81,462	12,758
1921	4,535,262	309,404	158,305	80,871	14,140
1922	5,356,994	334,107	161,905	86,979	15,816
1923	5,564,135	355,006	188,017	96,502	15,585
1924	6,049,529	387,145	209,663	104,291	18,711
1925	6,575,191	416,753	241,129	110,869	19,298
1926	6,851,965	454,326	256,945	129,934	21,399
1927	7,968,519	487,553	286,938	134,837	21,021
1928	8,632,182	563,026	281,024	156,356	n/a
1929	9,323,521	618,143	359,373	168,009	23,609
1930	10,054,094	675,934	404,733	166,962	24,810
1931	10,840,045	692,152	410,755	178,787	27,802
1932	10,917,097	n/a	356,942	187,595	n/a
1933	11,324,427	631,656	383,168	189,258	27,963
1934	11,282,441	638,115	410,731	183,860	26,988
1935	11,101,832	596,631	353,000	175,778	28,759
1936	11,033,330	603,314	351,247	165,271	26,404
1937	11,343,727	n/a	363,341	160,214	n/a
1938	11,623,419	706,856	424,372	158,055	28,862
1939	11,657,905	676,343	404,436	156,902	26,938

Table 6.2 reflects very clearly the shift in the balance of the business away from mortgages and towards Alliance's new status as an investment trust.

Despite the difficulties of the interwar years the Alliance Trust was able to maintain its ordinary share dividend and to keep faith with the shareholders. Dividends remained high, but it was the constant attention to building up the

Table 6.2 Revenue sources, 1927–1939

As at 31 January	Bond revenue (£)	Stock revenue (£)	Mortgage revenue (£)	Total revenue (£)
1927	177,835	195,681	113,035	486,551
1928	207,591	250,078	106,193	563,862
1929	220,231	297,614	101,798	619,643
1930	240,489	358,107	82,336	680,932
1931	246,069	401,068	55,728	702,865
1932	265,815	357,792	22,989	646,596
1933	255,256	318,305	22,039	595,600
1934	226,848	311,956	27,798	566,602
1935	204,426	361,205	27,030	592,661
1936	184,078	391,302	24,225	599,605
1937	180,891	453,640	20,532	655,063
1938	160,543	523,919	18,055	702,517
1939	141,776	508,899	19,116	669,791

reserve that created the real strength. It was a good position from which to approach the Second World War.

Annual General Meetings

Alliance Trust emerged from the First World War in good shape. Its capital and reserve were sound, although its investment portfolio was more heavily concentrated in government securities than it would have wished. Paradoxically this had the effect of accelerating the transition from being a mortgage company to being an investment trust. And it was this transition, more than anything else, which helped the company to survive the vicissitudes of the interwar years.

The shareholders who attended the annual general meeting in April 1919 were told that the consequences of war 'still bear heavily on the company's business. Taxation in the UK and US has increased and the higher rates of interest have diminished revenue'. However, investments in UK and other government securities exceeded £1m and securities amounting to £246,377 were still lodged with the Treasury.

A year later the shareholders were told that conditions in the mortgage business were good and that interest collections were high. These good conditions encouraged Alliance, and other mortgage companies, to expand their lending to farmers notwithstanding that the US government was making plans to establish associations that would become rivals to the mortgage companies. But the good times were not to last – at least not in the farming business.

In April 1921 the new chairman, Frederick Sharp, informed the shareholders that there had been a heavy fall in farm prices in the US and that this had affected collections. Nevertheless there had been a rise in net revenue because there had been a rise in the prices of securities that had more than offset the damage. Confidence in the future was strong, and plans were being laid to increase the company's share capital. A favourable exchange rate had also helped increase revenues.

The news about mortgages in 1923 and 1924 was much worse. Sharp indicated that progress had been made with the collection of arrears but they had soon been replaced with other arrears. American farmers had managed to increase their yields but the relationship of price to cost of production was 'very unsatisfactory'. Inevitably the number of foreclosures began to mount. There was, too, a realisation that real estate, if uncared for, would depreciate quickly and that it was necessary, therefore, to 'procure tenants and other persons to maintain our properties in good condition, so that when the real estate market revives, we may all the more readily dispose of them'. It never did revive, and the burden of finding tenants and managing real estate fell inevitably upon the agents.

US President Calvin Coolidge, in his inaugural address in 1925, referred to the general prosperity prevailing in the country and expressed the hope that this would soon spread to the agriculture sector. The reality was that the US economy was benefitting from buoyant industrial and commercial sectors while much of the agriculture sector was in the doldrums.

By this time Alliance's mortgage business had become the smaller of its enterprises. The investment business now accounted for 62% of invested funds and that was producing a strong revenue stream as well as demonstrating good capital appreciation. In 1925, however, stock markets went through one of their periodic readjustments and prices fell. This was seen as an opportunity to acquire good investments at depressed prices. Borrowing on debentures was increased and new capital was issued.

All this occurred in the middle of a debate amongst investment fund managers, with some taking the view that if fund managers took care of the capital then the revenue would take care of itself. Others adhered to the exact opposite view, believing that prices of investments were of no interest to those who purchased shares in investment trusts because their sole concern was the revenue. The Alliance view was that there was a key relationship between the price at which securities traded on the stock exchanges and the revenue that they were likely to generate. The directors concluded that, 'An intelligent stockholder, therefore, must always be interested in the question of the Annual Valuation, as well as in that of the Annual Revenue.'

The message from the directors to the shareholders was positive. They were reminded that investment was for long-term gain and not for short-term profits. They were further reminded that the company's long-term policy of increasing the reserve fund had been highly successful. The balance in the reserve had risen from £800,000 in 1919 to £1,440,000 in just six years. There was, however, a note of caution, and shareholders were told that the favourable investment conditions of the early 1920s could not be expected 'to continue indefinitely'. The shareholders who attended the meeting were well pleased with the report and re-elected the retiring directors.

Later in 1925 one of the directors, W. Norman Boase, accompanied the company secretary, Greenhill, on a tour of the North American agencies. He reported on his findings to the annual general meeting in April 1926. But the glimmer of light that he shone on the proceedings was a very small glimmer indeed. He assured the shareholders that the directors were handling the matter with great caution. Notwithstanding their care, the amount of real estate acquired as a result of foreclosures continued to increase.

Nevertheless the UK stock market continued to view Alliance Trust with great favour. And in proposing the re-election of directors, H.A. Pattullo noted that the stock market price of the company's ordinary shares in 1905 was £180 but it was now £515. This was very good news for ordinary stock shareholders. Pattullo, speaking for the shareholders, expressed the deep indebtedness of the shareholders for this 'economic miracle'.

In 1927 Sharp began the chairman's report with the bad news: 'We have had representatives from our mortgage fields in this country during the year and discussed the position fully with them, and we are devoting our best efforts to dealing with the problems before us.' Cotton prices had experienced further decline caused, perversely, by a good crop.

There was however cause for celebration when he moved on to discuss the investment side of the business – a growing portion of whose money was invested in British securities: 'It is a remarkable testimony to the strength and stability of this country's financial structure that a year which saw a General Strike threatening the foundations of our economic life and a Coal Strike which involved the semi-paralysis of industry for a great part of the year, should contribute nothing in the way of a panic on the stock exchange, but should, on the contrary, show the values of the Securities dealt in there as fully maintained.'

This was a cue to vote the directors an increase in their remuneration. Funds under management in 1923 were £5.5m. By 1927 they had increased to £8m, so the remuneration of the directors was increased from £3,750 to £5,100, and it was left to them to decide the proportion that each director should receive.

In 1928 Sharp drew attention to the fact that the reserve fund was now £2m and reiterated the company mantra that the buttressing of the balance sheet with an 'exceptionally large reserve' contributed greatly to the 'standing and credit of the company and the investment quality of its stock'. None of the shareholders took exception to this view.

There had also been good progress in Europe, Russia excepted. There was muted praise for France, which was achieving some success in stabilising its currency. Germany would shortly face some serious problems in making reparations payments, as her balance of trade had not produced the desired results. But it was the UK with which he was most impressed.

In 1929 the chairman returned to the performance of securities markets. In the United States Wall Street had been moving ahead strongly but there were beginning to be worries about instability:

Last year was one of great and varied activity in the Stock Markets. This activity took many forms. The memorable gramophone boom, from which the better concerns emerged more or less successfully; the notorious greyhound racing promotions which collapsed without recovery; the gambling in 1s. [5p] shares, and so forth. These were the features which perhaps dwell in the public memory, but what interested us most was the strength in the markets for sound investments which continued right up to the close of our year . . . the mere increase in market values which is here to-day and may be gone tomorrow, does not interest us very much. Ours is an Investment Trust, not a speculative concern or a liquidating agency, and our true object is the stability and expansion of our earning power. Still, even in this connection market values must not be disregarded.

Sharp went on to recount to shareholders the somewhat improved performance in the mortgage business. Only 18% of the company's assets remained there. He then returned to the opportunities that the current stock market situation presented. 'Conditions of considerable uncertainty prevail at present, but uncertainties are rarely absent from the horizon, and we have come to the conclusion that opportunities for profitable investment will currently arise during the current year.' Consequently a new issue of shares was imminent. Sharp's statement almost certainly does not mean that money was needed for immediate investment. More likely he, and his colleagues, were predicting a fall in an over-heating market and they wanted to be ready to take advantage of lower prices when the market correction occurred. He could not have predicted how dramatic that fall would be.

The annual general meeting in 1930 took place on 16 April. It was a time for reassurance. The Wall Street crash was doubtless uppermost in the shareholders' minds but Sharp reassured them. He told them that 86% of the funds were invested in stocks and bonds in 905 different investments and the directors had it in mind to increase the ordinary share capital still further. Revenues were holding up and, despite the great uncertainty he saw 'no reason to sound a note of pessimism so far as this company is concerned. We are in a strong position, and it is just in such days as these that one can appreciate the benefits of our strong Reserve policy and our safe margin of earning power.'

In his report he dwelt on the crash, its causes and its likely effects. Prior to that event the securities held by Alliance had shown a substantial surplus over book value and, while that surplus had diminished, a recent valuation showed that there was still a surplus and that the recovery in stock prices since the valuation date had further augmented that figure. He did not reveal the date at which the valuation had been made, but it was most likely to have been the end of the company's financial year – 31 January.

The news about the mortgage business was less promising. Little progress had been made in selling off real estate and there were numerous difficulties in doing so. The main problem was the depressed price of agricultural commodities, which made the purchase of farm land a doubtful economic proposition.

The chairman's report in 1931 was extremely gloomy. The 'economic weather has got worse instead of better' and an economic storm had broken over the world. He referred to the various opinions that were circulating as to the cause of the crash. His own view was that it had many causes. But he noted that since 1918 the population of the world had increased by about 10% while the production of raw materials had increased by 40%. Overproduction was therefore likely to be the root cause.

He was firmly of the view that readjustment would be 'extremely difficult'. He placed his hope in the 'invisible hand' and told the shareholders that 'the force of circumstances has a way of compelling mankind to effect it [readjustment] and we must hopefully rely on necessity once again playing its proverbial part in human affairs'.

Turning to the problems that the worldwide recession had created for the investment trusts, he stated the obvious: 'The results to be reported by industrial concerns during the current year can only reflect the troubles of the past, and defaults and reductions in dividends cannot fail to be the order of the day. Trust Companies . . . must pass through a period more trying than the most cautious pessimist ever anticipated. In the past they have reckoned that by a wide spreading of their investment risk, a stable revenue position could be maintained, as it was not to be expected that all the world would go wrong at the same time. But the unexpected has happened, and every part of the civilised world is in trouble.'

Further bad news came from the mortgage market where 'agricultural conditions were worse last year than they have been for quarter of a century and when we have not only poor crops but poor world prices, it is small wonder that we have been faced with reduced interest collections and a dull real estate market'.

It was a damning report, but Sharp was able to assure shareholders that Alliance had a strong reserve position and that, notwithstanding the drop in securities prices, the valuation of shareholdings was still above their book price. Compared to many others it was a strong position to be in.

Things were no better when the annual meeting took place in April 1932. The crisis continued and was made worse as many nations retreated into protectionism and 'all the obstacles to the healthy freedom of international trade-became more numerous and complicated'. Despite various government attempts in Britain and America to improve matters, there were no signs of a recovery. Britain had come off the gold standard and the country was then governed by a coalition of parties. In the US it was election year with all the uncertainties that that involved. The US banking industry was crumbling and Roosevelt, who would replace Hoover as president, was beginning to talk about a 'New Deal' for the American economy.

In his annual report the chairman could do nothing other than refer to the parlous state of the world economy and the likely impact that the

Depression would have on the company. Companies in which Alliance had invested would fail or default on their interest and dividend obligations. He confessed that he was buoyed up by the fact that Britain had a balanced budget, had come off the gold standard and was 'firmly and honestly facing the situation'. However he could not, as yet, detect any sign of recovery. The situation was made even more difficult when the bank rate came down to 2% and government securities were converted to pay lower rates of return. This had the effect of making investors look more closely at ordinary shares as the only means available to them to increase their income but, in the economic climate of the time, the trade-off of security in favour of income was challenging.

Other countries in which Alliance had invested were in a worse state than Britain. The German economy was in a very poor condition, due largely to its commitment to pay reparations after the First World War, and it was not long before Hitler became Chancellor.

Some other investment trusts had begun providing their shareholders with statements about where their funds were invested, and Alliance followed suit.

It was a strong position to be in. Not only was the portfolio spread throughout the world but 71% was invested in securities where the interest and dividends would take precedence over dividend payments to holders of ordinary shares. Not all investment trusts were similarly placed, and some of the newer trusts went out of business.

The turbulent nature of world stock markets gave rise to a debate about the usefulness, or otherwise, of investment trusts. In the light of this debate the chairman took the time to review the service that Alliance provided for its investors. He stressed the value, for a certain class of investor, of debentures, which provided almost cast-iron security and returns for investors who were risk averse. These were particularly suitable for trustees. Similar claims could be made for preference shareholders, and there were now more than 12,000 holders of debentures and preference shares on the Trust's register. Ordinary shareholders, he claimed, could not be displeased with the performance of the company either in the value of their capital or in the dividends that they had received. Somewhat surprisingly he did not mention the deposit-making service that Alliance offered and which attracted in excess of £500,000, mostly from local sources.

He went on to discuss the operation of investment trusts in general and said that the agglomeration of capital in trusts led to sound investment

Table 6.3 Distribution of investments, 1932

	Percentage
Great Britain	39.36
British Empire (exc. GB)	12.28
US	14.91
Europe (exc. GB)	16.57
Latin America	13.64
Asia and Africa (exc. British Empire)	3.24
	100.00%
Bonds and debentures	37.86
Preference shares and stocks	33.47
Ordinary and deferred shares and stocks	28.67
	100.00%

decisions and the avoidance of speculation, for the simple reason that the money was professionally managed. Moreover companies issuing new capital appreciated that investment trusts were well placed to operate in such a way that new share issues would be taken up. He concluded with the words, 'I am satisfied that the existence of an Investment Trust operating on sound lines is a help and a service to its shareholders and to the community.'

As if to prove his points he announced that the preference share dividends would be paid as normal and that the ordinary share dividend would be maintained at 25%. The maintenance of the ordinary dividend was all the more remarkable because it was based on an increased capital. The shareholders were surprised but delighted.

In 1934 it was reported that the depreciation on investments was then only 0.5% and that there were a few glimmers of hope on the mortgage front, but US government measures to assist farmers had not then had time to take effect. A year later the investments had appreciated and stood at 8% above book value, but so far as what remained of the mortgage business was concerned it was 'impossible to put a value on this part of the company's investment'.

In 1936 the shareholders learned that one part of the US government's plans to assist farmers had been declared unconstitutional and this had arrested the improvements that had begun in the mortgage business. 'Meantime the real estate market had become entirely unsatisfactory and collections of both principal and interest have become adversely affected.' Again, no reliable valuation could be put on the mortgage business.

A year later the chairman's statement reflected even more strongly the fact that the balance of the business had shifted and that the board's main concern was then with the investment side of the business. In his report he dealt with taxation difficulties in Britain and America and recommended that a portion of the £523,554 surplus should be placed in reserve to meet as yet unknown tax liabilities. But the news for shareholders was more positive than it had been for many years. Not only was revenue higher than it had ever been, but values were also higher, and these facts contributed to a picture of 'general prosperity brighter than any we have seen for many years'. Employment had risen and commodity prices had moved strongly ahead. But the chairman was not to have his head turned by healthy economic conditions. He noted that economic conditions were similar to what they had been in 1929 and questioned whether there was some danger that these healthy conditions might soon give way to another depression. On balance he did not think that there was such a danger as interest rates were low, there were no signs of overheating in the stock market and there was a lot of new investment – particularly in the armaments industry.

Other than a brief thank you to the 'representatives in America' the mortgage business was not mentioned.

The reports for 1938 and 1939 contained similar messages. In 1938 it was reported that stocks and bonds constituted 92.41% of the company's assets. The mortgage business had all but ceased to be of any importance.

In short, the Alliance Trust was a very different kind of business in 1939 than it had been in 1918. Yet it still had a very small management team which faced challenges in managing not just the business but the information that it needed to make good investment decisions. It got into the habit of preparing a diary of events every three months. In the diary for January–March 1939 the exchange rates for the dollar, franc and mark were tracked, as were representative stock prices such as British consols, US bonds and various UK and US industrials. Commodity prices were recorded together with trade statistics. World events were detailed including the fact that Britain and France had provided a security guarantee to Poland. By that time few were in any doubt that another war was imminent.

People and Property

People

One of the effects of the First World War was to make it difficult for older people to retire. Conscription into the armed services had denuded businesses of their young people and made it virtually impossible for companies to recruit new staff. The result was that older people remained in service beyond the date at which they might have contemplated retirement. Consequently, when the armistice was signed in November 1918, most businesses housed men who were eager to retire. Alliance Trust was no different from other businesses in this respect.

First to go was John W. Shepherd, who was manager of the Western and Hawaiian Investment Trust. He actually announced his retirement before the war came to an end. Commensurate with his retirement was a proposal, which was not being made for the first time, that the Alliance should take over the management of the Western and Hawaiian. There does not appear to have been a proposal to merge the two organisations. What was contemplated was that Alliance staff should simply run the Western and Hawaiian, with the latter making a contribution towards management costs. The proposal made sense, as the two companies shared several of the American agents and were similarly engaged in a transition from being a mortgage company to being an investment trust.

The proposal was agreed in April 1918, subject to satisfactory arrangements being made to share the expenses. It did not take long to come to an agreement. MacDougall, who was then secretary of Alliance, was appointed to the same role in Western and Hawaiian, and at the June 1918 meeting of the Alliance board it was agreed that Western and Hawaiian would pay £300 per annum to Alliance for salaries and £60 for heating, rates and other expenses. These calculations were based on the relative amounts of capital of the companies. Shepherd was appointed to be a director of Alliance. He did not tarry long, and resigned in May 1921 due to his 'increasing deafness, failing strength and loss or lack of nerve'. Western and Hawaiian was re-named the Second Alliance Trust.

In March 1919 Mackenzie decided that it was time for him to go. He was almost 73 and had been in employment for 55 years, of which 45 had been with Alliance Trust and its predecessors. He was not in good health and his doctor, who had been visiting weekly, had advised retirement and a life of 'ordered leisure'. He had been suffering from serious, unexplained headaches for six months. In his retirement letter he wrote, 'In my opinion my mental condition is such that it is quite impossible for me to pretend that either in strength, memory or judgement, am I fit to perform effectively the duties, or to sustain adequately the responsibilities of my high office.'

He went on to address MacDougall directly and to recommend him as his successor. He concluded:

> During long hours of weary wakefulness I have recognised painfully enough but quite clearly that our management and directors are not adequate to our capacity present and potential, and also my own inability to fulfil those functions of administration, which the directors and Shareholders are entitled to expect. The company must either be managed or liquidated and perhaps the latter might be the simple course. If however, our business is to be maintained, I would further and strongly advise the appointment of another official as your colleague and assistant. It is due to yourself and requisite in the company's interest that you should have an associate who would help you as materially as you have helped me and stand by you with the same loyalty and affection as it has been my privilege and comfort to enjoy in my association with you, all of which I gladly and gratefully acknowledge. I am also grateful in the same sense to the other members of our staff and cannot too strongly express my appreci-ation, of the most friendly spirit by which their services and assistance have been inspired, during so many years of devotion and loyalty both to our common employer and to myself personally.

The directors accepted his resignation with 'deep regret'.

Quite why he contemplated the winding up of the business is not clear. It may simply have been that his state of health made him depressed. There was certainly nothing in the condition of the business at that time to suggest that there were major problems. Moreover his letter suggests not just that the business had future potential but that MacDougall was the man to run it.

The suggestion that the business might be wound up does not seem to have been taken seriously, and MacDougall was duly appointed as manager and secretary. However, he did not retain the latter role for long, and in July 1919 Mackenzie's advice was followed when J. Kenneth Greenhill, BA, LLB was appointed as company secretary.

There were also major changes in the directorate. In December 1919 William Thomson asked for six months' leave of absence from the board on grounds of ill health. Later that month David Pirie, a Dundee merchant, was appointed as a director. Three months later the chairman, James Guthrie, died. He had been a director since 1884. Frederick B. Sharp then took the chair. At the end of 1920 W. Norman Boase and James Prain, Jnr, both manufacturers in Dundee, were appointed to the board. Thomson retired in February 1921. Thereafter there was remarkable stability in the board, and in the executive, for the remainder of the decade.

It is not possible to say very much about the staff of the Trust. No records remain. Photographs of the office in the 1930s suggest that there were no more than ten employees. It is clear, however, that Mackenzie's advice about the need to strengthen the senior management was heeded. Ernest D. Fleming was one of the senior men and was given responsibility for tidying up the mortgage business after Jones' retirement. George S. Spence, who was the company's 'chief assistant', died suddenly in 1925. Although there was no formal pension scheme his widow was given a pension of £350 per annum. Spence's replacement was John Pringle Bruce, who was appointed as assistant secretary in 1926. Bruce deputised for Greenhill during his trips to America and succeeded him as company secretary when Greenhill died in 1931. James Fleming Nicoll, one of the assistants, was then promoted to be assistant secretary. Promotion from within the company seems to have been normal practice, but as in all businesses with relatively small numbers of staff, it was a case of filling 'dead men's shoes'.

The provision of a pension to Spence's widow, in the absence of a formal pension scheme, suggests a paternalistic approach to the staff, and this was in evidence again when William Findlay, the cashier, was given 250 guineas and an inscribed plate on completion of 50 years' service. The provision of retirement pensions became the norm for staff retiring and widow's pensions for those dying in service.

In January 1929 Thomas Maitland, who had been absent from the board for several months, resigned on grounds of ill health. He had been on the board for 24 years and was the last of the old guard. MacDougall was promoted to the board as his replacement. At the same meeting in February 1929 Hugh F.B. Sharp, son of the chairman, was also nominated as a director, but as he was a salaried employee of the company, his appointment was deferred until it could be confirmed at an annual general meeting. Quite why MacDougall could be appointed by the directors, and Sharp could not, is not clear.

The promotion of Hugh Sharp to the board may well have been in antic-ipation of his father's retirement, but Frederick Sharp died in 1932 while still in harness. His replacement was David Pirie, who served until 1937 when James Prain assumed the chair. Strangely, the chairman did not always chair the annual general meeting, where the chair could be taken by any one of the directors.

In September 1937 John P. Bruce, the company secretary, died suddenly. He had been in the service of the company since 1896. James F. Nicoll became interim secretary but was not given the job. The role went to Alan Lindsay Brown, CA, from Edinburgh. Brown had worked for Baillie Gifford, an Edinburgh firm of fund managers, but had left for personal reasons (perhaps occasioned by the recent death of his wife). His appointment was announced within a fortnight of Bruce's death. A year later he was appointed to be assistant manager and secretary.

In the months between December 1937 and March 1938 the board suffered two major blows – first with the death of Hugh Sharp in the Castlecary train crash and then with the death of W. Norman Boase. Another member of the Sharp family, Harold Sidney Sharp, was appointed to the board in February 1938 but there was no replacement for Boase.

Throughout the interwar period the leadership of the company was in the hands of its manager, William MacDougall. He had assumed the role when Mackenzie retired in 1919 and had become a director in 1929. The difficulties that he had faced were substantial. Not only had he to manage his way through one of the worst commercial crisis that the world had ever seen, he also had to transform the company from its primary role as a mortgage lender into an investment trust. He achieved all this by sticking to first principles. The reserve fund was built up and maintained, investments were made in sound, revenue-earning companies and the people, in Britain and America, were treated well.

Property

The company's offices in the D.C. Thomson and Co. building at 22 Meadowside had been occupied by the Trust since 1907, but advice was received from the landlords at Whitsun 1922 that the lease would not be renewed when it expired a year later. It seems likely that prior knowledge had been obtained of the need to vacate Meadowside, as matters moved very quickly.

Thomas Duff and Co. were co-tenants in Meadowside and they had also received notice to quit. They joined forces with Alliance to purchase the property at 64 Reform Street, formerly known as Lamb's Temperance Hotel. This property, which was just across the road from Meadowside, was the building in which Alliance's annual general meetings had been held for many years.

The property was much too big – even for the combined staff of both companies – and they agreed that they would share the cost of purchase, with Duff paying two-thirds and Alliance one third. The purchase price was £33,000. The two companies then set about disposing of the portions of the property that were surplus to their requirements. The ground-floor offices and shops were sold to the North of Scotland Bank, Alliance Assurance Co. and Andrew G. Kidd and Co. The flats and attics were also sold, and when the accounting was finished £27,250 of the initial outlay had been recovered. Alliance Trust had therefore acquired its own property for the first time for an outlay of less than £2,000. As the Trust expanded in years to come it had to buy back what it had sold and eventually came into sole occupancy of the whole building, which it occupied until 2009.

Investments

As the First World War drew to a close there were signs in the stock markets that things were beginning to get back to normal. In August 1917 Alliance participated in underwriting a new issue for Lever Brothers for which the underwriting commission was the princely sum of £35 for a £2,000 commitment. There was a further underwriting opportunity in December to underwrite the new issue for Anglo Persian Oil. This opportunity came via Fleming. A few mixed securities were purchased but the amounts were small. Much larger sums continued to be placed in British government securities and Treasury bills.

In September 1918 it was reported to the board that shares had been purchased in a number of companies. They included

British Mannesmann Tube Company (for a new tube works
    at Newport, Wales)
General Electric Co. Ltd
Fife Tramway Light and Power Co.
The British Trusts Association Ltd
British Vegetable Oil Extraction Co.

Dunlop Rubber Company
North Wales Power and Traction Co. Ltd

The armistice in November 1918 brought a rush of new issues to the market, and Alliance participated in several of them. The Magadi Soda Co., based in Kenya, was one of Africa's largest soda ash companies, which, a few years later, was taken over by Brunner Mond – one of the companies that became ICI in 1926. It issued £500,000 of new shares. Alliance underwrote £11,000. Other large companies in which Alliance participated included Vickers Ltd, who issued new shares in order to allow it to acquire the capital of the Metropolitan Carriage, Wagon and Finance Co. Many of these new issues were oversubscribed and investment companies soon learned that if they actually wanted to own the shares, as opposed to just underwriting the issues, then they would have to bid for them themselves. The underwriting contract then seems to have changed to allow underwriters to buy shares 'firm' i.e. ahead of the actual issue.

The investment policy which had prevailed before the war was gradually reintroduced. Underwriting was an important part of the strategy but not the most important part. Shares were also purchased in a wide variety of companies in a geographically dispersed range of countries. British and American shares predominated but companies in the British Empire and South America continued to feature in the portfolio.

Moreover the type of companies in which investments were made reflected the changes that were taking place in the economy. Some of these changes had been discernible before the war. The growth of the motor car, tram car and electricity industries created an enormous demand for capital as did a substantial growth in new house building. This in turn generated demand for furniture, carpets and kitchen goods.

Standards of living were improving for the bulk of the population and new companies were created to satisfy increasing consumer and industrial demand. A growing number of these companies took advantage of the stock market to raise capital in a way that had not really happened before the war. Companies which were, or soon became, household names appeared in the investment portfolio, including Debenhams, English Electric, Bovril, British Dyestuffs, British Portland Cement, Wolseley, Stewart and Macdonald, Birmingham Small Arms and J. & P. Coats. Occasionally there was an investment in a really obscure organisation, as when 250,000 kroner was invested in the dated bonds of the Credit Association of Proprietors of Small Landed Estates in the Islands of Denmark.

The 8th Earl of Airlie, Chairman, The Oregon and Washington Trust Investment Company Ltd.

RIGHT. William Reid, Agent in Portland, Oregon, and serial entrepreneur.

BELOW. Ankeny Family, Portland, Oregon: the first borrower.

Robert Fleming, Director and investment guru.

John Leng, Director and newspaper proprietor.

No. $\frac{1681}{1731}$

CERTIFICATE OF INCORPORATION

OF

"The Alliance Trust Company, Limited."

I hereby Certify, That "THE ALLIANCE TRUST COMPANY, LIMITED," is this day Incorporated under the Companies Acts, 1862 to 1886, and that this Company is LIMITED.

GIVEN under my hand, at Edinburgh, this Twenty-first day of April, One Thousand Eight Hundred and Eighty-Eight.

R. GLEGG,
For Registrar of Joint Stock Companies.

Alliance Trust Ltd, Certificate of Incorporation.

John Guild, Director and Chairman
1888–1892.

Henry Drought, Agent in San Antonio,
Texas.

William Mackenzie, Company Secretary then Managing Director, 1888–1918.

Oregon and Washington Trust Building, Portland, Oregon.

Cowhands and Dundee Financiers, Texas, 1880s.

RIGHT. William D MacDougall, Company Secretary, Director then Chairman 1912–1952.

BELOW. Farming in the West, the Ellis family.

Farming in the West, the Fannin family.

Oil in Louisiana.

ABOVE. Oil in Louisiana.

RIGHT. Interior, Meadow House 1930s.

Interior, Meadow House 1930s.

Interior, Meadow House 1930s.

ABOVE. Interior, Meadow House 1930s.

RIGHT. Alan Brown, Company Secretary, Director then Chairman, 1938–1967.

ABOVE. Hugh Sharp, Director, 1929–1937.

ABOVE. David McCurrach, Manager,
Director then Chairman, 1946–1982.

Mrs Johanson, farming in Canada, 1946.

In making these acquisitions Alliance used a wide range of brokers and agencies. It was no longer dependent upon Fleming, although he continued to be a good friend to the Trust. Shares in North British Locomotive and United Turkey Red were purchased through the Glasgow brokers Penney and MacGeorge, and Buchanan, Gairdner and Tennant. There was also a trend to purchase shares in other investment trusts, the number of which increased substantially in the interwar years.

There was a degree of caution about overseas investments and most of these were acquired in companies that were already well known to the directors. The Dundee-managed, but Texas-based, Matador Land and Cattle Co. was a popular investment, as was New Zealand Loan and Mercantile, and the United States Trust Corporation.

The actual number of shares purchased in some companies was quite small and probably reflected the number of shares available from sellers. In October 1919 30 shares were purchased in Glasgow-based Clydesdale Bank just ahead of its acquisition by Midland Bank. But at the same time 2,000 shares were purchased in Imperial Tobacco and 1,000 in British American Tobacco.

Early in 1920 the pound began to fall against the dollar and substantial sums were brought back from the United States for investment in British securities. Some of the money, however, was spread more widely, with purchases of Chinese government bonds, French *rentes*, shares in the Rio de Janeiro Tramways Light and Power Co., an Argentine government sterling loan and a Japanese sterling loan.

The minutes record all the purchases and sales of securities but say nothing of how the decisions to buy or sell were made. Given that there were in excess of 900 investments it seems unlikely that MacDougall, as manager, would have sole responsibility for this aspect of the company business. It is clear that company reports were circulated around the directors, and it may well be that decisions to buy or sell were perhaps not made in a collective way, but certainly as a result of an exchange of views amongst some or all of the directors. Each monthly minute recorded between 20 and 40 share transactions.

As the 1920s progressed there was little sign of change in the investment strategy. The task was always to find good, secure, revenue-earning assets. There was a preponderance of preference shares and debentures over ordinary shares in the portfolio, reflecting the need for security. For example the minute of 22 December 1921 recorded the transactions detailed in Table 6.4.

The directors kept a keen eye on the portfolio. They received a report, together with details of purchases and sales, at each of their meetings and, from time to time, they considered special reports. At their meeting in August 1922 they examined and discussed a list of securities whose market values were substantially above book value, together with a list of redeemable debentures with short dates to redemption, especially where prices were higher than redemption prices. There was also a list of securities in default. They did not record their decisions. They were aware, however, that the introduction of corporation profits tax in 1921 had the potential to alter the investment landscape. Many trusts began to shift their investment strategy towards ordinary shares. The new tax also had the effect of making debentures and other borrowing more attractive as the cost could be set against the tax liability.

A year later they examined a list of their investments in Brazil and Argentina. In February 1925 it was the turn of power companies in the US and Canada, and of industrial ordinary shares. Although most investments were in the UK, the spread of investments across many countries was impressive. At the board meeting in June 1924 they recorded transactions in securities for the UK, US, Sweden, Borneo, Czechoslovakia, Australia, Argentina, France, New Zealand, Netherlands, Japan, East Africa, China, Switzerland, India and Chile. Most of these were traded in the London market.

The spread of investments across industrial sectors was no less impressive and included investments in steamships, collieries, tobacco, railways, rubber, batteries, land, sleeping cars, chemicals, foodstuffs, power, shops, shipbuilding, engineering, munitions, life assurance, government securities, banks, investment companies, oil, textiles, hotels and coffee.

The various new shares and debentures that Alliance Trust issued in the 1920s allowed total investments (including mortgages) to rise from £4.2m in 1918 to £10m in 1930.

When the Wall Street crash happened in October 1929 that was the occasion for the directors to look even more closely than usual at their American investments. At the board meeting on 11 October, 'A list of the company's holdings in American common stocks was submitted to and examined by the directors.' They evidently decided to look a little closer, and at their November meeting, 'An analysis on a percentage basis was submitted to and examined by the directors, the figures showing that [of] the Company's total invested funds 3% was in American common stocks, 7.8% in preferred stocks, 8.7% in Foreign Bonds quoted on the New York Stock Exchange, 2.1% and 14% in American Bonds and City Mortgages.'

Many of the American stocks that had fallen in value during the panic

Table 6.4 Securities transactions in December 1921

Purchases
Treasury Bonds 5% Series C
United Kingdom of Great Britain and Ireland 10 yr 5.5% Conversion Gold Bonds
Central Argentine Railroad 5% 10 year Conversion Gold Notes
Scottish Power Co. Ltd 8% Cumulative Preference Shares
Shell Transport and Trading Company Ltd Ordinary shares (syndicate)
Chinese Government 5% Gold Loan
Canadian Pacific Railway Perpetual 4.5% Consolidated Debenture Stock
Port of London 6% Inscribed Stock
Buenos Aires Western Railway 4% Debenture Stock
Lipton Ltd 6% Debenture Stock
Scottish Mortgage and Trust Company Ltd 5.25% Preference Shares and
    Ordinary Shares
Liebig's Extract of Meat Co. Ltd (OXO) 5% Cumulative Preference Shares

Underwritten
Straits Settlement Government 6% Inscribed Stock
Reading Electric Supply Co. Ltd 7.5% First Mortgage Debenture Stock
Government of India 5% Loan
Newcastle Upon Tyne Electric Supply Co. Ltd 6% Second Mortgage
    Debenture Stock
Midland Counties Electric Supply Co. Ltd 7.5% Mortgage Debenture Stock
Buenos Aires Western Railway 4% Debenture Stock

Sold
5% National War Bonds
Union of South Africa 6% Stock
Ceylon Upcountry Tea Estates Ltd 6% Mortgage Debentures
Cook Son and Co. Ltd 7% Cumulative Participating Preference Shares
A Pirie and Sons Ltd 7% 2nd Cumulative Preference Shares

---

soon began to regain what they had lost and this was an opportunity, in a rising market, for investors to make purchases. Alliance Trust made investments in Purity Bakeries Corporation, Radio Corporation of America, Revere Copper and Brass Inc., R.J. Reynolds Tobacco Co., Safeway Stores Inc., P. Lorillard Co., Kansas City Southern Railroad, General Mills Co. and General Cable Corp.

This was also the time for companies, especially investment companies, to examine more closely their arrangements for maintaining the security of their investments. In the spring of 1930 there was an extensive correspondence with lawyers regarding the safety of the company's securities while they were in the custody of American bankers. The solution was to insure the risk, which had not been done before.

Major failures in the United States banking system following the Wall Street crash caused a prolonged depression in the US economy. In the UK there were certainly many difficulties, but there were no bank failures and the recession did not take a hold of the British economy in the same way that it had in the US. There were certainly serious difficulties in some sectors, especially in the heavy industries, but there was sufficient resilience in other sectors of the economy to avoid a US-style depression. Consequently the Alliance Trust's investment strategy continued much as before.

By the end of 1931 F.W. Woolworth and Co. issued new ordinary and preference shares and Alliance participated in the underwriting. Sizeable amounts of the shares were purchased outright. Underwriting commissions increased to £6,326 in 1932 and were more than 50% higher than what was received for 1931. Occasionally there was a fall-out from the wider problems in the economy, as when the Mansfield and District Tramways Ltd in Nottinghamshire got into difficulties. Alliance Trust was trustee for the debenture holders and it was decided to abandon the tramway, lift the gear, repair the roads, install buses on the service routes and lease the buses from a hire-purchase company.

Having come off the gold standard in 1931 the rate of exchange for the pound against the US dollar improved until it was nearly back up to $5. This fact, together with emerging business opportunities, caused the directors to rethink their strategy of bringing money back from North America. In September 1933 $350,000 was sent to New York for investment in US securities. This seems to have been a solitary event, however, as the process of remitting money from New York to London, which had been the common practice in the 1920s, was soon resumed.

Early in 1934 the list of shares purchased included investments in furniture, rubber, clothes, oil, gold, newspapers, cinemas, government bonds, electricity, tea, foodstuffs, building materials and wallpaper. Alliance also participated in new issues for banks, brickworks, property companies and printers. There were also sales of government bonds, brickworks, oil, electricity and steel.

A major review of investment activity and policy took place in 1935. The board paper prepared for this event revealed that there were 1,136 different investments. The geographical distribution is revealed in Table 6.5.

It is a remarkable list, notwithstanding that most of these investments were purchased in London or New York. That such a small management team

Table 6.5 Geographical distribution of investments, 31 January 1935

	£	£	%
Great Britain		4,363,315	43.95
British Colonies			
Africa	331,613		
Australia	150,038		
Burma	105,203		
Canada	129,073		
F.U.S	84,540		
India	281,124		
Iraq	13,493		
New Zealand	77,347		
Palestine	13,899		
West Indies	20,614	1,206,944	12.16
North America			
USA and Colonies		1,517,922	15.29
Central America	65,005		
Cuba	51,705		
Mexico	19,155	135,865	1.37
Europe			
Austria	92,987		
Belgium	106,066		
Czechoslovakia	37,330		
Danzig	33,303		
Denmark	13,383		
Finland	71,795		
France	83,828		
Germany	416,171		
Greece	104,494		
Holland	66,307		
Hungary	71,126		
Iceland	14,658		
Italy	82,521		
Norway	21,251		
Poland	3,565		
Portugal	32,676		

Table 6.5 *continued*

	£	£	%
Romania	3,915		
Russia	3,018		
Spain	23,486		
Sweden	65,489		
Switzerland	2,745		
Yugoslavia	9,354	1,359,468	13.69
South America			
Argentine	410,730		
Bolivia	18,235		
Brazil	222,657		
Chile	204,636		
Colombia	54,941		
Paraguay	16,810		
Peru	19,402		
Uruguay	92,743	1,040,154	10.47
Asia			
China	67,089		
East Indies	36,764		
Japan	144,682		
Persia	8,700		
Siam (Thailand)	19,556	276,791	2.79
Africa (non British)		27,482	0.28
Total		£9,927,941	100%

could deal with more than a thousand investments, at the same time as putting a herculean effort into extricating the Trust from the mortgage business, suggests that there were long working hours for MacDougall and his team.

In September 1935 there was a clearing of the stables when a number of securities were declared to be of no value and were written off. Most of these were the Russian investments that had been purchased before the 1917 revolution. But they also included Mexican investments, mostly in railways. The nominal values of these write-offs was less than £30,000.

A few months later the review was still ongoing, and having consulted Edinburgh solicitors, Shepherd and Wedderburn, it was decided that, where partial sales of an investment had been made and a profit or loss had been realised, these sums should be carried to the contingent fund. The list of these realisations where gains had been made ran to nine pages and amounted to £954,256. The list of losses was 2.5 pages and amounted to £139,395.

Thereafter the investment policy settled back into its normal routine. At the board meeting in March 1936 the directors discussed a long list of company reports which had been pre-circulated. The list contained the following companies:

Bradleys (Chepstow Place) Ltd
Chartered Bank of India, Australia and China.
Cooper, McDougall and Robertson Ltd
Enfield Cable Works Ltd
Godfrey Phillips Ltd
Home and Colonial Stores Ltd
International Automatic Telephone Co. Ltd
London and Thames Haven Oil Wharves Ltd
Maple and Co. Ltd
Mercantile Bank of India Ltd
Moss Empires Ltd
National Bank of India Ltd
Pinchin Johnson and Co. Ltd
Radiation Ltd
Rawlplug Co. Ltd
Scottish Power Co. Ltd
Winterbottom Book Cloth Co. Ltd

The investment policy was highly active, and at the February 1937 meeting the minutes recorded that in the previous month Alliance had participated in 14 new issues and had made 47 purchases, 6 switches, 37 sales and 11 redemptions. There were a further 7 miscellaneous items which included capital reorganisations.

On the eve of the Second World War the directors examined the reports of 27 companies. Almost all of the companies in the list were British companies, and despite the imminence of war, only one had any direct connection with the armaments industry.

The Agencies

As the Great War drew to a close the agriculture industry in North America was in good shape. The war had brought increased prices, and land values were commensurately higher. It was a good time to be in the mortgage business. Returns on investment were higher than on bonds, which was a reversal of the pre-war position. As wartime lending restrictions were dismantled, the directors began to respond to the agents' eager requests for new money. In January 1919 they gave permission to the Memphis agent to lend money at 7.5%, which, after agent's commission and expenses, would yield 6.5%. The following month the inspector, Henry Jones, recommended that more money should be provided to the agencies for lending, and this was agreed. San Antonio received a new credit of $100,000 while Fort Worth got $50,000 and Memphis $75,000. Some loans were also taken over from the Scottish Canadian Trust, of which two of the Alliance directors, William Thomson and Frederick Sharp, were also directors. By April 1919 total mortgages were £2,469,301, which was a large increase on the 1909 figure of £1,394,403. This healthy situation was not to last, and as events unfolded it became increasingly clear that many lending decisions, made in the heat of post-war demand, had not been well judged.

In making some of the larger loans the Alliance was still in the habit of sharing these with partners of long standing. The Lasater ranch in South Texas, 'Falfurrias', required a loan of $100,000, and the Investors' Mortgage Security Co. provided $20,000, with Alliance providing the balance.

Thereafter the mortgage business is mentioned only occasionally in the minute books – notwithstanding that revenue from mortgages was still nearly five times as much as from investments in 1919. Attention was now more clearly focused on the transition to an investment business and the minute books reflect this trend. It was certainly the case that Henry Jones, the inspector, was a well-trusted employee and most of the agents had been in place for many years. They knew their business and did not require much prompting from Dundee. They were left to get on with it.

Macmaster and Jones both paid visits to Dundee in the summer of 1920. Jones had proposed to send a letter to the agents in which permission was granted to re-lend all monies gathered in repayments. The directors withdrew the letter and told him that 'no such advice should be given to the agents'. Jones was also told that stiffer rates were to be expected from the mortgage business and that 8% should be charged. An application from the Memphis agents for another credit was rejected. Macmaster and Jones were asked to submit a report on the state of the mortgage business. These are the first real signs that the directors were beginning to see the mortgage business as secondary to their preferred route of investing their funds in securities.

Alliance Trust was expanding, new capital was being raised, a new head office was acquired and a new manager, MacDougall, had taken over the reins. The decision would eventually be made to withdraw from the mortgage business. The reason for the decision is almost certainly that higher returns could be made from the investment business. After the deduction of agent's commissions the yield on mortgages had fallen to 5.75% whereas a good portfolio of securities could yield 1% more. Doubtless the decision to exit from the mortgage business was also hastened by the parlous state into which American agriculture fell in the 1920s. The post-war boom soon gave way to more difficult times and was marked by steeply falling commodity prices and land values. By the summer of 1921 22% of mortgages were in arrears. A year later revenue from investments exceeded revenue from mortgages for the first time.

H.P. Drought, from San Antonio, visited Dundee in the summer of 1921 to discuss the mortgage business and, at the same time, the Second Investors' Mortgage Security Co. announced that it had decided to withdraw from lending on mortgages. It was the first of the mortgage companies to make this decision but it was the first of many. And when MacDougall visited North America later that year the instructions that he received from his board were more about share dealings than about mortgages. When he visited Kansas City for discussions with Jones and his assistant, Leighton Myles, the outcome was to terminate Myles' appointment. Myles was given a year's notice but told that he could leave earlier if he could find another position. MacDougall's end-of-trip report revealed mounting caution about the mortgage business. Lending had been stopped in Portland and restricted in the other agencies, although there was a prospect of them getting some new money later in the year.

The Alliance Trust's appetite for mortgages was not dead but it was veering towards a more cautious approach. Early in 1922 the Investors Mortgage Security Co. offered to sell a parcel of its mortgages to Alliance, and the idea was actively considered before being withdrawn. One of the companies with which Alliance shared the inspector's costs was the United States Mortgage Co. In 1922 it applied for, and was granted, a reduction in its portion of the shared costs on account of the reduced amount of mortgage business that it was undertaking. There was beginning to be an exodus of companies from the North American mortgage business.

There were clear signs that the post-war boom in American agriculture was over. In March 1922 the board reviewed a report on mortgage arrears. It was the first of many that they would consider. On the positive side the war and post-war boom had been a good time for the Deltic Investment Company and it repaid all of its deferred debt in 1922. Alliance received £11,918. Some of that money was used to purchase new debentures of the Matador Land and Cattle Co. This was a company in which a substantial holding was built up over several years. Not all of American farming was in dire straits.

Nevertheless it required close monitoring and, notwithstanding that MacDougall had visited North America in 1922, Greenhill, the company secretary, was sent on a visit in 1923. On his return he submitted his report. It revealed that there was a large and increasing amount of arrears on the mortgage account. This revelation prompted a rethink about the accounting treatment of revenues. Until then it had been the company practice to take credit for accrued interest on 'regular loans'. But in view of the possibility that loans might become irregular, and that interest might not be paid, it was decided that, in future, only cash actually received would be credited to revenue account. A brief consultation with the local assessor of taxes followed, and he gave his blessing to this change.

Jones and MacDougall corresponded about what was to be done about the mounting arrears, and a number of options were considered, including selling some of the defaulting loans to the federal land banks. Nothing seems to have been done, and notwithstanding the growing difficulties, the Alliance Trust, together with the Second Alliance Trust, got into negotiations with the Investors' Mortgage Security Company in May 1924 to acquire $500,000 of mortgages in Dallas. The transaction was complete by August 1924, and 77 farm loans valued at $337,650 and 42 city loans totalling $162,000 were acquired. It was a mixed blessing. Many of these loans proved problematical in the years to come, but in acquiring them Alliance also secured the services of Robert Ralston and Co. as Dallas agents. Ralston and his partner William Dyckman were of inestimable value in helping Alliance to manage its way through the crisis ahead.

MacDougall's report in 1925 contained the following table (Table 6.6). However, it does not tell the whole story as the figure for real estate (i.e. forfeited lands) had already been written down by $546,389. There was also some abandoned land in Portland, Kansas City, Memphis and Winnipeg, the book cost of which was $65,953. Some two-thirds of all the mortgages were on land

Table 6.6 State of the Alliance Trust Mortgage Business, 1925 ($)

Agency	Regular	In arrear	Default	Real estate	Total
Portland	675,405	264,250	181,869	770,314	1,891,838
Kansas City	1,081284	328,800	532,120	364,350	2,306,554
San Antonio	1,342,638	97,700	148,300	317,500	1,906,138
Memphis	1,389,038	20,816	41,596	228,221	1,677,671
Winnipeg	413,778	326,970	258,910	108,835	1,108,494
Fort Worth	2,017,188	58,300	73,211	174,300	2,323,000
Dallas	400,000				400,000
	7,317,332	1,096,836	1,236,007	1,963,520	11,613,696

where cotton, wheat and corn was grown, so the prices of these commodities would be what determined the future of the real estate business.

Clearly the mortgage business was in decline, but the directors and agents could not have forecast that much worse was to come.

There were other signs that all was not well when a local correspondent in Stigler, Haskell County in Oklahoma was found to have committed a defalcation. Barrow, Wade, Guthrie, the North American auditors, were despatched to sort out the problem. They recommended the appointment of an experienced book-keeper in the Kansas City office, where responsibility for Oklahoma lending lay. It transpired that some of the loans in Haskell County were not, in fact, first mortgages but second and third mortgages which gave Alliance virtually no security. These loans were contrary to company policy and had been made by the sub-agent employed by the agent Holmes in Kansas City.

Given the mounting problems being experienced in the mortgage business the Alliance board stepped up its monitoring. Reade Ireland, who was Macmaster's assistant in Portland (and son-in-law), visited Dundee in 1924 – closely followed by Bolton Smith from Memphis. Ernest Fleming, from the Alliance staff, made the first of many visits to the United States in 1924.

Thereafter new lending was made only in exceptional circumstances. H.P. Drought, in San Antonio, was given permission in March 1925 to make city loans but only if the security was of the 'highest class'.

Throughout the remainder of 1925 and through much of 1926 various investigations and reviews were conducted into the mortgage business. The secretary and one of the directors, W. Norman Boase, went to North America to confer with agents as to 'the best means to be adopted for the disposal as early as possible of the company's real estate, to examine the position of the company's investment generally in the United States and Canada and to report'. Their concern was not just that many mortgage payments were in arrears but that some were so far in arrears that the agents had foreclosed on the mortgages.

All business was stopped in Tennessee in the summer of 1925, and by the end of that year it seems clear, although the decision was not recorded in the minutes, that a process of gradual disengagement from mortgage lending had commenced. The decision was made not a moment too soon, as farming conditions and the Great Depression would only make things much worse. The biggest challenge of the disengagement process would prove to be disposing of land that had become real estate on the company's books.

Henry Jones visited Dundee in the summer of 1926. He reported that some of the agencies, mainly Winnipeg and Portland, had been requesting to be allowed to renew maturing loans of good standing but the requests were refused. Agents in other places requested extensions to their credits but these too were rejected. The United States Mortgage Co., whose loan book was then down to about $250,000, managed to sell its remaining loans and was released from its obligation to contribute to Jones' expenses.

Towards the end of the harvest season in 1926, when the bulk of collections of mortgage payments would be made, the directors in Dundee were aware that the price of cotton had plummeted. They sent anxious telegrams to the agents enquiring as to the likely effect of the price fall on collections and, just as importantly, on the prospects for selling real estate.

There were more specific worries about the Kansas City agency, where the agent E.E. Holmes was in failing health and the agency was thought to be in an 'unsatisfactory condition'. The directors decided that responsibility for the agency's business should be transferred to Ralston in Dallas on the under-standing that he liquidate the business as speedily as possible. Holmes died a few months later. Floods on the Mississippi just at the time when the new crop was being planted only added to the directors' concerns. One of their number, Hugh Sharp, went to North America in 1927 to see what could be learned. By the end of that year the process of remitting money from the US and Canada back to the UK was well under way. Agents were instructed to try to sell blocks of their loans to other lenders but the American insurance companies, who were also heavily engaged in this business, were disinclined to buy many more loans. There was, however, one major success with this strategy when the Sovereign Life Assurance Company agreed to buy part of the loan book of the Winnipeg agency in 1929. A minor success was achieved later that year when some of the Memphis loans were sold.

The agents continued to receive small credits from Dundee but these were usually only sufficient to pay the agencies' expenses and the local taxes on real estate owned by the company.

In March 1928 a cablegram was sent to Jones which read, 'Refer your letter 9th February advise all agents excepting Dallas meantime that they are not to renew any loans falling due and are to cease investment of principal collections remitting all collections promptly to New York.'

The reason that Dallas was singled out was that when Ralston was engaged as agent an undertaking was given to him that he would have $500,000 to invest and the directors felt obliged to adhere to the agreement. They would come to wish that they could have abrogated it.

It was soon MacDougall's turn to revisit the agencies, and he went in the autumn of 1928. While he was away Greenhill, the secretary, and his assistant Bruce, had a meeting with the lawyers Shepherd and Wedderburn in Edinburgh regarding the possibility of separating the mortgage business and placing it in a separate company. The purpose of doing so was to enable the tax authorities to treat Alliance Trust as an investment trust. This suggestion had come from various quarters and it was given detailed attention. By December 1928 there was a lengthy discussion document on the subject that was under active consideration by the directors. The idea was eventually rejected. It was feared that the Inland Revenue might be hostile to the idea but there were also the practical difficulties of valuing mortgages and real estate.

The mortgage business was beginning to look like an intractable problem but it was not without its hopeful side. The agents continued to send positive statements about their expectations. But their expectations about crops and collections were seldom fulfilled. More positively, thinking began to turn to what might be done with real estate to make it generate revenue and to make it more saleable. In 1928 Bolton Smith in Memphis leased some of the company's real estate in East Carroll Parish, Louisiana, to oil prospectors. This was the first of many such ventures, some of which ultimately brought healthy returns to the company. Even when real estate was sold it was possible under United States law to retain mineral rights and this soon became established company practice.

The agents were ever hopeful that a revival was imminent, and continued to press Dundee for permission to renew existing loans and, on occasion, for more money to lend. In November 1929, in response to one such entreaty, Greenhill wrote a strongly worded letter to Drought in San Antonio: '... while giving due weight to the arguments which you put forward, the Board wish it clearly to be understood once and for all that the decision which the Company has come to the effect that the policy of re-investing is at an end and is replaced by one of liquidation, is a resolution which is absolute and irrevocable'.

The contraction of the mortgage business and the fact that agents were no longer allowed to make new loans impacted on their own incomes, and it was not long before rumblings began to be heard in Dundee about how dissatisfied the agents were with their remuneration. Early in 1929 the directors became aware that the agents in Portland and Memphis had been corresponding with one another about their commissions. In San Antonio, Drought brought matters to a head when he told MacDougall that he was now running the Alliance's business on an unprofitable basis. It was not long before the other agents were making similar comments and telling the directors that the management of real estate – a growing part of the business for all of them – was a lot more expensive than managing a loan book. Jones took the part of the agents in these exchanges.

MacDougall was not unsympathetic to their plight. He was also aware that if they resigned it would be virtually impossible to find suitable replacements except on terms which would be very much more expensive than were currently being paid. In December 1931 he addressed Shepherd and Wedderburn in Edinburgh on the subject: 'One of the main troubles which faces us in the Mortgage Business is the fact that in all our Agencies the business is getting into such a state that the remuneration which the Agents will earn in the ordinary course on present scales is too small to justify them in maintaining an organisation for the benefit of our business, and we think that every effort should be made to get some arrangement whereby the Agents should receive some kind of suitable remuneration.'

As the correspondence continued he wrote, 'we feel that it is in the interests of the Company to treat the Agents not only with justice but with generosity in order to get the best service from them'.

Various compromise arrangements were agreed before it was decided to reward the agents by paying them a salary, with extra commissions on the sale of real estate. Transfers of mortgages to the federal land banks were treated as sales and the agents were paid their commissions.

By 1931 the Depression had set in. The amount of foreclosures was rising and Bolton Smith in Memphis was told not to foreclose unless absolutely necessary. Loans were to be extended for as short a time as possible. Jones visited Dundee in November 1931 for discussions about how to cope with what now clearly a major recession that was worst in America but was affecting other parts of the world. The company policy was restated. Real estate was to be sold so long as the company could recover the principal amount that had been lent plus outstanding interest. It was recognised, however, that some real estate was of little value and Jones was told to sell it for whatever he could get.

Then they went through the agencies case by case. The outcome of their examination was that they decided to do almost nothing. The problems had become so intractable that they could find no way forward and no way out. Even the hoped-for increase in revenues from oil leases was proving to be a chimera. Overproduction of oil had made it necessary for the agents to allow the lessees to reduce their rentals from $1 to 50c per acre per annum. News was received in May 1932 that oil had been discovered on the Cormier land in Vermillion parish in Louisiana that had been leased to the Pure Oil Co. It was not, at that time, a matter for much celebration, although the find was to prove to be an important source of revenue for many years to come.

All the directors could do was to worry about the fitness of some of the agents to conduct their business. Douglass, in Fort Worth, in the face of falling revenues, was busy trying to diversify his activities and the directors were worried that he was not devoting sufficient time to their business. There was no alternative. It would have been impossible to find a replacement to take on the role. They decided to take no action.

In Portland William Macmaster was old and frail and was no longer devoting much of his time to business matters. He had been with Alliance since the beginning. His partner was his son-in-law, Reade M. Ireland, who was then vice-president of the Association of American Mortgage Bankers. Jones thought that he was fit to succeed Macmaster.

In some states there was a statute of limitations on loans, principally in Texas and Tennessee, where the loan would be cancelled after a number of years if payments had not been made and the loan was not officially renewed. Jones was told to get these off the books as soon as possible.

Correspondence was received from the auditors Barrow, Wade, Guthrie and Co., who were then based in Chicago. Their concern was that the Depression was likely to heighten the possibility of fraud and defalcation in the mortgage business. They were asked to provide a further detailed comment and an action plan. The correspondence that followed concluded that the directors had done everything possible to mitigate the risk of fraud. Barrow, Wade, Guthrie were thanked and then asked to reduce their audit expenses. Their fee duly fell from $8,500 to $6,000.

As the mortgage business diminished it was necessary to reduce the costs of running it. Cutting the audit costs was one strategy. Preparing for the retirement of Jones was another. But before that could be achieved it was necessary to have an alternative for keeping the agents in order and effecting an orderly withdrawal from the mortgage business. The task was given to Ernest D. Fleming from the Dundee staff. He already had experience of visiting North America, and in 1932 he was sent again – this time to Winnipeg and Portland.

He was back in Portland in 1934, reporting on the lending there and in neighbouring Idaho, where most of the lending from that agency had taken place. During the First World War sizeable loans had been made to 'dry wheat' farmers in Washington and Idaho where elaborate irrigation schemes had been constructed to ration water. Of the $511,000 invested in Idaho, $251,000 was already in real estate and only $137,000 of loans were being paid regularly. Much of this lending depended on wheat prices being $2 per bushel, and it took another war before these prices were achieved again. When Fleming returned in 1946 he was able to report on a much more prosperous outlook.

Meanwhile Fleming recommended that Ireland should succeed his father-in-law but the problem was that Macmaster did not see the need for his own retirement. Various pieces of correspondence said that Ireland should 'assert himself' but it was some time before Macmaster's retirement was agreed by all parties.

In Memphis, Bolton Smith was also ready for retirement. He was given a parting gift of $5,000 'as a memento of the long and faithful service rendered to the company by him'. His successor was to be a member of his staff, C.F.E. Williams. But Williams, like many of his contemporaries, had various business interests, including agencies for the Connecticut General Life Assurance Co. and Scottish American Mortgage Co., and wanted to move the business to Greenville in Louisiana. This was accomplished with some difficulty and, for most intents and purposes, the result worked well. The only serious problems were caused by the local politician, Huey Long, whose populist style of politicking created several concerns for foreign corporations such as the Alliance Trust. In May 1935 MacDougall wrote on the subject to Williams: 'At one time Hitler's initial propaganda was ignored and more or less jeered at . . . Senator Huey Long no doubt has in mind how dictators have come to the front in

Europe, and is possibly trying by every means in his power to get some sort of similar position in your country.'

Four months later Long was dead – shot in Baton Rouge by the son-in-law of a judge Long was attempting to remove from the bench.

Next of the agents to retire was the inspector Henry Jones. He had been appointed as assistant inspector in 1905 and inspector in 1909. In January 1933 the directors decided that the reduction in the scope and scale of the mortgage business made it no longer necessary to incur the heavy costs of maintaining the inspector's office in Kansas City. Jones was shocked to receive the news, but his health was indifferent and he soon came round to see the directors' viewpoint and received a retiring allowance of $4,000 per annum. Some of the agents, Ralston in particular, were reluctant to see him go. Jones generously offered to make himself available for any purpose for which the directors might find him useful. He did not live long to enjoy his pension, and died three years after his retirement.

Jones' departure necessitated a lengthy round of producing new powers of attorney for what remained of the North American mortgage business, and Ralston in Dallas was delighted to be made the attorney-in-law, which made him, in effect, the senior agent.

As economic conditions improved slightly in 1933 the agents put pressure on Dundee for more remuneration and the directors put pressure on the agents to sell more real estate. These countervailing pressures produced few results. The position was complicated towards the end of 1933 when there was a marked appreciation in the exchange rate and the dollar rose back to $5 to the £1. The directors instructed the agents to delay selling real estate until they had time to consider the situation. To mitigate the exchange rate risk the use of forward contracts was introduced and the process of bringing money home from North America was soon underway again.

Ireland had been given a one-year contract when he took over from Macmaster in Portland but in 1934 his contract was renewed at a salary of $8,000. Most of the Portland agency's business was no longer in Oregon, but in neighbouring Idaho, where substantial irrigation projects had created farms that were viable, but only just. Ireland employed a man called Ford to act as a sub-agent to look after the business there. The directors decided to pay him separately at the rate of $3,000 per annum. Given these overheads, and the precarious nature of the farming business, the directors were anxious to divest themselves of the business, and put increased pressure on Ireland to sell real estate.

A close watch was kept on the business and a board report was prepared every few months. These contained league tables and enabled the directors to monitor the deterioration in the business.

The Chaves Grant in New Mexico was still on the company's books and there was some desultory oil prospecting throughout this period. However, in 1935 there was some possibility that the grant might be sold to the US government for a Navajo reservation. However local interests eventually put an end to that prospect as such a sale would diminish the state tax rolls. In a letter to Drought in 1938 Ernest Fleming wrote: 'Our experience of the Grant has been that it is not much more than as an asset in name, and I cannot help thinking that had a pin been stuck at random in the map of the United States at the time the grant was made, it could not have been placed on a territory that has been less affected by the opening up and development of the West that has since taken place than this tract.'

Total oil revenue on Chaves from 1914 until 1938 was only $25,000. The only reliable income came from the sheep farmers but that was barely sufficient to pay the local taxes.

Inevitably some of the real estate was disposed of at a loss, and in April 1937 the directors learned that these losses amounted to £101,034. A mortgage and real estate suspense account was in existence and it was agreed to credit the account with £75,635 of unappropriated profits and a further £25,398 from the contingent fund.

Valiant efforts were made to dispose of land but sometimes the only way to do this was to grant a mortgage to a new purchaser. This had the merit of transferring the mortgage from 'real estate' to 'live mortgage' but it prolonged the date at which the Alliance Trust could extricate itself from the mortgage business. Moreover as agricultural prices turned sharply downwards at the end of 1937 the directors contemplated the possibility that they might have to foreclose on some of these new mortgages.

The other challenge was to manage and maintain the farm land that, as a result of foreclosure, had come into company ownership. Their objective was to preserve the land and its buildings in saleable condition. This was largely the responsibility of the agents, and various efforts were recorded of their diligence. Williams in Greenville planted legumes on land owned by Alliance Trust and then ploughed them into the land to improve its nutritional value and enhance the next crop. Ireland, in Portland, reported in 1935 that he had put new tenants into a property but they had only stayed for a year. He went to inspect the property after the tenant and his 13 children had gone, and reported, 'One can not imagine what damage a gang of children can do when the cold winters restrict them to the confines of the house.' He had to spend $1,000 to make it habitable.

By this time the New Deal, introduced by President Roosevelt in 1933, was beginning to have an impact, although it was very uneven. Complications were introduced by frequent changes to the legislation, slow payments, administrators who had never before held down a clerical job and inconsistent decision making.

The principal aim of the New Deal, so far as farmers were concerned, was to make them more secure by making it more difficult for lenders to foreclose. It ensured that their horses and equipment could not be taken away and enabled them to borrow money with which they could pay off existing loans. It was also designed to maintain prices by limiting production, by taking land out of cultivation and by enforcing a system of quantity licences for certain crops. The Alliance directors in Dundee generally welcomed this new policy, but they were also cautious and reserved judgement until they had some experience of how it would work in practice. They were worried, however, that the loans from the land banks would be insufficient for the purpose as they would only provide a sum equivalent to the current value of land and buildings rather than the historic value at the time when their mortgages were made. Perhaps they worried too much, for if the loans had been made on 40 to 50% of the valuation, then the government loans from the land bank or the Home Owners' Loan Corporation should have been sufficient to enable the farmers to pay off their debts.

It would not prove to be so simple. While mortgage companies had been lending to farmers to finance the purchase of their farms, bankers had been lending to them to finance the crop planting. The failure of thousands of banks in the Depression created confusion to add to the obvious economic distress. Freak weather conditions only made matters worse. Drought created dust storms and eventually the dust bowl. Poor crops over several years added to other problems such as crop infestations of boll weevil. In 1933 farmers in the Mississippi valley held back their crops from market in order to secure a higher price. This made collections of mortgage payments impossible.

By the summer of 1934 MacDougall was able to report to his board that, administrative difficulties notwithstanding, the company was benefitting from the existence of land banks. Louisiana was the exception and MacDougall wrote to Williams to find out why. The situation there was partially resolved when a new chairman of the land bank was appointed.

MacDougall wrote to Williams in September 1934: 'We quite recognise the difficulties with which you are surrounded in having so many complicated Acts which are supposed to help the cotton industry but which appear to have left a great deal of doubt as to their exact meaning and the way in which their object of helping the industry can be attained.'

Williams was thought to be doing a good job in Louisiana but his task was made doubly difficult by the fact that he was also looking after some oil leases, including the productive Cormier. American legislation had brought about 'exceptional circumstances complicated by oil leases and oil rights'.

In other agencies the story was broadly similar, although in Portland discussions with the Washington State Land Bank were helped by the fact that the vice-president, Henry Matthew, hailed originally from Angus – the county of Dundee. He was, however, no pushover, and discussions with him started after dinner and went on until 2 a.m.

As time went on the perception was that the land banks were becoming more conservative. Some of them had become overextended and had to be bailed out by the federal government. Others tended to favour loans on the better lands and were of no help to the poor farmers who really needed assistance.

Towards the end of 1934 the directors made it clear to the agents that they would accept whatever the land banks and other government agencies, like the Home Owners' Loan Corporation, would offer. Inevitably this meant incurring losses. Ralston was horrified by the prospect and asked, several times, for this policy to be confirmed. In October 1934 he wrote to Dundee, 'We know that our failure to make much headway in the realization of real estate is discouraging but conditions have been most unfavourable, such as the confusion caused by the agricultural programme, the insolvency of the landed population and a waiting attitude, in expectation of further deflation, by those who are able to make real estate investments.'

The latter point was a criticism of land speculators, who were a constant irritation to those trying to sell real estate.

By 1935 the mortgage business had diminished to the extent that virtually nothing about it was recorded in the board minutes. The focus of the directors was almost exclusively on the investment business. But that does not mean that nothing was happening. Some of the letter books containing the agencies' correspondence, passing in both directions, reveal not just that the manager and secretary were writing to the agents on a weekly basis but that there were still many difficulties to be resolved.

MacDougall with Bruce, who had succeeded Greenhill as secretary in 1931, also had a number of battles to fight with the Inland Revenue in the UK, but these paled into insignificance compared with those that had to be fought with the Internal Revenue in the US. In 1937 negotiations with the American tax authorities persuaded the directors to transfer £50,000 from the contingent fund to a special taxation reserve. The United States had introduced capital stock and excess profits taxes and there was considerable uncertainty not just about the Alliance Trust's liability for these taxes but about the manner in which that liability would be calculated. The Alliance Trust was duly recognised as a 'resident foreign corporation' – a recognition that was to be highly useful to the company after 1945.

'American independent public accountants' were employed to advise the directors. The problem was to separate out the US and rest of the world activities and which portions of capital and revenue could be attributed to each. There were various outstanding cases involving other companies that were under consideration by the authorities and the courts. They merely served to make matters even more complex. Inevitably there were varying interpretations of what the law said and required: ' . . . the company's advisers were unable to inform the officers and directors of the Company as to what constituted gross income from United States sources and from all sources for the purpose of determining the proportion of home office expenses deductible in arriving at net income from United States sources and . . . have been unable to obtain an authoritative ruling on that question from the commissioner of Internal Revenue'.

A compromise was eventually reached, but not before a considerable amount of time, effort and expense had been devoted to finding a solution.

And if the taxation position was confused and confusing, so too was the implementation of government strategy in the various states.

Ralston wrote from Dallas in August 1934 to complain that, 'all these laws being passed from time to time first by the Federal Government and then the States in their ardour not to be outdone passing almost conflicting laws, have left us in a position where we simply did not know and are not yet quite clear where we stand'.

The Bankhead Bill and the Frazier-Lemke Bill were only two of the pieces of legislation with which the agents had to grapple. Ralston claimed that the Bankhead Bill had 'worked untold hardship on all of our farmers'.

He was getting increasingly angry about the way that government policy was impacting on the farmers and his own business. In October 1935 he wrote to MacDougall and set out his concerns:

I fully appreciate that you do not wish to acquire any more real estate, but in several cases – particularly this one – I do think the borrowers have taken advantage of our leniency and our reluctance to acquire more real estate, for I think that you appreciate that I cannot say emphatically to one that if you do not do thus and so we shall foreclose, for once having made a statement of this nature and failing to carry it out, you are irretrievably lost.

Unfortunately our Federal Government, as well as our states, are encouraging delinquencies through moratoriums and legislation of this character just as, you will remember, the Frazier-Lemke Bill – a most drastic thing – was declared unconstitutional by the Supreme Court and in less than two months another practically as drastic has been passed and signed by the President. In the face of such action, naturally, the borrowers feel that the lending companies are disregarding the wishes of the President as well as the Congress, and that we are nothing short of Bolshevists for doing so.

All of the Insurance companies are reducing their rates from the present face rate to 5% voluntarily, and this does not help a bit in the present situation, especially as regards those who must have better rates on account of severe taxation.

These were challenging times, and the Alliance Trust's overall position was undoubtedly helped by the fact that the bulk of its funds were then invested in securities rather than in mortgages. Nevertheless there was still a substantial portion of company money in mortgages and a considerable amount of effort was devoted to ensuring that everything possible was done to minimise the losses that were being incurred.

The agents were particularly helpful in this regard. Their letters to Dundee are full of hard-headed statements about the current situation. In January 1933 Drought wrote from San Antonio with an update and some veiled advice:

Included in this long list of defaults are some borrowers who have for many prior years met all of their obligations promptly. During these difficult times they were able for a while to draw on their reserves, but they have now reached the point where their own resources are exhausted and they cannot obtain assistance elsewhere. Everything that the farmer or ranchman now has to sell must be sold at a price which is roughly about one third or one fourth of the price he was receiving when most of these loans were made. And these prices, giving little or no return above the cost of production, leave him nothing to apply on his obligations. As we consider it inadvisable to take over any more real estate than is necessary under present conditions, in all cases where we find that a borrower is working hard to take care of and cultivate our security, we are marking time in the hope that at least some of them will eventually be able to work out of their present difficulties and put their loans in good standing again. Generally it is quite important that the securities for the loans be cultivated and in many cases, if we should take over the property, we would no doubt find it difficult to obtain renters who would care for it as the owners are now doing. Within recent months inspections have been made of the securities for quite a number of loans which are seriously in default, so that we might have first hand information relative to their condition and in most cases we found that the properties were being pretty well cared for and that the sole reason for the defaults was the low price of agricultural products. Whenever possible, we obtained definite assurances from the borrowers that the land would be thoroughly cultivated this year and in a number of instances we have taken a crop mortgage of one third of the grain and one fourth of the cotton to be produced on the property in 1933. These shares, as you know, are the customary rent paid the landlord of a farm in Texas when he supplies only the land and are all we could expect to receive if we owned and rented the property.

Similar messages were received from the other agents. Even the auditors, Barrow, Wade, Guthrie wrote in the same vein.

The directors in Dundee were also well aware of the human costs of what was happening. In 1936 they took notice of a visit to Europe by the editor of the *Nation*, a US publication. Referring to the area around Greenville, Louisiana, MacDougall reported to Williams in Greenville on what he had said. He wrote that 'the standard of living down there, not only of the negroes but of the poor whites, either as renters or share crop, was worse than anything he had seen in his travels in Europe. If, he said, this was to be improved, it could never be done by growing cotton in competition with all the other countries now producing it, but would require that much of the acreage would have to be split up and proportioned out to negro and white families for growing diversified [crops] and truck farming for local consumption'.

Later that year the problems were compounded when the state authorities in Oklahoma raised an action of escheat against the Trust. Although this was a very ancient piece of English law which had its roots in the Old Testament concept of jubilee, several US states had it on their statute books. In Oklahoma escheat prevented any corporation from holding land for more than seven years if the land was not being used for farming or any other commercial purpose.

In July 1936 the Hughes County attorney in Oklahoma raised an action of escheat in respect of 680 acres on which Alliance Trust had foreclosed in 1926 and which it still owned despite having made various efforts to sell it. MacDougall and John Bruce, the company secretary, made depositions in front of a notary public in Dundee and these were sent to MacQueen and Kidd who were the Alliance's legal agents in Oklahoma. An enormous volume of legal wrangling ensued before the case was eventually dismissed upon Alliance paying $294. This sum and the attendant legal expenses, which were far higher, were debited to the mortgage and real estate suspense account.

When this account was looked at in April 1937 it revealed losses and irrecoverable expenses amounting to £101,034. It was decided that this could not be allowed to mount any higher as there was no real prospect of the mortgage business returning to profit. This amount was written off by applying sums from the contingent fund and unappropriated profits.

Oklahoma's efforts to enforce its escheat law were apparently a test case, and within months it had repealed the law and replaced it with a tax on the assessed value of land.

The policy of lending on mortgages had stood the Alliance Trust in good stead for many years but the exceptional circumstances of the interwar years had rendered it unviable. Despite the enormous difficulties the New Deal was probably, on balance, of help to the Trust in divesting itself of the mortgage business, but it could not provide a complete answer to the difficulties that were experienced. Moreover there were some positive signs. Oil was discovered on some of the land on which Alliance had foreclosed and revenues from oil leases provided a revenue stream for many years thereafter. Other pieces of real estate were managed successfully and Drought was given extra remuner-ation in 1938 based upon some land that he was managing profitably. Never-theless many years were to elapse before a line could be drawn under the mortgage business.

Chapter 7
The Second World War: 1939–1945

War Finance

Almost from the moment when hostilities were declared, the UK Treasury took hold of Britain's finances. Doubtless there were many civil servants in the Treasury offices who had been in service during the First World War who could well remember what had been done then. Moreover the British civil service's reputation for record keeping was second to none, and the records from 1914–18 had been retrieved from the archives and gone over in great detail even before war had been declared.

Prior to the declaration on 3 September 1939, the insurance and investment trust industries had voluntarily sent questionnaires to their members to enquire as to their holdings of foreign securities. They clearly anticipated that these would be requisitioned on the outbreak of hostilities.

The option of borrowing money for the war effort from the United States was not available, as the US Neutrality Act forbade the lending of money to belligerents. Moreover Britain had defaulted on some of its debts from the First World War, and the United States had legislation in place – the Johnson Act of 1934 – which prevented it from lending more money to defaulting nations. Therefore the only solution was for Britain to raise money in the United States by selling its assets. It was reckoned UK interests held 2% by value of all the stocks traded on the New York Stock Exchange at that time.

In August 1939 the Treasury was given the appropriate powers to requisition securities and control their transfer. Holders of overseas securities were required to register their holdings with the Bank of England. It was still permissible for the owners to sell these securities but the foreign currency proceeds had to be surrendered to the Treasury. From February 1940 until April 1941 several vesting orders were issued which compelled holders of foreign securities to surrender them to the Treasury. The securities were acquired for the exchange equalisation account and investors were compensated in Treasury bills.

This created difficulties for a number of investment trusts, as the yield on Treasury bills was less than they were accustomed to obtaining on their investments. Trusts like the British Assets Trust and the Scottish American Investment Company were seriously affected, as a large portion of their investments were in the United States. Alliance Trust was less seriously affected, as on the eve of war only 14% of its portfolio was in the US, including what remained of the mortgage business. Although it is not possible to be precise, it has been estimated that £45m was raised by the Treasury from the sale of US securities held by British investment trusts.[21]

The Treasury's hand on the Alliance Trust was felt strongly when it came to dealing with investments in securities. In April 1940 the Treasury began the process of requisitioning American securities from whoever held them in the UK. They were then to be sold in New York and the money raised was to pay for vital war supplies from North America. Alliance Trust gave up 21 stocks, including their investments in Philip Morris, Bethlehem Steel, Chesapeake and the Ohio Railroad. It was the first of many such requisitions. In January 1941 the company surrendered its holdings in Woolworths, Sears Roebuck, Ohio Oil, Goodyear and Liggett and Myers. These requisitions were followed in February by shares in Ohio Edison, Great Northern Railway and American Telephone and Telegraph, and in May by P. Lorillard, Gillette Safety Razor, Standard Oil of Indiana, International Telephone and Telegraph, and Pure Oil. This last company operated Alliance's oil interests in the Cormier Oil field in Louisiana.

The man entrusted with the task of selling these securities in New York was Walter Whigham of Robert Fleming and Co. in London. However, although he made a start, he was unable to complete the task, which then fell to T.J. Carlyle Gifford who had set up Baillie Gifford as a firm of solicitors and trust managers in Edinburgh before the First World War. Gifford had seen his firm grow to specialise in investment before the fund management and legal sides of the business separated.[22] After the war Gifford became a director of Alliance Trust and served until 1964.

Alan Brown, who was then assistant manager and secretary of Alliance

21 D.C. Corner and H. Burton, *Investment and Unit Trusts in Britain and America*, Elek, London, 1968, Ch. 5.
22 C.W. Munn, T.J.C. Gifford, in A. Slaven and S.G. Checkland (eds), *Dictionary of Scottish Business Biography, 1860–1960*, Aberdeen, 1990, p. 406.

had served the early part of his career with Baillie Gifford. One of his young colleagues there was David McCurrach, whom Brown brought from Edinburgh to work with Alliance. When Gifford was sent to America he recruited McCurrach to work with him in the British delegation in the United States, and McCurrach remained in the US for the remainder of the war before returning to Dundee.

The task facing Gifford and McCurrach in America was substantial and not without its difficulties. However, it was relatively free of controversy and the task was completed successfully.[23]

The Treasury did not confine itself to concerns over marketable securities. In January 1940 there was some doubt as to whether or not approval had to be sought from the Treasury's Capital Issues Committee for alterations to the Trust's short-term borrowing requirement. Legal advice had been sought but no firm conclusion had been reached. For the avoidance of doubt, and future problems, it was decided to seek approval. The Treasury responded quickly and approval was given before the end of the month.

That was certainly not the end of the matter, and within two months the Treasury wrote to 'recommend' that terminable debentures should be reduced. The company's response was to say that this was being done gradually. Thereafter Treasury requests to reduce terminable debentures fell into a pattern of polite requests. Before the end of 1940 the approval to renew the debentures was always given but 'subject to the company adopting measures which will have the effect of reducing the amount of these borrowings in so far as they find themselves able to do so'. This phrase was always tacked on to the end of these letters. These debentures were reduced during the war but only by a relatively trivial amount. Although Treasury permission had to be sought for all renewals, this does not seem to have been anything more than a formality. It is perhaps not surprising that the company was keen to maintain the level of debentures. As late as October 1941 debenture interest was still quite low, and they could be renewed for three years at 3% and for five years at 3¼%. It seems likely that the Treasury was keen for trusts to reduce debentures as they proved to be attractive to savers and were in competition with the government's own efforts to raise war funds by issuing various types of security.

---

23 R.S. Sayers, *Financial Policy 1939–45*, HMSO.

People

Fortunately MacDougall was still around to manage the company's affairs. He had joined Alliance Trust as secretary in 1912 and had succeeded Mackenzie as manager in 1919. Consequently when war broke out in 1939 he was well placed, as one of the most experienced fund managers in the country, to direct the affairs of the Alliance Trust. Not only had he witnessed the demands of the First World War but he had managed the Trust's affairs during the troubled interwar period. MacDougall was in his late sixties in 1939 and must have been contemplating retirement but he had an able helpmate in the form of Alan Brown, a chartered accountant, who had joined the Alliance from Baillie Gifford in 1937.

There were strong ties between the Alliance and Baillie Gifford. Hugh Sharp, the Alliance chairman until his untimely death in 1937, had been a member of the Baillie Gifford board, and MacDougall himself had been a director of Scottish Mortgage, which was managed by Baillie Gifford. Therefore Brown would have been well known to both men.

Brown was appointed secretary and assistant manager in 1938. He became joint manager, with MacDougall, in 1942, and was given a seat on the board the following year. His appointment to the board was prompted by the fact that Harold Sharp was unwell and had asked for four months' leave of absence. Brown continued as company secretary, reflecting perhaps the wartime conditions and the difficulty of bringing in younger men to fill positions.

James Prain, who had been a director since 1920, succeeded Sharp as chairman in 1937. He remained on the board until 1945 when he was succeeded as chairman by MacDougall. It was the first time that an employee of the company had become chairman of the board.

There were very few changes to the board during the war. In 1939 there were only four directors: James Prain (chairman), David Pirie, William MacDougall and Harold Sharp. Apart from Brown's appointment in 1943 the only other newcomer was Thomas H.H. Walker who joined in 1945. Pirie, who had been chairman from 1932 until 1937, and on the board from 1919, died in September 1943.

The records are remarkably silent on the staff of the organisation. Doubtless there were the same problems experienced by other businesses. Conscription came in quickly, compared with the First World War, and most organisations experienced a rapid exit to the forces with no prospect of finding qualified replacements. Consequently the burden of running the business fell on the shoulders of MacDougall, Brown and on older staff like the assistant secretary, James Fleming Nicoll and his colleague Ernest Fleming. Whatever the burden they were up to the task, and one measure of this is the number of wartime economic publications, from academics and others, in the archives. Clearly they were making great efforts to keep up to date with economic thinking and wartime exigencies.

The Agents

It did not take long before the prices of agricultural produce and land began to rise, which made it relatively easy for agents to sell much of the remaining US and Canadian real estate.

Early in the war Tom Drought in San Antonio was in serious discussions with the US government over the Chaves Grant. A deal was eventually done in January 1941 that transferred ownership at a price of $67,350. 'After charging all expenses (excluding commission and expenses on sale) and crediting $25,033 from oil leases it showed a loss of $2,000, or a net loss of $11,600 including all expenses commission etc. Three quarters mineral rights in the sale have been reserved.' (There is no truth in the company folk memory that this land became part of the Los Alamos development.)

The war greatly stimulated the search for oil, and in 1942 Barcroft, the agent in Greenville, reported that a new well had been brought in on the Cormier property. He pointed out to Brown in Dundee that it was the custom when this happened for owners to throw a party, dance or barbecue 'to show their appreciation of the drilling crew who dug and brought in the wells'. The same crew had brought in all the wells in the vicinity 'and were beginning to wonder if we were not going to do as others had done'. Barcroft had taken it upon himself to advance $150 for the purpose. Brown's response from war-ravaged Britain can only be guessed at.

By that time Barcroft, who was also agent for Scottish American Mortgage and the Connecticut General Life Assurance Company, was worried, at the age of 42, that he would be called up for military service. His worries were unfounded and he was free to pursue his various business interests. He was of considerable help in selling much of the real estate that remained on the company's books. The Deltic lands were sold in 1941, and some of the nearby, heavily wooded, Wyly land, which had been a drag on the company's finances for many years, he sold at the handsome price of $40 per acre in 1940. The Wyly account in the company's books, which for many years had been a source of anguish and red ink, was then showing a healthy surplus of £100,000. So successful was Barcroft in selling real estate that in 1943 MacDougall urged caution lest the lands be sold too cheaply. Given the upward movement in land prices he felt that Barcroft should take full advantage of the strong bargaining position in which he found himself. By 1944 there were six wells in production at Cormier, and Barcroft had also succeeded in selling 547 acres of the land, retaining only a small portion that preserved Alliance's rights of access to the wells.

McCurrach, who was then in Washington with the mission from the British Ministry of Supply, met Barcroft in 1943 and described him as a 'militant southerner' although he went on to say that he liked him. The main purpose behind McCurrach's meeting with Barcroft concerned the former's lack of knowledge of the mortgage business. MacDougall wrote to Barcroft in 1943 suggesting that the two men should meet: '. . . we feel strongly that it will be of great advantage to him and to us if before he returns to this country he was able to see something of the conditions at the various agencies and to meet our friends who look after our interests there'. It is clear, from this letter, that McCurrach was being groomed for higher things.

The two men discussed the agency's various issues and, in particular, the difficult Armstrong case in which the litigant was challenging the foreclosure the Alliance had effected on his property ten years earlier. The case had dragged on all that time and McCurrach regretted that there was no American equivalent of the British term 'vexatious litigant'. The case took a great deal of Barcroft's time but in 1945 it was eventually settled when the Supreme Court in Mississippi ruled in favour of Alliance. By that stage the case had been tried 'three times in Chancery Court, twice in Bankruptcy Court, twice in Supreme Court as well as twice in Federal Courts'. Alliance was awarded $93,000, which perhaps explained why the case had not been settled at an earlier stage.

As the war drew to a close Barcroft found it easier to sell the remaining real estate as 'There are a great many professional men, that is doctors, lawyers, and merchants, who have made a great deal of money during the past few years and are desirous of investing it or speculating with their money.'

Investments

There was no mention of the war in the minute books but a board discussion paper was prepared and there is no doubt that hostilities had a profound effect on the company's investment activities. The discussion paper stated that there was no possibility of preparing a comprehensive investment policy but it seemed 'desirable to have ready some outline . . . of how such a policy might be framed'. It was thought then that the war might last for three years so it would be necessary to concentrate 'on those fields where there is strong peace time industry, trying to select those companies whose activity might be stimulated, or at least not diminished, by a prolonged war'.

Consequently fixed interest investments were to be avoided, as there was likely to be inflation. Luxury industries such as hotels, cars, distilleries and high-priced stores were unlikely to prosper. Companies likely to perform well included those making bicycles and batteries as well as the more obvious war equipment manufacturers. It was also thought sensible to hold on to building and materials companies, as there was likely to be a lot of rebuilding after the war.

By the close of 1939 the bulk of the company's money was going into heavy industry and war-related activities, much of it in ordinary shares. But there was also a substantial proportion going into what may have been regarded as safer activities such as banking and insurance. At the same time investments in the more remote parts of the world and in areas vulnerable to German invasion were sold. Queensland gold bonds, Danish gold bonds and shares in Brazilian coffee were all disposed of. In the year to 31 January 1940 there were no purchases of European equities or fixed-interest investments and, in the same year, European investments totalling £254,000 were sold.

Notwithstanding that the American investments were gradually being given up to the Treasury the directors continued to monitor the annual reports of those American companies in which they had invested. There was little point in attempting to make further purchases as they would soon be forfeited. However, the possibility of investing in the American economy was not entirely closed. There were a number of British companies whose activities were largely in the United States and whose shares were unlikely to fall into the Treasury ambit. Foremost among these was the Dundee-run Matador Land and Cattle Co., and Alliance continued to purchase small numbers of its shares whenever they became available. This was not a new activity but the continuation of a policy that had been pursued throughout the interwar years.

Although the war caused substantial changes in the investment strategy the directors did not lose sight of the basic rules of running an investment trust which were to place their money in a broad range of industries and in good revenue-earning companies. One way to do this, which found favour in these difficult years, was to buy the shares of other trusts. This was not an entirely new strategy but the shares of other trusts became a growing part of the Alliance portfolio for no other reason than that it helped to spread risks and, in the process, bought into the knowledge and skills of other investment professionals.

There were very few new issues in the British stock exchanges and in 1941 it was reported that underwriting commissions at £468 were about one third of what they had been in the previous year. Nevertheless there were still lots of British companies whose shares were being actively traded, and Alliance bought those that were expected to perform well in wartime. In June 1941, in addition to a number of other trusts, they bought shares in food and drink companies (Peek Frean, Guinness), building materials (Olympic Portland Cement), banks (Lloyds, Martins, Midland) and newspapers (Daily Mail). These acquisitions were followed a few weeks later by Bairds and Scottish Steel, Commercial Union, Coatbridge Gas Co., Raleigh Cycles, Saxone Shoes and Spillers. The only purchase which can be thought of as in any way speculative was a purchase of shares in Harrods which, given the blitz, was in some danger of disappearing. This pattern of investment continued through the remaining years of the war. The only notable departure was in 1944 when preference shares in the Philco Radio and Television Corporation of Great Britain were acquired. This was the first mention of television in the company's records.

Some months later shares in Chartered Bank and HSBC which, in those days did most of their banking business in India and the Far East, were sold at a loss. There was a net loss on realisations for the financial year ending on 31 January 1942 of £117,456 which was debited to the contingent fund. But while investment conditions were undoubtedly difficult it is clear that the company was practising what came to be known as 'bed and breakfasting'. This was a practice to establish losses in order to minimise tax liabilities. In the month before the board meeting in January 1943, which approached the end of the company's financial year, there was a sudden upsurge in trading. But many of the shares that were sold were soon repurchased, thereby establishing a trading loss on many of them. The practice continued throughout the war years. Further modest losses on realisations were made in 1943 and 1944, and the sums were debited to the contingent fund.

As the war approached its end, government gave a great deal of thought to what would have to be done to restore prosperity to the country in peacetime. The further development of the welfare state was an important ingredient of public policy. But a great deal of thought was also given to the

Mr Nygren, pedigree cattle farmer, c. 1950.

Mr and Mrs Phancup, farming in Canada, c. 1946.

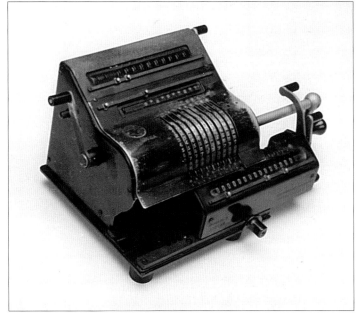

ABOVE. Reform Street, Dundee, in the 1950s. Meadow House is on the right of the picture. (Courtesy of D.C. Thomson and Co. Ltd)

LEFT. The company comptometer, c.1955.

Best Wishes from Meadow House

A "Corner
Taken from near "Arthur's Seat"

ABOVE. Interior, Meadow House, 1950s.

RIGHT. George Stout, Joint Manager then director, 1976–1987.

ABOVE LEFT. Lyndon Bolton, Joint Manager, Manager then Director, 1976–1995.

ABOVE RIGHT. George Dunn, Director then Chairman, 1970–1984.

LEFT. Sir Robert Smith, Director then Chairman, 1984–1997.

RIGHT. Gavin Suggett, Company Secretary, then Managing Director, 1976–2003.

BELOW. Board Room, Meadow House, c.1990.

The Investment Team, 1990s. *Back row* (left to right): Neil Tong, Matthew Strachan, Grant Lindsay, Ronald Hadden. *Front row* (left to right): Shona Dobbie, Gavin Suggett (Chief Executive), Alan Young.

The Savings Team, 1990s. *Back row* (left to right): Neil Anderson, Kevin Dann. *Front row*: Alisdair Dobie, Gavin Suggett (Chief Executive), Sheila Ruckley.

LEFT. Bruce Johnston, Director then Chairman. 1991–2000.

BELOW. The Board of Directors, 2002. *Left to right*: Nelson Robertson, Lesley Knox, Sheila Ruckley, Alan Young, Bruce Johnston, Gavin Suggett, William Jack, William Berry.

RIGHT. Sheila Ruckley, Company Secretary then Director, 1989–2006.

BELOW. The Accounts Team, c. 2000. *Left to right*: Sean Gillanders, Alan Hunter (seated), Roslyn Brown, Sharon Winter.

ABOVE LEFT. Alan Harden, Chief Executive and Director, 2004–2008.

ABOVE RIGHT. Alan Young, Executive Director, 1992–2006.

LEFT. Lesley Knox, Director then Chairman, 2001–2012.

The New Head Office, 2009.

Katherine Garrett-Cox, Director since 2007 and Chief Executive since 2008.

Alliance staff helping out at The Brae.

Alliance staff and friends at the Cateran Yomp, 2011.

Iain Smith, Investment Manager, with Tom Drought, agent in San Antonio, 2011.

Leadership Group, 2012.

rebuilding of the economy and, in particular, to the needs of British industry for investment capital. The suggestion that the function of capital allocation might be undertaken by a government department drew from the chairman, James Prain, a powerful statement of his opposition to all forms of national-isation which he delivered to the annual general meeting in 1944:

> In providing finance for the development and expansion of all forms of legitimate commercial activity, the Investment trusts, along with other financial institutions, have played their part in taking the initial risk either by subscribing to or guaranteeing the subscription to new issues of capital. If I understand it rightly, there is now a school of thought which advocates that these functions should be performed by a Government Department or be subject to some form of State control. This to my mind is a dangerous doctrine and one for which I can find no justification. Under peace conditions all our nation's old skill and resource will be required to meet the problems which specially face this country, and these qualities will only be brought out satisfactorily under a system of private enterprise. If that system is to work it must be untrammelled or the driving force will go out of it. I would remind those who in state control see a cure for all our economic ills that this country depends probably more than any other on the bold initiative of its industrial leaders. The fact that State control is exercised elsewhere does not mean that it would suit our requirements. Countries with ample agricultural resources and comparatively small export trade can afford to make economical experiments of a revolutionary nature without incurring the risk of starvation but we here depend for our bread and butter on being able to maintain our position in the markets of the world – and not a State controlled world, but a world of all sorts, and a competitive one at that. We should take thought, therefore, before we tamper with a system which with all its faults has so far kept us in the van of progress and I firmly believe will continue to do so.

Notwithstanding Prain's clarion call for the maintenance of free enterprise there was still a concern that the Macmillan Gap had not disappeared and a growing acknowledgement that a government initiative might be required to close it. Since the Macmillan committee had reported on company finance in 1931 there had been an acknowledgement that small firms could find it difficult

to raise capital – the so-called 'Macmillan gap'. There was, therefore, a determination on the part of government to make it easier for small firms to raise
money. As early as 1943 three committees (Treasury, Board of Trade and Bank
of England) were set up to consider the problems of post-war finance. But
there was no agreement, and the Committee of London Clearing Bankers took
the view that they could easily provide whatever finance was necessary. Months
of wrangling ensued but it was eventually agreed that two new organisations
would be established and the Chancellor, Sir John Anderson, made a statement
to that effect in the House of Commons in January 1945. The Industrial and
Commercial Finance Corporation (ICFC) was to be largely funded by the
banks and was to provide loans of under £200,000 to industrial and
commercial companies. Some of the banks took a good deal of persuasion
before committing themselves to assist this new enterprise. The larger organisation, the Finance Corporation for Industry (FCI), was to provide loans in
excess of £200,000 and its funding was to come from insurance and investment
trust companies, although 15% was to be held by the Bank of England.[24]

Matters moved forward quickly and a month later the Alliance Trust board
recorded that

> The proposals put forward by the Governor of the Bank of England
> to the Association of Investment Trusts, and explained verbally by the
> Governor to Mr James Prain [chairman of Alliance Trust], having
> been considered by the Board, it was resolved to support the proposals
> in principle and to indicate that, subject to the Board being satisfied
> with the scheme as finally adjusted and with the provisions of the
> Corporation's Memorandum and Articles of Association and
> Prospectus when issued, the company would be prepared to subscribe
> to the share capital to an amount not exceeding £150,000.

The creation of these two companies was the harbinger of a changed
relationship between government and the financial services industry. As
governments moved to the left across the world, businesses had to learn how
to deal with a new set of relationships and to factor government expectations
into their planning strategies.

------

24 J. Kinross, *Fifty Years in the City*, Murray, London, 1982, pp. 116–17.

Annual Reports and Annual General Meetings

The message given to the shareholders on the outbreak of war was one of caution and uncertainty. Moreover the amount of information that they received in the annual report was scanty. The report itself was reduced to a double sheet that could be folded in on itself and put in the post without an envelope.

At the annual general meeting in April 1940 the shareholders were told that collections and revenue had been good up to the outbreak of hostilities but since then there had been some deterioration, albeit that this had been counterbalanced by the exchange rate at which monies could be remitted to the UK. At that stage bonds and stocks comprised 93.66% of investments.

A year later the exchange rate was still providing some support for remittances from America but revenue was under pressure as a result of the war. The shareholders learned that, 'During the year there has been requisitioned by the Treasury a considerable part of the Company's American interests, the replacement of which by equally remunerative investments here presents some difficulty at the present time. This is but one of the many factors now operating adversely to revenue, and the immediate outlook therefore must be regarded as uncertain.'

There was also a problem of placing a realistic value on many of the investments and there was a similar problem with what remained of the mortgage business.

At the shareholders meeting in 1942 the chairman said quite plainly that the situation that had prevailed in 1939 was entirely changed. Nearly all of the American investments had been sold off and those that were left had been lent to the Treasury to provide security for a loan from the United States. In 1939 less than 20% of the company's funds had been invested in the US. Virtually nothing was left.

He regretted that the worldwide spreading of risks, which had been the hallmark of company policy, was no longer in evidence. He went on to admit that it had not afforded that 'measure of protection which might be claimed for it in times of peace'. Wartime necessities had dictated the surrender of the American assets but the turn of events had moved the company to lighten its investments in other parts of the world. Consequently the current position was that the revenue-earning assets of the company were, almost entirely, concentrated in the UK and the Empire. This had impacted on revenues, as had the investments in war bonds, which paid lower rates of interest than the company had been accustomed to receiving on its investments.

Notwithstanding this rather glum report the chairman was able to say that revenues were almost as high as the previous year and that the dividend would be maintained at its former level. The impact of taxation, however, meant that only £75,000 would be added to the contingent fund compared to £100,000 in 1941.

Prain went on to regret the difficulty of providing accurate valuations of the investments but he did express the personal opinion that they were broadly in line with book value.

The war was not going well and Prain told the shareholders what the consequences would be if India, Ceylon and Australia fell to the Japanese. If they fell then the loss, added to existing losses on investments in Japan, the Malay Archipelago and Burma, would be equivalent to about 5% on the ordinary shares of the company. The company would be able to absorb this without too much difficulty. But it was much harder to gauge what the effects of the loss of India, Ceylon and Australia would be on the British companies that traded in these countries.

Valuations for the mortgage business were even more problematical but there had been some good sales of larger estates which enhanced the profit figures. What remained of this business, however, were mostly poor quality lands that, together with penal rates of US tax on land held by foreign corporations, made sales at almost any price highly desirable. The only glimmer of hope for the mortgage business was the prospect of oil revenues from land that had been sold but in which the company had reserved the mineral rights.

At the meeting in 1943 Prain maintained the line that it was not possible to provide a realistic valuation for investments. Whilst stock market prices might suggest that there had been some forward movement, Prain took great pains to impress upon his shareholders that this movement was chimerical and was based on an officially controlled interest rate and on the drying up of overseas investment opportunities leading to the repatriation of money, which heightened the level of demand for British investments. Consequently no reliance could be placed on these values. Alliance policy remained to invest in companies from which a good dividend stream could be relied upon.

There was little to be said at the meeting in 1944 except that good harvests in North America, and high demand, had resulted in raised revenues and more of the company's real estate had been sold at rewarding prices. When the annual general meeting came round in April 1945, peace, and a winnable war, were widely anticipated. Consequently Prain's statement to the shareholders looked to the future. What he said was highly political but it is clear that feelings in Britain's boardrooms were not in harmony with the shifts that were taking place in the political landscape.

Prain called for realism in dealing with the economic problems that Britain would face after the war. The fact that many of Britain's overseas assets had been sold to pay for the war meant that foreign earnings would be greatly reduced. Consequently the need to export was vital to Britain's economic survival.

It was clear that 'the maintenance of productive efficiency is of the first importance' and 'capital must be forthcoming to provide the most modern equipment'. Prain felt that 'Too little attention is paid to this aspect . . . in our post-war planning which so far has been concerned more with unproductive expenditure, surely a matter of secondary importance.' Doubtless this was an allusion to the social reforms that had been announced, but it may also have referred to the maintenance of Empire on which much British resource was expended.

Prain believed that Britain's principal competitors understood these points, especially in the US where labour productivity was higher than in the UK. 'In this country the effect of legislation has been to starve industry of the funds it should have retained for its maintenance and development.' Capital investment had been 'discouraged'. Some improvement in provision for depreciation had been made but not enough. Overall he felt strongly that government was more concerned with 'dividing the golden eggs than with keeping the goose alive'.

In the post-war world these were indeed the themes that would dominate the political and economic scene for many years. Much of British industry's capital equipment was in poor condition after the war, labour productivity was modest, the balance of payments was adverse and the cost of social policy required what many saw as punitive rates of taxation.

Chapter 8
The McCurrach Years: 1945–1980

Part 1 1945–52

The coming of peace after six years of war found the Alliance Trust in better condition than many of its competitors. Having managed to divest itself of much of its earlier mortgage business it had entered the war with a relatively small amount of its funds invested in the US. During the conflict it had managed to sell many of its investments in what became the main theatres of war. It had found safe homes for its funds in UK and British Empire investments. It had managed to maintain its dividend at pre-war levels. It was, however, entering a new age in which new thinking, new ways of working and new relationships would be required.

Yet if the Trust was in reasonable shape the same could not be said for the British economy, which had been seriously weakened by the war. Moreover the economies of most countries in Europe were in ruins. It was clear from an early stage that the US would emerge from the war both richer and more important strategically, and that these gains would be achieved, at least in part, at the UK's expense. The agreement that Britain had entered with the US in 1942 for lend-lease ensured that, whatever emerged after the war, it would be a system that ensured greater free trade and capital movement. The UK and US were of a single mind that what was needed was a system that would ensure a smooth-running international trade and payments mechanism. They believed that the enormous foreign exchange fluctuations of the interwar years had done much to destabilise countries and make war more likely. So their desire to see a stable and open international trade and payments system was as much to do with the maintenance of peace as it was with the need to promote economic development. Out of their deliberations at Bretton Woods in 1944, where 42 other countries joined them, emerged the International Monetary Fund and the International Bank for Reconstruction and Development. It took some time for these institutions to become established and effective, and the needs of some countries for assistance were pressing. Consequently the US established the Marshall Plan in 1947 which provided assistance to many European countries, including the UK.

A Labour government had been elected in the UK immediately after the war. Given the popularity of Winston Churchill as a war leader his defeat at the polls was a surprise to many people. But others reasoned that the war had been won because the government, that Churchill had led, had been one that had taken firm control of the economy. If success on that scale could be achieved in wartime then there was a case to be made for arguing that government management of the economy might be just as successful in peacetime. Consequently a Labour government, dedicated to the nationalisation of several key industries and the creation of a welfare state, won the post-war election.

It took several years before Britain began to recover from wartime damage, and in the meantime the business community set about the process of rebuilding. There were those who foresaw imminent disaster for the British economy while others were of a more sanguine disposition. In 1947 MacDougall was not to be found in the ranks of the pessimists, but saw himself as a realist. 'While I do not subscribe to the prophecies of imminent catastrophe, failure to achieve the necessary level of production within the next two years will result in a very serious state of affairs and a drift to a lower level of the whole national life.' In the event he saw only half of the picture that was to emerge. For while the British economy went through many difficulties in the years to come it was also the case that living standards rose, employment was maintained at historically high levels and the performance of investment trusts exceeded the expectations of most people.

People and Economy

Before any post-war economic changes began to impress themselves on the Alliance Trust there were some significant alterations to the board and staff. Most organisations had managed their way through the war by making use of older employees, by doubling up roles and by employing temporary staff, including retirees and women. It was inevitable therefore that major changes would follow the declaration of peace, and Alliance Trust was no exception. Older men wanted to retire and places had to be found for younger men returning from the war.

MacDougall, who was then in his seventies, showed no signs of being prepared to make way for new blood. However, the chairman, James Prain, died in November 1945 and MacDougall was offered, and accepted, the role. At that point he resigned as manager, after 34 years of active service, leaving Alan Brown in charge on a daily basis. David McCurrach came back from Washington in 1946 and was appointed as Brown's assistant manager. Brown then relinquished the role of company secretary, and James F. Nicoll, a long-serving member of the Trust's staff, was appointed to that post. Ralph Fyfe Smith became his assistant. At the same time another long-serving staffer, Ernest Fleming – who had looked after the mortgage side of the business – retired.

Retirees, especially those with long service, participated in an informal pension scheme that was paid out of annual revenues. Long-serving retirees could look forward to receiving two-thirds of their retiring salary as a pension. But many companies had begun to establish formal pension plans for their staff that were properly funded and professionally managed. In March 1949 the Alliance board decided that it would follow suit, and Standard Life was approached to devise a scheme. The initial arrangement was open to all male staff over the age of 25 and under 60 who had at least one year's service. There were, at first, 13 members. The scheme was also open to women aged 30 to 55 who had at least three years' service, but the five women who worked for Alliance were all under 30. There were a further six men on the staff but five of them were about to retire and separate provision would have to be made for them. The pension was based on an average of the last five years' service, with pensioners receiving 1/60th of that average for each year of service. It was a non-contributory scheme and members were expected to retire when they reached the age of 65. The fund was established by May 1949 with Prain, McCurrach and Fyfe Smith as trustees.

There were a few changes on the company board. MacDougall's appointment as chairman was confirmed at the annual general meeting in April 1946. T.J. Carlyle Gifford, from Baillie Gifford, the man who had sold Britain's assets in America, then became a director. His appointment, together with those of Brown and McCurrach meant that there were now three Baillie Gifford men in the Alliance Trust hierarchy. This, however, was a connection that worked in both directions, as MacDougall had been on the board of Baillie Gifford from 1922. When he died in 1951 McCurrach took his place and served until 1982.

T.H.H. Walker's appointment to the board was short lived. He joined in 1945, but he last attended a board meeting in May 1946 and died a few months later. It was clear that the board had to be strengthened, and it was – first by the appointment of John Murray Prain, jute spinner and manufacturer in Dundee, and then by the addition of Sir George Cunningham. Harold Sharp, who had served from 1938 died in 1949 and was replaced by Col. Hugh B Spens, CBE, DSO.

Whilst he was manager MacDougall showed every sign of being the loyal company man – professional, hard working and quiet. But in his role as chairman he became vociferous and straight talking. His annual reports to the shareholders were full of forthright challenges to government policies and, at the same time, demands that government should do more to assist the economy. It was evident that the post-war Labour government of Clement Atlee would be interventionist to a far greater extent than any pre-war government. There was much talk of plans for the nationalisation of key industries, and many of the wartime controls on interest rates, dividends and rationing were not relaxed as quickly as many people in the business community would have wished.

MacDougall, naturally, was especially concerned about the efficient working of the capital markets. Controls on dividends, he felt, were unfair, particularly in a period of high taxation. In 1946 he said that, 'if the State intends to take the lion's share of the profits normally falling to the ordinary shareholder and leave to the latter the major part of the risk, these issues of ordinary shares under official sanction are not consistent with the accepted principles of fair dealing'.

But he was also concerned about grander matters. In 1948 he was worried that the government did not have sufficient control over its budget and that the country was in danger of living beyond its means. Although the Trust was doing well MacDougall was conscious of the fact that the performances of the Trust, and the national economy, were inextricably linked: '... it is no exaggeration to say that in the absence of aid under the Marshall Plan, this country would face in a matter of weeks a financial and economic crisis without parallel in its modern history. In the light of these grave adverse factors I should be remiss if I did not sound a note of caution and give a warning that our results of the past year may not be repeated.'

With this in mind Alliance began to rebuild its investments in the United States. 'The wide spreading of risks which was always regarded as the foundation of an Investment Trust's stability has been much restricted by the course of events in recent years, and in particular, in this country [the UK], by the encroachment of the State into a number of important fields of investment: if only for this reason we regard the increase in our interest in the

United States as a sound addition to the Company's portfolio.'

The British economy was in such a parlous state that the pound sterling was devalued in September 1949 from $4.03 to $2.80. Many other countries quickly followed this action but the dollar held firm and the devaluation was widely regarded as a success in giving the UK economy a more realistic exchange rate that would help to improve its balance of payments.

When the annual general meeting was held in April 1950 the benefits of devaluation had not filtered through and, although the value of sterling securities had fallen, the all-important dividends had held up well. MacDougall continued to sound a cautious note. Yet revenues continued to rise. At the shareholders meeting in 1951 it was announced that total revenues were almost £1million and the board recommended that the ordinary share dividend be increased from 33% to 40%. Notwithstanding this increase it was still possible to add £150,000 to general reserve and leave a substantial sum to be carried forward on the profit and loss account. MacDougall attributed much of the improvement to the increased portion of the funds that were invested in the United States but devaluation had helped, as had the implementation of double taxation relief on foreign earnings.

The Korean War also gave a boost to the economy but, in MacDougall's view, it was the wrong kind of boost. A year earlier he had hoped for 'signs of a return to more normal conditions in which one might expect a freer interplay of purely economic forces and some stability of money values'. He did not relish the fact that government needed to commandeer a large part of the country's material resources, nor did he savour the inevitable inflationary surge that this would give to the economy. He was concerned that this would lead to 'shortages, controls, rationing, increased taxation and even greater inflationary pressures'. In such conditions it was incumbent upon the Trust's management to try to take account of all of these distortions and pressures in the real economy and, in the process, to attempt to improve the Trust's income flow and its security.

MacDougall had attended his last annual general meeting. He died on 25 March 1952. He was 80. Nevertheless the report that he had drafted, and the board had approved, was circulated, as normal, with the annual accounts. He had been with the company for over 40 years and his colleagues recorded their 'deep sense of loss both of his wisdom and of the genial warmth of his personality'.

Despite his worries about the state of the economy MacDougall left the company in a strong condition. Revenues had exceeded £1m for the first time and the ordinary share dividend was increased from 40% to 50%. In view of this it was decided to issue 1,050,000 new shares as a scrip issue by capitalising reserves. Even so, MacDougall's natural pessimism had not left him, and his last word was about the 'grave uncertainty' facing the company and the country.

Notwithstanding the contributions to the post-war company made by MacDougall and Brown, it was McCurrach who made the greatest advances. He returned from his wartime duties in Washington in 1946 and remained with the company until 1982. At some point in his long career he committed his thoughts on the post-war company to paper. It rather looks as if he typed it himself, and only part of it has survived, but the fragment that still exists gives a trenchant and hard-headed view of the state of the company in 1946.

McCurrach took the view that the company faced some 'stark realities', all of which 'created barriers against the development of anything like coherent policies'. He was especially concerned that there was no research organisation within the company and that staff resources were wasted, as he saw it, in doing all the dividend and registration work manually. They also factored the large half-yearly terminable debentures. Although staff numbers had returned to their pre-war levels he did not feel that this kind of work was an appropriate use of their time. There was still sufficient left of the old mortgage business to consume the energies of three members of staff. To set up a research department, however, would cost money, and McCurrach was ever mindful of the pride that his company took in the modesty of its operating costs. In 1949 comparisons were made with the expense ratios of other trusts and the board confessed itself to be quietly pleased with the results.

He also commented on the fact that the company was 'highly geared' – a term that came to be used pejoratively but which, for most trusts, was the norm. For if the investment returns exceeded the debenture and short loan interest payments, which they usually did, then the dividend payable to the ordinary shareholders could be so much greater. McCurrach also took the view that this gearing was more apparent than real, as Alliance held fixed-interest investments in its portfolio that were approximately the same amount as the fixed-interest liabilities on its own balance sheet. In effect they balanced one another, albeit that the returns on the assets exceeded the payments on the liabilities.

These were vital considerations for investment houses, and the manner in which investment managers made their calculations were becoming ever more sophisticated. Alan Brown had a hand in inventing 'priority percentages' which calculated what percentage of revenues was attributable to each of the groups expecting a return from their investments. Brown was influential in persuading the rating agency, Standard and Poor's, to use them in their service cards.

Given that there was no research department, McCurrach found it remarkable that the company had over 1,400 different investments. At 31 January 1947 there were more than 660 fixed-interest and 750 equity investments. He took the view that this reflected a board and management structure that was 'to use the most flattering epithet, most curious'. The board may have had an officially minuted monthly meeting but in fact it met daily before lunch so that the directors were involved in every decision before, or as, it was taken. Consequently 'almost the whole morning was taken up preparing for the meeting, digesting the news from our multitudinous holdings and all the other news of the day. Even visiting brokers were occasionally admitted.'

There were a number of other issues upon which he commented in his paper. He was also preoccupied with the thought that there was no revenue estimate or forward cash forecast, and while actual cash collections were occasionally reported, it usually took several days to reconcile them to the investments before they revealed any real meaning. He was also greatly in favour of a change to the tax status of the organisation that would see it taxed as an investment trust. He was especially worried that the US tax position, especially with the introduction of double taxation relief, was not well understood. It particular he was concerned that his colleagues in Dundee did not know that Barrow, Wade, Guthrie – the company's US accountants – did not offer tax counsel. In the US this was left to specialist tax lawyers. Consequently no one had a defined responsibility for tax affairs in North America.

McCurrach may have been the assistant manager but the responsibility that he assumed for addressing the problems that he had identified went far beyond the power implied in his job title. He was particularly well placed to address the taxation issues as he had been involved, albeit peripherally, in the drafting of the double taxation agreement when he was still in Washington. Consequently he understood the benefits that the system was intended to provide for British investors in the US – benefits that had been ignored by most of the British financial press. So, while the tax position for investment in the US might have been favourable, the same could not be said for the capital position. The obstacle to the pursuit of a successful investment policy in the US was the existence of the dollar pool from which British investors had to buy any dollars, usually at a premium over normal exchange rates, before they could acquire assets in the US. The Alliance board took a bit of persuading that it would be worth paying the premium. Consequently their initial forays into the US market were, in McCurrach's view, somewhat tentative. These investments were conducted through Buckmaster and Moore in New York. The purchases were in the leading equities and in McCurrach's view, 'in far too modest quantities'.

At the same time as all this was under discussion at the board the British economy was clearly in difficulties, and people began to talk about the threat of devaluation. By the summer of 1948 foreign countries were shorting sterling in the expectation that devaluation would happen sooner or later. One senior member of the board regarded it as an act of disloyalty to even talk about the possibility of devaluation, but it happened in September 1949. Its effect was to increase the value of the Trust's US holdings.

Some of the other issues which McCurrach had outlined in his paper were relatively easily addressed. The lack of revenue estimates was perhaps the simplest to deal with, and there was soon in existence a system for estimating forthcoming revenues and for sharing information around the company.

The daily meeting of directors was soon dispensed with, first by reducing the meetings to two a week – Tuesdays and Fridays – and then by eliminating the Tuesday meeting.

It was a much more difficult task to weed out many of the smaller investment holdings and, in so doing, to reduce the total number to more manageable proportions. The market for many of these smaller companies was thin and it took some time to get them off the books. This reduction in the range of the portfolio was also conducted against a background of a debate about the proportion of investments that should be held in preference stocks.

The question over the company's gearing was more easily settled. The growth in the value of assets and earnings, and changing attitudes towards gearing, actually led to the issue of new debenture stocks to restore the ratio of borrowing to ordinary shares.

The absence of a research department was a more vexatious problem for McCurrach. He took the view that neither MacDougall nor Brown liked new faces. The exclamation mark that he added to the fact that MacDougall was re-elected chairman at the age of 79 indicates that he felt new blood was required. There were a number of 'old friends around doing the purely routine statistical work'. McCurrach clearly had ambitions for the organisation and, in doing so, may well have been ahead of his time, as most investment trusts were run in much the same way. The discipline of investment analysis was only beginning to emerge and some years would pass before McCurrach realised his ambition of having an investment research department.

Until that happened he personally filled the role of investment analyst. His regular papers for the board were often masterpieces of precision and concision. Nor did he confine his research to investment matters. He thought deeply about the macroeconomic environment and about how changes might impact on Alliance. In a paper dated December 1948, for example, he stress tested the company's position vis-à-vis its short-term borrowings. His primary concern was to see what would happen if all these deposits were withdrawn, but when he looked closely at the situation he was satisfied that the company had sufficient cash and 'near money' assets to deal with such an eventuality. The situation was helped by the fact that investments in the United States were settled in three days and could therefore be regarded as near money. In his paper McCurrach went on to examine the likely impact of such threats as a home political crisis, an international crisis, runaway inflation, government action to restrict credit and a moderate depression. He was persuaded that the Alliance Trust could ride out storms such as these. But crises such as a wholesale economic collapse or a general moratorium were doomsday scenarios.

Changes to the Companies Acts were passed in 1947 and 1948 and these made substantial differences to the ways in which many companies conducted their business. Shareholders were then entitled to much more information about the companies in which they had invested. In the case of investment trusts this enabled them to establish the net asset value (NAV) and the discount at which their shares traded. They were also to be provided with consolidated accounts.

Investments

When the war came to an end the board's mind-set might be described as 'getting back to normal', so there was no immediately perceptible change in the investment strategy. The board continued to analyse company reports. At a meeting in November 1945 they examined seven companies, including Montague Burton, Herbert Morris and South African Distilleries and Wines. They also continued their very long-term strategy of building up a large stake in the Dundee-run Matador Land and Cattle Company, of which MacDougall was chairman.

There was, however, a growing realisation that the world had changed and that getting back to the way the world had been was not an option. MacDougall began to think and talk about future investment policy. Changes in consumer taste, demand and supply issues, technological discoveries and movements of labour were all, in MacDougall's view, likely to change the nature and composition of the economy. 'And over and above these comparatively lesser uncertainties there hang, in the international sphere, the threat of general inflation, and, in the domestic sphere, the enigma of Socialist Government Policies.'

As the economy struggled to get back to normal after the hostilities there was a rush of new share issues and, in 1945, Alliance participated in the underwriting of shares for Standard Motors and Singer Motors. The following year they participated in the underwriting for many of the big British companies and some of the smaller ones: British Celanese; English Electric; Granada Theatres; Grosvenor House; Guest, Keen and Nettlefolds; Selfridge; Tayside Floorcloth; Tennant Bros., and several others. In 1947 it was the turn of Bowater Paper; de Havilland Aircraft; Davy Engineering and Thomas de la Rue.

It was also a time to cleanse the stable, and although there was a very modest payment on the Baku Consolidated Oilfields ordinary shares, which had been purchased before the First World War, the other shares in that company were written off as having no value. The Glasgow American Trust was in voluntary liquidation and these shares were also written off as being worthless.

Until this time the ordinary shares of Alliance had been quoted as £100 units, but in 1947 permission was sought from the London, Edinburgh and Dundee stock exchanges to trade the shares as £1 units. This was eventually agreed but not before a somewhat labyrinthine administrative process had been undertaken.

It was also an appropriate time to approach the Inland Revenue for a change in the Trust's basis of taxation. This move had been contemplated in 1928–9 but rejected. The change meant that 'capital losses and profits would be omitted in future from the Income Tax computations, provided the mortgage and real estate business was transferred to a subsidiary company'. Alliance Trust would henceforth be taxed as a pure investment trust, i.e. on revenues received. The directors believed that this move would ultimately be of benefit to the company, and the management was asked to make the necessary arrangements to meet the requirements of the Inland Revenue. McCurrach was especially keen on the idea. He believed that, notwithstanding recent increases in share values, they would go on increasing making it difficult to establish losses to minimise tax liabilities.

McCurrach believed that 'The swing to the left in Governments through-

out the world would appear to have, as a necessary consequence, a continuously rising trend in wages and prices accompanied by pressure to reduce the
earning power and cost of capital and the scope for investment.' His paper
concluded with the statement that, 'from every point of view, therefore, other
than the risk of a new Capital Gains Tax, the advantage appears to lie in a
change of status'.

One of the reasons for revisiting the decision not to change the taxation
regime in 1929 was because taxation at that time was only levied if the whole
holding in a particular investment was sold, making it wise to sell a large part
of a holding but not the whole thing. This seriously minimised the tax liability,
even if it meant that investment companies were left holding large numbers
of small-holdings. This position was changed in 1937 when the Inland Revenue
withdrew this concession.

The transition to the new arrangements was not achieved without
difficulty. It was a highly significant change with many implications and it was
therefore a time to proceed cautiously. Opinions were received from King's
Counsel and from the London lawyers, Linklaters and Paine, which raised
difficulties, and the change was not accomplished until 1948 when the Inland
Revenue made some concessions. McCurrach paid particular tribute to the
assistance provided by Sir Arthur Fforde who conducted the negotiations with
the Inland Revenue and who did 'a miraculous job'. Changes to the
memorandum and articles of association would not be required. Nor was there
a need to set up a subsidiary company to manage what remained of the
mortgage business. The delay had been caused by the possibility that, in
making the change, there would have to be recalculations of prior years'
taxation. Fforde asked that Alliance assemble a substantial analysis of all transactions in years past that would be sufficiently persuasive to impress the
Revenue that, in every respect, the Alliance had conducted its affairs like a
normal investment trust. In the end the Inland Revenue agreed that no
reassessment of prior years would be required because the tax to be paid on
capital gains for the last two years approximated to what would have to be
paid if the last seven years were to be reassessed under the new arrangements.
McCurrach described this as a 'long, laborious and extremely tense process
and its vital importance for the future of the company, one might almost
suggest its continuance as a Trust, cannot be exaggerated'.

There was, however, a need to change the memorandum and articles of
association to allow the company to establish and administer its new pension
fund for employees.

There was very little left of the mortgage business, although net profit from real estate was recorded in 1949 as £7,582. Nevertheless the business was still sufficiently large for the US tax authorities to recognise Alliance Trust as a US resident. This produced tax benefits – it exempted the company from the 15% withholding tax – and enhanced the rate of return on American investments, with benefits to the company and the balance of payments. In the middle of 1948 money was still being brought back from New York and Montreal. But there would soon be a renewed interest in American investments, notwithstanding that the exchange control regulations had brought about an investment currency pool which meant that companies wishing to invest overseas had to buy dollars from this pool. An excess of demand over supply of investment money meant that there was usually a premium to be paid for the currency.

Notwithstanding the existence, and price, of the dollar pool, there began to be renewed interest in investment in the United States. Brown went there in the closing months of 1947. His main reason for going was to visit the agencies and he went to Winnipeg, Portland, Fort Worth, Dallas and San Antonio. The principal role of these agencies was now to manage the mineral rights that had been retained when real estate was sold, although small amounts of land remained on the agencies' books. As a result of his visit the company gave up its licence to conduct business in Arkansas. A little later the certificates of authority to do business in Mississippi and Missouri were also relinquished. It was 1950 before the authority to do business in Oregon was relinquished, as all the real estate there had been sold.

McCurrach, with his greater knowledge of the United States, was keen for Alliance to restart investing in American companies. Brown seems to have been warming to the idea. While he was in the US Bankers Trust in New York advised that they wished to reduce their loan to Alliance. This caused something of a rethink about the strategy. A growing number of US companies were being quoted on the London Stock Exchange, and Alliance opened an account with the Bank of Montreal's London office for the 'purpose of handling the company's purchases of American Stocks on the London market'.

The changes in tax status and renewed interest in investments was accompanied by a serious rethink about the company's cash and short-term borrowings position, and how it was managed. There was a long-established practice of acquiring short-term borrowings from banks and local businesses. This was a very cheap means of raising funds, as funds could be acquired for between 1% and 1.5%. But, in December 1948, the board reviewed a paper which suggested that these borrowings might give an inaccurate impression to investors of the state of the company. The board however took the view that this was a long established practice, that investors knew about it and, therefore, there was no need to alter established business practice, especially as the company held short-dated British government securities to cover the bank borrowings. Nevertheless they did decide that rules had to be established. They determined to limit the amount of its short-term borrowings to £750,000 and that no more than 10% of borrowings should come from any one lender. It is doubtful if this last suggestion was ever put into practice as, a few months later, a call loan facility of £150,000 was negotiated with the Bank of Montreal.

The Bank of Montreal and Bankers Trust were approached with a view to 'obtaining assurances of their support [on the security of dollar and sterling investments deposited with them] in the event of need arising for sudden substantial short loan calls'. In effect the prospect of short-term borrowings being needed in a hurry was slight as the minutes recorded that 'In recent months the enquiries for short loans have exceeded the amount which it has been deemed necessary to accept.'

The position at the end of November 1948 is revealed in Table 8.1 (a) and 8.1 (b).

The short-term money coming from local industries came from a wide variety of sources but the bulk came from just a few companies:

The rates for terminable debentures were 2% for two years and 2¾% for five-year money. Clearly if money could be borrowed at from 1% for short loans and 2¾% for debentures then, given the average 4.5% returns that could be made on investments, it would have been a very myopic fund manager who failed to see the opportunity for profit. In the Alliance's own case the surplus made by taking short-term borrowings was enough to pay all the management expenses.

The paper presented to the board concluded that 'the only circumstances where any serious embarrassment could arise are runaway inflation or total economic collapse'. It went on to say that the policy could only work well because of the 'day-to-day contacts of the management with local industrialists . . . afforded a degree of protection on that account through forewarning of the intentions of lenders'. To add even greater security it was suggested that bank loans be obtained from a wider range of banks.

The ability to borrow on short loans and terminable debentures gave Alliance the ability and flexibility to acquire investments whenever opportunities presented themselves. Yet there are indications that investment strategy

Table 8.1 (a) Short term borrowings at 30 November 1948

	£
UK bank loans	226,000
Short loans	606,000
Total call Loans	£832,000
Terminable debentures	1,803,000
Total short term borrowings	£2,635,000
Value of gilt edged holdings	£227,000

Total call borrowing and cost of interest (excluding NY)		Gross interest (£)
606,000	Short loans at 1%	6,060
112,500	Bankers Trust overdraft at 1.5%	1,687
47,060	Bankers Trust overdraft at 1¾%	825
67,300	Royal Bank overdraft	2,019
£832,860	Total short loans	£10,591

Table 8.1 (b) Local industry sources of short-term borrowings
at 30 November 1948

	Source		Largest
Jute	£153,000	Jute Industries Ltd	£65,000
Coal	65,000	Coltness	£25,000
Linoleum	105,000	Nairn	£75,000
Miscellaneous	203,000	DP&L (shipping)	£70,000
Pension funds	20,000	Jute Compensation Fund	£20,000

was anything but opportunistic. On the contrary, the carefully considered and well researched papers that McCurrach prepared for the board indicate a careful, well-considered and professional approach to money management. One of the earliest papers that he produced, before spending the war years in America, was on the American company Climax Molybdenum, an alloy producer. The report discussed the demand for the product, the past performance of the company, the competition and the political environment – all on two pages. He was particularly aware of the competition from other alloys, especially tungsten, much of which came from China. However, in view of the Sino-Chinese war, he was afraid that the Japanese might dump their product on the market to raise foreign exchange and so produce unwanted competition for Climax Molybdenum.

When McCurrach returned to Dundee in 1946 he possessed immense knowledge of the American economy. The first paper that he produced was on the rubber industry. In it he evidenced not only a well-considered opinion on the likely demand for rubber but a detailed knowledge of the condition of the Malaysian estates where it was produced. He was aware that the shares were likely to be the subject of speculation and recommended that Alliance's rubber shares should be sold. He was also acutely aware that, as the largest consumer, the US held 'a very big stick which she may not be too much inclined to keep behind her back'.

But if his knowledge of American business was second to none, his understanding of British conditions was somewhat dated. The matter was soon remedied by a visit to London in May 1946. Doubtless, in view of his American experience, the London financiers were just as keen to meet him as he was to meet them. He visited Greenwells; Capel, Cure; Earnshaw, Green; Cazenove; Laing and Cruikshank; Hoare; De Zoete and Gordon; and Myers, as well as a number of more minor houses.

The discussions ranged over a myriad of companies as well as over matters of international significance. The London investment houses were worried, for example, that General Peron might nationalise Argentina's railways, but in view of the deteriorating financial position in the country, the prospect was thought to be receding, which made the bonds more attractive.

McCurrach was back in London later that year for further discussions with his contemporaries. Companies under consideration included Debenhams, Universal Asbestos, Whiteways Cider, Pressed Steel, Beechams, Rank and Great Universal Stores. Some of McCurrach's contacts expressed the view that Isaac Wolfson, who had established Great Universal Stores, was a brilliant man, but they were worried that he had become a 'one-man-show' and might overreach himself. This view was not universally held.

By the summer of 1948 the policy of purchasing shares in American companies was underway. Shares were acquired in the London market in Boston Edison, Brown Brothers, Caterpillar Tractor, International Harvester and Sears Roebuck. Added to this were US treasury bonds. Most of these investments were in common (i.e. ordinary) stock. In a somewhat convoluted book-keeping entry, these acquisitions were quoted in the books as New York prices converted at the rate of $4.88 : £1.

Shares were also acquired in New York, but not before the Bank of England gave its permission for the reinvestment of company dollars that had been acquired through repayment of mortgages and real estate sales.

These American purchases did not preclude other acquisitions and, at the same time, shares were purchased in British, and British-controlled companies, including Albion Motors, Bowater's Newfoundland Pulp and Paper Mills, Cunard, Nyasaland Railways and Whitbread Breweries.

At the annual general meeting in 1949 the distribution of assets still showed a heavy concentration in the UK. Although there had been some forward movement in the acquisition of American securities they still comprised less than 9% of the portfolio.

An attempt to increase the company's borrowing in New York in 1950 was halted when the Bank of England refused to give permission.

Later that year McCurrach paid a visit to the United States where he

Table 8.2 Distribution of investments by region, April 1949

	Fixed interest %	Equities %	Totals %
United Kingdom	26.88	49.88	76.76
British Empire	1.85	7.14	8.99
USA	0.94	7.21	8.15
Latin America	1.39	1.26	2.65
Europe	0.57	0.75	1.32
Other	1.06	1.07	2.13
	32.69	67.31	100.00

renewed old acquaintances and took the opportunity to ascertain their views on the political situation and the state of the American economy. The papers that he wrote on his return are both wide-ranging and informative. They also urged caution. The United States was getting into election mode and Wall Street was worried about inflation. There were concerns that President Truman, in his enthusiasm to get re-elected, would buy prosperity at any price, although McCurrach thought that he would do the 'right thing' and choke off any inflationary boom. Wall Street was by no means unanimous in its views, with the brokers backing expansion and the bankers pursuing a more cautious line of argument.

The paper on the United States is all the more remarkable because it addresses issues that later came to be concerns in the United Kingdom. The bankers, for example, were worried about the entry into the market of large numbers of small investors. This was usually taken to be a danger signal because they tended to place their money in 'openended' trusts which, since they had to repay on demand, might compel the fund managers to sell large blocks of their holdings 'without regard to market consequences'. There were also concerns about the market becoming distorted because of the rapid growth of pension funds. 'This may lead the Life Assurance companies to press successfully for freedom to buy common stocks as the only way to invest all their funds'. If this happened the impact would be to give these funds a powerful and influential place in the stock markets. As time went on the position of unit trusts and pension funds in the UK had precisely the impact that McCurrach detected in the US markets in the 1940s.

McCurrach's intellectual approach was undoubtedly that of the open, enquiring mind which, when the evidence suggested it, he was prepared to change. The paper on the United States was quickly followed by one on Canada. It was twelve pages long and concluded that while the situation in Canada was improving there was still a need for caution. A copy of the paper was sent to the Trust's American bankers, the Bank of Montreal, where it was read by their chief economist, Mr Hackett. His response to McCurrach was sufficiently persuasive to impress upon him that his earlier view was too gloomy. Consequently 'on the grounds of spreading investment risk and good potentialities it is suggested that moderate purchases be made of high grade Canadian equities'.

McCurrach could be remarkably prescient. As early as 1951 he wrote a paper on the growing threat of Japanese manufacturing to British production. More often his papers stressed his firmly held belief that investment in the

United States would, in the long run, prove to be a sound idea. His paper on the US repeated his concern about the need to control inflation. This was also a worry in the UK. In October 1951 his paper on the forthcoming general election expressed the view that Labour government had not worked. He felt that there had been too many new policies and changes to existing policy. Consequently the recent rise in stock market prices had 'taken on the nature of a movement of despair – that a stake in real possessions, regardless of current yield prospects, was the only last resort against inflation. Thus, although the hope of a general election may have had some place in sentiment, the fact or prospect of inflation has constantly outweighed the extremely adverse political climate.' He went on to argue that if the Conservatives were elected they would deflate the economy so prices would fall and it would be sensible to sell equities. This was an argument for investing more in the United States although, if Conservative policies were successful, it might be the case that, in a year or two, this policy could be reversed.

In the closing months of 1951 McCurrach was impressed by the 'astonishing unanimity' of both parties in the US about the favourable prospects for long-term growth and stability. That fact, and the changing taxation regimes on both sides of the Atlantic, required a rethink of investment strategy. At that time the US strategy was to invest defensively in cyclical and growth stocks. McCurrach proposed that the American investments should henceforth be invested largely in growth stocks. This required some switching. The types of industry proposed for new investments included electrical manufacturing, electronics, office equipment, ethical drugs, rubber manufacturing, growth chemicals and crude oil. Switches were also proposed out of the defensive industries: tobacco, grocery chains, food manufacturing, shoes, household equipment and chemicals. It was also proposed to switch out of less progressive metropolitan utilities into utilities in growth areas. Quite simply, McCurrach felt that there was an opportunity to pursue a more adventurous investment strategy.

Overall this was a busy time for the executives and the board. In July 1949 the minutes recorded that since the last monthly meeting, Alliance had been involved in 30 new issues in addition to which there had been 25 purchases, 15 sales, 2 exchanges and 5 redemptions. The business was growing and a start was made in 1950 to buying back some additional space in the building in Reform Street. Alliance would eventually acquire the whole building.

In all this activity McCurrach was playing a more important role. As we have seen, he was the author of many of the board papers and research reports. It is clear that on matters of UK and US taxation he was the acknowledged expert. And when an extraordinary meeting of the shareholders of the Matador Land and Cattle Company was called in July 1951, to discuss a possible takeover, it was McCurrach who was sent to represent the Alliance. The Trust had been building up a large holding in the shares over many years, and at that time held 3,360 shares. It was to prove to be a highly profitable investment.

The Agencies

Notwithstanding that Alliance had given up the right to transact business in a number of American states, it nevertheless continued to hold rights to various mineral interests, especially oil. For this reason agents were still under contract in places where Alliance no longer held any real estate. Reade M. Ireland, for example, was still the agent in Portland.

Brown visited all the agencies in 1951 and reported to his board that he found them all to be in satisfactory condition. They had all been audited on a regular basis by Barrow, Wade, Guthrie and Co., but shortly afterwards that firm merged with Peat, Marwick and Mitchell. The relationship was then brought to an end and local firms of accountants were appointed to conduct audits in their own states. The amount of business being transacted in the agencies was quite small and it was no longer necessary to incur the expense of hiring a large firm of accountants to conduct the audits. Appointments were duly made in Winnipeg, Portland, Fort Worth, Dallas, San Antonio and Greenville.

However, an entirely different strategy was followed when it came to legal matters in the United States. The business was originally given to the New York lawyers Sherman, Sterling and Wright, who were recommended by the Bank of Montreal. It then went to the large New York firm of Debevoise, Plimpton and McLean, of 20 Exchange Place, one of whose partners was an expert on UK and US tax matters. They were appointed to file all state and federal tax returns. As time went on this firm became much more than a filer of returns. They became trusted advisers on many matters of interest to Alliance Trust and, in McCurrach's words, 'extracted us from some US tangles which had built up'. Unusually for a firm of lawyers they also undertook the collation of figures from the agencies.

The most active of the agents in this period was Tom Drought of the firm H.P. Drought and Co. in San Antonio, Texas. He made valiant efforts over many years to make something of the mineral rights that had been retained on the Chaves Grant. Most of the land had been sold to the US government in 1941, but Alliance retained a share of the mineral rights and it was these that Drought was determined to develop. There was quite a bit of interest from prospectors and speculators but the degree of their interest seemed to vary with the price of oil.

In 1945 Drought persuaded the hopefully named Richfield Oil Co. to take a lease on 6,400 acres. Before drilling they had to build a road into this remote area so that they could manoeuvre their rig into position. Once this was done they began drilling almost immediately and by the summer months weekly reports of progress were being received in Dundee. Excitement was rising but, as so often happened with these speculative developments, granite was struck at 7,143 feet and the well was abandoned. Richfield Oil submitted a quit claim and left.

Drought was still hopeful that other areas of the Chaves Grant might bear fruit, but he was sanguine enough to realise that Richfield's failure might deter others from making the effort.

Close behind Drought in terms of the efforts being made on Alliance's behalf was the agent in Greenville, Peter Barcroft, who rejoiced in the nickname 'Bones'. As the war came to a close Barcroft was able to report that the long-running Armstrong case had finally concluded, with Armstrong paying $97,000 to Alliance. The litigation had lasted for ten years.

Barcroft continued the good progress he had made in the war years in selling off real estate. By 1948 only the Cormier oil field and some of the Wyly lands remained on his books. He was of the view that these holdings would 'require nursing for a long time to come'. In addition there were two outstanding loans in Mississippi and one in Arkansas. He was asked to try and have the loans refinanced by another company. It took him a year but he eventually succeeded in getting other companies to acquire them.

Selling the remaining real estate soon became more problematical. MacDougall was keen to take the timber from it which, he reckoned, would make it more saleable, but Barcroft advised otherwise. This was because the cost of clearing the land was likely to be greater than the land was worth due to the expense of hiring machinery, which was in short supply, and the difficult labour market. The remaining parts of the Wyly lands were in relatively small lots and were scattered over a wide area where the roads were in poor condition. At least one prospective buyer came to look but was never seen again. In 1951 Barcroft appointed a local man, Noel Marcom, to look after the Alliance interests. Thieves had been stealing wood from the property and Marcom had caught them at it. Barcroft told him that he 'did not expect him to get himself shot over a wagon load of sawed wood'.

Both MacDougall and Barcroft were keen to hold onto the Cormier property, which was producing good amounts of oil in a rising market. Barcroft went for a site visit early in 1948 and reported to Dundee that government controls on production were not a major concern as the price of oil had been rising. The pressure in the wells was still what it had been several years earlier so they thought that they would go on producing for many years to come.

They were concerned, however, about the activities of the Texas Gulf Company that had put down a deep well on the edge of the Cormier property. It was decided to keep a watchful eye on this development and, if it produced oil, then a deep well would be put down adjacent to it on Cormier property 'to prevent them from draining off our oil'.

The relationship with Barcroft was businesslike but it was also friendly. The letters often contained personal references to games of golf that had been played, to families and to other personal matters. When Barcroft mentioned that his long-standing secretary was to retire in 1949 he hinted that Alliance might recognise her service in some way. Brown sent her a letter and a cheque for $800.

Part 2 1952–67

Economy

This period began with the economy feeling the effects of the programme of nationalisation that had taken place under Labour and with the impact of the Korean War. It also heralded the return of a Conservative government to power at Westminster. There were some who expected that this government, under Winston Churchill, would reverse the public ownership policies of Clement Attlee's Labour administration but it did not do so. It was, after all, a wartime economy, in which controls were necessary. Yet even after the Korean War came to an end there was no serious movement to privatise the nationalised industries.

There were other changes afoot that impacted on the British economy. The Empire began to be dismantled as country after country gained its independence. This had the effect of changing patterns of trade. Britain tended to suffer from a balance of payments deficit and the situation was not helped by former Empire members who took their trade elsewhere. Britain's economic difficulties were compounded by the fact that economic growth was trundling along at approximately half the rate experienced by other European countries.

Despite the difficulties, however, employment was maintained, as a matter of economic policy, at a historically high rate. There were labour shortages in some areas that led to growing rates of immigration. One consequence of this was that standards of living continued to improve and, as they did so, people bought the consumer goods that were increasingly available in the shops. The austerity of the wartime economy was left behind as the demand for comfort and convenience took over. The second consequence was that the need for capital grew and opportunities for investors developed at a speed that had never been experienced in the past.

A great boom in equities prices began in the US, quickly followed by the UK and other European countries. The boom went on, with minor interruptions, until 1968. Yet there were sufficient uncertainties in the economy, and sufficient problems, for chairmen of investment trusts to go on sounding their warning noises on an annual basis only to have to express their surprise at the continuation of the boom the following year. They knew, however, that one day it would come to an end. Before that happened, however, more than 40 new investment trusts were formed. It was becoming a very competitive market.

When the first Labour government under Harold Wilson was elected in 1964 it was already clear that there were mounting problems in the British economy. The balance of payments was at the heart of the difficulties, and various politicians, led by James Callaghan, attacked overseas portfolio investment as a major source of the payments imbalance. What followed was one of those periodic spats between those who criticised 'the City' for ignoring Britain's needs and those who took a contrary view and defended it. Lord Cromer, a member of the Baring family, pointed out that more money was coming home in dividends and repatriations than was going out. But the City's staunchest defender was Harold Wincott, writing in the *Financial Times* in February 1966:

> First, then, it seems to be sheer ignorance that is responsible, and here what we call 'the City' must be to blame. Secondly, there is the instinctive feeling that you have to have a massive industrial complex, employing a highly expensive chairman, dozens of multi-lingual

salesmen giving themselves ulcers chasing orders all over the world in planes, dirty great computers, tens of thousands of horny handed sons of toil working in factories, millions and millions of pounds of imported raw materials, before you are really 'worthwhile'.

Whatever the rest of us are to do, the leaders of the nation ought not to distort or misrepresent figures simply to justify age old prejudices or ignorance.

In a direct reference to the success of Alliance Trust he went on to remark how overseas commentators 'see how we deliberately set out to cripple people who can turn $2m. into $86m. in less than 20 years. They must think we're stark, staring mad.'

Government was not listening, and various taxation measures made life more difficult for investment trusts to the extent that in March 1967 the *Scotsman* recorded that investment trusts had taken a hammering and they could not be recommended to investors as it was widely expected that share prices would fall further due to the government's taxation policies.

People

McCurrach's hard work brought him promotion. He was appointed joint manager with Alan Brown in March 1952 – just a month before MacDougall died. Immediately following the announcement of MacDougall's death McCurrach was appointed to the board, while he and Brown continued as joint managers. Brown was also appointed to be chairman of the company. The next 20 years were to be the most remarkable that the company had ever experienced.

It was not an auspicious start for Brown as chairman. The UK and US were embroiled in the Korean War. These were worrying times. The war might have been on the far side of the world but it was an ideological conflict between the forces of communism and capitalism represented on one hand by Russia and China, and, on the other, by the United Nations. Although the war ended in stalemate in 1953 there was always the concern that it might escalate into a nuclear war. While war might be good for some types of businesses, it had the effect of diverting economies away from long-term investment in companies which were likely to pay increasing dividends over the long term – which was what interested most investment trusts.

When the Korean War came to an end, western economies settled into a remarkably long period of sustained growth that was reflected in rising stock market prices and enhanced dividends. Most fund managers had a natural disposition to be cautious, and there were many who believed that this period of growth would not last. However, relatively full employment and rising living standards ensured that it did. And while the American economy made faster progress than most others it was not long before European economies, including the UK, also settled into a period of sustained growth. It was, therefore, a time of great opportunity for fund managers.

At the board meeting on 29 August 1952 there was a full attendance. None of the directors had served before the Second World War. The board then comprised:

A.L. Brown
T.J.C. Gifford
J. Murray Prain
Sir George Cunningham
Col. Hugh B. Spens
D.F. McCurrach

It was an important meeting. In addition to the normal investment business the board gave serious consideration to its involvement in underwriting. The traditional practice had been to participate in whatever the London issuing houses were offering. But as there had recently been only small financial gains from this activity they decided that the past policy of maintaining 'an active underwriting position should cease and that in future only manifestly sound offers should be accepted without regard to the effect which this new policy may have upon goodwill in the new issue business'. This was undoubtedly a measure of the Trust's growing strength and importance in financial markets. The fact that it could take this decision and not concern itself if it got left out of future issuing business is some measure of its high standing in financial markets.

Brown then went off on sick leave for three months, leaving Gifford to chair the meetings. Brown returned to his duties as executive chairman the following January. Decisions about what to buy and sell seem to have been made by him and McCurrach. The role of other board members is unclear, although it is known that, for some time, conversations took place with them on a very regular basis and that some would drop into the office almost every day. It is likely that with men of the stature of Gifford on the board, their role would have been highly influential. Only the formal board meetings were recorded in the minutes and in those the directors received a list of purchases, sales, rights issues and other transactions that had taken place since their last meeting.

From time to time they gave consideration to the direction of company policy and, before a decision was made, they would consider a paper on the subject. Most of these were written by McCurrach. In July 1954, for example, the minutes record that, 'A memo. giving a comprehensive study of the relative sizes of the Company's major Investments that had been circulated was examined and discussed. A number of suggestions for increased holdings were made and it was agreed in general that the United States individual holdings could be considerably enlarged at suitable times.' This decision was made despite the fact that the dollar premium that had to be paid for investment funds was then fluctuating between 14% and 16%.

McCurrach and Brown seem to have worked well together. Their partnership continued until Brown's death in 1967. Given the renewed commitment to investment in North America, Brown went on a fact-finding trip in 1956 and McCurrach went the following year. McCurrach gained an assistant in February 1961 with the appointment of George Alexander Stout. As part of his induction to the role he and McCurrach visited the United States the following month. Their fact-finding visits to the United States became a regular practice, as they had been in an earlier part of the company's history. McCurrach went again in 1963.

There were few changes to the board in these years. The company's long serving auditor Charles N. Thomson, DSO, OBE, TD, DL, CA joined in 1956. This appointment forced the resignation of his firm R.C. Thomson and Murdoch, CA, as auditors. In 1961 he was joined by his namesake Brian H. Thomson from D.C. Thomson and Co., publishers in Dundee, who were the largest shareholders in the Trust.

The company was entering one of those periods when, after a period of great stability in the board and executive, there were a number of changes. T.J. Carlyle Gifford was advanced in years and occasionally tendered his apologies for the board meetings. As he was over 70 the Companies Act required that a special resolution be passed at the annual general meeting to allow him to be re-elected. He retired from the board in 1964, which was also the year in which Sir George Cunningham died. Cunningham's replacement was Sir William Walker, TD, DL, of Sandford, near Wormit in Fife, but there was to be no immediate replacement for Gifford. It was not until 1967 that George T.

Chiene, DSO, MC, TD, WS, another Baillie Gifford man, was appointed.

In July 1965 Brown intimated that he wished to retire from the joint managership on reaching the age of 70 later that year. This was agreed, but he retained the chairmanship while McCurrach continued as sole manager. Brown did not live long to enjoy his semi-retirement. He died in January 1967.

At that time Alliance was still a small company so far as staff numbers were concerned. When Lyndon Bolton, a future managing director, joined the organisation in 1963 there were only 19 staff.

Agents

Tom Drought in San Antonio was, once again, the busiest of the agents as he strived to interest mining companies in the Chaves Grant. He had some success. In 1952 he was in deep negotiations with an oil company over a possible lease. But, ultimately, it was not oil that was the main focus of attention in this period, but uranium. There had been some discoveries in other parts of New Mexico and the US government encouraged mineral companies by buying all their output and stockpiling it. The price was attractive to the companies and, beginning in 1955 with the Canoncito Uranium Corporation, Drought soon had the whole grant leased out to the uranium companies. A decade later, however, interest in uranium mining evaporated when the US government withdrew its incentives.

Black and Armstrong were the agents in Manitoba and their activities extended into the province of Saskatchewan. There were still a number of outstanding mortgages in these areas and a certain amount of real estate that Black and Armstrong were trying to sell. It was slow going. The wheat business was strictly controlled by the Canadian Wheat Board and they would accept only limited deliveries of wheat at any one time. The consequence of this was that farming incomes were modest and unpredictable. In 1956 the comment was made that the first payment from the Wheat Board would 'hardly pay the expense of harvesting'. Added to this problem were the difficulties created by severe weather. The correspondence from Black and Armstrong throughout the 1950s records one problem after another.

In a situation like this it was inevitable that the sale of real estate would be slow, and when sales were made the transactions often involved a down payment with further payments coming in over a number of years. Sometimes these payments were irregular, involving much correspondence as Black and Armstrong endeavoured to explain problematical situations to Dundee. The situation was helped to some degree by the activities of the Veterans' Land Department that helped to finance land purchases by former servicemen. By 1964 matters had improved sufficiently that Alliance's licence to operate was given up in both provinces.

The agents there seem to have had a lot of leeway in their conduct of Alliance's affairs as, on one occasion, they paid $565 for a new chicken house on a farm. They had done this because the old chicken house had fallen down but, as the farmer was a good operator and a regular payer, they had assumed responsibility for the investment with the farmer providing the labour.

As in other places Alliance had retained mineral rights on land that it had sold, but in 1966 the total revenue from these in Canada was only $7,440. Three years later a number of oil companies had given up their leases, leaving Alliance to pay the taxes on land that was producing no revenue.

It was a happier situation in Louisiana where the Cormier field continued to provide a regular, if somewhat erratic, stream of revenue. In 1958 heavy rains led to East Carroll Parish, where Cormier was situated, to be declared a disaster zone and Barcroft was given permission to do what he could to provide assistance to the people there.

The Suez crisis in 1956 had produced a sharp rise in oil prices and, with it, a renewed interest in exploration. A new deep well was sunk at Cormier that was planned to go down to 16,000 feet but it was abandoned after six months. The decision was then made to sell the mineral rights at Cormier, at least down to the productive level of 10,000 feet. The reason given was not the disappointment of the deep well but taxation. Brown explained in a letter to Barcroft, 'we have to suffer a much greater load of taxation in this country on our royalties than would fall on a resident of the United States and we do not receive the benefit of double tax relief which we obtain in respect of the dividends on common stocks.' The sale to Barlu Oil was completed in January 1958, but not before an independent assessor's report had been obtained on likely future output. In total the Cormier field had produced revenues for Alliance of $1,644,581. It was almost the end of a long saga whose origins were a loan for $22,000 in 1919 upon which only one payment had been made. The loan was foreclosed in 1923. Alliance had then operated it as a rice plantation for 15 years, making a net profit of only $9,367. It was not until 1930 that some of it was leased for oil exploration. Following the sale to Barlu Oil in 1958 Alliance retained rights to minerals below 10,000 feet. Sadly no oil has been discovered below that level.

Barcroft continued his efforts to dispose of real estate, and a further 320 acres of the Wyly lands were sold in 1953 at $40 per acre. Two years later he received an offer for the remaining 839 acres. The offer price was only $30 per acre but the prospective purchaser was deemed unreliable and his offer was refused. Other purchasers were soon found, albeit that some of the purchases were for a down payment and a mortgage stretching over several years. The final tract of land was sold in 1957 although Brown thought that there was still some land to sell. His thinking was based on the documentation obtained in 1897 when Alliance foreclosed on William G. Wyly's 16,302 acres. But Barcroft persuaded Dundee that the original surveys had been unreliable and Brown agreed to draw a line under the matter.

By that stage Barcroft, although still not an old man, was becoming increasingly frail. In 1951 he had had a falling out with his main employers, the Connecticut General Insurance Co., and they sacked him. Thereafter he had a rather sad end to his career and tried to make a living as an agent for an oil company and then as a realtor – neither of which provided the comfort for his old age that he would have wished for. He had diabetes and was unable to get about as he had once done. Although it was not company policy to provide pensions for agents, the board decided, in view of Barcroft's service, to provide him with a pension of $3,100 per annum which was the equivalent of his annual salary. Notwithstanding his retirement he kept an eye on the few matters that had to be attended to and the last mortgage payment on the Wyly lands was received in 1967.

There was an even longer wait for the final mortgage payment in Idaho. Reade Ireland died in 1956 and his assistant Gordon Boyle of L.A. Hartert and Co. in Fergus Falls, Idaho was appointed agent – there being virtually no business left in Oregon. By that stage there was very little real estate to dispose of in either state. There had been four years of good sales. As in other places, Alliance had reserved mineral rights on properties it had sold, but the opinion of Standard Oil of California was that, given the volcanic nature of the area, it was unlikely that there would be oil in Idaho.

Investments and Shareholders

In MacDougall's final annual report to the shareholders in 1952 he had recorded the fact that the value of investments had risen despite a small fall in the value of British securities. The rise was due to a surge in American share prices that then comprised 28.76% of total investments. The fact that this was remarked upon is an indication that serious thought was then being given to share values as well as to the more traditional concerns with revenues. This is not to say that concerns about prices had overtaken those about dividends in company thinking. But share price rises were often so large that they could not possibly be ignored. Comments upon what was happening dominated the business press.

In 1955 Brown told the shareholders that the market value of company investments was £28m, while in 1954 they had only been £20m. As far as he was concerned this was just cause for issuing a cautionary message and for reiterating the mantra about the need to invest in good dividend-paying stocks.

The 'constant policy' is to concentrate 'on those investments which we believe offer either the best prospects for future growth or wide and secure cover for their current dividends. In this way we can reasonably hope to continue to share fully in the prosperity of industry during periods of expanding business while moderating as far as possible the effects on our income should business recede.'

There was a similar message a year later when the shareholders were told that the valuation of the company's bond and stock investments showed 'an appreciation of 133.8% on the figure at which they stand in the balance sheet'. Brown and McCurrach decided to enhance the company's liquidity position as a guard against the expected downturn in markets: '. . . we should concern ourselves less with the absolute value of a portfolio at any chosen moment than with its progress over the years and, still more, with the income which it earns and may be expected to earn'.

Shareholders were provided with a table that was given as an index, taking 31 January 1946 as 100 (see Table 8.3).

If anything, Brown was even more of the cautious pessimist than MacDougall had been. He told the shareholders that 'if our present economic difficulties are correctly diagnosed as being the product of an excess of prosperity and capital creation, we may look for its correction to be followed by a period of stability and more measured expansion'. But by 1957 he had begun to wonder if his caution was well judged. 'It has become trite to observe that one cannot look for a further rise in dividend income and the annual warning has been continuously belied by events.'

Such success brought an increase in the share price, and in 1959 the *Financial Times* suggested that the £1 ordinary shares should be divided into four 5s (25p) shares, as this would make them more attractive to the 'common man'. The board took heed and the shares were duly converted.

Table 8.3 Index of investment and earnings valuations 1947–1956
(1946 = 100)

31 January	Valuation	Gross income	Ordinary stock earnings
1947	116	111	114
1948	113	123	136
1949	109	122	134
1950	99	125	145
1951	110	138	178
1952	110	156	228
1953	112	164	215
1954	126	169	237
1955	176	190	277
1956	177	217	330

The stellar performance of Alliance was then drawing complimentary comments in the press. In March 1959 the *Stock Exchange Gazette* commented that 'it is often thought that size brings about diminishing returns in the way of asset performance, but there are few managements that would not settle for [Alliance Trust's] five year asset record. Those who purchased their holding ten years ago will have seen their capital multiplied fourfold and income increased more than three times.' A year later it took the view that Alliance 'sets a standard which is difficult to beat'. There were similar comments in the *Investors' Guardian*. Alliance's reserves were then four times the amount of equity capital and, for the first time since 1937, new money was raised with the issue of £3m of debenture stock. Even the *Scotsman* was moved to praise the Alliance management, with the comment in April 1961 that 'Even in Edinburgh financiers talk with hushed breath about the power of Reform Street.'

In 1964, twenty years before it created the FTSE 100 index of shares, the *Financial Times* produced a list of Britain's top 100 companies. Alliance Trust came in at 73rd place, ahead of such companies as Guardian Assurance, Cable and Wireless, Glaxo Group and Royal Exchange.

This period also saw the start of a process by which the shareholders were provided with much more information than they had ever received before. During the war the annual report and accounts had been reduced to two pages and contained no more than a profits statement, a balance sheet and a few brief comments from the chairman. Earlier reports contained not much more, and there had been occasional requests from individual shareholders for more information that were always resisted.

It would be an exaggeration to say that there had been any kind of shareholder revolution but many companies began, in the post-war years, to produce more elaborate reports that conveyed more information about their activities. Some of the English trusts had led the way in this regard, and the first table of investments was published by an English trust as early as 1908. To some extent this development had been accelerated by the new Companies Act which had been passed in 1948 and which required more disclosure, but many companies began to see the advantages in providing the shareholders with more information and went beyond the legal requirements. The financial press was also growing in importance, and companies like Alliance were likely to receive frequent requests for information or comment from journalists.

In the case of the Alliance Trust there was a fundamental rethink about what to provide, and Table 8.4 opposite, which stopped short of revealing the companies in which the funds were invested, was published with the annual report. The information provided a breakdown by sector and region of where the funds had been invested. It revealed the extent to which the company had committed itself to the United States.

The provision of such detailed information was a serious break with traditional practice, but it proved to be popular with shareholders and it was not long before the board was contemplating communicating with shareholders more than once a year. Nevertheless Brown's statements to the shareholders remained full of highly detailed information about tax rates and movements in figures, and failed to reveal very much about strategy. The decision to communicate with shareholders twice a year was finally made in 1964 at the behest of the London Stock Exchange, when it was decided to provide an unaudited valuation of the company's investments as at 31 July and a forward estimate of revenue for the remainder of the year.

By the end of the decade investment strategy had shifted away from cyclical fields towards 'stable and conservative trades and industries'. So the portfolio was heavily invested in banking, insurance, food, drink, tobacco and, in the United States, public utilities. Many, if not most, of the British public utilities had been nationalised.

Table 8.4 Distribution of Investments Based on Valuation (Percentages) (31 January 1956)

	United Kingdom %	British Common- wealth %	United States of America %	Other countries %	Total %
Insurance	2.21	–	–	–	2.21
Banks, trusts, finance and land	6.93	0.76	1.62	0.11	9.42
Public utilities	–	0.48	7.84	0.18	8.50
Railways	–	–	2.12	0.14	2.26
Brewers and distillers	3.07	0.30	–	–	3.37
Tobacco	1.85	0.04	1.04	–	2.93
Food manufacturing	3.70	–	1.29	0.09	5.08
Retail trade	3.61	0.11	1.40	0.09	5.21
Textiles	2.08	0.02	0.55	–	2.65
Paper, printing and periodicals	4.28	0.36	1.39	–	6.03
Chemicals and drugs	2.29	–	1.88	–	4.17
Electrical manufacturing	3.12	0.08	1.37	0.30	4.87
Motors, aircraft and allied trades	3.98	0.23	1.30	–	5.51
Rubber manufacturing	0.98	–	0.60	-	1.58
General engineering	4.98	0.05	1.58	–	6.61
Iron and steel	2.52	–	2.04	0.03	4.59
Building and construction	2.35	0.08	3.23	–	5.66
Miscellaneous manufacturing	2.09	–	1.19	–	3.28
Shipping	0.84	–	–	–	0.84
Gold and diamonds	0.01	1.23	–	–	1.24
Base metals	0.46	2.10	1.45	0.32	4.33
Oils (incl. international companies)	2.19	0.35	3.40	–	5.94
Others	2.32	0.65	0.24	0.51	3.72
Total	55.86	6.84	35.53	1.77	100.00

Fixed interest	10.09	
Ordinary	89.91	
	100.00	

Brown was quite clear that, 'These more conservative investments sometimes seem to lack the glamour of large speculative possibilities but our main pre-occupation is improvement in the quality and amount of our income and these investments still hold the promise of steady earnings growth in meeting the persistent world-wide rise in individual living standards and populations.'

There appears to have been something of a lag between British and American shares but, by the end of the 1950s, British equities were fast catching up with their American competitors. This development encouraged Brown and McCurrach to shift their investment strategy back towards the UK so that by 1960 the portion of funds invested in North America, which had risen to 44.22% in 1958, had fallen to 34.5%, while the money invested in the UK had risen to 59.6%. Nevertheless in both investment arenas the bulk of investments were in consumer industries rather than in heavy, cyclical or capital-intensive industries. By 1961 Brown was able to report that there were 225 sterling ordinary and 120 dollar common stock investments.

Some serious thought was also being given to the needs of investors, and there was a plan to create a Third Alliance Trust. The scheme involved the Alliance Trust and the Second Alliance Trust in providing the initial capital. There would then be a placing of shares with institutions, followed shortly thereafter by a public offering of shares. In this way the need for, and the cost of, underwriting would be avoided. Linklaters and Paine in London were asked to investigate the legal and taxation niceties. Hoare's were asked to advise, and they were quite enthusiastic, but someone, probably Brown, pencilled a note on their report that they were bound to be enthusiastic as they stood to make money out of it if the launch went ahead. However, Linklaters and Paine discovered some difficulties over legal and taxation issues. The scheme was dropped when McCurrach discovered how opposed to the idea Brown was. In a letter to T.J. Carlyle, Gifford he wrote that 'As a manager I should find it very difficult to proceed with any major operation which my own chairman and co-manager so strongly disliked.' Nevertheless the idea was not lost and a new trust, the Claverhouse Investment Trust, was eventually established, in 1963, by Robert Fleming and Co. McCurrach became a director but the Alliance Trust was not itself involved.

At the annual meeting in 1964 Brown reported that there had been some unusual swings in stock markets in the UK and US. This had been the subject of much comment in the financial press, which must have compelled Brown to offer his view. 'It would scarcely be possible, even if it were desirable, in a

fund of our size seeking diversification and pursuing longer term policies of
steady income growth, to make sufficiently rapid and massive changes of
investments to take advantage of what may be purely temporary swings of this
kind.' It is highly likely that the swings were taking place as a reaction to
political changes on both sides of the Atlantic.

In the UK a Labour government, under Harold Wilson, had been elected
for the first time in 13 years, and in the United States it was also an election
year. Lyndon Johnson had succeeded to the presidency following the assassi-
nation of John F. Kennedy and was standing for re-election. Presidential
elections had a habit of making investors nervous until it became clear who
would be elected and what the direction of policy would be. Johnson was
strong on social policy, which made the business community nervous,
although he went on to establish a good working relationship with business
people.

The middle years of the 1960s were a period of great activity. The uncertainty caused by frequent changes in the taxation regimes on both sides of the
Atlantic caused considerable anxiety and produced a heightened degree of
caution in the investment strategy. As early as 1965 Brown expressed his
concern about impending changes to the taxation regime, although he stopped
short of criticising the Labour government. There was also a worry that some
double taxation relief on US investments might be lost. 'We are investors
seeking income, preferably growing income. We change our investments only
to that end. We are not securities traders and do not seek short-term capital
gains. Our business is to invest – long term. Our investments represent our
whole capital and we are prohibited by our Articles of Association from
distributing any capital profits (a prohibition agreed with the Inland Revenue
as a condition of our present tax status).' He went on to complain that insufficient information was available about the proposed capital gains tax to enable
the board to adjust the investment strategy 'rationally or coherently'. As a
defensive measure investments in ordinary shares had been reduced and the
proceeds used to purchase fixed-interest government and local authority
securities.

A year later the shareholders were told that there had been a complete
disallowance of taxes paid in the United States that had 'rendered some
categories of investment there wholly unsatisfactory'. Consequently $8m had
been brought back to the UK.

January 1967 was the last occasion on which the purchases and sales of
securities were recorded in the minute books. On that occasion the purchases

included a wide range of leading British companies including Shell, Westland Aircraft, Associated British Picture Corporation, BP, British Shoe Corporation, Burmah Oil, Charrington United Breweries, Debenhams, General Electric, Great Universal Stores, John Lewis Partnership, News of the World, Rank Organisation and several investment trusts. The list went on to detail several US acquisitions, including the familiar favourites, Automatic Retailers of America, Mclean Trucking and Worthington Corporation. In future the investment activities were included in a transactions book that, despite the fact that it was to be kept under the 'same strict security arrangements as the Minute Book', has not survived.

The nature of the purchases of British stocks, and the preference for fixed-interest investments, was a sure indication that all was not well with the British economy and that safety had to be sought in well established and steadily performing companies. McCurrach's first statement as chairman in 1967 made the situation abundantly clear. He was still keen on American common stocks and believed that further earnings growth could be obtained by maintaining these investments, but at the same time he was unhappy about British government policy that required forfeiture of 25% of the dollar premium if any of these shares were sold. This was all part of government policy to bring dollars into the Exchequer. So, too, was the 'voluntary' ceiling on overseas investments which, to McCurrach's great annoyance, applied not just to the US and other countries but also to the British Commonwealth. He told the shareholders that Alliance had had to contemplate situations where the combined cost of capital gains tax and the dollar surrender had exceeded 20% of the value of the investment. Moreover this was 'an almost insurmountable impediment to rational judgement ... to have to surrender one-fifth of one's earning capital, payable almost immediately in cash, as the price of a simple switch however prudent'.

The situation was not helped by other aspects of government policy such as the freeze on dividends. It was then abundantly clear to those countries which held sterling as part of their reserve that it was not a robust currency and they began to move their money elsewhere. On 18 November 1967 the government gave up on its efforts to maintain the value of sterling and devalued, so that its exchange rate fell from $2.80 to $2.40.

Part 3 1967–1980

Economy

The 1970s were a torrid time for the British economy. The devaluation of the pound sterling in November 1967 did little to improve the situation. The Labour government under Harold Wilson (1964–70) failed to solve Britain's economic woes. The stop-go policies that had been pursued by the Conservatives in the early 1960s had been succeeded by a series of national economic plans under Labour, but neither party's strategy had produced the desired results. Economic growth in the UK was about half of what it was in other European countries and inflation was showing a disturbing upward trend.

While trade was falling with the Commonwealth it was actually growing with the European Economic Community (EEC), but Britain's attempts to join in 1963 and 1967 were blocked by the French. It was not until 1973 that Britain was admitted to the Community, but by that time there were real danger signs that serious trouble was ahead.

It was in that year that a variety of economic factors came together to create one of these dislocations in an economy that make it look as if everything is going wrong at the same time. The oil crisis started with an embargo imposed by the Organisation of Petroleum Exporting Countries (OPEC) and was followed by severe price increases. Poor industrial relations led to strikes and these, together with the oil crisis, led to the imposition of a three-day working week.

Inflation was already running at high levels and a housing boom was suddenly choked off in 1973 when the Bank of England raised interest rates to 13%. This created great difficulties for many of the smaller banks – many of whom failed in what became known as the secondary banking crisis. A government policy document, 'Competition and Credit Control', published in 1971, had endeavoured to control credit and, at the same time, to encourage banking institutions to be more competitive. But the combined effect of these contradictory policy objectives led directly to the crisis.

Whilst many of these issues were confined to the UK there were others that impacted on other economies. By 1973, the Bretton Woods system of international money management that had been set up after the Second World War had collapsed, and the US dollar, which had become the major reserve currency for most countries, had been devalued.

Inevitably these events led to a stock market collapse. The long boom in equity prices, which had lasted through the 1950s and 1960s, came to an abrupt end. There had been signs of this in 1968 but the 'dash for growth' instituted by the Heath government in the early 1970s had produced a rally. The crash affected all of the world's stock markets. Between January 1973 and December 1974 the Dow Jones index lost 45% of its value and the American economy went into recession. Inflation in the US was recorded at 12.3% in 1974.

In the UK matters were even worse. The London Stock Exchange's FT 30 index lost 73% of its value during the crash. The already troubled economy went into recession, and it was not until December 1974 when a rent freeze was lifted that the property market recovered and stock market prices began a dramatic improvement that saw them rise 150% in 1975. Nevertheless while the US authorities managed to get inflation there under control the British authorities failed to do so and rates of 25% were experienced in 1975. It was an era of stagflation. Britain became known as 'the sick man of Europe'.

These were difficult and frustrating years for investors. Not only had they to cope with the crisis in the economy but the tax regime and exchange control regulations made for an exceptionally problematical period. In the ten years after a new tax regime was introduced in the mid 1960s, the Alliance Trust ordinary share dividend increased by only 45%, while the UK retail price index advanced by 170%.

The national press gave investment trusts a hard ride. In *The Times* on 13 March 1974 an article on trusts declared that, 'If ever a sector needed a champion, it is the investment trust sector. The disillusioned army of investment trust shareholders may not yet quite be on the brink of mutiny but there have been enough rumblings of discontent over the past few months to suggest that the start of a bull market will need to be clearly in sight before the end of this year if things are not to start getting out of hand.' The article went on to suggest that trusts should either liquidate themselves or mutualise so that they could become unit trusts. Neither of these strategies would be easy to achieve but 'the best hope of quick relief for some companies . . . may well be a bid from a financial group needing to expand its asset base'. Similar articles appeared in the *Sunday Telegraph* and *Investors' Chronicle*. It was undoubtedly a frustrating time for the trusts. Not only had asset values collapsed but the discount at which their shares traded had increased to alarming levels. McCurrach expressed his frustration in an article in the *Glasgow Herald* on 21 September 1974. He took the view that current share values were absurd but matters would not improve until the political fog was removed.

When McCurrach reported to the shareholders in 1977 he said, 'We have seen two completely new tax systems, a temporary ceiling on overseas investment, a drastic broadening of the currency premium surrender system and, for almost the whole decade, either dividend limitation or a total freeze.'

Better times were ahead, and the discovery of oil and gas in the North Sea greatly assisted Britain's economic recovery. As early as 1971 Norman Lamont (a future chancellor of the Exchequer) approached Alliance on behalf of Rothschild and invited participation in an exploration company that was eventually called City Oil Exploration Ltd. In an article in the *Investors' Chronicle* in October 1978 George Stout celebrated 'the beginning of the pay off for the hard decisions taken a number of years ago on North Sea Oil investment. In many instances it has been a long gestation period with little or no return. Scottish trusts have been significantly involved both directly through drilling consortia and indirectly in the oil service companies.'

The 25% foreign currency surrender system was abolished in January 1978 and almost the first action of the Conservative government that was elected in 1979 was to abolish exchange controls, which had been around since 1939. The investment currency pool was also terminated. City opinion had been betting that this would not happen.

The abolition of these controls was not entirely good news for investors as the loss of the dollar premium had the effect of reducing the value of the American investments, and there were those who saw this as yet another hammer blow meted out to investors by governments. Investment trusts, including Alliance, saw the discount on their shares increase to high levels. Nevertheless the longer-term impact was more positive, as capital was able to flow more freely into investment opportunities.

McCurrach's was not the only Alliance voice speaking up on behalf of the investment trust industry. In giving evidence, in April 1978, to the Wilson Committee on the Functioning of Financial Institutions, George Stout maintained that many small businesses sold out too early thereby preventing investment trusts from helping them to raise capital. He took the view that if the original owners of a business held on and developed the business before bringing it to market then the trusts would be able and willing to supply their capital needs.

Two months later Stout was heard again to defend the investment trust movement when he warned against the takeover of trusts by pension funds. As the biggest pension funds were those of the nationalised industries he was concerned that they would soon end up controlling a large part of British industry. The *Sunday Times* agreed, and in an article on 25 June 1978 warned that 'perhaps the most troubling element is that the pension funds go for the larger, better run quality portfolios instead of mopping up the confusing detritus of also rans'.

People

Alan Brown retired from his role of joint manager upon reaching his 70th birthday in August 1965. He retained the role of chairman but he did not live long to enjoy his semi-retirement. He died in January 1967. The tribute paid to him by his fellow directors was fulsome. They recorded that he would be remembered for his 'constant attention to the interests of the Company and its staff, for his firm grasp of investment activities and the range of his financial experience and acumen, for his kindliness and unfailing sympathy, for the soundness of his judgement and, above all, for his unwavering integrity'.

David McCurrach was appointed chairman. He was the third manager to succeed to the chairmanship. His reports to the shareholders were every bit as arcane as Brown's had been but at least they were more informative. The new Companies Act required directors to provide a great deal more information than had been provided in the past, and most boards of directors saw the merits of this development and gave a great deal of careful thought to what needed to be done and how it would be presented.

Brown's replacement on the board was George T. Chiene, who was a member of the board of Baillie Gifford. His appointment kept alive the long-standing connection with the Edinburgh firm. Chiene became chairman of Baillie Gifford later that year.

McCurrach's appointment as executive chairman finally gave him the power to make alterations to the staffing of the organisation and to build a management cadre. George Stout had been his assistant since 1961. Peter Millar and Lyndon Bolton were also appointed as assistant managers in 1968. Other young men who would play a significant part in the future of the organisation, including W. Grant Lindsay, joined in this period. In his search for new blood McCurrach went as far as the London Business School, where he approached a young Gavin Suggett, who initially declined to join Alliance although he came on board two years later.

There were no women in the management team but there was a small sign that women would play an increasingly important role when the pension scheme was altered in 1971 to allow people of both sexes to become members when they were 21.

Further change was ahead. In 1972 McCurrach was given the new job title of managing director while George Stout and Lyndon Bolton were promoted to be 'managers' of the company. Gavin Suggett joined shortly after this in the role of assistant company secretary. R.D. Skene was still secretary, but R. Fyfe Smith who had been joint secretary had retired.

Despite the fact that he had a rather domineering personality McCurrach had succeeded in attracting, and keeping, significant talent to the organisation and this new blood would play a highly significant part in the future of the company.

These arrangements did not last for long. McCurrach retired as managing director in 1976. The board recorded their 'warm appreciation' of his services. It was a less than fulsome tribute to a man who had steered the company through some difficult times. The brevity of the tribute may, of course, be explained by the fact that he remained chairman for another four years and there would be another occasion for a more extensive eulogy. George Stout and Lyndon Bolton were appointed as joint managing directors while Suggett became joint secretary with Skene. When Skene retired Suggett became secretary, and in due course assumed duties beyond those normally associated with that role. He acquired responsibility for deposit taking, oil royalty business and the treasury function. In this latter role he was responsible for managing the company's cash flow and ensuring that funds were available for investment when needed. This required him to keep up to speed with interest rates, exchange rates and liquidity management. To do this he maintained an extensive list of contacts with bank treasury departments and money market intermediaries.

New people were coming into the company although, in 1974, the total staffing numbered only 21 people. There were six in the investment department, two in company secretariat, six cashiers, three clerks, three secretaries and a caretaker. It was very much a family atmosphere although the hierarchy of rank was well observed – even when one of the senior managers took to wearing a miner's helmet during the miners' strike. His adoption of this headgear was not to establish his sympathy for the miners' cause but rather to shed light on his work during the electricity blackouts. Other members of staff used candles.

A table tennis table was available for staff to use. It was located on the third floor, but play was not allowed on board days as the table was immediately above the board room and the light fittings there would shake when the table was in use on the floor above.

There was also a certain amount of formal entertaining when senior managers would entertain staff either at their houses or at a restaurant – the Craw's Nest in Anstruther being one such venue. Occasional staff outings to enjoy the delights of Burntisland were eagerly anticipated.

In most respects the working atmosphere was relatively formal. Staff seldom got to speak to members of the board. Men were required to wear business suits and women were not allowed to wear trousers. Working conditions were relatively spartan and reflected the company's preoccupation with saving costs. Underwood manual typewriters were standard equipment for the typists, and a young clerical worker could expect to serve five years as office junior before being promoted to be a typist, whose duties would include maintaining daily logs and typing purchase orders and board papers.

Many members of staff had long service and it was expected that those who joined the company would serve their whole career in it. The prospect of a good pension was certainly an attractive feature of employment in Alliance but it was not the only factor at work. The dearth of similar employment opportunities in Dundee was a powerful factor in the career choices that people made. A job with Alliance Trust was seen by many as a job for life. It was not until the late 1980s that this began to change, as it did in many other financial services companies.

New technology was also being introduced at this time. A telex machine was installed in 1969 whose purpose was not just to relay information but also to transact business with other businesses across the world. This was the preferred means of communication for many of the American, and, increasingly, the British finance houses.

In 1974 Gavin Suggett won a competition to have use of a Honeywell computer time-sharing terminal that was to be used to develop a computer package to forecast cash flows which would, in turn, accelerate investment decisions. The £1,000 prize was sponsored by Honeywell, Post Office Telecommunications and *Accounts Weekly*. By means of a telephone call to Edinburgh Suggett could link in to a 'super-centre of computers' in Cleveland, Ohio. It was the beginning of computing in Alliance Trust, and Suggett was not only to lead future computing developments but he also wrote much of the software himself. Two years later he was appointed joint secretary with R.D. Skene.

At that time the company occupied only the second floor of Meadow House. Jute and insurance companies, a bank and a firm of civil engineers occupied other parts of the building. That situation would soon change.

The new Companies Act, passed in 1968, required directors of limited companies to declare their other directorships, and the list produced by the Alliance Board reveals a wide spread of board positions in national and local companies:

Table 8.5 Board directorships

David McCurrach
Claverhouse Investment Trust Ltd
Scottish Mortgage and Trust Co. Ltd
Baillie Gifford
Second Scottish Mortgage and Trust Co. Ltd
(He was also a member of the investment advisory panels of Rolls Royce Ltd and Courtaulds Ltd.)

J. Murray Prain
William Halley and Sons Ltd
Royal Bank of Scotland Ltd
Scottish Life Assurance Co.

Charles N. Thomson
Douglas Fraser and Sons (London) Ltd
Douglas Fraser and Sons (Jute) Ltd
Fraser Machine Tool Finance Ltd
Giddings and Lewis-Fraser Ltd
Giddings and Lewis-Fraser, Sales Ltd
Arbroath Herald Ltd
D.S. Bryson Ltd
R.G. Kennedy and Co. (Textiles) Ltd
M.C. Thomson and Co. Ltd
Hotel Seaforth (Arbroath) Ltd
McTavish Ramsay and Co. Ltd
Alexander Shanks and Son Ltd

Brian H. Thomson
John Leng and Co. Ltd
Scottish Canadian Trust Ltd
Scots Magazine Ltd
Southern Television Ltd
DC. Thomson and Co. Ltd
W., D.C. and F. Thomson Ltd

Sir William G.N. Walker
Clydesdale Bank Ltd

Dundee, Perth and London Shipping Co. Ltd
Andrew Gray Ltd
Jute Industries (Holdings) Ltd
Nairn and Williamson (Holdings) Ltd
Scottish Television Ltd

George T. Chiene
Edinburgh and Dundee Investment Co. Ltd
Lloyds and Scottish Ltd
Royal Bank of Scotland
Scottish Capital Investment Trust Ltd
Scottish Central Investment Trust Ltd
Scottish Life Assurance Co. Ltd
Scottish Mortgage and Trust Co. Ltd
Second Edinburgh and Dundee Investment Co. Ltd
Second Scottish Mortgage and Trust Co. Ltd
Western Reversion Trust Co. Ltd

All directors were also directors of the Second Alliance Trust. The connections of the directors, together with their experience, gave to Alliance a remarkably wide access to knowledge and understanding of many other sectors of the economy.

Just after this list was prepared, George W. Dunn, CBE, DSO, MC, TD, BL of Letham House, Arbroath joined the board. He was a director of Wm Low and Co. Ltd and 23 other local companies. He was joined in 1974 by Professor Christopher Blake, MA, PhD from the Department of Economics in the University of Dundee. The board, therefore, was entirely composed of men from East Central Scotland

The annual general meeting in 1971 was asked to approve an increase in the total remuneration of the board from £18,000, at which it had been fixed in 1957, to £21,000, but it was explained that this was not to pay more to individual directors but simply to enable the number of directors to increase to seven. It was noted that 'should the number of directors revert to 6 the remuneration also would be allowed to return to the previous figure.' The Alliance Trust's reputation for careful husbanding of resources was, by then, well established and well recognised, and the remuneration of directors did revert to its former level when J. Murray Prain retired from the board in 1973.

The directors met on Fridays when the talk, at least before lunch, was on investment trust matters. They were therefore kept fully up to date with the

Trust's affairs and, like all boards of their time, they were not best pleased when something happened to upset the routine of their business.

An increasing amount of regulation had to be dealt with, whether it came from legislation or from the stock exchange, and this really marks the beginning of a trend towards major changes in corporate governance. In 1977 the stock exchange's model code for securities transactions by directors of listed companies was adopted. It stated that any proposed transactions in the shares of Alliance Trust had to be intimated in advance to the company secretary who, in turn, had to present it to the board or to the chairman. Alliance got into the habit of recording all the dealings of its directors in its own shares in the board minute book – even when they participated in the dividend reinvestment scheme.

The directors were happy to participate in schemes devised by the Association of Investment Trust Companies that were designed to make the industry more transparent and more readily understood by existing and potential customers. In 1969, following a sizeable publicity campaign, it began to publish monthly comparative statistics of net asset values for a range of trusts. Only 96 of the Association's 283 members agreed to participate in the scheme, for there were still some old-fashioned attitudes around about what should be in the public domain.[25] Alliance Trust was one of the companies that agreed to participate. In 1978 there was a proposal to further develop these statistics by including figures for, inter alia, total return on investments. Alliance was less happy about this proposal. They did, however, agree to support the Association's concept, and financial arrangements for, a 'council' for the securities industry.

The directors were less sanguine about another document that emanated from the Association in 1976. 'The directors, having considered the memorandum entitled "The Future of Investment Trust Companies: The advantages and disadvantages of unitisation and liquidation", issued by the Association of Investment Trust Companies, resolved that no recommendations should be made to shareholders at this time.'

Stout and Bolton were appointed to the board in 1978 and each purchased 800 ordinary shares that were then in 25p units at a price of 221p per unit. Both already had other board membership. Stout was a director of Claverhouse Investment Trust and City Oil Exploration Ltd while Bolton was a director of TSB Trust Co. Ltd.

———

25 J. Newlands, *Put Not Your Trust in Money*, Chappin Kavanagh, London, 1997, p. 291.

Performance

The company was growing strongly. In May 1970 the *Investors' Guardian* produced a statistical list of British investment trusts that, at net asset value of £96.2m, revealed Alliance to be the biggest of the trusts. The only other trusts over £60m were Foreign and Colonial at £94.9m and British Assets Trust at £70.2m.

McCurrach's efforts to ensure that Alliance was adequately staffed inevitably meant that more office space was required. The company occupied the second floor of Meadow House and in 1970 space was repurchased from the Titaghur Jute Factory Ltd. In 1977 the offices occupied by A. and S. Henry and Co. was acquired for £55,000.

The company's growth was also reflected in the appointment of Royal Bank of Scotland as registrars for the debenture stock in 1968, which removed a great deal of tedious work from the office.

A third measure of that growth lay in the fact that when the auditors A.W. Mudie, CA, resigned in 1975 they were replaced by Messrs Thomson McLintock. No longer would a local firm of auditors suffice for such a large company; only a large national firm would be able to undertake the task.

In 1968 the Trust recorded a fall in revenues from £3,214,000 to £2,986,000, although the dividend was maintained at 20%. In his report to the shareholders McCurrach reviewed the problems that the company faced under the new taxation regimes in Britain and America.

The paradox in this was that the valuation of investments had risen massively and then stood at £107,646,000 – the first time that they had broken through the £100m barrier. Over the year, leading ordinary share indicators in the UK had risen between 32 and 35%. In the US the rise was only 6.5%, but when this figure was adjusted for devaluation, and the higher dollar premium, then it too became 35%. McCurrach's view was that rises of this magnitude were 'a matter more of concern than of comfort' because they represented 'a general lack of confidence and a flight from money'. He attributed this to the new rigidities of the tax system, especially the restraint which capital gains tax placed on potential sellers, and to devaluation itself. Such were the uncertainties amongst investors, including investment managers, that there had been a flight to safe investments, with the result that prices had been driven upwards.

McCurrach went on to argue that the activities of companies such as Alliance were, despite what the Treasury believed, actually beneficial to the national economy and the Exchequer. He produced figures to prove his point which demonstrated that the investment strategy pursued by the company enhanced not only the revenues coming into the Treasury, but also the flow of foreign currencies, with benefits to the balance of payments.

He was also concerned that dividends paid out to the Trust's own shareholders meant that money was leaving the organisation, and shareholders then had to decide what to do with it. He reasoned that it would be far better, and certainly more sensible, for the money to remain with the Trust. He began to plan therefore for the introduction of a dividend reinvestment plan which, when it was introduced, was unique to the Alliance Trust and remained so for many years. McCurrach himself made good personal use of the new facility.

By the late 1970s the British economy was still experiencing difficulties and money had to be borrowed from the International Monetary Fund. Nevertheless the worst of the decade was over and businesses were looking for new opportunities and new ways of doing business. The Stock Exchange introduced its new settlement system 'Talisman' in 1979 and Alliance applied for an account. But thought was also being given to new opportunities that presented themselves to Alliance. The company was very liquid and the difficult economic times made it difficult to find suitable long-term investments for the shareholders' funds. It was about this time that George Stout received an approach from Baillie Gifford in Edinburgh with a view to a merger. But there was no support for this from Alliance, whose thinking was moving in other directions.

In 1979 the decision was made to get into the leasing business. The banks had, to a large extent, exited this market, leaving room for new initiatives but again it was taxation considerations that made this a particularly attractive prospect. High inflation, high interest rates and a shrinking shareholder base all combined to require new thinking from the company's executives.

At the board meeting in January 1979 it was decided to establish Alldee Leasing Ltd as a wholly owned subsidiary. All the directors of Alliance were to be directors of Alldee, with the addition of Gavin Suggett, who was the driving force behind this new initiative. He had already had discussions with interested customers who were ready to do business with the new company. The share capital of Alldee was £10,000 in £1 shares which was subscribed by Alliance. A loan of £30,000 was also provided. In its first year of business the new company transacted £3.4m of contracts. A similar, but smaller, company, Secdee, was established as a subsidiary of Second Alliance Trust.

One of the arguments for setting up Alldee Leasing was that Alliance was paying corporation tax at 52% on its foreign and interest income. This drew comment from institutional shareholders, especially the National Coal Board Pension Fund, who, if they held these assets themselves, would not be subject to the tax. But the economic difficulties of the late 1970s had led the government to introduce 100% capital allowances – partly to mitigate the high tax rate but really to stimulate investment. This had caused companies like Alliance to become involved in leasing, whereby they could defer their tax and provide leasing facilities to those companies needing investment but who did not have the money to invest or were not paying corporation tax. Suggett, using his computing skills, was able to demonstrate to the board that the proposed business was not only viable but had real profit potential. He went on to use his contacts at the London Business School, the Equipment Leasing Association and amongst brokers to get the business underway. The first substantial lease was for British Gas to acquire a mainframe computer.

Other factors that made the Trust's entry into the leasing business a good idea were the fact that it was highly liquid, had good computing skills and the taxation arrangements for this new business were a good match for those of the Trust. There was also an emerging broking network that helped to bring lessors and lessees together.

That was by no means the end of the search for new business opportunities. The secondary banking crisis in 1973–4 had led, eventually, to the passing of a new Banking Act in 1979. Suggett saw further opportunity and persuaded the board to apply for a licence under the Act so that Alliance could conduct a deposit-taking business.

Agents

The agencies were little mentioned in the board minutes for the simple reason that they had little to do. That is not to say that they were not important, but their main task was to manage the company's mineral interests, which still existed in several locations and in several states.

The last of the real estate was disposed of in Idaho in 1962 but it was not finally paid for until 1968. It was not until October of that year that McCurrach wrote fulsomely to Boyle to thank him for his efforts in disposing of landed assets. The final payment on a mortgage had now been received, and Boyle was thanked for 'the most helpful and understanding way in which you have pushed ahead with the winding up process'.

This event marked not just the end of the mortgage business in Idaho but its end for the Alliance Trust. The decision to extricate itself from this business, which had been made in 1925, had taken 43 years to implement. All that remained in Idaho, and elsewhere, were several hundred rights to minerals. No one in Idaho or Dundee entertained much hope of discovery in that northern state and Boyle was asked to advise when these rights might properly be abandoned.

Boyle himself advised McCurrach that he thought that the mineral rights had no value. The response that he received was not to his liking. He was told that the company was actively considering abandoning the rights. Despite his earlier opinion, Boyle argued for retaining them and told McCurrach that his firm, L.A. Hartert and Co., would protect them. There were 43 mineral leases in 1968, although none of the properties appear to have produced any oil or other minerals. Despite the fact that the bank account was closed in 1975 there was a renewed interest in drilling two years later. Prospectors wanted ten-year leases but the maximum that Alliance would grant was for five years, as they wished to deter speculators who preferred to leave the oil in the ground to appreciate in value. Alliance was more interested in seeing drilling activity with the prospect of royalty payments.

Some drilling took place in Idaho but no oil was discovered and the correspondence with Boyle petered out.

There was a not dissimilar situation in the other agencies. Many of the rights owned by Alliance were leased, but few were being explored and fewer were in production. In Manitoba Black and Armstrong reported regularly on the nine titles they held but only three were leased. In Fort Worth Alexander and Martin recorded that all 14 properties in their care were leased. In Louisiana the rights to the Cormier field had been sold to Barlu Oil in 1957 but the company had retained rights to any oil that was discovered below 10,000 feet. It also retained ownership of 105 acres on the surface so that access could be provided for future drillers. Fred W. Bates and Associates of Lafayette, Louisiana was commissioned to survey the holdings and reported that there might be good reserves under the Gueydan salt dome, i.e. the area on which the Cormier field was situated. Barlu Oil took the view that there were no more discoverable reserves. Bates was retained to look after the company's interests but no more oil was ever found.

Meanwhile in San Antonio, Drought had been giving some thought to what might be done with what remained of the Chaves Grant. By 1973 there were six speculative wells with another on the way and, while they had all shown traces of oil, none had produced in commercial quantities. The decision by the Organisation of Petroleum Exporting Countries (OPEC) to increase substantially the price at which they would sell oil gave a tremendous boost to exploration as politicians came to realise that oil was a strategic commodity and that Middle Eastern sources might not be relied upon in the long term. In 1975 Drought arranged six leases covering 43,260 acres in favour of the Northern Mineral Oil and Gas Company. The leases were later extended to cover the period to 1989. Early in 1976 he decided to appoint a mining engineer or geologist to report on coal mining prospects on the Grant. The report was received a year later but it does not seem to have been favourable, as the board did not record a decision. Gavin Suggett wrote to Drought at Christmas 1976 to say, 'In some respects I suppose we are back to where we started on the "Grant" and must continue to pursue any leases, although our exploration must have diminished the chances of these.' Alliance's rights to the minerals on the Grant were due to expire in 1989 and it looked as if time was running out. Nevertheless Drought's efforts bore fruit. Revenues from the Grant that had been only a few thousand dollars per annum in the late 1960s had grown to average $40,000 in the late 1970s.

In 1979 it was the turn of Oklahoma, and the board decided to fund a report on the mineral interests there. The agent at that time was the First National Bank and Trust Company of Tulsa and it was left to them to appoint an appropriate person to conduct the survey. Every year they sent a list of the Alliance's holdings but there never seems to have been much effort to encourage exploration and production, which was in sharp contrast to the efforts made in Texas and New Mexico by Tom Drought.

Notwithstanding this fact it was the Tulsa Bank rather than Drought that took over the Fort Worth Agency in 1973 when the agent there retired. Drought wanted to consolidate the Texas business in his own office but the feeling in Dundee was that it was better to have an institution, rather than an individual, as agent.

Overall the mineral interests had long since ceased to be a matter of great interest to the board or the company. By this time Gavin Suggett had joined Alliance as assistant secretary and it fell to him to look after the mineral interests. It was not a large part of his job, yet the fact that there might be potential was never overlooked and a watchful eye was kept open for any possibilities – especially in view of the fact that oil, its supply and price, had become such an important factor in world affairs and that its price rose dramatically in the 1970s.

The early months of 1980 found Suggett planning a trip to the United States to prepare a paper for his board. There was a heightened interest in the mineral rights and this was a fact-finding visit. Among the options being considered was a more active participation in the oil market, and thought was being given to making some new purchases.

Investments

The investment decisions that were made in McCurrach's first few months as executive chairman in 1917 reflect the troubled state of the British economy. They were mostly in blue chip companies that had a good track record and prospects for paying good dividends. They included Bowater Paper, Imperial Tobacco, Shell, Westland Aircraft, Associated British Picture Corp., BP, British Shoe Corp., Burmah Oil, Charrington United Breweries, Debenhams, General Electric, Great Universal Stores, John Lewis Partnership (Preference), News of the World, Rank Organisation and several investment trusts. The US purchases included Automatic Retailers of America, Mclean Trucking and Worthington Corporation. Many of these companies had long enjoyed a position in the Alliance portfolio. This was the last occasion on which the purchases and sales of investments were recorded in the board minute book. Thereafter the directors received a separate list of transactions for the previous month that they approved and the chairman initialled each page.

Investment decisions were made by McCurrach and his investment managers, based largely upon information received from brokers, but the directors were kept fully informed and McCurrach was often asked to explain his, and his team's, acquisitions and disposals.

Such was the worry that the long boom of the 1950s and 1960s was coming to an end, and that there was bound to be a downturn, that a special reserve to be called 'Provision for Diminution in Value of Investments' was created. There was also an increased emphasis on buying preference shares rather than equities. The creation of this new reserve marked a turning point in the company's history. In earlier years the changes in stock market prices of the company's securities were not something that the board would become overly concerned about. They often stated that the company was interested in purchasing good dividend-paying stocks with potential for dividend growth. Changes in stock market prices were of little interest to them, but such were the fluctuations in stock market prices in the 1960s and 1970s that they could no longer be ignored. In other senses investors were beginning to concern themselves about these changes, especially as inflation began to take its toll on real values.

In an article in the *Investors' Chronicle* in December 1965 Harold Wincott raised the question, not for the first time, of the need for investment trusts to cater for different types of investor. The article created quite a stir in the investment trust world and it received very active consideration in numerous boardrooms. An article in *The Times* soon followed, which argued that, partly due to changes in the taxation system, unit trusts were proving to be a more popular investment channel for savers than investment trusts. It went on to be mildly critical and said that investment trusts had to sort out their problems before investment in them could be recommended.

Some trusts responded to this by launching 'split capital' funds, where one group of shareholders enjoyed the benefits of the dividends while others benefited from increases in capital values. Alliance gave serious thought to launching its own split capital trust in the autumn and winter of 1965. Under the heading of a project called 'Athol', McCurrach drafted several papers on the subject and even went so far as to draft a letter to shareholders. Linklaters and Paine, the London lawyers, were consulted and advised on the taxation implications. Barings were engaged to advise but were very lukewarm about the idea. It was then that the project was abandoned, as it was not thought to be in the best long-term interests of the existing shareholders. Moreover they would be asked, if the scheme was launched, to choose between their existing holdings and the new trust without the benefit of a market price on which to judge the new offering. Given the bumpy ride that the stock market experienced over the next 15 years the decision not to go ahead was probably the right one.

The net profit on realisations of bond and stock investments for the year to 31 January 1967 was credited to the new Provision for Diminution in Value of Investments. There was an immediate need for this new reserve not only to credit the last year's surplus but to credit the sums of £7,187,674 and $19,822,734. These had arisen because the new tax regime that made the Trust liable for capital gains tax allowed investment companies to choose a date at which their investments would be valued for taxation purposes. Rather than value them at their original cost, the board elected to value them as at the budget date in 1965 when the new tax had been announced. The sums credited to the new reserve, therefore, were the appreciation in investment values from that date until the Trust's balance date in 1967.

The shareholders who attended the annual general meeting in 1967 learned that the outlook was not good and that, as a consequence, ordinary shares were being sold to be replaced by the safer preference shares. Overall fixed-interest investments had grown from 8.6% of the portfolio to 15.2%, as fears mounted about the state of the economy. This development was only partly the result of these fears; it was also in response to changes in the taxation system. As events unfolded it seems that this cautious approach was appropriate.

Shares in American companies remained in favour, notwithstanding that the American economy had its own problems, as inflation appeared to be getting out of control. Investment in the United States was also increasingly problematical – partly because of the loss of double taxation relief, the introduction of capital gains tax and the dollar premium surrender. McCurrach said that he 'made no apology . . . for concentrating on the grievous injury to our U.S. investment operations by the restraints and taxes put on by the present Government or for asking stockholders to glance at a small corner of the jungle of Capital Gains Tax.' In paragraph after paragraph he fulminated against this tyranny and again provided figures to show how advantageous the Alliance's American investments were to the British economy. At least some of the 16,200 shareholders must have wondered why investors in an investment trust had to be tax experts just to understand the nature of their investment. It was a theme to which McCurrach returned in 1969 when he said that the market was so confused by taxation and other changes that there was less confidence in the accuracy of figures.

He went on to assure the shareholders that although there were still large investments in many British companies, these were the better run companies which had been selected for their good management and dividend-paying record. Moreover many of them had large overseas activities and so were not dependent on whatever happened to the British economy.

Later in that same report he returned to these themes but also had in his sights the government policy of restricting growth in company dividends to 3.5%, which was part of the prices and incomes policy designed to control inflation.

Year on year, 1968–9, the Financial Times All Shares Index (FTA Index) actually increased by 39%, although the leading shares index went up by only 23%. The Alliance performance, where funds were heavily concentrated in the leading shares as a precaution against the expected downturn, was 29%.

Some switching out of equities into government securities helped to counterbalance the downturn in British equities in 1969–70 but the net asset value per share, which had peaked at £2.49 in 1969, was down to £1.88 in 1971, although that was still higher than it had been for most of the 1960s.

McCurrach still fulminated against exchange control regulations and the dollar premium surrender that he believed inhibited investors from having the flexibility to deal with their assets in the optimal way. 'I must yet again repeat the hope that these artificial and damaging burdens will be speedily removed.'

Nevertheless these problems did not deter American investors who were coming to Scotland in increasing numbers and buying shares in investment trusts. The major attraction according to *Duns*, an American investment magazine, was 'the Scottish Trusts' relative insulation from the exaggerated swings of market mood'. Nor had they suffered as much in the downturn as had the 'go-go and hedge funds'. This was a two-way street. For, as the Americans were investing in Scotland, the Scottish trusts were in some of the regional markets in the US, such as Atlanta, Baltimore and Houston, looking for shares that were not yet fashionable. McCurrach had been interviewed for the *Duns* article and expressed the view that while Alliance was still keen on American investments, Japan, which was then entering more fully into the world economy, 'frightens us to death. Business is too much in the hands of government and the whole structure and objective of their society is something alien and inscrutable to us.'

In 1971, governments on both sides of the Atlantic were working out how to deal with cost inflation without plunging their economies into recession. McCurrach felt that the 'forces set up have had damaging results for employment, trade, profits, interest rates and investment values'. The Americans had started to reflate their economy but the new British administration under Edward Heath 'so far seems less inclined to flinch'. McCurrach was very much on Heath's side in the fight with the unions who, he felt, were acting against their own best interests. His view was that more capital investment was needed to bring growth back into the economy and that was not going to happen so long as there was so much industrial unrest.

By that time up to 25% of the portfolio was in fixed-interest securities but he was ready to reinvest in equities 'on any real signs of stability'. He was wary and very conscious of what he called the risk factor in equities, which were no protection against inflation and which suffered doubly when that was combined with recession.

But taxation changes introduced by the Heath government in 1971 produced a speedy recovery and there was a very strong bounce back to asset price levels that had prevailed in 1968. McCurrach told the shareholders that he was pleased with the increase in values, although he stressed that the Alliance had never 'surrendered to the total cult of capital performance in disregard to the growth and quality of our earnings. We have thought both the interests and the wishes of our shareholders to be better served by our seeking also consistently rising true earnings and dividend payments.'

The position in equities had been restored, rising from 37.9% to 48.6% of the portfolio, which was the highest level that had been reached since 1965. At the same time investments in the United States had been reduced and $2m had been brought back to the UK. McCurrach had strong words for the US administration which, he felt, was being inconsistent in trying to revive the US economy while, at the same time, trying to restore the strength of the currency. In a televised broadcast on 15 August 1971 President Nixon had performed a volte-face in economic policy. McCurrach saw the barrier of complex statutory wage and price controls which the Americans introduced as 'a strange and disturbing sight in the bastion of free enterprise'. In the *City Press* on 16 September he went further and described President Nixon's new policies as 'a tragic threat to co-operative international economic liberalism'.

By contrast, he said that the British economy was much better placed to face the future. There was ample unused capacity in the economy, a balance of payments surplus, rising productivity, slowing inflation and good prospects for profits. The currency was strong and the UK was in the process of finally becoming a member of the Common Market. He was bullish about the future. In view of what happened next it is difficult to escape the conclusion that there were parts of the picture on which he had not focused.

When he reported in 1972 it was clear that asset growth had come to an abrupt halt, although it had not yet gone into reverse. However, the company's year end was 31 January and the annual report was issued in March. And whilst asset values may have looked little changed from the previous year McCurrach told the shareholders what they probably already knew – that since the end of January there had been 'wide movements in all markets'. His message to the shareholders was rather gloomy.

The Bretton Woods system of currency management that had been established after the Second World War had fallen apart, the US dollar had been devalued and, consequently, the world lacked a reliable reserve currency. McCurrach still felt that inflation was an ever-present menace in the US and that the UK was in a better position to deal with its economic problems. But 'the attitude of Unions is menacingly obstructive'. There was no doubt in his mind that only a political solution could address the world's difficulties.

As an investment manager, McCurrach's own answer to the issues facing Alliance Trust was to look beyond currencies and economies to managements and products. This meant, quite simply, that there would be a renewed, and intensified, interest in how individual companies were assessed with a view to whether their shares should be bought or sold. When macro-economic indicators could no longer be relied upon to provide directions then the individual management of companies, and the likely demand for the products and services they produced, had to serve as the only signpost to investment-grade assets.

Investment income actually held up well in the crisis but the same could not be said for capital values. As the world's stock markets plummeted the value of net assets fell from £137.6m to £109.5m. The FTA All Share Index fell by 27%. Not surprisingly the press again attacked the investment trust movement saying that they 'have lost for ever their appeal and their function as an institutional service to investors'. And once again McCurrach rose to their defence. He saw the large discount at which investments trusts traded against their asset values as nothing new. It was also to be seen as an opportunity for investors to acquire assets that would appreciate substantially as markets recovered and the discount narrowed.

He was particularly blunt about the journalists' use of some imagined 'ideal' standard by which to judge investment trusts because this so-called standard 'concentrates wholly on capital rewards ignoring income and often disregarding the risks of alternatives'. In a well argued riposte to the journalists he went on to demonstrate that Alliance Trust's had, in all respects, outperformed the market. He produced figures to show that in the previous ten years the London market had fallen by 3% and the New York market had risen by 9%. In the same period Alliance's net asset value had increased by 68%. Nor had this capital growth been bought at the cost of revenues and dividends. The latter had increased in London by 69% and in New York by 36%. The Alliance dividend had increased by 82%.

It was a strong performance of which McCurrach could be justifiably proud. Part of the problem was that there had been a large number of trusts formed in recent years, often with very narrowly defined investment criteria, and the ire of the journalists was directed at them rather than at the older, broadly based trusts such as Alliance. Yet all too often they had failed to make this distinction in their articles – preferring instead to discuss investment trusts as if they were one homogeneous group.

McCurrach was too experienced an investment manager to be panicked by the turn that events had taken or by the comments of journalists. He was experienced in the turns of the business cycles and had dealt before with such serious difficulties. He concluded his annual report with the words, 'I do not suggest any very early recovery either in net asset value or in discounts, at least until interest rates start to fall, but I do strongly suggest that altogether too much is being made of what is a recurrent, and one believes, transitory, phenomenon.' His caution, as well as his long view, was a measure of his experience. The crisis got worse before it got better.

The Alliance response to the crisis was to move out of equities and into gold, short-dated gilts and almost anywhere else where money could be invested with a view to protecting its value. That included investments in Deutschmarks and German equities. A statistics paper presented to the board in November 1974 revealed something of the extent of the turmoil and of the speed at which investment strategy had to be changed. It gave some detail of the main categories of investments at 30 June and 29 October 1974 before concluding with the following synopsis (see Table 8.6).

Table 8.6 Distribution of assets (totals by percentage)

| | | 30 June 1974 | | 29 October 1974 | |
		%	%	%	%
Equities	Sterling	41.5		35.3	
	Foreign	40.3	81.8	38.5	73.8
Gild Edged			6.8		–
Fixed Interest		4.6		5.1	
Cash			6.8		21.1
			100		100

The paper went on to provide figures that demonstrated the scale and scope of the changes that had taken place in the Alliance portfolio. Over that same four-month period, some £2.7m of US equities, £1m of British equities and £6.2m of gilt-edged had been sold. There had been modest purchases of non-sterling equities and German fixed-interest, but the fund was extremely liquid. Net equity sales over that four-month period had been £3.2m.

The 1975 report stated that more than half of the company's assets were invested overseas so there was some protection against further falls in the sterling rate of exchange. McCurrach reported that the year had been 'one of turmoil, national and international, political and social, economic and industrial, and above all in the financial markets of the world'. It was, he said, 'a year of near disintegration of all financial standards and values. It was time, therefore, to offer some reassurance to shareholders by restating Alliance company policy.

The quadruple objectives of the company were: 'First to protect capital against possible disasters of Stock Market collapse or of bankruptcy, corporate or even national. Second, to preserve the real value of capital against erosion by rampant inflation . . . Third, to increase the company's revenue collections and dividend distributions. Fourth . . . to be in a position to take advantage of any real permanent recovery.' In saying this McCurrach recognised that these aims and objectives were not always going to be mutually consistent and that the achievement of one might mean some sacrifice in another.

He went on to explain what Alliance had done to cope with the crisis and concluded with a clear statement about the root of the problem. Governments of all political hues had failed to control inflation. 'It seems forgotten that while recession is curable and its very real pains may be eased, continuous high inflation corrupts and corrodes irreversibly ending in chaos. Inflation is a drug. Taken in small doses it stimulates, insensibly it becomes an addiction; finally it is a tyrant and a killer. The future, therefore defies analysis.' He was clearly very conscious that the figures he produced to demonstrate how well Alliance had performed, compared with the market, were not what was uppermost in some investors' minds. They were even more concerned with the corrosive effect of inflation on their savings.

It was a fast-moving situation. The secondary banking crisis in the UK had added another dimension to the crisis. McCurrach was now more sanguine about economic prospects in America, which had finally got inflation under better control. He was increasingly impressed by prospects in Germany. The consequence was that investments had been moved into these countries and the non-sterling proportion of investments was then 51.9%.

McCurrach closed his report by stressing that Alliance still had no foreign currency loans. These had been considered from time to time but rejected. Other trusts had borrowed money overseas, especially in America, but the dangers of having to repay these loans at a time when sterling was depressed or devalued persuaded the board not to tread that particular path. It was a wise decision as, only two years later, an article in the *Sunday Times* regretted the fact that shareholders in some trusts had lost out as a result of such borrowings.

The report in 1976 revealed a much more comfortable position. There had been a dramatic recovery during the year 'not simply . . . in security prices but in fundamental economic, political and even social factors'. Concerns about hyper-inflation and bankruptcy had ceased to be 'imminent fears' and it was then possible to think about 'returning calm and reconstruction'. The net asset value of Alliance had increased from £1.64 per share to £2.48. Other indicators showed equally impressive results. Investment trusts were, once again, finding favour with the business press, and equities were finding favour in the portfolios of investment trusts.

Alliance had got out of gold stocks just before their decline and back into equities in time to catch the rising market. And while revenues had suffered a little in the process the board was still able to recommend a small increase in the annual dividend.

Good use had been made of the new reserve for the Diminution in Value of Assets. When the markets eventually went into free fall in 1973 there was a net loss on sales of investments, recorded in 1975, when the provision was debited with the sum of £2,930,266. However the markets rebounded quite strongly and the reserve was credited the following year with £2,296,178.

For the first time, in 1976, shareholders were provided with a list of actual share transactions in the larger holdings. The major purchases were in leading British companies such as Beecham Group, British American Tobacco, ICI, General Electric, Rank Organisation and Royal Insurance but with the addition of two German banks, Deutsche and Dresdner. The major sales were Sears Holdings and S.S. Kresge (K-Mart) and Tandy Corporation, although French government bonds were also sold. The sale of the American securities incurred a cost in dollar surrender premium of £933,000 which gave McCurrach a further opportunity to remind his shareholders that this was 'an arbitrary tax not upon profits but upon normal day-to-day activities' which had 'a distorting and paralysing effect on investment management'. He was well aware that the only way to avoid this imposition was by borrowing in foreign currency, but that brought its own risks, which he was not prepared to embrace. This policy had been considered but 'as consistently, deliberately and to date fortunately, rejected on the ground of high risk and tenuous reward'.

By that time the dollar surrender premium had been part of the UK's fiscal system for ten years, and throughout that period McCurrach had been consistent in his opposition to it. He called again for its abolition 'The conditions, the magnitude and above all the management impact have changed so much, creating a tangle of distortions and devices, that I make no apology for insisting that its abolition has become a matter of national importance.'

The move back into UK equities was timeous. In 1977 McCurrach was able to report that there had been very good rises in dividends both in the UK and US, and the fall in sterling against the dollar had produced a further £246,000. Yet the market had gone down and the net asset value had fallen, as a result, by 6%.

McCurrach had, by then, retired from active management, although he remained as chairman, and this gave him the opportunity of a retrospective on his ten years as chairman and managing director – years marked by great turbulence in world economic affairs or, as he put it, the world had been 'turned upside down'. He began with a characteristic criticism of the tax system and the dollar premium surrender that would have been no surprise to any of the shareholders who were regular readers of the annual report. He went on to remind them that there had been regulatory changes to the banking system and a dividend limitation policy. 'In the wider world there were two sterling devaluations followed by a final "float", two major dollar crises, two major world stock market slumps, the collapse of the Bretton Woods world monetary system, the temporary resurrection of gold, the driving out of Keynesian demand management by the monetarists, and the greatest world inflation in modern history followed by the worst recession since the 1930s.'

Against that background he felt that there was some merit in Alliance Trust's own record, which showed that there had been an unbroken record of increases in dividends that was far ahead of the indices. This, together with an even greater rise in net asset value and a sizeable increase in the Alliance share price, was a strong performance in the face of such adverse economic conditions.

McCurrach was clear that this success had only been achieved by major policy changes on a scale, and with a frequency, that had never before been contemplated or 'thought proper for conventional investment trusts'. In the process a variety of options and alternatives had been considered and, mostly, rejected. These included offshore funds, overseas subsidiaries, foreign borrowings and split capital funds, although he confessed that Alliance had an open mind about some of these options in the future. Throughout these difficult years the core policy to which Alliance had adhered was 'the pursuit of both income and capital growth, neither ever wholly surrendered to the other'. He admitted that while this had denied them dramatic short-term successes, it had also protected the Trust from the extremes of the major downturns and produced a balanced growth. The figure of which he was most proud was dividend growth, which was 86.4% better than that experienced by holders of F.T. Industrials.

But he did not believe that the British economy, far less the world economy, had resolved all of the difficulties. He thought that 'The future seems as confused as the past.' There was a possibility, he believed, that the effects of North Sea oil and gas might be so beneficial that the country would be deterred from making the changes that were otherwise deemed to be necessary, and that were being pressed for by the International Monetary Fund from which the UK had recently borrowed large sums of money.

Nor was the world economy showing any signs of stability. There were still many countries with 'yawning balance of payments gaps and huge mountains of unstable debt'. The risks remained great but he was sure that the potential of the UK stock market was as great as anywhere else.

Again it was a well-assessed appraisal of potential. When he reported in 1978 McCurrach was able to tell shareholders that the UK stock market performed well, compared with others, and that the company's net asset value had reached an all-time high. Investments in the US were the lowest they had been since 1951.

It was with some self-satisfaction that McCurrach recorded the demise of the hated investment currency surrender that he regarded quite simply as a tax and not as a legitimate component of exchange control. He was also pleased that there were signs that revenues from the North Sea would be put to good use to 'fuel and lubricate structural changes in government and industry, in attitudes and institutions'. Overall he was optimistic that the changes that were afoot would bring about a climate that was likely to be more helpful to capital formation.

Although he had given up the managing directorship there were no signs that McCurrach's interest in business was diminishing. His annual report for 1978 included a review of government reports and enquiries into various aspects of the financial system. He was especially interested in the interim report of the Wilson Committee on the Functioning of Financial Institutions which, he detected, contained strands of recognition that capital needed fair incentives and that the City was well equipped and ready to find money for investment in the economy. He went on to express his concern at the trend towards the dominance of the life and pension funds as owners of the greater part of the nation's marketable assets. This was a development he viewed as being undesirable and which should be stopped. It was a development that would come to bear heavily on investment trusts.

Inevitably his concluding remarks were another blast at the inequitable way that capital gains tax (CGT) was applied to investment trusts. He applauded the activities of the Association of Investment Trust Companies that had been campaigning to draw these inequities to the attention of government. As it then stood CGT was applied to the transactions in securities of investment trusts, and the effect of this was to diminish the earnings of shareholders in trusts even if they were exempt from the tax as individuals. The Inland Revenue had attempted to respond to some of the criticisms by publishing a discussion paper which proposed a 'tapering relief' but McCurrach dismissed this as, to make it work, 'would need a machinery of unmanageable complexity' which, he believed, underlined the need to exempt trusts from the tax, leaving individual shareholders to pay whenever they sold their investments in the trusts. There was no doubt in his mind but that this was a 'fiscal wrong' that should be corrected as quickly as possible.

As recovery continued in the closing years of the 1970s McCurrach was able to report rising dividends and improved capital performance, although he was still not overly sanguine about the prospects for the international economy. In view of the uncertainty Alliance maintained a high level of liquidity and McCurrach confessed that returns would have been higher had this not been the case. Nevertheless he believed that it was the right thing to do and this was borne out by the fact that in 1979 the year-end valuation and the net asset value were the highest in the company's history.

In the 1980 annual report McCurrach announced his retirement from the chairmanship of the company, although he also announced that he would continue as a board member for a further two years. His tenure at the company had been traumatic but successful. He ended on a high and clearly delighted in the fact that all the main indicators of performance were showing good signs. Even income from oil royalties was at an all-time high. Only the overall valuation of the portfolio was down a little on previous years, but this was entirely explained by the disappearance of the currency premium that had gone when exchange controls were abolished as almost the first act of the Thatcher government elected in 1979.

The ending of exchange controls produced a collective sigh of relief throughout the investment community. It provided them with much greater flexibility and easier calculations when investment decisions were to be made. McCurrach must have felt that at least some of his personal campaign had been successful. He reported to his shareholders that Alliance had taken advantage of the greater flexibility now available and had 'added almost £6 million to our Far East and continental equities and over £2 million to German bond holdings, while reducing exposure to U.K. equities by £5.3 million and U.S. equities by £2.6 million'.

McCurrach reserved his final report for a strongly worded statement about the dangers of inflation and the problems caused by indexation. In the UK and in other countries governments had tried to deal with inflation by indexing wages and benefits. McCurrach conceded that, in its initial phase, this was a sensible move because it protected the weak, but it was now institutionalised and he felt the curse of inflation was being exacerbated. As he put it, 'We have reached the stage where we are all the victims of our own simple arithmetic, but at compound interest.' It was, quite simply, a threat to the living standards of the strong and the weak. Moreover, it 'threatens to sterilise all new productive investment'. Devices put in place to cope with inflation had the effect of clogging 'true capital creation, by diverting whatever savings flow there may be away from it'.

He welcomed the steps that the new government had taken to combat inflation but he felt that Thatcher had not gone far enough. He went on to call for complete fiscal neutrality for all savers, especially individuals and investment trusts who struggled against the tax advantages that were available to pension funds, life assurance companies and building societies. Ultimately he wanted to see a 'revival of the flow of personal saving for direct investment'. Only that would lay 'the ground for solid advance'.

He concluded his report with a review of the performance of the Trust since he became joint manager in 1952.

McCurrach recounted the turbulent times through which the Trust had passed during his time in charge and concluded that the long-term investor 'has been not merely protected against inflation on both income and capital, but well rewarded'.

His final remarks were a word of thanks to the management team who were now supported by the 'most advanced technical apparatus'. His past and present colleagues on the board were thanked 'for their counsel, for their tolerance and for their support'.

McCurrach retired with a job well done but he was not immune from criticism. His record over the long term was exceptional but the shorter-term perspective painted a somewhat different picture. The Association of Investment Trust Companies (AITC) had begun to provide comparative figures showing the total return on net assets over five-year periods and on this basis the Alliance figures for the period 1975–80 showed the company in

Table 8.7. Comparison of Alliance performance with increases
in main indicators, 1952–1980

Alliance Trust ordinary dividends	13.7 times
FT Index dividends	5.2 times
Alliance Trust net asset value	14.0 times
FT Index	4.1 times
Alliance Trust share price	10.1 times
Cost of Living Index	6.1 times

a poorer light. The average return for all trusts was 227.8 while the Alliance
figure was only 187.8.

The reason for this lay in the distribution of assets that the Trust had
acquired in the early 1970s when the economy was in turmoil, a bear market
had left equity investments looking like a very high risk and banks were
looking particularly weak. In January 1974 total assets were £109 million, and
of this £12 million was in cash and gilts while £10m was represented by
currency premium. These were wise investments that helped the Alliance
weather the economic storm in better shape than most of its rivals and to
outperform them in all respects. In retrospect in would have been better to
sell these assets in 1975 and invest in the UK market. While there were
numerous changes in the portfolio between 1975 and 1980, they did not fundamentally alter its makeup. Consequently the Trust did not perform so well in
the second part of the 1970 as many of its rivals and by 1980 the discount of its
share price to net asset value was a historically high 34.9%.

George Stout's paper on the subject of investments, in February 1980,
raised a concern that Alliance still had less of its portfolio in equities than
many of its rivals and that there was a consequent danger that performance
over the coming years might continue to look weaker than that of other trusts.

Stout knew that this position would mean that Alliance would perform
less well than other trusts in a rising market and better in a falling market. Yet
he was also acutely aware that over a longer term Alliance had performed
consistently better than other trusts. His preoccupation, and that of Lyndon
Bolton, was how they could repeat Alliance's market leading performance in
the years to come.

Stout also raised a cautionary word in another paper that he wrote for the
Accountants' Magazine in February 1979. In it he surveyed the history of the

Table 8.8. Portfolio composition – Alliance Trust and average
of other Trusts, 1980 (percentages)

	UK Equity %	US Equity %	Other Equity %	Fixed-interest %
Alliance Trust	57	21	9	13
Average of Trusts	68	21	10	8

investment trust movement and expressed particular concerns for the future. He took the view that, 'The onset of Government budget deficits on an international scale, burgeoning money supply growth and rampant inflation . . . created a new set of conditions with which the system of private capitalism has found it difficult to cope.' He adhered to the widely held view that public sector borrowing had 'crowded out' the private sector from financial markets and that, given that government needs had to be met whatever the cost, there was therefore no objective criteria against which to measure the cost of borrowing. In the UK, public sector debt had more than doubled from 1968 and then stood at over £90bn. Industrial companies had been unable to pay the levels of interest on their borrowing that government was able to pay, and consequently there had been no net issue of loan capital by British companies between 1975 and 1979.

He went on, in a manner very reminiscent of McCurrach, to rail against major tax changes, savage taxation on investment income, foreign currency controls and dividend limitation. All of these had combined to make the running of investment trusts 'a mind bending exercise to managers and a headache of incomprehensibility to the private investor'. It was little wonder therefore that investment trusts had been losing shareholders. Evidence to the Wilson Committee on the Functioning of Financial Institutions had revealed that the percentage of ordinary shares in British companies that were owned by individuals had declined from 54% in 1963 to 33% in 1978. Such had been the changes that had taken place in the investment environment that individual were being advised to give up managing their own portfolios in favour of institutional schemes. Funds were then pouring into life assurance companies and pension plans which were heavily incentivised by tax concessions. The future for investment trusts looked bleak, for the implications were severe and they had already become takeover targets for pensions funds. More would follow.

Shareholders

These were difficult times for shareholders in many companies and there were numerous comments in the financial press about the demise of the individual shareholder and investor, as institutional investors increasingly dominated share registers in many companies. This was an inevitable consequence of the rise of company pension schemes. Individual shareholders, however, could still be found in large numbers in the ranks of the investment trusts whose initial appeal to individuals still held sway, i.e. the provision of a professionally managed diversified portfolio.

In his annual report to shareholders in 1969 McCurrach reported that the number of ordinary shareholders on the Alliance Trust register was then 16,200, and about 90% of shareholders were individuals. He went on to say that this number had been increasing at a compound rate of 11.5% per annum for ten years and that only 8% of shares in the company changed hands every year. Three years later he reaffirmed the traditional Alliance policy and said that 'although the management has consistently sought capital appreciation it has never surrendered to the cult of capital performance in disregard of the growth and quality of the earnings'.

He noted, too, that since 1963 the proportion of all ordinary shares on the London Stock Exchange that were held by investment trusts had increased from 10.5% to 13.6%. Financial journalists had increasingly called the function and usefulness of investment trusts into question, so he concluded with a sideswipe at them by saying, 'None of these figures seem very consistent with the picture, sometimes painted, of a group of institutions failing in their function.'

Figures prepared for the Diamond Committee in 1975 provide a snapshot of the Alliance Trust and its ordinary shareholders compared with other trusts (see Table 8.9).

Shareholders, by this time, were being provided with a growing volume of information. In addition to lists of the ten largest investments in the UK and US there was also a page in the annual report that gave a breakdown by sector and country, although not by company, of the classifications of investments.

On January 31 1969 (the annual balance date) the ten largest investments in the UK were (see Table 8.10).

The report in 1971 also revealed that there were 123 sterling ordinary, 182 sterling fixed-asset and 93 dollar common stock investments. Although still a

Table 8.9 (a) Analysis of Alliance ordinary shareholders
(as at 31 December 1974)

| | Numbers (000) | | | | Proportions of total capital | |
	All Trusts		Alliance		All Trusts	Alliance
Identified Persons	663	88%	17.4	86%	40%	55.6%
Banks and nominees	49	6%	1.6	8%	24%	25.1%
Identified Institutions	38	5%	1.1	5.5%	36%	18.8%
Overseas	7	1%	0.1	0.5%	0%	0.4%
Total	757	100%	20.2	100%	100%	100%

Table 8.9 (b) Analysis of Alliance Ordinary Shareholders
(Institutional Shareholders)

| | Numbers (000) | | Proportions of total capital | |
	All Trusts	Alliance	All Trusts	Alliance
Insurance Companies	7,385	224	18%	4.5%
Investment Trusts	2,581	57	4%	1.4%
Unit Trusts	398		3%	
Pension funds	2,242	32	2%	0.8%
Charities and others	22,194	811	7%	12.2%
Total	34,800	1,124	34%	18.9%

Notes:

Although Identified Persons are numerically slightly lower than average in Alliance, their percentage holding is very substantially larger, implying relatively larger average individual holdings.

Conversely Identified Institutions are numerically slightly above average but hold almost half as much capital as average, implying relatively small average institutional holdings.

Within the total for Identified Institutions, Alliance holdings of Insurance companies are only a quarter of the average, and the position for Investment Trusts, Identifiable Unit Trusts and Pension Funds is similar. On the other hand 'Others' are well above average. These consist of Industrial companies, Lloyds, the Public Trustee, Trade Unions and others, all of whom may be regarded as strong holders.

Nominee holdings do not affect these conclusions; as a proportion of capital Alliance was close to average: they are known to include Unit Trust holdings.

Table 8.10 (a) The ten largest investments by value in UK-registered companies (as at 31 January 1969)

1. Shell Transport and Trading Co. Ltd
2. Imperial Tobacco Co. Ltd
3. British American Tobacco Co. Ltd
4. Allied Breweries Ltd
5. Thorn Electrical Industries Ltd
6. Glaxo Group Ltd
7. Lesney Products and Co. Ltd
8. Gestetner Holdings Ltd
9. Beecham Group Ltd
10. Bass Charrington Ltd

Table 8.10 (b) The ten largest investments by value in US-registered companies (as at 31 January 1969)

1. Tri-Continental Corp.
2. S.S. Kresge Co. (K-Mart)
3. International Business Machines Corp.
4. International Telephone and Telegraph Corp.
5. Anheuser-Busch Inc.
6. General Motors Corp.
7. Avon Products Inc.
8. General Cable Corp.
9. Washington Associates Inc.
10. Pabst Brewing Co.

much diversified portfolio, it was a very different one from earlier phases in the company's life when, for example, in the 1930s it contained more than 1,000 different investments.

In addition to these lists, shareholders were also provided with a table showing, year by year, the ten-year record of the company. These showed, inter alia, the figures set out in Table 8.11.

These figures are indicative of a remarkable performance, and they placed

Table 8.11 Key performance figures, 1960 and 1969

Year	Gross revenue (£)	Ordinary dividend (%)	Value of net assets (£)	Net asset value of 5s share
1960	2,402,076	11.33	42,410,211	16/10 (84p)
1969	3,773,624	23.14	125,845,603	49/11 (£2.50)

the Alliance in a position where it faced the economic difficulties to come from a position of real strength.

However, the Alliance, like all investment trusts, was facing mounting competition from unit trusts. These open-ended funds were able to advertise their products whereas investment trusts had only their shares to sell, and company law prevented them from advertising. The Alliance's way of dealing with this was to start a Dividend Investment Plan in 1969 in which investors could allow their dividends to be reinvested in company shares. Alliance was the first of the investment trusts to introduce such a scheme and, for some unexplained reason, it remained the only one for several years. It is certainly the case that the economic troubles of the 1970s might have deterred other companies from copying the system and shareholders might have been reluctant to commit to it in view of the wide fluctuations in the stock markets. But by the closing years of the 1970s those who had been the first to reinvest their dividends in the scheme would have been well satisfied with the results.

The economic circumstances of the early 1970s certainly did not deter new investors in Alliance shares and by 1976 the number of shareholders on the register had risen to 21,000. This was in stark contrast to the experience of companies in other sectors of the economy where there was growing concern about the diminishing numbers of private investors and the increasing dominance of institutional investors – principally life and pensions companies. Nevertheless the downturn in the numbers of private investors eventually began to hit investments trusts and by 1979 the number of shareholders on the register was down to 18,135. McCurrach blamed this on the taxation regime but also on 'new styles of financial journalism, of professional advice and even of many investment management objectives'. These, he believed, 'laid increasing, and finally exclusive emphasis on rapid growth, short term performance and quick capital gains'. These factors eclipsed what he believed to be the true function of investment trusts, which was 'the provision of a service to the private investor for the safe and productive *long-term* management of his investment capital'. What he failed to mention was the impact of inflation on savings and the fact that it made more sense for many people to borrow rather than save in an era when inflation was rampant and house prices, in many areas, were advancing even more quickly than the published rate of inflation.

Whatever their motivations for investing in Alliance shares the shareholders articulated a need for more information. This was not unique to Alliance, and most companies responded by providing not just what the Companies Acts required but what they thought would be of interest and value to shareholders. Clearly there was a balance to be struck between the provision of information to shareholders and what might be commercially sensitive and of use to competitors. By the closing years of the 1970s the Alliance annual report had become a much more informative document than it had previously been. It contained a list of the 40 largest equity holdings, together with a figure for the value of each holding. Typically these investments accounted for just over 50% of all equity holdings. There was also a table like a trading account that listed the value by market at the beginning of the year, added purchases, subtracted sales and provided a closing balance. A further table showed the percentages of each class of investment by industrial sector with another division, which showed investments in the UK, US, Europe and 'elsewhere'. The penultimate page of the report contained tables with ten-year overviews of the Dividend Investment Plan and the main performance indicators, the final column of which was net asset value. The last page was a proxy voting form for the annual general meeting.

The nature and content of the report was a total transformation compared with what would have sufficed only 20 years earlier and it went well beyond what the Companies Acts required. To a large extent the change was led by the Association of Investment Trusts which recognised the changes that were taking place in investment and savings habits and did what it could to promote the services of its members, recognising in the process that investors were becoming more sophisticated and that they required more information to enable them to make better-informed choices. There is no doubt however that they were also stung into action by the criticism that investment trusts had attracted in the financial press – criticism which often failed to distinguish between the different types of trust and the varying ambitions of investors.

Chapter 9
Resurgence and Innovation: 1980–1996

These were difficult but successful years for Alliance Trust. The economic woes of the 1970s left a legacy of problems, not the least of which were a high rate of inflation and low economic growth. The Conservative government that was elected in 1979 set about trying to improve matters. Almost its first action was to abolish exchange control regulations. A programme of privatisation of nationalised industries followed. Both measures provided a dramatic stimulus for investors. A third strand of government policy was to make the financial services sector more competitive, and this led to dramatic restructuring as financial services companies engaged in takeovers and the traditional dividing lines between different types of financial institution disappeared. 'Big Bang' in 1986 brought to an end a number of established relationships in the City of London, not least fixed commissions, and made trading much more competitive. New players came into the market, many from the US and Europe, and transformed London into what it had once been – the world's largest financial centre.

Progress, however, was far from smooth. Black Monday in 1987 was one of the largest downturns the stock markets had ever seen and the recession in the early 1990s was on a truly global scale.

Between 1984 and 1994 more than 100 new trusts were established in the UK, raising £2.5bn in capital. Nevertheless there was a net outflow from the sector caused by takeovers and conversions into unit trusts. Many of the new trusts were very specialised. One even concentrated on second-hand insurance policies. Others specialised in particular regions of the world. Large general investment trusts like Alliance became increasingly rare.

Against this background Alliance Trust moved forward. Full advantage was taken of the new trading opportunities but not without also taking cognisance of the challenges posed by inflation and economic cycles. Alliance also saw the beginning of a quiet revolution. With a move into leasing and then into a range of savings products the very nature of Alliance Trust began to change.

The People

The new chairman was local solicitor George Dunn, who took over the reins from David McCurrach at the annual general meeting in 1980. Given his age – he was 66 – it is unlikely that he was seen as anything more than a stop-gap chairman. It was the first time since 1945 that the chairman had not also served as managing director of the company. Dunn's annual reports to the shareholders were a good deal more subdued than those of McCurrach. He was much less inclined to rail against the problems of society or the difficulties being endured by investors. Rather, he contented himself with a review of the Trust's performance and the changes that had occurred in the world economy during the year. He was quietly pleased that the company was now free of capital gains tax – a freedom for which McCurrach had campaigned ever since it was introduced in the mid 1960s.

The board in 1980 comprised:

George W. Dunn,
Professor Christopher Blake
Lyndon Bolton
David F. McCurrach
George A. Stout
Brian H. Thomson

Formal board meetings were held monthly, but there was also an informal meeting on Fridays. These meetings lasted between 30 minutes and an hour and were continued over lunch in the Eastern Club. The role of the board was to advise and counsel. Day-to-day operations were in the hands of the executive.

McCurrach finally retired when he reached the age of 70 in 1982 and was warmly thanked by the board for the enormous contribution that he had made to the company for over 40 years. His replacement on the board was Douglas Hardie, a Dundee resident who was deputy chairman of the Scottish Development Agency and a director of the Clydesdale Bank.

Dunn did not remain in the chair for long, and he retired on reaching the age of 70 in 1984. The new chairman was Robert C. Smith, CBE, MA, LLD, CA, a man of very wide business interests and experience, but who was best known for his role as liquidator of Upper Clyde Shipbuilders. Smith had joined the board in 1981 at a time when he was not personally known to the other directors. However his public reputation and his experience on the boards of companies such as Standard Life, Wm Collins and Burmah Oil ensured that he was a popular choice.

By that time George Stout and Lyndon Bolton had been in charge on a daily basis since 1976. They divided the responsibilities, with Stout being responsible for the US and Asia while Bolton concentrated on the UK and Europe. Stout retired in 1988 but not before writing a short history of the company. The Inland Revenue decided that this publication was not a book, but advertising, and, as such, was liable for VAT. Suggett decided that this was worth a fight and successfully challenged the decision.

Lyndon Bolton was then appointed as managing director and Gavin Suggett, who was company secretary, joined the board. The management team was then realigned with the appointment of W. Grant Lindsay, Ronald Hadden and Alan Young, all employees of some standing, as managers. Sheila Gates (later Sheila Ruckley) joined as company secretary.

There followed a period of relative stability in the management and in the board. Brian Thomson retired as a director in 1989 and was replaced by Andrew Thomson. D.C.Thomson and Co. was amongst the largest shareholders in the Trust. Bruce Johnston, a chartered accountant, who was a director of many companies including City Centre Restaurants and Mid Wynd International Investment Trust (a Baillie Gifford company), joined the board in 1991. Alan Young was appointed an executive director the following year. Three years later Young assumed responsibility for investment policy formulation and implementation through his team of six portfolio managers. Douglas Hardie retired in 1994 and was replaced by William Berry, who was chairman of Scottish Life and senior partner in Murray, Beith and Murray, WS.

Gavin Suggett was appointed to the new post of deputy general manager in 1992, and two years later he became joint managing director with a view to succeeding Lyndon Bolton when the latter retired in 1995.

The annual general meeting that year recorded the fact that Professor Christopher Blake, an economist in the University of Dundee and chairman of Wm Low and Co., who had been on the board since 1974, had retired the previous October.

The total number of staff employed in the organisation had been almost 30 in the early 1970s but this had fallen to 17 in 1984. The decline was partly due to the outsourcing of shareholder registration to the Royal Bank and partly to the efficiency gains from computerisation. It was not long however before staff numbers started rising again due to the success of the leasing business and the early growth of Alliance Trust Savings. By 1990 there were ten people employed in the investment side of the business and their responsibilities were divided by industrial sector.

Investments

The 1980s started with high expectations. What Dunn described as 'firm stock markets' actually delivered growth of 14.8% in the UK and 13.5% in the US. Gross revenue exceeded £10m for the first time. Alliance was heavily invested in energy and electronic technology stocks and so did even better than the indices. A stake was taken in Gate Microsystems – a Dundee-based company that was the leading Scottish dealer in Apple and Commodore computers. Suggett joined its board in what he described as 'a new departure for us'.

Dunn was able to report in 1981 that the net asset value of the company's investments had risen by 17%. Even the *Financial Times*, on 23 March 1981, celebrated the fact that investment trusts had been in 'a dark tunnel from which they are only just emerging'. Freedom from capital gains tax and exchange control regulations had enabled Alliance to dispose of certain stocks like General Electric and Southland Royalty where 'the stock market price appeared to run well ahead of the fundamentals'.

Nevertheless, despite the success, the chairman recorded a discordant note, at least so far as prospects for the British economy were concerned. Dunn felt that there was 'an ever smaller number of companies' which measured up to the long-term growth potential that Alliance sought. There were better opportunities in the US and Japan. Consequently an increasing proportion of the company's funds were invested in these countries. Nevertheless 28 of the top 40 largest investments were still in British companies.

Dunn's view was echoed in one of Stout's board papers in October 1982. His view was that the lack of good investment opportunities in the UK had persuaded investors to put their money in the big privatisation issues. Alliance had done this and had outperformed the average for investment trusts by a significant margin. The worries that Dunn had confided in a board paper two years earlier about growth prospects in the world economy were unfounded and net assets had increased by 36% in the previous twelve months.

This did not mean that Dunn thought all was well in the world. He had concerns about some of the trusts that specialised in a narrow range of investments. His view was that 'specialisation is bunk, these are dangerous times and we think it best to be as diversified in outlook as possible'. In an article published on 21 May 1983 *The Times* acknowledged that while specialist investment trusts were all the rage it could not be denied that some of the older generalist trusts, including Alliance, had performed really well.

David McCurrach finally retired from the board in 1982 and the annual report recorded the company's appreciation of his 'wise counsel'. He had been a 'tower of strength to the board'. The report also showed that performance had been satisfactory.

Of greater concern was the state of the world economy. There were worries that inflation was not under control in many countries and this was leading to instability in international financial affairs. In particular there were nagging concerns that the US budget deficit could only be financed in a non-inflationary way by maintaining high interest rates. This, it was thought, presented problems for other economies, including the British, where the maintenance of exchange rate parities with the dollar required a continuation of high interest rates which would be a check on growth.

This was a time to reassure shareholders that Alliance policy was on track to deliver 'a steadily increasing income return allied to reasonable capital growth'. The diversification of its investments, both geographically and industrially would ensure, they were informed, that the corrosive effect of a poor economic outlook and high interest rates would not impact unduly on the Alliance performance. Business conditions in the US and Japan were not as attractive as they had appeared a year earlier and some assets were converted into cash that was held as foreign currency.

The new style of annual report, which made its first appearance in 1982, gave shareholders an overview of conditions in each of the major markets in which their funds were invested and of the scale of transactions in each area. There were particular concerns about the prospects for consumer spending in the UK, so investments in breweries, tobacco and stores were reduced. Some of the money realised by these sales was invested in twenty smaller companies where 'the expertise, determination and flexibility of the management is particularly evident. There were even some investments in unquoted companies, including Advent Technology and other young companies which specialised in 'computer and related technologies especially in Scotland'.

Notwithstanding public policy problems in the US it was felt that there was still enormous potential in the country although there was also an awareness that the economic balance was shifting from the north-east to the south and west. It was there that the new industries of computers, communications, medical services and aerospace were to be found and it was there that Alliance placed a growing proportion of its funds. Nevertheless the major US investments were still in oil and oil-related services. The importance of oil to the North American economy was further reflected in the fact that Alliance's remaining holdings of mineral interests were both growing in value and producing increasing revenue. There were still almost 500 properties extending over 130,000 acres in Texas, Oklahoma, New Mexico, Idaho and Canada. These had been valued for the balance sheet at £1m, yet they produced royalty income of £127,000 while bonus payments and rentals on leases brought in a further £125,000 which was credited to capital reserve.

Only 4.9% of Alliance's funds were invested in Japan, in companies such as Kyoto Ceramic, Fuji Photo and Nippon Electric. But there were fears that a domestic recession and international protectionist measures against Japanese goods might damage the economy. Consequently no plans were laid to increase the commitment to Japanese companies.

In the report to shareholders in 1983 Dunn expressed his puzzlement that despite the fact that the world was still grappling with major economic problems the investment fraternity had had a very good year. Company policy was then being explained as a balanced growth of both income and capital, so there was increasing emphasis being given to the importance of the net asset value of Alliance shares, which had increased by 40%. Dunn felt that this was due to careful management by his colleagues, not just in stock selection but in currency exposure. He went on to say that, 'Stock markets are often in a decline when industrialists are at their most cheerful and optimistic. Conversely . . . the deeper the industrial problems become the more enthusiastic are financial markets. An explanation would seem to be that stock markets are motivated more by expectations and monetary influences and less by current levels of business activity and profit.'

He also felt that, especially in the UK, although inflation and interest rates were finally falling, investors were faced with higher prices as too much money chased too few good investments. 'Where the market's enthusiasm seems to have run ahead of reality we have taken substantial profits and retired to the sidelines.' He was also worried about the state of technology stocks in the US. High valuations had been put on many stocks but he took the view that many of the new companies coming to the market were of poor quality, and he interpreted this as a sign that the market had become overextended and was due for a correction. However, 'with substantial reserves in short-term deposits we are well placed to take advantage of any significant setback'.

There was continuing interest in investment in Australian infrastructure and renewed enthusiasm for unlisted Scottish companies such as Aberdeen-based engineering company the John Wood Group.

The remarkable growth of world stock markets continued into 1984. Dunn, in his final report, took pleasure in informing shareholders that in the past three years the Alliance net asset value had more than doubled but the UK stock market had risen by only 73%. The disparity between these figures he explained by the fact that 62% of the Trust's assets were invested in overseas assets and in countries where the stock market growth had been even greater than in the UK. Much of the growth was in the US where 47% of assets were invested and where there had also been an appreciation of the dollar against sterling. Price movements in the UK stock markets of these magnitudes made the Alliance cautious about current market levels. In the US it had become clear that 'the market's exuberance was outrunning the ability of even the best companies to deliver on earnings and dividends'.

These levels of growth had not gone unnoticed by investors, and Dunn was pleased to record the fact that an examination of the company's share register revealed, for the first time in many years, an increase in the number of private investors. He was also able to welcome, for the first time, a number of US institutional investors.

Robert Smith, in his first annual report to shareholders in 1985, continued the good news. Markets had continued to move forward and dividends from both British and American companies demonstrated impressive rates of growth. Consequently gross revenue rose by 19%, and earnings, helped by the start of a progressive reduction in corporation tax, went up by 28%.

Notwithstanding that the US government continued to grapple with a high budget deficit and a growing balance of payments problem, the value of the dollar continued to grow against other currencies. The US economy also demonstrated healthy levels of growth in output, unlike the British economy, which had not yet begun to benefit from some of the policy changes introduced by the Thatcher government.

Smith took the opportunity to review progress and to record that over the past five years the Trust had 'continued to balance the income and growth requirements of our stockholders'. He paid tribute to the 'skill and concentration on our affairs of a compact and effective staff and management team'.

It was not just the investments in securities that were producing bigger revenues. Oil and gas revenues from North America were £435,000, helped in part by the enhanced value of the dollar but also helped by the increase in exploration activity. It was not just North American oil in which Alliance was interested. A lively commitment had been made to North Sea oil exploration and to oil industry service companies. Alliance was a large investor in City Oil Exploration Ltd.

The leasing business, which had started in 1979, and oil exploration were somewhat peripheral to the main business of investment, which continued to perform well, aided by progressive reductions in the rate of corporation tax. In the 1986 report Smith recorded another strong revenue performance and confidently predicted that more was to come. However there was something of a hiatus in the growth of asset values, which Smith attributed to the adjustments that many economies were making to rid themselves of the burden of inflation. He noted that many investment decisions in the recent past had been based on the assumption that inflation would continue at high levels and 'For a time the ingenuity of the international financial system, in devising ever more sophisticated credit instruments for borrowers, postponed the inevitability of a correction.' But a collapse in oil prices and the problems experienced in the banking systems of many countries in dealing with Third World debt suggested that this was a time for pursuing a cautious investment policy.

Smith was clear that 'The present climate in international trade and finance makes it a particularly inappropriate time for specialisation, whether by currency or by industry, or for investing exclusively for either capital or for income growth.' Alliance would continue to pursue a balance of these objectives.

It would not be easy. Smith's comments about the US economy revealed concerns about weaknesses in agriculture, oil, consumer products and banking. The strength of the dollar had weakened the ability of American industry to compete on world markets, although this had been well contained. Despite this, some areas of the stock market had held up well. But there were other signs that the US economy was getting out of balance. Levels of personal savings had fallen to an all-time low and the expansion of debt to finance consumption had been growing at a precipitous rate.

The large leading companies whose profits were most predictable, in which Alliance was heavily invested, did well as US investors began to seek safety. And the Federal Reserve lowered interest rates and expanded the money supply as a support to the sectors that were experiencing difficulties. Yet there were also some new opportunities as the Bell Telephone system was broken up and seven new regional companies were created. Alliance invested £14m in

Pacific Telesis, Bell South and US West. Nevertheless Smith's tone was cautious. He believed that the US stock market was overpriced and 'In this environment it still seems too early to consider change to a more aggressive posture of investment.'

Meanwhile conditions in the British economy had begun to improve. The miners' strike in 1984 had damaged confidence, but otherwise the British economy had at last begun to put behind it the difficulties that it had experienced during the 1970s. Alliance still had about 40% of its portfolio in British stocks, and a recent spate of takeovers and mergers had provided some capital growth. The UK investments were being very actively managed, and disposals amounting to £39m had produced profits of £21m.

However Smith was concerned that the stridency with which some of the takeovers were conducted might deter investors and choke off the renewed interest in investments by private individuals. He was also a little worried that the balance sheets of newly merged companies revealed 'inherent risks'. His overall impression of the UK economy was mixed. Chronic unemployment, balance of payments difficulties and high levels of wage increases did not bode well for the future.

At the time when Smith's next report was written, in the early months of 1987, the worries that he had expressed a year earlier had not materialised in any major way, but nor had they disappeared. Indeed both the US and UK economies had done rather well. Dividend increases from both economies had averaged more than 10%. The value of Alliance's net assets had grown by 26% and Smith was able to announce a further increase in the dividend to shareholders. Stock market prices around the world, with the exception of Germany, had been 'spectacular'.

The surge had been fuelled by liquidity 'on an unprecedented international scale and . . . by generous supplies of credit'. The dollar had depreciated against other currencies, which had made US exports more competitive and had enabled it to expand employment by 2 million in 1986 alone. In the UK, rising property and stock market prices and the impact of the privatisation of government-owned enterprises had 'engendered a sense of financial well being'.

However, underlying that sense of well-being was the knowledge that economic fundamentals were still not well balanced. Moreover consumer behaviour in the financial services markets was changing. 'The present strenuous pursuit of short term interests,' declared Smith, 'be they in investment values, fees, commissions or bank and consumer lending is

occurring against a background of strong monetary growth, radical internationalisation and restructuring of financial organisations and a decidedly
immature regulatory system'.

Nor was all going well in the Far East where, in a reversal of its earlier
strategy, Alliance had been investing a growing proportion of its funds. The
Japanese stock market had grown 12% in a year, but growth was patchy and
there were marked differences between sectors. Moreover efforts to reduce the
value of the dollar had made Japanese exports to the US more expensive and
trade had suffered. This had impacted on the share prices of major exporting
companies. Consequently real growth in the economy was expected to slow
down.

The Australian economy was also posing difficulties, partly because of its
links to the US dollar but also because of a difficult balance of payments
problem.

Overall the impression given in the 1986 report was of trouble ahead. But
it was some time in coming. The 1987 report recorded a further increase in
income, dividends and stock market prices in both the UK and US. In the US,
Alliance's investments were concentrated in companies which would do well
despite the weakness of the economy. Some of these investments, including
Merck, Philip Morris, Abbot Laboratories and Wal-Mart, had increased by
more than 50%. Others such as IBM, which had suffered from increased
competition, saw the holding reduced. Funds were being moved into regional
telephone companies, and the oil portfolio, which had been virtually elimi-
nated, was steadily being rebuilt.

The major challenge for investors in the US economy was to make sense
of, and work out the likely implications of, changes to economic policy.
Reaganomics was the name given to a slew of new economic policies introduced during the presidency of Ronald Reagan. They emphasised low taxes,
reduced economic regulation, low social services spending, higher military
spending, low interest rates, low inflation and large budget deficits. There were
also measures of protection for some American industries. Although the
market had moved ahead smartly this was a time for caution, and Alliance
sold equities and invested in US treasury bonds.

There was a not dissimilar story in the UK economy. Alliance policy was
to concentrate on companies whose management was strong and which had
good growth prospects and sound finances. In Japan, however, there were
other types of problem. High levels of liquidity drove stock market prices to
historically high levels at a time when many of the economic fundamentals,

such as economic growth and company profits, were falling.

The collapse of oil and gas prices in 1986 inevitably affected the company's revenues from that sector. Total income from the mineral interests in the United States was only £190,000. There was better news from the leasing business, which benefited from strong demand. Pre-tax profits were up to £1.8m. But this was a business that was greatly influenced by tax systems, and the phasing out of first year capital allowances was an ominous sign.

Overall it is difficult to escape the conclusion that the world economy was running into difficulties. There were numerous signs that the markets had been overheating, and a number of high-profile scandals in the US in the early months of 1987 lent a sense of speculative mania to markets that were trading at historically high levels. Even junk bonds had been trading well. Alliance sold numerous investments and held the money as liquid assets. It proved to be a good decision. The crash came on Monday 19 October. Stout expressed the company view, albeit inelegantly, when he wrote 'The boom brings the punters in and it becomes heady and that's when we think about taking some cash.'

The crash began in Hong Kong before spreading westwards to Europe and eastwards to the United States. By the end of October the stock market in Hong Kong had fallen by 45.5%, the UK market was down 26.4% and the US market fell 22.7%. Other markets fared equally badly, with New Zealand probably the worst hit with a fall in excess of 60%. The events of Black Monday itself marked the largest one-day decline in stock market history. However, despite the severity of the crash, it was something of a chimera, at least so far as long-term investors were concerned. By the end of 1987 the markets were slightly ahead of where they had been at the beginning of the year. So while the increases of 1987 had been lost the longer-term trend was still positive.

Alliance was able to increase its dividend although net asset value was down over the previous year. This was largely a result of a further decline in the value of the dollar. As a result of this decline funds were withdrawn from the US and invested in UK equities.

The annual report in 1988 marked the company's centenary. The celebrations were quite modest. Instead of holding the annual general meeting in the head office in Reform Street it was held in the Stakis Earl Grey Hotel. George Stout's history of the company was published and given to shareholders, and £100,000 was spent in upgrading the head office building and facilities, which, with the exception of the Clydesdale Bank branch on the corner of Reform Street was then wholly owned by Alliance. In the conclusion to his annual statement Smith said: 'We embark on our second one hundred years, which recent events suggest may be quite as adventurous and as testing as the first, committed to the philosophies of independences of mind, consistency of style and integrity which we believe have our stockholders respect and which have stood them in good stead over so many years.' He offered assurances to the shareholders that Alliance had a well-diversified portfolio that demonstrated a 'flexible international spread of risk'. The 'euphoria' which had pervaded stock markets had evaporated, but conditions were still volatile and required vigilance to ensure the company could continue to deliver a 'steady growth in income and capital'.

Ivor Guild, great-grandson of the first chairman, congratulated the company on its performance and made special reference to the judicious decision to liquidate assets prior to the crash. Amongst those attending the lunch was James McIntosh Patrick, the well-known local landscape artist.

Table 9.1 Forty largest equity investments, 1988

Company	Value (£000)	Main activity	Country
Shell	18,214	Oil	UK
Philip Morris	14,219	Tobacco	US
BT	9,912	Telephones	UK
Dun and Bradstreet	7,743	Business Services	US
Beecham Group	6,779	Drugs and Toiletries	UK
Johnson & Johnson	6,509	Hospital supplies	US
BellSouth	6,252	Telephones	US
Morton Thiokol	5,458	Chemicals	US
Abbot Laboratories	5,404	Drugs and services	US
Wal-Mart Stores	5,332	Discount Stores	US
Pacific Telesis	5,200	Telephones	US
US West	5,057	Telephones	US
Farmers Group	4,894	Insurance	US
ASDA-MFI Group	4,776	Food Retailing	UK
Great Universal Stores	4,757	Mail Order Shopping	UK
Stakis	4,709	Leisure	UK
Slough Estates	4,662	Property	UK

Company	Value (£000)	Main activity	Country
National Westminster	4,643	Banking	UK
British Petroleum	4,577	Oil	UK
Humana	4,353	Hospital Services	US
Prudential	4,199	Insurance	UK
Merck	4,097	Drugs	US
Legal & General	4,090	Insurance	UK
PepsiCo	4,018	Food	US
Marks and Spencer	3,849	Multiple Stores	UK
Unilever	3,795	Food	UK
Wolverhampton Breweries	3,794	Brewing	UK
Reckitt & Colman	3,606	Food	UK
Rentokil Group	3,606	Pest control	UK
Nynex	3,578	Telephones	US
Security Services	3,573	Security	UK
Trusthouse Forte	3,450	Leisure	UK
BAT Industries	3,403	Tobacco	UK
Marsh & McLennan	3,364	Insurance Broking	US
EMAP	3,228	Publishing	UK
Britoil	3,226	Oil	UK
Electrocomponents	3,212	Electrical parts	UK
Barclays	3,204	Banking	UK
Bristol-Myers	3,141	Drugs and Cosmetics	US
Grand Metropolitan	3,065	Leisure	UK

It was a well-balanced portfolio that saw the company through the next series of challenges. The investors were now receiving much more information than they had received in the past and Smith was at pains to remind them that the company policy was 'aimed at producing a steady growth of both income and capital'. Greater interest was being taken in economies other than the UK and US, notably in Japan and Australia but, as the above table reveals, investments in these countries were still a small proportion of the total and no individual investment was particularly large. Moreover there was a conscious decision to make investments in smaller companies, as there was a belief that strong growth in the future was more likely to come from that direction. This in itself was perfectly sensible, but it also reflects the shift that was taking place from a complete emphasis on dividends to a more balanced approach with the objective of capital growth as well as dividends.

The Berlin Wall came down in 1989, and the investment community immediately began to consider the needs of Eastern European countries. The Alliance approach, however, was predictably cautious.

In the report for 1990 Smith wrote:

> Even if one dares to hope that the frighteningly complex political changes can be managed in an orderly way the economic problems are no less daunting. The trading and financial assistance required from the 'Western' nations may well divert growth away from some of the geographical and product areas, where it has been profitably concentrated in recent years, into more basic activities whose profitability will be, to say the least, uncertain.
>
> It will be a stern test of the willingness of the strong and affluent to provide relevant help to support the fragile economies now so publicly exposed, both internally and externally, behind the crumbling political walls, and most of the mechanisms and relationships, which had been taken for granted as stable and permanent, even if feared or detested, are now suddenly vulnerable and unpredictable.
>
> Caution in the face of uncertainty, not pessimism, would be an appropriate stance, for the new opportunities that will unfold are immense, and we are confident that our portfolio is well diversified geographically and concentrated in companies able to adapt to changing circumstances. We are effectively fully invested, though with minimal borrowing.

The cautious approach was wholly appropriate and Alliance contented itself with some investments in German companies that were thought to be well placed to take advantage of the opportunities in the east. Yet a year later Smith spoke to shareholders of the 'dissipation of many hopes for the USSR and Eastern Europe'. Moreover, 'The euphoria which surrounded the removal of the barriers between East and West, both within Germany and other countries, has been replaced by a more cautious assessment of the human, administrative and economic problems which must be addressed before the infrastructure of the East can be brought up to Western standards.'

It was also a troubled time for the British economy. Although progress had been made, inflation was not yet wholly under control and high wage settlements did not help that battle. The arrival of a new prime minister, John Major, and a new chancellor, Norman Lamont, added to the uncertainty, as did a number of factors on the international horizon such as the Iraqi invasion of Kuwait. Smith was seriously worried that the UK had entered the European Exchange Rate Mechanism 'at a particularly demanding level for the pound' with the result that interest rates remained high at a time when they should have been coming down to assist a 'fast weakening domestic economy'.

As in all times of weakening economies, investors were alive to the possibilities of identifying attractive prospects. Smith told the shareholders that, 'As companies seek to repair the damage to their own balance sheets by raising equity capital, or where share prices are depressed owing to special factors, we expect to use such opportunities gradually to commit some of our own cash balance to the market.'

Recessionary times were experienced by many world economies in the early 1990s. Japan, which until then had been a much envied model of economic success, was particularly badly hit. Early in 1991 it was reported that the Japanese stock market had fallen by 38%. Further falls were to follow. But by then Alliance had divested itself of most of its Japanese investments – a fact that was noted with an expression of relief by the *Scotsman*.

In the report to shareholders in 1992 Smith was able to say that, despite the state of the economy, earnings had risen by 7%. There were concerns, however, that the recession was giving every sign of being protracted. A year later he was able to report that net asset value had increased for the fourth year in a row. Much of the improvement had come from the strength of the dollar following sterling's departure from the European Exchange Rate Mechanism in September 1992, and cash reserves were being held in foreign currencies as it was widely expected that sterling would exhibit further weakness. The Japanese yen was not one of these currencies in which the reserves were held. The Japanese economy was still in turmoil and further falls in its currency and stock market were widely anticipated. Only the US economy was showing signs of improving health.

The fragile state of many economies made life difficult for investment managers, as did the enormous swings in interest rates that were occurring in many countries. In the UK the Bank of England base rate peaked at 14% in October 1990 but was down to 5.25% at the start of 1994. Consequently other market rates had also tumbled. Paradoxically the level of personal savings was rising and people were turning increasingly to the stock market as a repository for their savings. The challenge they faced was not to let inflation erode their savings. Inflation in the UK (the retail price index) had fallen from 9% in January 1991 to 2.5% in January 1994. Investment trusts were the simplest and most obvious way for individuals to secure an investment in a broadly based, professionally managed portfolio. Consequently they grew in popularity, and the number of ordinary shareholders in Alliance Trust was over 27,000, an increase of nearly 50% in two years.

Alliance Trust was able to weather the market pressure because it had a defensive portfolio and by this time, no gearing. It was well equipped therefore to ride out any economic storms.

Inflation was still the major problem being faced in many countries. Central banks began to apply a monetary squeeze by keeping interest rates low to choke off inflation. The result was to cool bond and stock markets. Smith was relieved that 'for the first time for very many years, a gentle slow down in the rate of growth [of prices] can be achieved without pushing the economies into recession. This would be a very satisfactory result.' For the short term Alliance had been selling assets, holding cash and investing small amounts in companies in developing countries.

By 1994 there were signs that the world was coming out of the recession. Alliance had steered its way through very successfully and had enjoyed a growing net asset value and rising dividends. The rise in the net asset value had been consistently ahead of the FTSE 100, although this was due mostly to improving market strength in the US rather than in the UK.

Smith's final report, in 1996, recorded that the company was doing well. Equities had risen strongly through 1995 and new industries, such as biotech, were beginning to emerge with growing demands for capital. Alliance compared itself with the FT All Share Index, against which it had performed favourably. Yet this success had been achieved against a background of economies enjoying very mixed fortunes. The US was doing well but there was still no evident recovery in Japan. In Europe several countries had been adversely affected as they adjusted their economies in preparation for entry into European Monetary Union.

As this phase in the company's history drew to a close, the major source of information and recommendations about investments continued to be the brokers. One bundle of papers dated 1995 contains recommendations from Cazenove, S.G. Warburg, Flemings, Hill Samuel, SBC Warburg Dillon Read and HSBC. But technology was also beginning to make its presence felt and Alliance also made use of Reuters, Datastream and Extel. But the real age of technology was, as yet, some way in the future.

Mineral Interests

Mineral interests continued to bring in a worthwhile, if somewhat irregular, flow of income. A 1984 paper, written by George Stout, revealed that there were 491 separate holdings, amounting to 128,899 gross acres, almost all of which were in the US. Much of this acreage was shared with other interested parties, and if their share is deducted then the Alliance holding was 72,848 net acres. The largest gross holding was the 47,239-acre Chaves Grant. Only 121 of the properties were producing oil, gas or coal, and a further 118 were leased but not producing anything. In 1983 the total revenue received was $498,000, of which $316,000 came from Oklahoma, $100,000 from San Antonio, $81,000 from Fort Worth and just $1,700 from Idaho.

Prospects in Oklahoma were good as Alliance held rights in the southeast part of the state which had, as yet, been little explored. Several leases were due for renewal and Stout expected to get higher prices for them. Much of the San Antonio business, which was managed by Tom Drought, consisted of the Chaves Grant in New Mexico. When the land had been purchased by the US government during the Second World War it was a condition of the acquisition that the mineral rights should not be held in perpetuity but that they should expire in 1989 – unless discoveries were made and production begun. This seemed increasingly unlikely, although a great deal of prospecting had been done but nothing commercial had been found. Moreover it had been proposed to designate the land as an area of 'protected wilderness' that would make life more difficult for anyone who wanted to drill for minerals. This was the only holding which Alliance did not hold in perpetuity. Drought managed to have the ownership of mineral rights extended to 1999.

There was very little activity in Idaho and none at all in the Canadian holdings. Alliance still held rights to the deep part of the Cormier plantation (below 10,000 feet) in Louisiana but there was no effort being made to drill such deep wells.

It would have been a relatively easy matter to dispose of all the holdings by selling most and abandoning the rest. This did not happen. Indeed there was some appetite for acquiring more holdings. The agents in Tulsa and Oklahoma had been alerted about Alliance's interest in purchasing mineral royalties 'should they become available at a realistic price'. But the agents in turn cautioned Stout against this as there was, at that time, such an oversupply of capital looking for good investments that it was unlikely that any could be obtained at a sensible price.

It was decided to hold on to what they had. It was an operation that could be run at a very modest cost and, so long as it brought in a healthy income, it was worth more than it could be sold for in the market. Communications with the agents were easier and were then being conducted largely by faxes and phone calls.

The idea of acquiring other interests was not immediately given up. The year after Stout's retirement in 1987 Bolton visited Drought in Texas. Nevertheless Drought's advice was that as Alliance 'has done so well in equities it is difficult to make a case for going off in another direction'. On his return to Dundee Bolton's advice to his board was that Alliance should not seek additional direct investment in the oil and gas industry, 'at least for the present'.

Corporate Governance

Running a company in 1980 was a relatively uncomplicated business. There were certain requirements of the various Companies Acts with which boards of directors had to comply and certain matters which annual reports had to reveal. Other than that company boards were free to run their businesses as they saw fit, always assuming that they complied with the law. However, the period between 1980 and 1996 saw various changes that forced companies to comply with new regulations and, even where there were no regulations as such, there were new expectations that companies would be organised and managed in certain ways. Computing was beginning to make a serious difference to the ways in which companies were administered, and to reflect this trend Alliance recruited Robin Thomson in 1983 to develop and run new systems. IBM had provided the hardware but all companies experienced teething troubles in the early days – whoever was their provider. To fix a problem on one occasion, an IBM engineer made an overnight trip from Manchester to Dundee in a taxi.

The first legal change came in 1981 when the 1980 Companies Act required public limited companies to style themselves as plcs. Consequently Alliance became The Alliance Trust plc. This required changes to all company station-ery and the acquisition of a new company common seal.

Over many years Alliance Trust had evolved a form of corporate gover-nance that suited it well. The appointment of George Dunn and then Robert Smith as chairmen in the early 1980s brought to an end a long period when the chairman was also the chief executive of the company. This separation of powers anticipated the Cadbury report on the 'Financial Aspects of Corporate Governance' that was published in December 1992. Adrian Cadbury's committee had been appointed as a result of a series of problems in the corporate sector. The affairs of Maxwell Communications, Bank of Credit and Commerce International and Polly Peck had created a feeling that all was not well in company boardrooms.

Following the publication of the report, companies were at pains to reassure their shareholders that they were compliant with its terms and recom-mendations. Alliance Trust was no exception, and the annual report thereafter included a section on governance matters. The Association of Investment Trust Companies had published guidelines for investment trusts based upon Cadbury's recommendations. Shareholders were reassured that the purpose of implementing the recommendations was to add an additional layer of security to the business while, at the same time, allowing the flexibility which enabled the company to 'benefit from investment opportunities and take appropriate business risks where conflicts inevitably arise between risk and return'. In reality Alliance already conformed to most of Cadbury's recom-mendations. The matter was discussed in detail at a board meeting on 30 November 1994 when length of service and size of shareholding were the main issues. The outcome was that Smith, as chairman, drew up a programme for rotations and retirals of directors.

There was already a division of powers that would ensure that the roles of chairman and chief executive were separate. There was also a majority of non-executive directors on the board, who would make up the entire membership of the audit and the new remuneration committees. The audit committee terms of reference were revised. There was no nominations committee but the whole board decided matters that would normally have been dealt with by such a committee.

There was also a segregation of duties to ensure that no one individual could execute a transaction 'from inception to completion'. Staff other than those who arranged settlement made investment decisions and no information technology staff handled funds or administration.

The third element was reporting and internal communication. The board met formally every month and informally most weeks. Consequently senior staff would have access to them on a regular basis. At board meetings regular reports on liquidity, investment changes, income flows and performance were examined and commented upon.

The final element was monitoring. The board as a whole conducted high-level monitoring and the audit committee reviewed the effectiveness of internal controls, liaised with the external auditors and set the agenda for the internal auditors. Alliance Trust (Finance) Ltd was subject to supervision under the 1987 Banking Act and the Personal Investment Authority regulated Alliance Trust Savings.

The reality was that Alliance had to make very few alterations to its corporate governance structure to comply with the recommendations of the report. So far as the shareholders were concerned the addition of a corporate governance section to the annual report was the major change, and the conse-quence was that shareholders received some more information about the company than they had received in the past. They learned from the audit committee report, for example, that executive directors and senior investment managers had two-year service contracts, which was regarded as appropriate 'given the nature and location of the company's operations in Dundee'. The challenge of dealing with governance issues was undoubtedly helped by the fact that this was an area in which Lyndon Bolton displayed conspicuous talents.

There were a few internal changes that the board agreed to introduce. A provision was made to have a committee of the board if something urgent arose between scheduled board meetings. Provision was also made for directors to take independent professional advice at the company's expense. In addition there was a revision to the terms of appointment for non-executive directors. Formal letters of appointment setting out the terms and conditions of service were, in future, to be issued to new non-executive directors.

Undoubtedly the Cadbury Report induced a change of mindset in board-rooms, with the result that more attention and care was given to board actions and the relationships between directors and executives than had been the case in the past. Cadbury's recommendations were widely adopted, not just in UK boardrooms, but in many other parts of the world.

The report was also a spur for the Alliance board to take time to look at others aspects of the way in which the company was run. Early in 1993 new technology costing £100,000 was purchased, which included an IBM AS400 computer. Before the year was out a major review of the company's banking arrangements had been carried out. In addition Alliance complied with new listing rules from the London Stock Exchange. There was also the regulator, the Securities and Futures Authority, to deal with. In many ways, therefore, running a company, especially a financial company, was becoming an altogether more complex business than it had ever been. The Bank of England regulated the Alliance Trust Savings business. In March 1992 David A. Reeves of the Bank of England's supervision division wrote, 'Generally we were impressed by the quality of staff, and the "hands on" style of management. The visit did not reveal any major supervisory concerns . . . Alliance has probably crossed that indefinable line from being a less formal "hands on" institution to being one where formal, written controls and procedures become the norm.'

All the changes that had taken place brought rewards and awards. In 1991 Alliance won the *Sunday Telegraph* investment trust group of the year award. This was the first of a series of prizes from the *Telegraph* and other newspapers. In presenting the *Telegraph* prize in January 1993 Hamish Buchan described Alliance as 'a triple A gold standard investment trust for the private investor'. The following month the *Financial Times* said that Alliance 'in recent years provided exactly the kind of investment performance that most small shareholders crave'. It went on to quote Bolton as making 'no apologies for establishing long term relationships with companies and making close contacts with their managements'.

Shareholders

Alliance prided itself in its history and in the fact that it had a very large number of individual investors. But, for many years, investment trusts had placed money in each other's shares as a way of spreading their own risks by buying into the expertise of professional money managers. This trend had never been viewed as in any way threatening, and there was very little experience of trusts buying the whole business of other trusts, although there had been a few mergers over the years.

That situation began to change towards the end of the 1970s. In 1979 the Wood Mackenzie *Investment Trust Annual* reported that, 'In the last two years, we have seen 18 takeovers, 4 unitisations, 7 liquidations and 5 mergers which has reduced the capitalisation of the sector by just under £500 million, or 11½ % of the current market.'[26]

Two large Edinburgh managed trusts, British Investment Trust and Edinburgh and Dundee Investment Company, disappeared as a result of takeover bids. The major predator was the National Coal Board Staff Superannuation Scheme (NCBSSS), which took over the British Investment Trust.

It was the growth of other large institutional investors, such as pension funds, which brought this dimension to the industry. For many years the largest investor in Alliance shares was Dundee publishing firm D.C. Thomson and Co. Ltd who were Alliance's near neighbours. But in January 1981, at Robert Smith's first board meeting, the directors were told that the National Coal Board Staff Superannuation Scheme and Mineworkers' Pension Scheme had acquired a 9.06% stake in Alliance shares. This stake continued to grow and had reached 12.21% in the summer of 1981 and 14.1% four years later. By that time US funds were buying Alliance shares and Stout went to the US to investigate their intentions. His findings are not recorded but it must be speculated that they expected Alliance to be the subject of a takeover bid.

Alliance must have felt that it was in real danger. A certain amount of nervousness was experienced by the staff who learned of the NCBSSS' accumulation of shares by virtue of their work in maintaining the share register. Bolton went to see the pension managers and came away with the impression that they did not intend to make a bid for Alliance. So the danger passed and the NCBSSS eventually staged a successful bid for Globe, Britain's largest investment trust, in 1990. What made investment trusts a suitable target for large pension funds was the fact that their shares usually traded at a discount to the market value of their investments. So when NCBSSS took over Globe it liquidated the assets and realised a larger sum of money than it had paid for the Trust. The NCBSSS holding in Alliance Trust was gradually sold off.

The changeover from limited company (Ltd) to public limited company (plc) was also the time when substantial changes were introduced into the annual report. The report that was issued to shareholders in 1982 was a radically different document from its predecessors. Shareholders were treated to head and shoulders photographs of the directors and senior management. There was also a profile of the company in which investors were provided with

26 J. Newlands, *Put Not Your Trust in Money*, London, 1997, p. 303.

a rationale for investing in the Trust that even managed to make a virtue of the discount of the share price measured against the value of the investments. 'The Alliance provides a good vehicle for obtaining the necessary investment spreads to reduce overall risk, as well as providing stockholders with all the advantages of professional management. Virtually all income is distributed as dividends and it is usually possible to buy stock at a discount to the value of the underlying assets.'

The profile also contained a brief history of the company, a statement about the mineral rights and their earning power, a note on the leasing company, a statement regarding the deposit-taking facility and a comment on the dividend reinvestment scheme. The most significant aspect of this profile, however, was what was said about the investment strategy. 'The bulk of the £200 million portfolio is invested on a long term basis in top quality commercial, financial and industrial concerns spread throughout the major free-world economies. In the main these investments are marketable and changes in investment policy are achieved by moderate movements of funds from one investment to another. About half the portfolio is overseas with an emphasis on North America where the company has a long standing expertise.'

In reality the requirements of the Companies Acts were gradually making annual reports somewhat impenetrable for many investors and this new company profile, together with the statement of 'financial highlights' that followed must have been a welcome innovation for many shareholders. They were also treated to a much lengthier statement about investments by region, with separate sections on the UK, US, Japan and other territories that were accompanied by well-chosen photographs of the investments in action. The 1982 report contained photographs of, inter alia, a Securicor messenger, the Castle Peak power station in Hong Kong, air traffic controllers at work with Plessey's radar system, the Coylumbridge hotel swimming pool, Dawson International's knitwear and Rentokil operatives controlling pests.

All in all it was a radical makeover for the annual report and was clearly a genuine effort to improve the flow of information to shareholders. It did not happen as a result of shareholder pressure, as the number of shareholders who attended the annual general meetings was still tiny and the numbers who, despite being invited, corresponded with the company secretary was vanishingly small. The new annual report, therefore, not only provided investors with enhanced information but also, as company law prevented the Trust from advertising its shares, became the major source of information for new investors. The Thatcher government was making great efforts to encourage a 'shareholding democracy', and investment trusts, unlike unit trusts that could advertise their products, needed some means of making the public aware of their existence. The new annual report certainly helped in that regard and, although it took a little time, there followed a very healthy increase in the numbers of new shareholders.

Nevertheless the 1984 report revealed that individuals held just over 40% of the shares while other trusts and institutional investors held the remainder. Compared with other trusts, however, this was a high figure, and compared with other public companies, where the average amount of stock held by individuals was only 28%, it was gratifyingly large. Although some US institutional investors were welcomed onto the register for the first time there was, nevertheless, a widespread concern that individual shareholders would eventually be crowded out and that conflict might arise between the expectations and requirements of the two groups of shareholders.

The company's dividend reinvestment plan continued in existence but did not attract a great deal of support from shareholders. In 1984 only 9% of the new shareholders on the register signed up for this service. Consequently it was given something of a push in 1985 when the chairman's statement revealed that 'An original subscriber with 1,000 stock units worth £1,745 in December 1969 would have held, at January 31 1985, 1,566 stock units worth £9,900.' A form was duly enclosed with the annual report to encourage new subscribers to sign up for the scheme. The modest uptake for the scheme may not have been either a surprise or a disappointment as, for many shareholders, their dividend from Alliance would have been an important part of their income for the year that they needed for living expenses.

In 1986 Smith was able to tell shareholders that the government's encouragement of stock exchange investment by private individuals had led to 'a renewed awareness of the merits of investment trusts'. There were then 13,675 ordinary stockholders on the register, of whom over 1,100 had joined during the year – a considerable increase on the experience of earlier years. More than 10% of the new shareholders chose to participate in the dividend reinvestment plan. Notwithstanding that there were good reasons why the uptake was relatively modest, the executive took the view that the scheme could be improved by making allowance for regular savers, and in January 1987 shareholders were sent details of a new scheme that allowed shareholders 'to add to their holdings on a regular or occasional basis, at very modest cost'.

Stout's impending retirement gave rise in 1987 to some speculation about what would happen next and, as ever, there was thinking about a new shape, and even a new locus, for Alliance. Smith took the time to put the record straight and to set the agenda for the future. At the annual general meeting that year he advised shareholders that the company is 'to remain in Dundee and continue to be managed by our highly competent and adequately supported investment team whose attention is directed and concentrated solely on the interests of our stockholders'.

This 'is against the recent trend of delegating investment management under contract to one of the composite investment houses who have a wider range of management interests in marketing unit trusts and securing pension and other funds under their control. It has been a carefully considered and not just a wilfully stubborn decision.'

There was a similar theme from Smith at the centenary annual general meeting in 1988. He acknowledged that there had been much talk in other trusts of changes in policy, much of which was driven by institutional investors who were keen to 'unlock the discount'. He told the shareholders that rights issues and share splits had been considered by the board but that it was believed that there would be no advantage for shareholders so it was not done. As new shareholders were coming onto the register it was thought that the current high share price was not a deterrent. He did concede that the matter would be kept under review.

The consistent message that the shareholders received was that the Alliance would hold fast to its traditional organisational structure and ways of doing business. In 1991 Smith restated the strategy when he said, 'Lyndon Bolton and his fellow managers will continue to steer a course which will not naively assume fair weather all the way, but will allow for the possibility of markets being becalmed and the probability of sharp storms, and we believe that such a policy is what our stockholders want of us.'

It was a strategy that served the Trust well in the recession of the early 1990s.

Alliance Trust Finance and Alliance Trust Savings

Alldee Leasing had now been renamed Alliance Trust (Finance) Ltd (ATF) and was making remarkable progress for such a young company. The dividend to the parent company at £50,000 in 1984 did not make much impression on overall profitability but interest payments on money borrowed contributed £476,000. A year later an exceptional profit of £836,000 was made as a result of the changes to the rates of corporation tax. Consequently over £1m was added to the company's reserves, of which £240,000 was capitalised. This brought the original £10,000 investment 'more into line with the size of the business'. The profitability of this business was higher than had been expected, with margins over 8%. This was due to a number of factors, including high demand, good portfolio building and initial conservatism in the original assessment. In 1983 some bank borrowing was required but this was easily and relatively inexpensively acquired due to the AAA rating of the Trusts. Selling the business was contemplated at that point but there were better arguments for retaining it, especially as the commercial banks were not much interested in competing in this market.

A major factor in the success of the leasing business was the way in which the taxation system worked. The rules changed frequently as chancellors of the Exchequer tried to encourage investment by businesses, and leasing grew in popularity as capital allowances and deferred taxation proved to be increasingly attractive to growing businesses and local authorities.

A major review of leasing was conducted in 1983, by which time there had been four years of active engagement in the business. Alldee Leasing had written £16m of business, which was more than had been envisaged at the outset but it had been profitable and had earned net returns of 8%. It was anticipated that these good returns would continue to be earned as Alldee now had a well-established place in the market. The only serious constraint was the irregular supply of funds. The existence of the leasing business was also a stimulus to investment in Alliance Trust's computing capability and when Suggett's computing prize ran its course the board was happy to continue the trend towards computerisation, with particular support coming from McCurrach and Brian Thomson. It was the savings side of the business, rather than the investment side, which required the heaviest investment in computing.

The growth of Alldee Leasing and the addition of the savings business led, in 1986, to some restructuring in the organisation. ATF had been established with the leasing companies as its subsidiaries. Alliance Trust Savings was added shortly afterwards, as was the banking licence that enabled deposits to be used to finance the leasing business. ATF was 75% owned by Alliance Trust and 25% by Second Alliance Trust. It was consistently profitable. Suggett's paper for the board at this time concluded that retaining this business outweighed the case for disposing of it. By 1989, however, competition was making it more and more difficult to sustain that argument. Of 300 quotations given out in 1990, only 56 new contracts were taken up. Nevertheless the business was still profitable and the quality of contracts was maintained at a high level. A lot of the contracts were for the supply of computer equipment in both the public and private sectors. Much of the remainder was for vehicles and, in the public sector, for refuse management equipment. Suggett was later to joke that Alliance was Britain's largest owner of wheelie bins. Early in 1993, however, plans were well advanced to dispose of the business and it was gradually sold off. It had, quite simply, become less profitable due to lower interest rates, changed taxation and heightened competition.

One of the reasons that the press was less than kind to investment trusts in the 1970s and 1980s was that the restriction on advertising imposed by the Companies Acts caused them to become also-rans in the savings and investment market. The number of shareholders dropped markedly, and large institutional investors built up substantial shareholdings in a predatory fashion. More than one financial journalist predicted a doomsday scenario for the trusts.

David McCurrach had introduced a dividend reinvestment plan in 1969 that had enjoyed only modest success but there was nothing else that would have allowed savers to invest their money with investment trusts other than by purchasing their shares in the open market. Given the wide availability of savings schemes from other financial institutions, and the tax advantages enjoyed by building societies and pension plans, there was a real danger than investment trusts would simply wither away or be the subject of takeover bids from insurance companies or pension funds. This was the problem that taxed the minds of directors and executives in trusts across the country.

The solution came from the oldest trust – the Foreign and Colonial, which introduced a savings scheme in the early 1980s that was followed by many other trusts. Alliance was keen to get involved but was not entirely convinced that the schemes would escape legal challenge. There was also the problem of what it would cost to set up a scheme similar to those being developed by its competitors.

The Alliance answer was to set up Alliance Trust Savings (ATS) and to provide all computing and administration internally. Even the computer software was written by in-house staff. ATS was popular with investors and soon built up a strong client base which was later helped by the introduction of personal equity plans (PEPs) in 1986.

The launch of ATS certainly had the desired effect of raising the profile of Alliance but there were serious questions at board level. Some of the directors were worried about where it was leading and what the implications were for the Trust. There was a particular concern about the amount of regulation that was involved. Suggett and his colleague Sheila Ruckley got to the point where they offered to do a management buyout, but this was rejected out of hand. Thereafter the board got behind the project, which then went from strength to strength.

ATS was created to provide a service to the Trust. It paid its own way and was profitable from the outset. The growing revenue was used to finance expansion, and while the growth of the business did create management challenges, these were overcome and ATS managed to avoid the difficulties that other trusts suffered such as service breakdown, brand damage and management failure. At first the rate of growth was limited by the ability of the organisation to put in systems, train people and develop management abilities fast enough to run the operation efficiently and keep it moving forward.

In some ways ATS was the opposite of the Trust. It required little capital but needed many people and activity while the Trust had a large capital, could be managed by few people, and could endure periods of low activity. Nevertheless this created a synergy between the two that has endured.

Nigel Lawson's 1986 budget introduced PEPs as part of a wider policy to encourage individuals to buy shares. These investments were free from capital gains tax and the income was free from income tax. Alliance decided to take the initiative amongst investment trusts and offer a PEP, 'again at a very low cost, to our investors'. Initially, at least, the investment trusts felt that they were not being treated fairly by the Chancellor, Nigel Lawson. The problem was that the rules stated that only trusts that had 75% or more of their investments in UK securities could benefit from all the provisions of the scheme. As Alliance was heavily invested overseas this meant that those who purchased the Alliance PEP could not do so to the full amount permitted. Lawson's view was that there was no good reason for subsidising the acquisition of shares in foreign companies. His successor Norman Lamont took only a slightly more generous view and altered the rules to allow Alliance PEP holders a larger share of the allowance.

Despite these limitations demand was high and by 1990 there were eight members of staff employed to administer ATS. There was little advertising, although a newsletter was published from 1989. Interestingly, demand was especially high amongst finance professionals from London. In 1990 John Major, in his only budget as Chancellor of the Exchequer, announced TESSAs that were to complement PEPs and be a low-risk, tax-efficient savings account. Alliance took up this challenge with some enthusiasm, and by 1992 they were so popular that a separate newsletter was published to keep investors up to date with developments. This was still an age of high inflation and interest rates. TESSAs attracted a rate of 11%.

As the business developed much thought was given not just to how to recruit new investors but on how to communicate with them. The formal business style of the past was to be left behind and letters to customers were to be 'friendly, informative, plain English and not condescending'. Amongst the phrases to be avoided were 'I would inform you'. There was also a change of name from AT Savings Ltd to Alliance Trust Savings Ltd to 'aid identifying the company more closely with the parent'.

The most problematical area for the new service was regulation. The regulator, the Personal Investment Authority (PIA), was a relatively young organisation struggling to live up to its responsibilities and trying hard to ensure that its guidance to the organisations that it regulated was fit for purpose. This led to a certain amount of frustration amongst the regulated companies. They needed to know where they stood. In December 1994 the company secretary Sheila Gates wrote to the PIA with a long list of questions. Of special concern was whether the PIA would regard ATS as product providers or advisers. To avoid confusion she told them what she thought the answer should be: ' . . . it would give me enormous comfort to know that we are not regarded as "advisers" as this was one of the great areas of confusion when we were operating under the FIMBRA rules'. She made it abundantly clear that ATS was not providing advice to investors. The PIA was not to be hurried, and Martin Tuckwell replied a month later that Gates' questions would be taken into account when PIA finalised its Training and Competence scheme. No date was provided for when this might be achieved and the question about advisers had still not been resolved by Easter of 1995.

As Alliance Trust Finance had a banking licence its regulator was the Bank of England. At a regulatory visit to Dundee in July 1995 a wide variety of issues were discussed, including money laundering, IT systems and segregation of duties. There were no matters for concern.

Chapter 10
Growth and Instability: 1996–2012

The years between 1996 and the present were fraught with difficulty. Yet, until a worldwide recession began in 2008, they were also years of great opportunity. Some sectors of the economy, such as technology, grew strongly, if erratically. There were numerous crises – in Asia, in split capital trusts and in corporate governance. There were also substantial changes to the regulatory environment.

The challenge for organisations such as Alliance Trust was to steer a way through these difficulties as smoothly as possible and take advantage of opportunities when they arose. Foremost amongst these was the possibility of diversifying the company's portfolio and expanding the savings business, which it did.

Consequently there were substantial changes to the ways in which the organisation was managed and controlled. A new head office building and new ways of incentivising staff went together with a growth in the scale of the business and the need to compete against rivals and retain the loyalty of shareholders. There was also a compelling case for merging with the Second Alliance Trust and this was duly accomplished. Moreover external pressures from those whose interests were short term forced Alliance into a bruising battle with external pressure groups which, if they had been successful, would have fundamentally altered the Alliance business model.

Substantial changes also took place in the ways in which people saved and invested their money. This was therefore a period of enormous creativity in financial management as many new savings channels opened up. But, at first, the investment trusts did not do well and various efforts were made to present their advantages to the investing public. The manner in which this was done was not to the liking of Alliance and, for several years, it withdrew its membership of the Association of Investment Trust Companies.

The People and Property

Gavin Suggett became chief executive when Lyndon Bolton retired in 1995. He had been with the company since 1973. In that time he had gained experience of investment, treasury, oil and mineral rights, administration and investor relations. He had been primarily responsible for introducing computer technology and for building up Alliance Trust (Finance) Ltd and Alliance Trust Savings.

There were further changes in 1996 when Robert Smith retired as chairman, to be replaced by Bruce Johnston, who had joined the board in 1991. Nelson Robertson, who had recently retired as chief executive of General Accident, became a director at this time.

The board then comprised:

Bruce W.M. Johnston, Chairman,
Gavin R. Suggett, Managing Director
Alan M.W. Young, Executive Director
Andrew F. Thomson (retired 2001)
William Berry
W. Nelson Robertson

A few months earlier Smith had received a letter from a shareholder congratulating him on the performance of the company but pointing out that most of the directors had only small holdings of shares in the Trust. He also noted, apparently with some regret, that most of the directors were chartered accountants or lawyers and few were residents of Dundee. Smith replied, 'In the past one might have looked around the Eastern Club for a suitable new recruit when a retirement from the board was imminent, but the pattern of business in Dundee is largely changed in the past twenty years and the heads of the indigenous businesses are more often professional managers than family successors.' He went on to say that there was still a strong local bias in the board, with directors resident in Dunkeld (himself), Newport on Tay, Blairgowrie and Dundee.

Four years then elapsed before there were further changes. In that year Sheila Ruckley, who had been company secretary since 1989, became an executive director and William Jack, former managing director of CGU Life, joined as a non-executive director. Jack was really the last of the local people to be appointed to the board. Thereafter directors were appointed from further afield.

Much of the work of the directors was routine. There was much monitoring work, some management assessment and a wide-ranging economic paper to be considered at each meeting. In 1998 thought was being given as to how to manage the agenda better and to the possibility that there might be more executive directors. The changes that took place were driven by a number of factors, including increased regulation and corporate governance requirements as well as the growing size and diversification of the business. As part of the trend towards more formal management systems a remuneration committee was appointed.

Over this period much consideration was given to matters of corporate governance, but the world was changing. No longer was it possible for company boards to organise and manage their companies entirely according to their own judgement. A whole raft of reports and recommendations, first started by the Cadbury report, induced a compliance mindset in British boardrooms. Cadbury was followed by Greenbury (1995), Hampel (1998), Turnbull (1999) and Smith (2003). All this produced the Combined Code of Corporate Governance, which was regularly revised – most recently in 2011 – and in addition there were modifications to the Companies Acts, together with major changes to the regulatory framework with the creation of the Financial Services Authority. It was a heady mixture for directors to deal with, whether they were members of the executive or not.

The board was further strengthened in 2001 by the addition of Lesley Knox, who had a wealth of experience in fund management and who had been governor of the British Linen Bank. She became chairman in 2004 and served until 2012. Christopher Masters, former chairman of Aggreko, joined the board in 2002 and David Deards, who had taken over the finance function, became an executive director in 2003.

The appointment of Masters and Deards followed a rethink about the board structure in relation to the needs of the business. The facts that Alliance was a self-managed trust, that it was growing strongly and that senior executives were closely involved in what would have been board-level decisions in other companies led to the view that more senior executives should be directors. But, with good corporate governance in mind, and in order to maintain a majority of non-executive directors, it was decided to increase the maximum number of directors to nine. It was also agreed that there should be a rethink about the remuneration of directors and executives, as a paper from the consultants Watson Wyatt, the company's remuneration advisers, revealed that current levels were well below market levels, despite recent increases in responsibility.

The arrival of so many new people at board and executive level was the occasion for a strategy meeting that took place at Ballathie House Hotel in Perthshire in January 2003. The substance of the discussion at the meeting was around the proposition that, 'Our objective is to provide the core investment for those who wish to build a long term store of increasing value.'

Almost all matters were on the table: investment strategy, gearing, fixed interest, greater scope for ATS, pensions, the need to understand stockholders better, remuneration and branding. Specifically excluded from discussion were buybacks, share splits and amalgamation. Gearing was discussed but there was little enthusiasm for it and, on this issue, Suggett was particularly opposed. It was also noted that there was no executive bonus scheme, despite this being common practice in other companies. Moreover, this ran contrary to the Greenbury code on corporate governance. But underpinning the whole discussion was the idea that the Trusts and ATS 'should operate as an integrated whole as part of the wider savings movement'.

With Suggett's retirement imminent the decision had already been taken that the new chief executive would come from outside the organisation. Alan Harden joined the company late in 2003 and, following Gavin Suggett's retirement, became chief executive and a board member in 2004. He had been greatly attracted by the fact that Alliance was a self-managed fund which meant that 'one group is not prejudiced in favour of another'. There was much speculation in the press that he would soon go on the acquisition trail and this was doubtless prompted by his own pronouncement when he said that Alliance needed more talent in private equity and property. His immediate focus, however, was on 'creating long term value for shareholders'. Harden was an attractive proposition for a company that was dealing with change in a rapidly shifting market and which understood that its business model needed modification. His particular strengths lay in his experience of running asset management businesses and leading change, having worked for Citigroup, Standard Chartered, HSBC, Abbey Life and Barclays. He had worked in a variety of countries in the Far East and had been voted Global Fund Leader in 2002.

Harden went on to make many modifications but the company had already embarked on a process of transformation. As Suggett prepared to retire he recalled how, when he had joined in 1973, there was one electronic calculator and eight slide rules to serve a staff of 18 people. By 2003 there were 165 computers and 130 staff. A graduate recruitment scheme was started in the mid 1990s in recognition that companies like Alliance had to compete for high quality staff. There was also a recognition that the staff were ageing, so new blood was required on the investment team and successful efforts were made to recruit experienced people from other companies.

It was in 2004 that Gordon McQueen, a banker who had been finance director of Bank of Scotland, became a non-executive director. A year later the board gained the services of Clare Salmon, who brought a wealth of experience in marketing financial services, and in 2006 Janet Pope, who had joined the company as chief executive of Alliance Trust Savings, became an executive director. She did not remain for long and left in 2008.

When the annual report was published in 2007 the board comprised:

Lesley Knox, Chairman
William Jack
Christopher Masters
W. Gordon McQueen
Clare Sheikh (Salmon)
Alan J. Harden, chief executive
David Deards, executive director
Janet Pope, executive director

All of the non-executive directors had joined the board since 2000. The fact that many of the directors lived and worked some distance from Dundee brought about the end of the weekly Friday board meeting. Thereafter board meetings took place on a monthly basis until 2010, when that practice was changed and the board met six times a year over two days.

Katherine Garrett-Cox joined the company on 1 May 2007 as an executive director and as chief investment officer. She had wide-ranging experience of the investment world that she had gained in Morley, Hill Samuel and Aberdeen Asset Management. Her appointment surprised many of her colleagues and contacts in London who viewed her move to Dundee as a loss to the City. They said that she would experience difficulties in attracting good people to work with her in Dundee. That proved not to be the case. That this was so was doubtless helped by the fact that facilities were created that allowed some of the investment team to work in offices in Edinburgh and London.

Shortly after her arrival William Jack retired from the board and was replaced by Hugh Bolland. He had spent much of his career with Schroders and had experience of investment in many parts of the world. Both Sheila Ruckley and Alan Young retired in 2006. Gordon McQueen resigned in March

2008 and was replaced by John Hylands, who had recently retired as finance director of Standard Life.

Although Robert Smith had made the point that it was difficult to recruit board members from the Dundee area, there seems little doubt that becoming a director of Alliance Trust was an attractive prospect for highly qualified people from further afield.

There were other changes in 2008 that saw Alan Harden's resignation, to return to the Far East, and the appointment in August of Katherine Garrett-Cox as chief executive. As the economic crisis deepened in many parts of the world it was perhaps not an auspicious time to become a chief executive. She, however, took a contrary view, as there are always good investment opportunities to be found in times of economic difficulty. Shortly after her appointment she described the economic environment as 'uncharted waters'. She went on, 'Markets are extremely volatile and there is a level of uncertainty that many of us have not seen in our lifetimes.'

Robert Burgess joined the board in 2009 on his appointment as chief executive of Alliance Trust Savings. He served until 2012. David Deards also resigned as finance director and was replaced, early in 2010, by Alan Trotter. Clare Sheikh (Salmon) retired from the board in 2011 and was replaced by Timothy Ingram, who had recently retired as chief executive of Caledonia Investments plc. And Consuelo Brooke joined in 2011. She had more than 40 years' experience with various investment companies, including her own, C. Brooke Investment Partners Ltd. Hugh Bolland and Timothy Ingram retired from the board in 2012. Early that year it was announced that Karin Forseke, deputy chairman and senior independent director of the Financial Services Authority, would succeed Lesley Knox as chairman. Forseke had been chief operating officer of the London International Financial Futures Exchange (LIFFE) in the 1990s and from 2003 to 2006 she was chief executive of D. Carnegie and Co., a Swedish investment bank.

Such major changes in the board and executive inevitably brought with it changes in the structure and methods of management. In 1998 a Trust Management Committee had been established with the purpose of 'improving the monitoring and management of the Alliance Trust's activities through the provision of better internal communications'. The initial meeting took place on 31 July 1998 with ten senior people in attendance. There was a wide-ranging agenda that included such matters as the Hampel report on corporate governance, executive pay and incentives and technology matters. The consultants Hay MSL were already advising on this. Future meetings dealt with regulation, compliance and the introduction of the internet and email. In the latter case the point was made that, in the past, senior managers would have seen all incoming mail but with the increasing use of email this was much more problematical. The point was forcefully made by Gavin Suggett that incoming mail belonged to the company and not to individual members of staff. The internet and email were duly set up at the end of October 1999. However problems with suppliers and apprehension amongst staff combined to ensure that the introduction of these technologies did not go smoothly. At the January 2000 meeting there were doubtless deep sighs of relief that the much feared millennium bug had not materialised and therefore had not had the destructive effect that many had anticipated. It was time to get back to normal business. Grant Lindsay was concerned that important information from Credit Lyonnais and Flemings was being missed because cookies which speeded up access to some websites would have to be accepted onto Alliance computers before this information could be received. This was against the company's rules as there was always the possibility that they could be used to remove information as well as to accept it. Later that year a trial began of a website. There was also a great deal of discussion at these meetings about the deteriorating relationship with the Association of Investment Trust Companies.

When Harden joined the company in 2003 one of his early initiatives was to establish an Asset, Liability and Income Committee (ALICo) to manage the company's assets. It was chaired by Alan Young, the investment director, and it considered 'many factors such as political trends, operating environments and investment themes in order to construct a range of scenarios and review their financial implications. From this the committee agreed a central view of the most likely scenario over the short, medium and long-term. It also examined the potential risks to the central view and formed a view on the "best" and "worst" cases to provide some fix on the probabilities of possible but less likely scenarios which would affect our investment strategy.'

There was also a serious rethink about how the portfolio was to be managed, and this led to a major change. The Committee announced that, 'we have returned to managing the overall portfolio by geography, while we have retained and will enhance experience gained at the global sector level by appointing dedicated global analysts. The various segments UK Large Cap, UK Small and Mid Cap, Europe, US Large Cap, US Small and Mid Cap, Japan, Asia Pacific and the Rest of the World, are divided across the seven investment managers. This structure allows more efficient monitoring for the purposes of tracking performance and managing risk.'

Given the growing importance of the Far East, plans were made to establish an office in Hong Kong. In explaining why this was to happen Harden harked back to the early days of the company: 'The Asian markets today bear a striking similarity to those in North America where, over a hundred years ago, my predecessors took the courageous decision to invest and ensure that the company had representatives locally.' The Hong Kong office was to be the base for a number of Asian funds. Anthony Muh, who had previously worked alongside Alan Harden at Citigroup, was appointed to run the operation, and in autumn 2006 the Premier Alliance Trust Japan Equity Fund and Premier Alliance Trust Asia Pacific Equity Fund were launched.

The company's memorandum and articles of association underwent revision, as they had not been substantially upgraded since the 1930s. It was also a time for more investment in technology and people. An incentive scheme for executive directors and senior staff was introduced based upon company and individual performance.

These changes produced a rise in the expense ratio (management expenses as a proportion of funds under management) but Harden told the shareholders that at 0.33% it was still amongst the lowest in the sector. Moreover, he was firmly of the view that Alliance and ATS, in particular, were in need of new investment and this could not be achieved without an increase in expenses. He went on to reassure shareholders that Alliance had not lost its focus on cost control but that it was necessary to commit to investing in the company's own infrastructure to ensure that it was not left behind by developments in the savings and investment industry. The target that he set himself, so far as costs were concerned, was to remain in the lowest 25% of Alliance's peer group. Further rises were experienced but the ratio was maintained in the lower quartile. But the business press did not like what it saw and in September 2007 the *Scotsman* headline asked, 'Has Underperforming Alliance Lost Plot?' The new strategy that was being pursued, including diversification into property and private equity alongside more aggressive growth plans for ATS, did not attract much praise, and the board's dogged refusal to buy back shares was blamed for the share price discount being twice the industry average.

The growth of the business, especially in ATS, and the new technologies that were in use resulted in a marked growth in staff numbers that by 2004 had reached 100 and by 2007 had grown to 297. This was far too many to be accommodated in the old building at 64 Reform Street. Consequently staff occupied a further two buildings in other parts of the city. Inevitably this led to communication difficulties and additional cost. It was not long therefore before the decision was made to acquire new premises. It was not the first time that the matter had been considered. In the early 1990s the idea of having a new building on the waterfront had been considered but Dundee's planning authorities preferred to retain the chosen site for an incoming business. Discussions about a new building resumed in 2006. The company did not move very far. The place chosen for the new head office was just a few hundred yards from Reform Street. It was the print works site formerly occupied by Burns and Harris in West Marketgait. The plan was known as project Wren, the architects were RMJM and the builder was the Miller Group. The new building, which accommodated all of the Dundee staff on one site and allowed for future expansion, was opened for business in spring 2009.

The considerable growth in staff numbers also brought a requirement for increased staff training, and the Alliance Trust Academy was established in October 2006 to provide internal training. External courses such as the Investment Administration qualification that was provided by the Securities and Investment Institute were also supported for the first time, and links were established with the local Abertay University.

The training programme had numerous elements, including leadership and management skills modules. Line managers and the leadership team participated in management development modules that were designed to fit the different stages of growth. Subjects included Managing Change and Innovation; Leading, Inspiring and Influencing; and Developing People. Leadership development remained a priority for Katherine Garrett-Cox, and two new groups were established in 2010 – one for senior leaders and one for emerging leaders. Development programmes were set up for both.

In addition to an enhanced focus on training, the problem of staff communications was also addressed by having regular 'town hall' meetings to which everyone was invited, and where presentations were made on company developments and staff had the opportunity to question senior executives. These meetings were further augmented when a company intranet was launched, by which staff were kept updated on developments within the group. An employee opinion survey was also instituted which an independent company was appointed to conduct. Participation rates were high. In 2010 more than 70% of the respondents said that working for Alliance gave them a sense of pride. Other comments included a need for better communications and an increased understanding of how the performance of individuals was matched to their rewards.

The way of the world was that staff also had to be incentivised with a bonus plan, and a new long-term incentive plan, which was introduced in 2007, incorporated 'a performance hurdle which is intended to ensure that only where shareholders see the benefit of a return on their investment which significantly outstrips inflation will management start to benefit from the plan, and full awards under the plan will only be made for genuinely outstanding returns'.

The additional focus on training and communications in the enlarged group was vital to meet the needs of a growing business in a highly competitive business environment. But there were other, external, pressures that required a management response. Mounting public engagement with environmental issues required businesses to think seriously about their green footprint. The announcement that Alliance was to move to a new office was an appropriate opportunity to engage with public bodies whose responsibility was to assist private companies to reduce their carbon emissions. Consequently the Scottish Executive's Energy Policy Team was consulted on the environmental, waste and resources issues connected with the building project. The company was able to report in 2011 that its CO_2 emissions had fallen by 29% and most of this was achieved as a direct result of moving to the new head office.

There was also a social dimension to working for Alliance. A staff social committee organised various events, and staff were encouraged to volunteer to assist at The Brae – a Riding for the Disabled centre. In 2011 the first Cateran Yomp took place when 53 members of staff got involved in a 52-mile overnight walk through the hills of Perthshire in aid of ABF the Soldiers' Charity. Funds also went to the Prince's Scottish Youth Business Trust. A sum of £282,000 was raised. Alliance also decided, in a reversal of policy, that it would match funds raised by staff for local charities and it was also able to secure additional funding from the Scottish Community Foundation.

Although Alliance had not made charitable donations it was not averse to assisting charities where it could and, in this regard, Alan Harden became a director of the Scottish Community Foundation during his time with Alliance.

Much merriment and a little concern arose in 2003 when a letter was received from Alliance Capital Management Corporation, 1345 Avenue of the Americas, New York. This was, effectively a cease and desist order. The American company considered 'its [trade] marks to be very valuable and is prepared to enforce its rights against infringers'. It went on, 'We are disturbed by your company's use of the 'Alliance Trust' mark.' This would, they believed, create confusion. 'We believe that your company may be attempting to benefit from the goodwill and reputation that the public has come to associate with Alliance.' Alliance Trust was told to cease their use immediately. The letter went on in vaguely threatening tones.

George Stout was then brought out of retirement to swear an affidavit in defence. He revealed that, at some point in the 1960s, 'I learned that the banking department of Donaldson, Lufkin and Jeanrette, which was run by Bill Donaldson – an old friend of the Alliance team – had been given the trading name of 'Alliance Capital'. I was advised that the name 'Alliance Capital' had been chosen in honour of the relationship with The Alliance Trust and because of the good name that The Alliance Trust had.'

He went on to say that Alliance Trust did not undertake any investment management for third parties and was therefore quite different from 'what appears to be the operations of Alliance Capital'. No more was heard about the matter. Nor did the Trust contemplate serving a cease and desist order on Alliance Capital!

Investments

The annual report for 1997 revealed changes that had taken place in the investment portfolio over the preceding year. The overall position suggests a broadening of the portfolio compared with earlier times as well as a renewed interest in British securities. At the same time investments in Japan were causing concern.

The UK stock market had done well, although most of the appreciation had happened in the second half of the year. Despite this the economy was, at best, unpredictable and, with an impending election, investors were becoming nervous. Nevertheless sterling was riding high and unemployment was low. Alliance favoured investments in companies that were not likely to be exposed to major changes during a downturn in the business cycle. Investments in utilities were sold and the money invested in companies that were showing long-term development prospects like Bank of Scotland, Carlton Communications and Marks and Spencer.

In the closing years of the century the situation in Europe was complicated in those countries that were preparing to join the single currency. The extent to which they had to adjust their economies before joining varied considerably, and such changes often had implications for the attractiveness of their equity and capital markets. The position was further complicated by the strength of

Table 10.1 Changes in investments, 1996–97
(all figures in £000s)

	UK	Europe	North America	Far East	Total
Valuation at 31/1/1996	642,547	114,539	298,059	134,426	1,189,571
Purchases	24,175	19,473	16,571	35,214	95,433
Sales	45,574	13,976	27,476	24,973	111,999
Appreciation	89,291	16,532	35,419	(8,354)	132,888
Valuation 31/1/1997	710,439	136,568	322,573	136,313	1,305,893

sterling, which caused a reduction in the sterling value of any growth in European stocks. Notwithstanding this fact Alliance found good cause to invest in several leading German companies such as Bayer, Deutsche Bank, Mannesmann, Siemens, and SAP.

There were few worries about the US economy whose common stocks markets accounted for 47% of the value of the world's equity markets. In 1996 there had been a 24% increase in the price of stocks, which, in other circumstances, might have sounded a cautionary note, but all the fundamentals of the economy were showing positive signs. Inflation and the budget deficit were at historic lows. Employment was growing strongly. Investment in new technologies was driving high productivity growth. President Clinton had been returned to the White House but with a Republican Congress. It was time to take some profits, especially in companies which had done well but which might suffer from a strong dollar. Consequently Anheuser-Busch, Toys R Us and 3M were sold and the money was invested in smaller oil and financial services companies. The fastest growing stocks were in the electronic technology sector, but the rate of growth suggested that this was a bubble and Alliance chose not to participate. It was a wise decision.

The Japanese economy, by contrast, was still not doing well but Alliance had little exposure there. It was a similar tale in Korea and Thailand. But Hong Kong had recovered from worries about the impending Chinese takeover, when British rule would cease, and investors were now contemplating the development possibilities there. Alliance added to its holdings of HSBC, Hutchison Whampoa and CITIC Pacific. There were also new holdings in

Table 10.2 Classification of all investments
by region as at 31 January 1997

	%
UK	52.1
Europe	10.2
North America	23.8
Far East	9.9
Total	96.0
Other investments	4.0

Australia and Malaysia. The strength of sterling, however, muted any rise in prices in overseas stock markets. For example a 6% rise in Australian stock prices converted into a 2% rise in sterling terms.

Consequently Alliance's investments were still heavily concentrated in the UK. Of the top 50 investments 37 were in the UK and 10 were in the US, with one each in Germany, Sweden and the Netherlands. In percentage terms 86% of the top 50 investments by value were in the UK, with 10% in the US. It was a very different picture from the one that had prevailed in earlier stages of the company's history.

An examination of the top 50 investments does not, however, tell the whole story. Table 10.2 reveals the bigger picture.

The reason for the differences in figures when comparing the top 50 investments with the total portfolio is simply explained by the policy of seeking out and investing in smaller companies with growth potential. While larger companies could be relied upon for their steady dividends there was also merit in seeking out companies that had the potential to grow.

The UK general election in 1997 returned a Labour government for the first time in 18 years but, despite the fears of some, the economy continued its upward momentum. The new Monetary Policy Committee at the Bank of England increased interest rates several times. 'Confidence was re-inforced by a 2.5% inflation target, a rapidly shrinking government borrowing requirement and the new government's repeated commitment to tight fiscal control.' There was a welcome for the fact that corporation tax was to be reduced and advanced corporation tax was to be abolished on dividends, but there was also an understanding that other 'more subtle effects will tend to increase corporate costs over the next few years'. Amongst these was the decision to remove the ability of companies to reclaim tax credits in their pension schemes. There was a concern, too, that a rash of mergers, buybacks and special dividends meant that companies, on balance, were giving more money back to their shareholders than they were raising from them. Even the Association of Investment Trust Companies was pushing the idea of share buybacks but Alliance was resolutely against the idea.

In Europe, Alliance increased its investments in Spain, Portugal, Switzerland, Austria and Hungary. Preparations were well under way in Europe for the launch of the euro in 1999. In the US things were also going well but there had been a number of large company mergers that had led to a shortage of quality equities.

Good equities were in high demand as there had been a flight to quality caused by the failure of a number of currency and equity markets in the Far East, where stock markets and currencies had collapsed in a number of countries, most notably, Thailand, Indonesia and Malaya. Hong Kong managed to maintain its currency peg against the dollar and so the losses in its stock markets, although still large, were not as disastrous as in other countries. Alliance saw long-term values in these markets but was reluctant to reinvest until a new economic model for the region had emerged. This had not yet happened and Alliance had sold all its bank holdings, except HSBC. By the end of the financial year Alliance had disposed of many of its other holdings, but had retained modest stakes in a number of companies with strong franchises in the expectation that they would eventually benefit from the recovery when it came.

The crisis in the East prompted a rethink about how the portfolio would be managed and the annual report in 1999 reflected the changes that took place. Gone were the continent-by-continent commentaries. These were replaced by sector-by-sector descriptions of the changes that had taken place in investment policy over the past year. Doubtless the increasing globalisation of the world economy had also contributed towards this change in approach. During 1998 some new portfolio managers had been added to the team of investment managers. Their responsibilities were to concentrate on global coverage on an industry-by-industry basis, 'to match the increasing internationalisation of business and the further integration of Europe. It was envisaged that these changes would improve long-term investment returns as portfolio managers were encouraged to 'focus their skills and attention on the prospects for industries and companies, make comparisons across markets and take the best opportunities available'.

The company's strategy was restated:

> We aim to achieve our investment objective by holding and developing a widely diversified portfolio of minority equity stakes in commercial enterprises worldwide. These investments are chosen for their potential ability to deliver long-term returns. Diversification is aimed at ensuring that the aggregate return from the portfolio as a whole is not unduly affected by the performance of any one company, sector, country or currency. Investments are therefore held for a combination of reasons: financial strength, the quality of management, the prospects for the sector and the broad factors relating to the socio-economic and political environment in which the company operates.

As the century drew to a close there were in excess of 380 individual holdings in the portfolio. There was also an acute awareness that fundamental changes were taking place in the world economy and that these would impact on investment opportunities, especially prices. Demographic factors were top of the list and the fact that the 'baby-boomer' generation was now in its fifties, with money to save and invest, was already having a substantial impact, especially in the US. In 1998 these people had helped put $160bn into US equity mutual funds – the standard American vehicle for retirement provision. That particular part of the 1999 report concluded with a look forward to 2008, which was the year in which the bulk of the post-war baby boomers would retire. This was expected to have major implications for national economies, especially in those countries where pension provisions were unfunded and paid out of current revenues.

Technological change was also entering a second wave of development. Alliance continued to be sceptical about the values being placed on many of the companies in this sector. Yet technology in the workplace could not be ignored. Most people now worked with a personal computer, and the use of emails and the internet was adding a new dimension to people's working lives. This was especially so in the investment world where the internet fast became a major research tool when information was sought about new and existing investments. The use of Datastream and Bloomberg enabled the investment team to respond easily and quickly to market movements, although brokers continued to be an important, if declining, source of information. If anything, the problem was a surfeit of information.

Over the years the focus for the Alliance portfolio had evolved from basic industrial sectors to the higher value-added areas of services, and this trend continued. In geographical terms there was a balance between markets that had performed well in capital terms, such as the US, and those where valuations were 'somewhat less demanding but where interest rate cuts were expected to have a positive effect on economic recovery'. The problem was to identify suitable companies, and it was only at this time that opportunities in France and Italy had come to match those in the traditional markets of the UK and US.

A great deal of the Alliance's income came from UK companies, and impending changes in the taxation system were giving rise to uncertainty, but Bruce Johnston was able to reassure shareholders that the company was confident of the long-term reliability of its income flows.

As competition became more aggressive in many sectors of the economy, boards of directors concentrated on these pressures by cutting costs, concentrating on their most profitable activities and looking for new opportunities. This was most evident in the oil, utilities, health care and pharmaceuticals industries. In the retail sector, however, lifestyle and fashion changes were creating great difficulties for some, while others, such as sellers of mobile phones and personal computers, were doing particularly well. Yet some companies in the technology sector struggled to make much headway and Alliance retained a sceptical position on technology stocks. Its position was realistic, as there was a dramatic collapse in these stocks in 2000.

Some banks were suffering badly under the pressure of bad debts in emerging economies, increased competition, downward pressure on margins and new technologies. Asian banks, in particular, were in a process of restructuring and recapitalising. Japanese banks were still facing the need to restructure their whole economic system. Western banks were doing a little better as credit quality improved, but competition for new business was intensifying. As different sectors moved in diverse directions and there were growing numbers of challenges within sectors it became increasingly difficult to pick appropriate investments. Johnston reported that Bank of Scotland and Lloyds TSB, which had dramatically reduced their cost-income ratios, sat 'comfortably in the innovative and cost effective camps'.

Looking back over the 1990s, the 1999 report included some performance comparisons against the Alliance outcomes, assuming that all income was

Table 10.3 Performance comparison (1 and 10 years)

	1 year (%)	10 years (%)
Alliance Net Asset Value	+12.5	+272.1
International General Investment Trusts (NAV)	+12.2	+245.5
FTSE All Share Index	+9.1	+251.5
US Standard and Poors 500	+31.6	+464.2
FT/S&P World Index (ex UK)	+26.1	+343.9
Tokyo	−2.7	−41.9
Halifax 30-day deposit account	+4.5	+84.4
Retail Price Index	+2.4	+49.4

(Source: Association of Investment Trust Companies)

reinvested. Table 10.3 is a copy of that comparison.

The Asian economies, to which Alliance had little exposure, recovered quite quickly from their crisis, Europe was buoyant and the US economy was doing well. The annual report in 2000 spoke about the 'ninth year of expansion'. There was also a reference to the phantom millennium bug which, it was widely believed, would cause computer systems to crash and which made fortunes for many 'computing consultants'. In the event there was no problem but the amounts of money spent on 'solving' the problem was doubtless a useful injection of cash for many companies in the technology consulting business.

The improving international economy, especially in the East, persuaded Alan Young, who was the director responsible for investment policy and implementation, that Japan was once more a good investment prospect. Consequently he allocated £31m to take advantage of opportunities in the 'new Japan', principally technology and telecoms companies. A further tranche of money was invested in Europe now that the euro had been successfully launched.

The downturn in technology stocks that occurred in 2000 was a warning sign that uncertainties were never far away. The US government had already moved to lower interest rates in an effort to maintain business confidence and Johnston was in no doubt that the road ahead might be rocky. Nevertheless he felt comfortable with the fact that Alliance had no gearing and that it had a flow of income that would support a growing dividend. Moreover he was sure, now that many businesses operated on a global scale, that Alliance's widely diversified international portfolio would provide real returns and a store of value without 'excessive positioning risk'.

As the Alliance entered the new millennium it was in good shape. Bruce Johnston assured the shareholders that the Trust's 'fundamental approach to investment has again delivered value'. With the impact of the precipitous falls in the technology, media and telecommunications sectors having largely been avoided, the Alliance portfolio outperformed in nearly all of the markets in which it was invested. He reminded shareholders, in the 2001 annual report, that Alliance still had no gearing and an expense ratio of only 0.14%. This placed the Alliance in a good position that would enable it to 'secure the long term real returns which . . . are offered by equities'.

Yet while Alliance was secure the same could not be said for the world economy. The 2002 annual report, published at the beginning of the year, sounded warnings about the possibility of the major world economies facing a 'synchronised recession'. Johnston felt that the 'corporate sector was plagued by the excesses of acquisition and technology driven expansion, over borrowing and doubtful accounting practices, and stock markets were depressed by crystallising risks and falling returns'.

Against this background it was inevitable that the Trust's net asset value would fall although, once again, the dividend was increased. It was also inevitable that investors would become anxious. Johnston, however, pointed out that the Trust's cautious investment policy over the years had enabled it to avoid the worst of the excesses that had been experienced elsewhere. He further reassured them that the Trust's conservative accounting policies, its cost containment and avoidance of borrowed money all contributed to ensuring that Alliance was able to ride out the storm.

Inevitably the state of world stock markets raised doubts about the prospects for equity investors. Johnston thought that this questioning about the wisdom of investing in equities would continue for some time, at least until the excesses of the past few years were purged from the system. When that happened it would be possible to pick up investments at modest prices. In short he, and his board, were firm in the view that the 'genuinely long term investor' would find equity investment rewarding, provided that risks were diversified.

The decision-making process about what to invest in was becoming more and more complex. Changes in economic and fiscal policies in many countries, and differences in accounting standards, had to be monitored and the amount of information available about possible investment targets was growing strongly. Alliance Trust's own annual report was, by 2002, a substantial document running to 47 pages. Other companies provided even lengthier reports. The internet was fast becoming a major source of information and opinion. There were around 400 different investments in the Alliance portfolio. Consequently there was a need to increase the staff, and by this time there were 19 investment staff on the payroll. Inevitably this added to the costs of running the business. As late as 2002 the expense ratio was still only 0.19% of total assets.

When the 2002 report was written there were only a few hopeful signs that recovery was on the way. US interest rates had been cut and there had also been some relaxation of fiscal policy. There was little sign yet that corporate spending was increasing but that was usually the consequence of an easing of government policy. Worries over inflation and the euro constrained European central banks from taking the bold measures taken by the American authorities. Elsewhere in the world economies remained mired in recession.

The collapse of Enron in 2001 gave rise to calls for greater regulation of businesses and tighter accounting standards. This was a familiar response that happened every time there was a collapse of a major company, especially when it was clear that market rules and company law had not always been observed. The collapse, coming at a time of depressed economic conditions, probably slowed down the recovery. Fortunately Alliance had never invested in Enron and the impact of its failure on other shares in utilities companies was relatively modest.

Revenues for oil producers and other extractive industries declined dramatically and the Organisation of Petroleum Exporting Countries (OPEC) moved to restrict production. However this was against a backdrop of the United States striving to increase domestic production of oil and gas to counter its strategic weakness of being reliant on Middle East oil. This was a signal for Alliance to invest in companies such as BP and Burlington Resources that had large stakes in North American energy fields.

In the UK, Alliance continued its policy of being invested in good dividend-paying companies such as Persimmon Homes and Wolseley Group, but in other sectors it was all about stock picking, as in engineering, electrical and general industrial stocks there was no consistent level of performance. Some sectors were particularly badly hit by the economic downturn. Advertising, tourism and consultancy services all experienced contractions, while others, such as telecommunications, struggled to find new customers.

If the problems of the international economy were not problems enough, in 2002 the investment trust industry was hit by the split capital trusts scandal. Many of these trusts were run on a model that worked well when the economy was expanding but when contraction set in they made serious losses. Alliance had contemplated setting up a split capital trust in the 1960s but had ultimately set its face against the idea and had never considered it again. In an article in the *Scotsman* in October 2002 Bill Jamieson described Alliance as 'the most boring business in Britain'. In the middle of the split capital crisis it was intended as a compliment. 'Alliance seldom gets much coverage for its values and for what it does. But today, amid the split cap hullabaloo, it especially deserves it.'

Johnston hoped that, 'common sense will prevail and that the root of many of the problems in the marketplace – the incentivised selling of long-term products on short-term criteria – which it has been our policy to avoid, will be tackled without damaging the strengths which companies such as our own have displayed for over a century'.

In referring to the various corporate scandals of the time he said, 'These disclosed many irregularities, not only in basic accounting practices, but also in the corporate structures and governance of several high profile companies. Overly optimistic pension assumptions and the value destroying effects of dilutive options-based reward structures have also emerged. Moves to address many of these have been made quickly in the US, but the transitional process is still painful.'

He went on to reassure shareholders:

> The Company has faced major uncertainties many times in its 115 year history, but it has been able to prosper with remarkably little change to the corporate structure on which it stands. Unfortunately, the good reputation of investment trusts has been damaged recently by the problems of some of the split capital sector and, although we are not involved in the scandals, we are bound to be affected by regulatory changes proposed. Proposals for greater disclosure of risks and exposures are sensible, but care needs to be taken where change could damage operational efficiency and investment flexibility. Employing our own staff and retaining our ability to respond to change will be as vital in the future as they have been in the past.

The scandal gave another downward twist to the already depressed markets. Share prices fell for the third successive year.

A watchful eye was kept open for new investment opportunities, and exposure to China was increased largely because of the 'prospects for increased consumer activity in the region as a whole'. The position in Japan, however, was a lot more cautious and the view was held that Japanese banks were 'probably insolvent'. There were no holdings. The view on other banking systems was more generous, but still cautious. 'Economic uncertainty makes credit quality remain a key issue. Exposures have generally been well managed thus far and widespread systemic issues seem unlikely, due to the growing use of loan syndication, securitisation and credit derivatives.'

It was better news for Johnston's final report as chairman in 2004. The economy had started to recover and equities were in favour once more, although currency movements, including further depreciation of the dollar against sterling, had the effect of reducing the value of returns on US investments. Johnston was also candid about aspects of investment policy that had impacted on Alliance's performance. He thought that the Trust had been too cautious on Japanese banks and on IT hardware where exposure was quite modest. Nevertheless Alliance's net asset value had increased by 22.5% over the year and this was a matter for quiet satisfaction.

Despite the recovery there were still a number of factors at work in the world that were likely to impact on investment opportunities and returns. War in Iraq, the flu-like Sars epidemic in China and the US budget and trade deficits were just some of the factors that investment managers factored into their decisions. These challenges brought about a substantial change in the investment management team, with responsibilities divided on a geographic basis rather than by industrial sector.

More than 50% of the Alliance portfolio was measured on a global basis, which meant that investment opportunities were evaluated without taking domestic boundaries into account. This approach enabled the Trust to focus on important industry trends that were occurring across the world and to value investments on an international basis. The issue of where a company was listed was of lesser importance. There were, however, some sectors of the economy, such as retail, where this approach was not appropriate and they continued to be managed on a national or regional basis.

The appearance of the annual report received a makeover in 2004 and there were further changes in 2005. It was Lesley Knox's first report as chairman. It was also Alan Harden's first full year as chief executive and the annual report contained a chief executive's statement for the first time.

Of particular concern at that time were changes to the regulatory environment being proposed by the Treasury that would have made shares in investment trusts 'regulated products'. The effect of this would have been to expose them to a framework similar to that for open-ended investment companies. The Alliance view was that this would be of no benefit to share-holders who already enjoyed protection under the Companies Acts and the UK Listing Authority rules. The Trust argued the case with the Treasury and contributed to the response made by the Association of Investment Trust Companies (AITC). It was at this point that Alliance saw the value in rejoining the AITC, which it had left several years earlier after a disagreement about an advertising campaign that would have doubled Alliance's expense ratio. The proposed changes never came to pass.

Harden took the view that the Alliance's investment strategy, which was then based on industrial sectors, needed to change. He believed that 'geography and geographical environment is a more defining factor on corporate performance'. Consequently the equity team, under Grant Lindsay, was re-jigged to give managers a clear geographical mandate. That was by no means the end of the changes that Harden introduced. For he was keen on asset classes other than equities such as property, private equity, fixed interest and cash.

One of the early decisions made by the Asset, Liability and Income Committee (ALICo), which Harden established, was to diversify investment policy. There was still great faith in equities but there was also a realisation, based on experience over the past few years, that there were many risks involved. Consequently it was decided to extend the portfolio into property and private equity. The significance of these changes can be exaggerated, but only 3% of the portfolio was to be invested in property. Harden was well aware that the extent of due diligence required when investing in property or private equity meant that decisions could not be rushed.

This diversification of the portfolio was in response to worries about possible oil price rises, the dangers of a hard landing in China, a slowdown in the UK housing market and the depreciation of the dollar. ALICo monitored 'thousands of economic statistics from all the major economies' in its quest for the best investments.

When the annual report appeared early in 2006 it recorded the fact that Alliance had experienced a very good year. Net asset value had increased by 24.6%, the share price had risen by 27.3% and capital growth had been £395.5m. An increase in dividend was announced.

There was, however, a growing worry about the health of the US economy. The view was expressed that it appeared to be approaching a watershed. There were signs that house price increases might slow and that might affect consumer spending. There were also concerns about US deficits and worries that the Asian nations might reduce their preparedness to purchase US government bonds. Interest rates, which were reaching their peak, might lead to further pressure on the dollar.

There had also been a continuation of the changes that had earlier been initiated. The Hong Kong office had been opened and the staff there were soon managing two new funds. Harden said, 'The re-alignment of our funds onto a geographic basis, coupled with the formal asset allocation process through the new Asset, Liability and Income Committee (ALICo), has sharpened our ability to achieve these results without diminishing our cautious approach to risk.'

There was further diversification of the portfolio with small investments in private equity, property and in the financial services subsidiaries. The private equity firm, Albany Ventures, which specialised in early stage technology and life sciences, was acquired. The addition of these new elements in the portfolio resulted in an internal restructuring of the business so that four divisions were created. These were equity, private equity, property and financial services. The latter included ATS. The old mineral rights in North America, which were still bringing in a healthy income, were included under property. Private equity included an investment in Fleming Family Private Equity, which re-established a link to the Fleming family that had been so important to the Alliance in its very early days.

Throughout this time the stock market continued to rise but there were growing fears that it was over-heating, and the Alliance appetite for such risks was very modest. Consequently the equities percentage in the portfolio was reduced. Other trusts continued to ride the bull market with the result that their performance appeared to outstrip that of Alliance. In his statement to shareholders in 2007 Harden conceded that perhaps Alliance had reduced its equity portfolio too early. A year later, however, the depths of the crisis were becoming more evident and it was clear that the defensive strategy was exactly what was needed. Nevertheless Alliance was in a position to continue its decades-long strategy of increasing the dividend. Harden, in his pre-results statement, made it clear that Alliance was focused on the long term. There had been a significant change in investment strategy and Alliance was focused on just 200 equity investments.

There was also a wider concern about what indices it would be appropriate to set as a measure against which the Alliance performance might be judged. It was decided that the retail price index (RPI) would be the most appropriate.

On that basis the Alliance shareholder return was 7.5% compared with an RPI of 4.2%.

The storm broke in the autumn of 2007 when concerns about US mortgages led to a tightening of the wholesale money markets. This resulted in several UK banks, including Northern Rock, getting into difficulty, but it was the failure of American banks Bear Sterns in March 2008 and Lehman Brothers several months later that ignited the crisis and necessitated a UK government bailout for Royal Bank of Scotland and HBOS.

Inevitably the stock markets, which had risen through 2007, took a sharp fall in January 2008. By this time Katherine Garrett-Cox was installed as chief investment officer and she had begun to further diversify the portfolio in pursuit of a policy that was 'intended to improve our ability to generate returns for shareholders at all stages of the economic cycle'. To assist this process there had been investment in 'more sophisticated information technology for both stock selection, using quantitative screening tools, and risk management software as well as more detailed performance attribution'.

Despite the fact that the dividend continued to increase Alliance attracted some adverse criticism. The *Daily Telegraph's* Money supplement, in August 2007, feared that Alliance was losing its 'famously thrifty ways'. The article went on to note that the Alliance share price had underperformed the FTSE 100 index and the FTSE Investment Trust index. The article also noted that the company was hiring more staff, mostly in ATS, and was planning a new building. The prospect of a new corporate headquarters always makes financial journalists very nervous.

There was criticism, too, from some institutional investors who, ignoring Alliance's relatively good performance in the crisis, were more interested in what Harden described as 'financially engineering the share price to their benefit'. It was not the first time, nor would it be the last, that some investors applied pressure to get Alliance to buy back some of its own shares with the objective of reducing the discount. He was, however, pleased that 'the analysts who work for private investors were very positive. Those guys understand what we are doing – it is an evolutionary process and that is to our benefit.'

Lesley Knox was proved to be absolutely right when she told the shareholders, early in 2008, that 'we are looking back at a year of market turbulence and forward to one which seems likely to be just as difficult'.

When the 2008 annual general meeting came round it was revealed that Alliance had increased its revenues by 21%. At the same time net asset value had fallen by 4.7%, although this was less than the fall in the All Share Index.

Several months later Alan Harden's resignation was announced and he returned to the Far East as chief executive of ING Investment Management. An article in the *Sunday Herald* (13 July 2008) claimed that many analysts preferred 'more focused global generalist investment trusts . . . to Harden's flashy but underperforming creation'. Reuters took a less critical approach and a longer-term view. It talked of ambitious plans for progress, the fruits of which had not yet made their way through to the share price. The Reuters correspondent went on to raise the question of what Harden's successor might do: '. . . the question will be whether to continue Harden's expansion of the company into the myriad of areas he had developed, including self invested pension plans (SIPPs) administration, the launch of a fund supermarket and more fund launches or opt for a simpler structure with a focus on returns from its listed holdings'.

The promotion of Katherine Garrett-Cox to the top job was greeted warmly by the financial press. She knew that the opinions and pronouncements of the financial journalists carried weight and that there were mixed views about the direction of Alliance policy. She announced that there would be a review of strategy 'in which there would be no sacred cows'. An early victim of this review was the Hong Kong office, the closure of which was announced in December 2008 in order to centralise investment decision-making in the UK. Garrett-Cox went to Hong Kong to tell staff the news in person. Nevertheless some of the plans for new initiatives were well advanced and ATS launched its new fund supermarket in September 2008. In announcing half-yearly results a month later she advised shareholders that the focus would be on the main business and that the development of new initiatives would not be fast.

All this was happening against a backdrop of the worst global financial crisis the world had seen for 80 years. The failure of banks and other financial institutions was accompanied by government efforts in many countries to shore up their systems in an endeavour to prevent further collapse. The UK was one of the worst affected countries, and even companies like Alliance, which were not close to the maelstrom, found it wise to trim their sails. Staff numbers were cut by 12% and investment policy changed so that more than 20% of Alliance assets were in cash or near cash. The challenge in such situations is always to make good decisions for the long-term interests of the company rather than just react to the current crisis.

The emphasis was henceforth to be on the core business, but that did not mean that new initiatives were to be ruled out. Nor did it mean that some of the new business developments of recent years were to be forgotten. There was a commitment to building the asset management business that was expected to complement the Trust's own activities and help to enhance investment performance. This was not without controversy, and the *Herald* (21 December 2008) was worried that this might distract fund managers from their investment activities. There was also a concern about what was likely to be a high marketing spend to get the business established.

As the 2009 annual general meeting drew near there was comment in the *Scotsman* (20 April 2009) about what was likely to happen next. 'A key aim of the group this year will be to build its appeal as a core investment and as a "bedrock" share for portfolios.' Nevertheless two new open-ended funds were launched – a North American equity fund and a UK equity income fund, in each case based closely on the Trust's existing equity portfolio in these regions. The principle objective was to attract new investors. A permanent office was opened in Edinburgh to cater for the private equity team and to assist in company visits and research. And in September that year Alliance recruited a fixed-income team from Scottish Widows Investment Partnership.

These new developments may have had some financial commentators wondering what was going on but, in reality, Alliance was being true to its history in moving with the times, as it had done in the 1920s when moving out of mortgages and looking for new opportunities in a crisis when prices were low. These were difficult times, and in the financial year to 31 January 2009 net asset value fell by 19.5% but the All Share Index had fallen by 27.8%. The Alliance had a history of outperforming the market when times were tough.

Financial markets were nervous through 2009 to 2012, with currency instability, sovereign debt problems, fears over the euro and a constant apprehension about the possibility of a double-dip recession. Alliance continued its cautious investment policy and cost-cutting measures. Staff numbers fell by 14% between 2009 and 2010. But it also dipped its toes into borrowing, and by September 2009 was 2% geared, with Katherine Garrett-Cox reported as saying that she would be happy with gearing up to 10%–15%. In the 2011 report she indicated that net gearing was then 11%. Earlier that year the board had decided to close the private equity business, reversing one of Alan Harden's diversification initiatives.

The 2011 annual report also revealed that Alliance Trust Asset Management was making good progress in only its second year of operation. The main source of funds was third-party investors and there were five equity funds and one fixed income fund. The monthly income bond then managed £83m of funds against £12m a year earlier – a clear indication that the market valued Alliance's investment abilities. Late in 2011 the business was rebranded as Alliance Trust Investments. A Global Equities Team under Ilario Di Bon was established to manage this part of the business, and on 29 December 2011 they launched a new fund – the Global Thematic Opportunities Fund.

In 2010 the board reviewed the key performance indicators and agreed that, in future, the success of the company would be measured against its peer group – the AIC Global Growth investment trust sector. Various measures were to be considered, including changes in net asset value, total shareholder return, dividend growth and the cost base. All these were to be ranked over periods of time ranging from one to five years.

Banking and Savings Operations

The banking and savings operation were run by Alliance Trust (Finance) Group (ATF), which was 75% owned by Alliance Trust and 25% by Second Alliance Trust. The leasing business was finally sold off in 1996. The decision was driven by the good price that was on offer and by the fact that the banks had re-entered the business and competition was driving down profit potential. Société Générale purchased two of the companies. The consequence was that ATF was then over capitalised. To make use of the money in the group the sum of £12m was loaned to the parent companies to 'reduce the effective capital and to allow the funds to be invested elsewhere'. The remaining funds were invested in gilts and short term deposits to cover the client deposit balances, which had increased by 20% in the year to 31 January 1997 and then stood at £32m.

Alliance Trust Savings (ATS) administered the PEP and the savings scheme. The PEP had been particularly popular, and the value of the clients' assets in ATS then stood at £400m. Nearly half of the 55,000 shareholders had come to Alliance via the PEP scheme. Further improvements had been made to the administration of ATS in 1996, and the result was a reduction in dealing costs for clients. The introduction of the CREST share dealing system had undoubtedly facilitated the changes.

The scale and nature of the changes that were taking place in the savings market required careful thinking about the future role of ATS and its relationship to the Trust. In June 1997 the new chairman, Bruce Johnston, wrote, 'ATS has developed over recent years from what may originally have been seen as essentially a support service to the Trusts into a business which has considerable potential as a profit centre in its own right. The wide range of investment choices available under the PEP and recently revamped Investment Plan, combined with the formidable reputations of the Trusts and moderate costs, have combined to create products with great appeal to our market of more substantial, perhaps more sophisticated, longer term investor.'

Rapid growth was clearly placing strains on management and accommodation. Moreover increased regulatory and risk controls were placing increasing burdens on management time. Something had to be done, and Suggett's response ran to nine pages. In this paper Suggett reviewed the history of ATS and acknowledged that the advent of PEPs, and their success, had caught everyone by surprise and had created problems for management. Telephone calls were running at a rate of 300 per day and plans were already in place to double the size of the switchboard. The possibility of outsourcing some of the work had been considered, but Suggett was clear that 'the responsibility for providing the service to the client cannot be outsourced'.

In 1997 plans were being laid for the further expansion of ATS based upon an extrapolation of growth over the preceding five years. This was, of course all being undertaken against a very uncertain future – the new ISA was an unknown quantity and the future of PEPs was completely unknown. The plan clearly stated that adding value was the main priority and attention would be given to telephone dealing, extended hours, improved marketing and staff recruitment. It was anticipated that staff numbers would increase from 38 to 80. The 1998 review of ATS revealed that the decisions made a year earlier had been well judged. Turnover and profits were substantially higher and the product range had been enhanced with the inclusion of a pension plan.

ATS eventually acquired its own authorisation under the 1987 Banking Act and its capital was increased, in 1999, to £10 million. It was beginning to demonstrate considerable growth potential, as Table 10.4 reveals.

Unlike many other players in the financial services market, ATS was free from the baggage of legacy products. It was, to all intents and purposes, a new business and it was no idle boast to say that 'Unlike many of the "new model" businesses in this sector, ATS is not only self funding, but profitable.' It derived benefits from being in Dundee – especially in the recruitment and retention of staff. Its location also helped in controlling costs. Good progress was being made in developing an online offering. It was expected that this would be particularly helpful in developing the savings scheme that, in future, would be called the Investment Plan.

Table 10.4 Alliance Trust savings growth by product in year to 31 January 2000

	Investors		Investors' assets	
	Numbers	Change (%)	£m	Change (%)
Investment Plan	6,659	+19	85	33
PEP	20,717	+5	774	11
ISA	6,959	n/a	34	n/a
Pension Plan	820	+55	23	155
Total	29,071	+13	916	19

At the same time there was a barrage of criticism in the press about the large generalist investment trusts. This prompted some serious thinking about branding and the organisation's position in the market. The existence of ATS gave Alliance the opportunity to do something about these issues without having to worry too much about the dangers of advertising the Trust itself, which would have breached company legislation. ATS provided a vehicle for raising the company's profile.

Yet this development was not achieved without some internal difficulties. The cultures of the Trust and the savings business were somewhat different and there were tensions between the staffs of the two divisions. This led the chairman, Bruce Johnston, in 1998 to pen a footnote to a board paper in which he wrote, 'The balancing of morale and motivation of Trust and ATS personnel is a sensitive area (from both directions) and does and will continue to require considerable top management attention.' At the root of this issue seems to have been the amount of money that was spent on technology for ATS operations while the Trust, by comparison, received little. Subsequent board papers revealed that the decision had been made to view the trusts and ATS as an integrated whole – 'all part of the Alliance brand'. The amalgamation of Alliance with Second Alliance Trust was then under consideration, as was a stock split which would have the effect of making Alliance shares more accessible to investors.

Growth in the business brought increasing complexity, and at a joint management committee meeting in 1998 the subjects under discussion included reconciliations, share exchanges, compliance, procedures, record keeping, complaints, monitoring, internal audit, pensions applications, AITC, CREST, taxation, staffing, training, computing, budgets, TESSAs, PEPs, ISAs, customer relations, performance, disaster recovery plan, health and safety, operations, interest rates, internet and property. It was a long meeting.

Changes introduced by the new Labour government from 1997 had brought new PEPs to an end, although the amount invested in these continued to increase as a result of returns being reinvested and transfers from other providers. The replacement product was the Individual Savings Account (ISA). This was a more flexible product than the PEP, as it allowed a broader range of investments than the stock market listed securities to which holders of PEPs were limited. It also allowed a much higher amount of saving in these tax-free investments. As these had only recently been announced when the 2000 report was published, there was little to be said about them except that Alliance Trust's offering was the first investment trust ISA to meet the government's CAT standard (for charges, access and terms). The expectation was that demand for the ISA would grow at least as quickly as demand for the PEP.

The Alliance pension plan was still only available for the self-employed, although access was being extended to people in non-pensionable employment. As Alliance's core business was long-term investing, there was a feeling that pensions provision sat well alongside this, and high levels of growth were anticipated to expand the healthy uptake that had already been experienced. A spring 1998 article in *Investment Trusts* magazine recorded that a great deal of consultation had taken place before the launch and that the plan was 'very attractive'. At that time there were only six investment trusts offering pension schemes. The annual report for 2002 recorded the fact that the uptake for the Alliance pension was strong and further growth was anticipated. It was also recorded that this service was unique amongst investment trusts.

In 2000 it was reported that Alliance had decided not to participate in a generic advertising campaign for investment trusts which was being run by the Association of Investment Trust Companies (AITC) because, to have done so, would have doubled the expense ratio. This decision led to Alliance's departure from membership of the organisation. In a letter to Michael Hart at the Association (20 September 2001) Suggett set out the reasons for Alliance's resignation. Alliance, being the largest of the Trusts in membership, would have borne the bulk of the cost of the campaign. The Alliance share was £250,000, which would be subject to VAT but not allowable for tax purposes. Moreover, 'As you know we are not really geared up to appeal to commission sensitive IFAs and unlike many management groups do not have a sales force on the road cultivating contacts and selling whatever is in demand from a portfolio of branded funds. Therefore the AITC marketing campaign did not really fit in with our own set up.' Suggett was concerned that AITC was changing from being a trade association to a marketing organisation. He went on, 'We are sceptical as to the effectiveness of generic marketing particularly for such an assortment of members and our conclusion was that, for both the short and longer term, our resources were better spent elsewhere or at least passed onto stockholders in the form of dividends.'

The decision to leave AITC had certainly not been taken lightly and Suggett had spoken with a number of industry leaders on the subject. In April 2001 he had written to Alex Hammond Chambers to say 'the industry is so diverse now – we see very little community of interest with splits [split capital investment trusts] – that we really do wonder whether we shouldn't just accept the reality that the AITC is no longer geared towards self managed trusts and resign as did 3i a few years ago'.

The Alliance departure from AITC did not mean, however, that no thought was being given to raising the company profile. In his report to shareholders in 2001, Bruce Johnston celebrated the fact that the growth of Alliance had largely been achieved by word-of-mouth recommendations. ATS had reached the £1bn in funds invested and 11% of Alliance shares were held in ATS plans. There was nothing that Alliance could do, as a public company, to promote its own shares but it now had a powerful investment vehicle in ATS and it was decided 'from a business and corporate viewpoint to raise the profile'. This was in direct response to changes in society. The tactic was more than a response to the competitive challenge from unit trusts. (In 2001 unit trusts were managing £250bn as against the £70bn managed by investment trusts.) It was widely acknowledged that the UK population was ageing and that state provision for pensions was declining. It was also well understood that more people were making provision for their retirement through private pensions and other savings schemes. Consequently Alliance's strategy would become more focused on 'the provision of an integrated savings and investment business for stockholders'. Such a strategy required a more active publicity profile and the Trust set about running investor seminars, conducting visits and developing press contacts. In the past, much of this type of activity had been run on a collaborative basis by the AITC. Alliance discovered that 'it is far more difficult and time consuming than we anticipated to source appropriate venues and that it takes more pairs of hands than we realised to make sure things go well on the day'.

From this point onwards the savings side of the business was given greater prominence in the annual report. In 2001 it recorded that:

> There have been remarkable changes in the savings industry over the last decade. Demand has been stimulated, competition opened up, regulation improved and better information provided. There is now a more level playing field but change is nowhere near complete and we see huge opportunities for cost efficient suppliers in this market. CAT and Stakeholder standards are only a very crude start to the process. ATS has built itself a secure position free from the baggage of history, has a business model that works, and faces an expanding market for long-term investment. This should ensure a good long-term future.

When the annual report was written early in 2001 it was becoming clearer what the new possibilities for ISAs and pensions might be. The new rules were due to come into force in April that year and Johnston was confident that Alliance's savings product would experience an upsurge in demand as the rules changed to permit more flexibility and greater amounts of savings. ATS grew 19% that year. Consequently it was necessary to be prepared. Increased recruitment, training, technology and accommodation placed Alliance in a good position to benefit from the increased demand. Staff numbers now exceeded 100 across the whole group.

ATS Online was set up and a new department was created to bring together and expand product development, events management, marketing and sales activities. Other changes were also afoot. Various changes in legislation allowed Alliance, inter alia, to offer its pension products to anyone, even to children. It was also offered via other providers but badged under their name. Its low costs were what attracted most people. Nevertheless the various changes that were taking place in products, combined with the poor state of the international economy, made investors wary; although there was strong growth in demand for the ISAs and pensions, there was also a decline in the amount invested in PEPs, which resulted in a reduction of 4% in managed funds between 2001 and 2002.

Such rapid development of ATS took up a great deal of management time. Early that year it was announced that the business would be managed as three departments. Investment would be headed up by Colin Beveridge, with savings under the leadership of Kevin Dann and central services in the care of Neil

Anderson. Later that year a separate business plan for ATS ran to 35 pages, with 54 pages of appendices. An investor relations implementation plan ran to 61 pages, much of which was actually taken up with regulatory concerns. The corporate goals were stated as being: 'To grow its business through the provision of savings products for investors on a non subsidised basis by the parent companies (The Trusts) ... We will promote ATS through advertising, other media and contacts with journalists.'

A great deal of research had been done so that the company had a clear view of its client base. It had discovered that 'Most of the ATS investors are in the populous south of England and anecdotal evidence suggests that an ATS investor tends to be relatively high net worth, well educated, cost conscious and with a suspicion for traditional selling methods and forms of distribution. Other anecdotal evidence, however, suggests a broadening of the client base, a feature which has gone hand in hand with the development of the pension and initiatives such as promoting the pension and investment plan as a means of saving for children.' Only 19% of investors were in Scotland.

Slightly more than half of investors in ATS had heard about Alliance Trust via a magazine or newspaper article, while 87% were attracted by low charges and 51% by the range of investment choice.

It was an increasingly competitive market but Alliance was making good progress and staff numbers for ATS had grown to 54, of which 24 were in client services department. The products available in 2002 were:

Alliance Select ISA
Alliance CAT ISA
Alliance Select PEP
Alliance Select Investment Plan
Alliance Select Pension

The following year, 2003, the business plan told a similar story and stressed the increasingly competitive nature of the market. Plans were laid for more growth and staff were becoming more 'sales aware'. SWOT analyses had been undertaken to ensure that everyone understood the strengths, weaknesses, opportunities and threats that underpinned and challenged the organisation.

ATS took every opportunity to advertise its services and when an invitation came from Ernst and Young to speak at a seminar in 2003 it was accepted with alacrity. Suggett told those who attended, 'ATS is unusual. It allows you to structure your own portfolio to suit yourself and it charges only on the basis of what you ask us to do. Your costs therefore depend on how active you are, not on how large or how successful your portfolio is. We make no annual charge.'

The presentation went on to talk about transparency, shareholders coming first, strong governance, low-key marketing, risk and cost control, conservative accounting and depth and experience. The in-house nature of operations was also stressed.

The quality of what ATS was doing was widely recognised in 2003 when 'in reader-nominated awards from *Investors' Chronicle* and *What Investment*; and from the *Guardian/Money Observer*, in whose Consumer Finance awards we scored best overall on all criteria of friendliness, quality, flexibility, competitiveness, efficiency and performance in the category of stocks and shares ISA/investment provider. ATS's own research shows that the majority of new customers take out a savings plan with ATS after personal recommendation from a relative or friend.'

By 2005 the increased investment in technology and systems drove down the surplus made by ATS but the improvements in service were well received by savers who could then choose variable investment levels within their plans. When the investment in new technology was completed customers could transact their business by any method, whether online, by phone or by post. Further technology changes were in train and Harden was aware that costs would increase, but he was confident that the business would grow and that current levels of investment would be 'more than justified by future returns'.

The year 2005 was ATS' 20th year in business. It had become a full member of the London Stock Exchange and the process of giving effect to customer orders, which used to take the better part of a day, could now be transacted in ten minutes.

Further changes were afoot with the acquisition of London-based Wolanski and Co. Trustees Ltd, a specialist pensions administrator which, in addition to bringing additional expertise and customers, also brought a new set of relationships with intermediaries. This subsidiary was renamed Alliance Trust Pensions Ltd and the administration was moved to Dundee. It required, at that time, a heavily manual administrative system, and with the introduction, and popularity, of self-invested pension plans (SIPPs), strains began to show in the administration. This required a temporary stop to the acceptance of new business while new, more automated systems for handling the administration were installed.

By 2007 ATS had 44,000 customers, a 30% increase over four years, and was continuing to invest in new technology, including online share dealing. There was also a move to get third parties to use ATS platforms and there was some success in this when Allianz Global Investors, Close Investments Ltd and Montanaro decided to make use of this opportunity.

A year later the problems in the world's financial system had begun to take hold but there was, as yet, little recognition of what would follow. The private equity business had doubled in size in the past year and revenues from property had increased. ATS had improved its revenue by 19% and its new technology platform was working well. *Investors' Chronicle* awarded Alliance its 'Best Investment Trust Manager' award.

However, the financial crisis, which involved the reduction of base rate to a historically low 0.5% created problems, not just for ATS but for the whole financial system. Costs were rising quickly, while revenues diminished, leaving the organisation in an unprofitable condition.

When Rob Burgess, a seasoned banker, arrived to run ATS in 2009 his primary objective was to get ATS back into profit but he was also focused on enhancing the quality of service. To achieve these objectives there was a need to further develop the back office technology. Automation would turn ATS into a low-cost scalable business and further growth was necessary to bring in revenues that would offset the loss of revenues that had been caused by falling interest rates. The objective, which was soon achieved, was to have an almost paperless back office system.

Growth came from several sources – marketing, the maintenance of a low-charging infrastructure, a growing reputation for good service and enhanced consumer choice. The i.nvest platform enabled savers to choose investments from 21,000 securities in 18 countries and 21 exchanges. ATS had also become of the leading providers of SIPPs in the UK. Improved staff training added greatly to the quality of service. In excess of 9,000 new accounts were opened in 2011.

These enhancements also brought younger customers to ATS, and many of them purchased shares in the Trust itself. Until then the age profile of account holders and shareholders had been getting older. This progress was greatly helped by the fact that in 2011, in excess of 400 friendly mentions had been made in the press. Personal recommendations also helped to bring in new customers. Financial commentators and intermediaries were, increasingly, opening accounts in their own names.

Shareholders

Alliance had always concentrated on keeping its costs as low as possible and was the envy of the rest of the investment trust industry in this respect. In 1998 the shareholders were informed in the annual report that management and administration costs as a percentage of total assets were only 0.13%. This fact was not lost on stockholders and the upward trend in the numbers of new holders, which had begun in the 1980s, continued. In 1998 there were 30,402 names on the register. However, many, if not most, of the shareholders had been with the company for a lengthy period of time and it was well understood by the board that shareholders relied on their dividend for their standard of living. Consequently the board saw it as their responsibility to provide a relatively predictable and increasing income stream.

But the difficult economic conditions around the turn of the century created an environment in which many companies, not just in the financial sector, were returning funds to shareholders in share buyback operations. This possibility was considered by the Alliance board but rejected. Their argument was that to do so might raise questions of fairness amongst shareholders. It would also 'dilute the historic strength of the closed end aspect of trusts in depressed markets', i.e. the flexibility to take advantage of low prices in antic-ipation of an upturn.

There had been a great deal of debate in the financial press about share buybacks (especially from institutional holders), the future of investment trusts, discounts, takeovers and the role of marketing. Suggett's view was that these matters kept coming up because 'there is an issue between the short and long term holders' (of shares). The Alliance position was that the organisation was being run in the interests of long-term shareholders. The board and executive of Alliance gave close scrutiny to what was being said and came to the conclusion that no change should be made to the structure of the company. It was felt that the Alliance as an investment trust, together with Alliance Trust Savings, 'captures the best of both the investment and savings business'. There was a particular satisfaction that Alliance Trust Savings provided a steady flow of new shareholders, and by this time more than 11% of the Trust's shares were held in savings plans. Nevertheless press criticism continued, especially in the light of returns that were being made by the split capital investment trusts where there were two categories of shareholders – one of which benefited from the dividends while the other benefited from capital growth.

Fund managers wrote to Suggett to try to persuade him of the advantages of buybacks. In 2001 James Carthew of Advance UK Trust wrote to Bruce Johnston to say that he would be voting against the directors at the AGM because of their refusal to countenance share buybacks. In 2002 Steve Brown of Hermes wrote to make the case for share buybacks and referred to what he saw as Alliance's indifferent performance over the past five years: 'It appears to us that share repurchases are a crucial factor in sustaining the stability and performance of the investment trust industry. Not only does the ability to repurchase shares restrict discount volatility but it offers liquidity to those wishing to sell whilst providing NAV enhancement to those retaining their shares.'

Suggett's response was robust. 'Certainly buy backs do not seem to have generated a total performance in the peer group which is obviously superior to that of the Alliance.' He went on, 'We have no argument with the managers' business model but we do always point out that their objectives are, in part, diametrically opposed to those of our own – they favour high fees, more funds under management, gearing, new issues, income enhancing accounting policies, a minimum of stock holder communication and "house" brand promotion paid for by the client. The split capital trust fiasco is hopefully the worst manifestation of these commercial pressures.'

Such a response could have left no doubt in Brown's mind that Alliance was not about to shift its position. The split capital scandal in 2002 caused some journalists to revise their thinking about large general trusts like Alliance. Tom Dalton, who had once criticised Alliance for the large discount, ate some humble pie when he wrote, 'The trusts were out of favour as they were not seen as fashionable for they had a low weighting in the Technology, Media and Telecoms sectors, had no gearing in place, and as a result were deemed to be dull and boring . . . Technology, Media and Telecoms sectors fell dramatically out of fashion, and many trusts with high levels of gearing suffered sharp falls in share price. Investors have come to appreciate the so-called 'dull and boring' trusts that are unlikely to spring any unpleasant surprises'.

In a board paper written in the summer of 2003, Suggett averred that, 'One of the lessons learned from the last few years has been the importance of being open and absolutely clear where we stand. The experiences with Hermes, Advance and other active institutions pushing for buy backs, mergers, gearing, changes of boards etc. show that standing up to them and having nothing to hide is important.'

But the prospect of share buybacks did not entirely disappear, and at the time of the merger of Alliance Trust with Second Alliance Trust in 2006 it was decided that, to ensure that support amongst institutional investors for the merger was forthcoming, the company should ask for the power to buy back its own shares for the first time. Although the powers were acquired, Harden was against the practice and there was, at that time, no real intention of exercising them. Harden's view was that better use could be made of the money, including an increase in the dividend.

The matter was again under consideration the following year but market turbulence at the end of 2007 suggested that a delay would be wise. It was not until October 2009 that the powers were eventually used when shares worth £15.4 million were purchased from Norges Bank Investment Management and more, to the value of £19.7 million, were acquired from D.C. Thomson in March 2010.

During 2006 the decision was made to merge the Trust with the Second Alliance Trust. The idea had been discussed and rejected several times in the past, most recently in 2003. Economic conditions were favourable, and as Alliance moved into new asset classes it made sense to merge the two trusts rather than try to manage subsidiary companies whose share capital was split between Alliance and Second Alliance. Second Alliance had begun life as the Hawaiian Investment and Agency Company in 1880. Responsibility for its management passed to the Alliance Trust in 1918 and shortly thereafter its name was changed to the Second Alliance Trust. Since then it had been managed by the same team that ran the Alliance and, as time went on, its investment policy and strategy differed not at all from the larger company. One consequence of the merger was that the Trust was recognised as one of the UK's largest companies when it was admitted to the FTSE 100 index in February 2008. But that was not the only reason, and Alliance entered the FTSE 100 as a result of its performance and ahead of other companies that had been on the FTSE reserve list – companies such as easyJet and Burberry. Harden described the move as 'morale boosting'.

The merger was arranged when Second Alliance shareholders received Alliance shares. There was also a 10 for 1 share split. The costs of merger amounted to £4.5 million and this caused some adverse comment. It was pointed out that this cost was less than a fifth of 1% of total assets.

Moreover there were sound management and economic reasons for the merger. As the companies moved into new areas like property, there were undoubted economies in a single company, as to do otherwise would require complex structures for joint investments. There were also sound arguments from a regulatory perspective, as a merger would make the group structure more readily comprehensible in the eyes of a regulator. Savings in management time was a further benefit to be derived from managing a single entity, especially where there was a commitment to developing the business of ATS. In addition, the fact that Second Alliance Trust was quite small made it vulnerable to a takeover bid. Hedge funds were already taking an interest and Standard Life had sold a large block of shares to them. The arguments in favour of a merger were compelling and, when the merger was eventually announced, the reaction from the financial press was welcoming. They also asked why it had not happened before. The reaction from shareholders was equally favourable, with in excess of 99% voting in favour.

But before all this could be achieved there was an enormous amount of work to be done. The Alliance prospectus that was sent to shareholders ran to 70 pages, with a further document of 77 pages. The equivalent document for Second Alliance shareholders reached 54 pages. This was all prepared by Sheila Ruckley and her small team, together with legal advisers. The task was called Project Blue. Before a merger could take place the memorandum and articles of association of both companies had to be updated, as they had not been revised since the 1920s. To protect the interests of shareholders both Alliance and Second Alliance acquired separate advisers – J.P. Morgan Cazenove in the case of Alliance, while Dresdner Kleinwort Wasserstein acted for Second Alliance. It all took time and it was necessary for the Project Blue team to maintain strict confidentiality, even within the company office. Consequently the team operated in an office with a locked door.

It was described as a merger but the reality was that Alliance took over Second Alliance. The main effect of the merger was to create the UK's largest generalist investment company.

Ruckley retired shortly afterwards. At around the same time Donald McPherson joined, as company secretary, from Scottish Power.

Other changes introduced at the time of the merger included a decision to pay dividends quarterly and a name change for the company by dropping 'The'. The company was henceforth called Alliance Trust plc.

In the 2007 report Knox told the shareholders: 'The merger was the natural outcome of a working arrangement put in place decades ago by our prede-cessors. It took an enormous amount of time and effort during the first half of the year but we are already seeing the benefits of the simpler structure.' The economies were substantial, not least in that it was then necessary to maintain only one shareholders' register.

The newly merged company continued to attract new shareholders. The major attraction was undoubtedly the steadily increasing dividend, now paid quarterly. It had long been company policy to return as much as possible of the surplus to them, and in 2007 the 40th consecutive increase in dividends was declared. Many of the new shareholders came via ATS, where the flexibility and simplicity of the investment medium was a major attraction.

Late in 2010 the question of share buybacks arose yet again when Laxey Partners, an Isle of Man-registered, but London-based, hedge fund wrote to the Alliance Board and announced that it would try to press Alliance into introducing an automatic discount control mechanism. Laxey held about 1.4% of Alliance Shares and its interests were avowedly short term, in contrast to those of the Alliance board and many, if not most, of the shareholders. The stage was set for a battle which, given Laxey's past record, would be fought out in the media, and the financial journalists sharpened their pencils. The board letter was followed up, in January 2011, with a letter to all Alliance shareholders. The initial letter had been rejected and Laxey now demanded that certain resolutions be put to the forthcoming AGM. Laxey were only able to do this by splitting up their holding across over 100 different shell companies set up for the purpose – a tactic they had used against British Land in a previous campaign almost a decade earlier.

Laxey raised two concerns. The first and more substantive was with the share price discount to net asset value (NAV) which, in the Alliance case, was then about 16%, compared with an industry average of less than 8%. Laxey wanted Alliance to adopt a 'hard' discount control mechanism, where the company would be compelled to buy back its own shares whenever the discount was wider than 10%. Laxey pointed out that some other investment trusts already operated similar mechanisms. Alliance had in recent years overcome a longstanding distrust of share buybacks and had made use of the power, first granted by shareholders in 2006, on a number of occasions since 2009. However the board believed the mechanistic approach, now proposed by Laxey, would hinder its ability to make these decisions on investment grounds.

Laxey was also concerned about the manner in which holders of Alliance shares in ATS exercised their votes at the AGM. They claimed that the manner in which this was done gave a large block vote to the directors, even in cases where the ATS members had not indicated their intentions. In fact, Alliance explained, the directors' holdings only represented a small proportion of those ATS members who gave voting instructions. Alliance countered that the arrangement was intended to ensure that the views of individual shareholders, who made up a large proportion of the company's share register but rarely voted, were properly represented and encouraged them to use their votes. In practice, however, the arrangement made no real difference to voting outcomes and the company stated that henceforth only those votes that were actually cast by ATS members would be counted.

The financial press was divided about what to say. First into the fray was *Investment Week*, which came out on the side of the Alliance board and its shareholders. Their journalists took the view that shareholders were looking for 'safety, security and steady returns in terms of the share price and/or dividend pay-outs'. This was contrary to Laxey's claim that 'the share price is the most important element for shareholders'.

It was not long before the battle became somewhat personal, with Colin Kingsnorth, who ran Laxey, claiming in the pages of the *Daily Mail* that Alliance Trust had 'lost its way' and needed to 'modernise'. The very substantial changes in the Alliance Trust business model that had been made since 2004 were quietly ignored as Kingsnorth pursued his objective of getting the Trust to buy back its own shares with a view to reducing the discount – presumably with a view to him selling his shares at a substantial profit once his objective had been achieved. Kingsnorth made no bones about this – the *Daily Mail* wrote that Kingsnorth was 'completely open about the fact that he won't hang around for the long term. Laxey would be happy to sell its stake in the next couple of months "so long as we achieve what we want to achieve."'

Clearly Alliance had a fight on its hands. Its position was somewhat undermined when on 16 February 2011 Citywire speculated that Alliance might drop out of the FTSE 100 index, one effect of which might be to widen the discount. A few days later the *Sunday Herald* revealed that two of the funds under Laxey's management traded at discounts greater than the 16% of Alliance and had not been able to maintain their own discount control mechanisms. The paper took the view that this undermined Kingsnorth's credibility.

The press continued in this vein for some time, but much of what they forecast came to pass. Alliance did drop out of the FTSE 100, notwithstanding that its share price had been growing strongly and outpacing the index. Some 10m shares in Alliance changed hands in one day as FTSE 100 Tracker funds offloaded their holdings. The discount did widen to 18%. This was an opportunity for Alliance to buy back some of its shares. From early February onwards Alliance bought back its own shares on an almost daily basis in what it described as a 'step-change'. On a single day in mid March it bought back 3.2m shares, representing almost 0.5% of its share capital. This gave practical expression to Katherine Garrett-Cox's oft-quoted statement that 'share buybacks are now in our DNA'.

Many of the newspaper articles and comments on various wire services gave the impression that Alliance had never purchased its own shares, but this was not the case. There was certainly a time when the company was hostile to the idea but at the time of the merger with Second Alliance Trust the board had decided to ask shareholders to give them share buyback powers. Subsequently, in 2009 and 2010, Alliance had entered into large one-off buybacks. In the 2010 annual report the chairman, Lesley Knox, made clear that this power would only be used when the board 'judged it to be in the interests of all shareholders'. She went on that this would only be done 'following rigorous consideration of the merits of the transaction from an investment perspective, and taking into account both market conditions and our own investment process . . . this should not be confused with adoption of a discount control mechanism'.

Kingsnorth returned to the battle and criticised Katherine Garrett-Cox for allowing her name to go forward for membership of Deutsche Bank's supervisory board. Alliance's expense ratio also came in for criticism, as did Garrett-Cox's remuneration package. He also claimed credit for Alliance's announcement in mid March that it was exiting from the private equity business that it had entered only a few years earlier, although in fact this was simply a reflection of the company's strategy of focusing on quoted equity investment. On 18 March David Prosser in the *Independent* argued that if 'the discount doesn't start coming down soon, the critics' case becomes compelling'. The balance of opinion seemed to be shifting in favour of Laxey.

There was some support for Alliance from the *Herald* and other newspapers, which quoted Association of Investment Companies' figures and reminded their readers that Alliance Trust was 'among an elite group of investment trusts that have increased their dividends every year for the last four decades'. Correspondence followed that the costs incurred by investment trusts were measurably lower than those of unit trusts. Garrett-Cox's own response to Laxey focused on the needs of long-term shareholders and stressed the importance of dividend increases which, that year, had increased by 3% when the FTSE All Share Index had fallen by 3%.

As time went on there was greater discussion about what Laxey actually wanted. Its primary objective was that a discount control mechanism should be used which would automatically come into operation when the discount rose above 10%. They also wanted changes to voting rights at annual general meetings. They went on to attack Alliance's expense ratio and this drew a stern rebuke from Alliance's chairman, Lesley Knox, who pointed out that Alliance followed industry standards and that its expense ratio was in the lower quartile of equivalent organisations. She was also concerned that Laxey's proposals were only in the interests of short-term holders of shares when most of Alliance's investors held their shares in excess of 15 years.

By late April, Kingsnorth was claiming victory for Laxey but he had reckoned without the intervention of other institutional investors. In the first week of May, Brewin Dolphin, who owned 5% of Alliance shares and were previously rumoured to be supportive of Laxey's campaign, came out in support of the Alliance position.

Laxey stepped up the battle by objecting to Alliance's executive remuneration scheme. But Kingsnorth must have felt that he was on the back foot when newspaper articles started to point out the potential pitfalls of discount control mechanisms. Andy Adams in the *Scotsman* on 17 May pointed out that in extreme markets 'investment trusts with discount control mechanisms could be forced into aggressive buy back activity and, in the process, be forced to sell investments to buy back its own shares'. Such a scenario was clearly not in the best interests of shareholders and was likely to make matters worse.

The annual general meeting was scheduled for 20 May. At the meeting it was announced that Lesley Knox would be standing down as chairman before the next AGM as part of a longstanding board succession plan. More than twice the customary number of shareholders turned up and a two-thirds majority voted down Laxey's proposals.

Interactive Investor described the battle as 'a draw' but the Alliance board was doubtless content that it had not been shackled with a mandatory discount control mechanism. Its policy of buying back its own shares continued. In the 2011 annual report Lesley Knox announced that further buybacks had taken place and that the company intended to maintain its flexible approach. Notwithstanding that several million of the company's shares had been bought and cancelled, the impact on the discount to net asset value was quite modest.

She also announced that the dividend was to be increased for the 44th consecutive year.

Undaunted, Kingsnorth returned the following year. This time he wanted Alliance to allow another fund management company to manage the investments. When this became public knowledge Alliance received a friendly but unwelcome offer from Aberdeen Asset Management to do just that. They were politely rebuffed.

When it came to a vote at the 2012 AGM on 27 April, Karin Forseke's first as chairman, some 79% of the votes cast were in favour of the board's position. Kingsnorth retired from the fray, saying that it was 'extraordinarily unlikely' that he would bring further motions to an AGM.

Throughout this period shareholder engagement was given a high priority. Companies, of whatever kind, must always have their eyes on who their shareholders are and what they want from their investments. Alliance was no different. Through a series of shareholder meetings, and at the AGM, the views of shareholders were listened to and acted upon. In addition, the work of ATS was a highly effective way of bringing new investors into the company. And, despite the activities of hedge funds, Alliance maintained its long-term strategy of steadily increasing its dividend. It did not see itself in the company of investment companies who sought high returns in risky situations. It sought good dividend-paying investments with growth potential, as it always had. As Katherine Garrett-Cox succinctly put it, 'Successful companies keep their eye on the horizon, not just on the bottom line.'

Bibliography

R E Breeden (ed.), *Trails West*, National Geographic Society, Washington, 1979

D Brown, *The American West*, Pocket Books, London, 2004

Richard Burns, *A Century of Investing – Baillie Gifford's First 100 Years*, Birlinn, Edinburgh, 2008

Richard Burns, *A History of Scottish Mortgage*, Privately printed, 2009

D C Corner and H Burton, *Investment and Unit Trusts in Britain and America*, Elek Books, London, 1968

P L Cottrell, *British Overseas Investment in the Nineteenth Century*, Macmillan, London, 1975

W F Crick, *War-Time Financial Control*, Macmillan, London, 1941

L Giffen, *How Scots Financed the Modern World*, Luath Press, Edinburgh, 2009

J C Gilbert, *A History of Investment Trusts in Dundee, 1873–1938*, P S King and Son, London, 1939

R Graham, *Britain and the Onset of Modernization in Brazil, 1850–1914*, Cambridge University Press, 1972

C K Hobson, *The Export of Capital*, London 1963

W Turrentine Jackson, *The Enterprising Scot: Investors in the American West after 1873*, Edinburgh University Press, 1968

W G Kerr, *Scottish Capital on the American Credit Frontier*, Texas State Historical Association, Austin, TX, 1976

D Lasater, *Falfurrias: Ed C.Lasater and the Development of South Texas*, A and M University Press, Texas, 1985

John Leng, *America in 1876 and Aspects of American Life*, Dundee 1877

Neil McKendrick and John Newlands, *F and C: A History of Foreign and Colonial Investment Trust*, Chapin Kavanagh, London, 1999

R C Michie, *Money, Mania and Markets*, John Donald, Edinburgh, 1981

M G Myers, *A Financial History of the United States*, Columbia University Press, 1970

R Napier, *Anatomy of the Bear*, CLSA Books, Hong Kong, 2005

J Newlands, *Put Not Your Trust in Money*, Chapin Kavanagh, London, 1997

J Newlands, *1907–2007, Murray International Trust PLC*, privately printed, 2008

W M Pearce, *The Matador Land and Cattle Company*, University of Oklahoma Press, 1964

E Rauchway, *The Great Depression and the New Deal*, Oxford University Press, 2008

R S Sayers, *Financial Policy 1939–1945*, HMSO

J Scott and M Hughes, *The Anatomy of Scottish Capital*, Croom Helm, London, 1980

Gordon Small, *D.C.Thomson and Co. Ltd: Its Origins and History*, Dundee, 2004

Gordon Small, *The Lengs: Dundee's Other Publishing Dynasty*, Tay Valley Family History Society, Dundee, 2010

B Smith, *Robert Fleming, 1845-1933*, Whittangehame House, Haddington, 2000

G Stewart, *Jute and Empire*, Manchester University Press, 1998

Claire E Swan, *Cowboys and the Dundee Investors*, Abertay Historical Society, Dundee, 2004

C A Whatley, *Onwards from Osnaburgs:Don and Low of Forfar 1792–1992*, Mainstream, Edinburgh, 1992

L J Williams, *Britain and the World Economy 1919–1970*, Fontana, London, 1971

Appendix 1:
The Pre-Alliance Balance Sheets

Oregon and Washington Trust Investment Co Ltd

	Dividend	Capital	Debentures	Interest Income
30.6.1875	6.00%	£25,437.00	£44,151.00	£2,933.00
31.12.1875	7.00%	£25,313.00	£74,360.00	£4,172.00
31.12.1876	9.00%	£25,981.00	£108,656.00	£12,121.00
31.12.1877	10.00%	£45,741.00	£155,766.00	£16,780.00
31.12.1878	10.00%	£50,000.00	£132,000.00	£17,316.00

NB 7% in 1875 is for six months

Oregon and Washington Mortgage Savings Bank Ltd

	Dividend	Capital	Debentures	Interest Income	Deposits
31.12.1877		£6,630.00	£1,783.00	£1,131.00	£10,856.00
31.12.1878	6.00%	£9,793.00	£4,624.00	£1,920.00	£11,799.00
31.12.1879	6.00%	£12,080.00	£14,524.00	£2,606.00	£11,664.00
31.12.1880	8.00%	£12,000.00	£33,271.00	£5,061.00	£16,193.00
31.12.1881	10.00%	£12,000.00	£47,800.00	£6,906.00	£19,232.00

Reserve	Net Revenue	Mortgages	Investments	Interest Paid	Management Expenses
	£1,150.00	£65,280.00	£4,785.00	£1,129.00	£676.00
	£1,828.00	£85,158.00	£9,554.00	£1,536.00	£674.00
£485.00	£5,183.00	£134,907.00	£16,466.00	£4,767.00	£1,436.00
£5,515.00	£7,832.00	£155,766.00	£18,821.00	£6,310.00	£2,664.00
£7,505.00	£6,746.00	£173,313.00	£7,144.00	£6,978.00	£3,668.00

Reserve	Net Revenue	Mortgages	Investments	Interest Paid	Management Expenses
	£481.00	£12,501.00	£681.00	£305.00	£531.00
£150.00	£668.00	£19,403.00	£1,947.00	£875.00	£872.00
£250.00	£1,007.00	£27,260.00	£2,056.00	£870.00	£1,064.00
£500.00	£1,522.00	£50,133.00	£5,348.00	£910.00	£1,767.00
£1,600.00	£2,518.00	£41,740.00	£4,319.00	£556.00	£1,410.00

Appendix 1: *continued*

Dundee Mortgage and Trust Investment Company Ltd

	Dividend	Capital	Debentures	Interest Income
31.5.1877	6.00%	£37,425.00	£140,261.00	£8,936.00
31.5.1878	9.00%	£49,952.00	£239,821.00	£22,109.00
31.5.1879	10.00%	£70,000.00	£285,341.00	£27,647.00
31.1.1880	7.00%	£118,000.00	£490,000.00	£44,474.00
31 1.1881	10.00%	£226,387.00	£510,724.00	£64,326.00
31.1.1882	10.00%	£288,000.00	£504,680.00	£68,637.00
31.1.1883	10.00%	£300,000.00	£527,356.00	£81,426.00
31.1.1884	10.00%	£300,000.00	£559,513.00	£68,924.00
31.1.1885	10.00%	£300,000.00	£556,527.00	£71,243.00
31.1.1886	10.00%	£300,000.00	£559,233.00	£68,300.00
31.1.1887	10.00%	£300,000.00	£560,000.00	£72,770.00
31.1.1888	10.00%	£340,000.00	£519,485.00	£72,515.00
31.1.1889	10.00%	£340,000.00	£535,126.00	£68,341.00

Dundee Land Investment Company Ltd

	Dividend	Capital	Debentures	Interest Income	Deposits
29.11.1879		£15,000.00		£299.00	£14,143.00
30.11.1880	5.00%	£29,720.00	£22,870.00	£1,558.00	£12,622.00
30.11.1881	10.00%	£40,100.00	£75,280.00	£2,794.00	£14,828.00

Reserve	Net Revenue	Mortgages	Investments	Interest Paid	Management Expenses
£1,875.00	£2,746.00	£177,711.00	£33,387.00	£4,305.00	£1,364.00
£2,500.00	£9,897.00	£269,219.00	£12,729.00	£9,987.00	£1,711.00
£15,000.00	£12,953.00	£318,187.00	£25,126.00	£13,015.00	£2,772.00
£35,000.00	£19,813.00	£587,980.00	£53,899.00	£18,352.00	£5,876.00
£50,000.00	£32,564.00	£691,852.00	£40,582.00	£25,509.00	£7,877.00
£66,000.00	£38,503.00	£727,861.00	£95,335.00	£27,379.00	£9,695.00
£80,000.00	£40,613.00	£669,170.00	£133,316.00	£29,269.00	£9,086.00
£87,500.00	£36,939.00	£699,683.00	£193,925.00	£25,994.00	£8,517.00
£87,500.00	£36,156.00	£686,276.00	£193,370.00	£25,637.00	£10,048.00
£97,500.00	£40,990.00	£719,300.00	£180,053.00	£25,345.00	£10,618.00
£108,000.00	£35,881.00	£740,298.00	£125,169.00	£25,050.00	£10,906.00
£115,000.00	£38,351.00	£783,571.00	£111,888.00	£23,643.00	£10,967.00
£125,000.00	£41,349.00	£829,497.00	£121,028.00	£22,297.00	£4,387.00

Reserve	Net Revenue	Mortgages	Investments	Interest Paid	Management Expenses
	£78.00	£24,837.00	£3,906.00		£224.00
	£1,736.00	£50,719.00		£448.00	£259.00
	£4,304.00	£101,577.00	£11,575.00	£2,908.00	£798.00

Appendix 1: *continued*

Dundee Investment Company Ltd

	Dividend	Capital	Debentures	Interest Income
31.12.1882	6.50%	£62,500.00	124,447.00	2,280.00
31.12.1883	0.00%	75,000.00	174,223.00	8,033.00
31.12.1884	0.00%	75,000.00	174,457.00	10,546.00
31.12.1885	5.00%	75,000.00	174,973.00	11,506.00
31.12.1886	5.00%	75,000.00	174,800.00	14,042.00
31.12.1887	5.00%	75,000.00	175,000.00	13,588.00
31.12.1888	5.00%	75,000.00	175,000.00	14,788.00

Reserve	Net Revenue	Mortgages	Investments	Interest Paid	Management Expenses
	7,354.00	40,745.00	99,283.00	6,265.00	1,882.00
2,500.00	6,058.00	69,332.00	86,920.00	7,600.00	1,331.00
5,000.00	5,358.00	81,220.00	85,157.00	8,084.00	1,116.00
8,000.00	5,964.00	114,949.00	85,601.00	8,365.00	847.00
10,000.00	13,835.00	150,010.00	66,781.00	8,344.00	1,053.00
19,500.00	6,309.00	168,550.00	68,557.00	8,357.00	953.00
21,500.00	7,295.00	163,570.00	68,781.00	7,898.00	812.00

Appendix 2:
Alliance Trust Balance Sheets

	Dividend	Capital Paid	Debentures	Reserve	Reserve Investment	Interest Income
1893	12.50%	£525,000	£599,312	£195,000	£193,545	£76,809
1894	12.50%	£595,000	£539,602	£195,000	£191,707	£69,744
1895	12.50%	£711,778	£503,896	£200,000	£200,138	£63,241
1896	8.00%	£775,000	£511,740	£200,000	£200,486	£67,207
1897	8.00%	£775,000	£529,915	£200,000	£201,721	£69,628
1898	8.00%	£775,000	£523,955	£200,000	£201,462	£67,916
1899	8.00%	£775,000	£529,095	£200,000	£201,026	£68,435
1900	8.00%	£775,000	£517,820	£200,000	£201,598	£71,650
1901	8.00%	£825,000	£539,900	£203,125	£200,871	£75,025
1902	8.00%	£825,000	£546,390	£215,000	£203,176	£81,097
1903	8.00%	£825,000	£581,335	£235,000	£214,956	£84,451
1904	8.00%	£907,590	£616,725	£280,000	£236,204	£92,691
1905	8.00%	£959,712	£595,865	£345,000	£300,581	£102,769
1906	10.00%	£1,000,000	£651,560	£370,000	£345,130	£112,304
1907	10.50%	£1,047,088	£661,447	£400,000	£369,915	£122,518
1908	12.00%	£1,118,512	£677,005	£425,000	Inc in Inv	£126,440
1909	12.00%	£1,176,280	£881,365	£450,000		£140,100
1910	13.00%	£1,200,000	£950,425	£500,000		£154,768
1911	13.00%	£1,200,000	£1,180,905	£535,000		£163,204
1912	15.00%	£1,200,000	£1,352,320	£575,000		£186,074
1913	17.00%	£1,350,000	£1,680,457	£685,000		£209,936
1914	18.00%	£1,440,771	£1,797,219	£780,000		£236,924
1915	19.00%	£1,500,000	£2,205,765	£800,000		£256,020
1916	19.00%	£1,500,000	£2,271,636	£800,000		£276,964
1917	19.00%	£1,500,000	£2,074,601	£800,000		£278,258
1918	19.00%	£1,500,000	£1,927,368	£800,000		£270,948
1919	19.00%	£1,500,000	£2,146,389	£800,000		£276,768

Net Revenue	Mortgages	Investments	Investment Valuation	Property	Interest Paid	Management Expenses
£47,427	£975,036	£194,483		£117,169	£25,112	£5,227
£42,924	£941,775	£71,319		£130,484	£22,667	£4,953
£35,539	Inc in Inv	£1,186,240		Inc in Inv	£20,827	£5,458
£40,061		£1,255,475			£19,988	£5,603
£42,101		£1,268,332			£19,577	£6,091
£43,153	£1,082,979	£179,434		Inc in Mort	£18,409	£6,214
£45,024	£1,016,538	£244,856			£17,994	£5,746
£49,539	£993,562	£275,785			£18,616	£6,287
£56,055	£923,526	£410,009			£19,289	£6,075
£66,897	£918,475	£439,801			£19,289	£6,492
£65,959	£942,855	£458,231			£19,948	£7,180
£75,454	£1,011,280	£526,469			£21,501	£6,411
£81,381	£1,063,687	£508,522			£22,047	£6,411
£82,188	£1,152,959	£490,455			£22,207	£6,846
£89,661	£1,219,559	£463,616			£23,131	£7,315
£92,925	£1,293,969	£917,716			£22,876	£7,199
£96,905	£1,394,403	£1,113,775			£30,072	£8,232
£107,002	Inc in Inv	£2,608,976			£36,181	£8,024
£110,130		£2,831,507			£39,855	£7,502
£121,705		£3,098,920			£49,763	£7,888
£129,919		£3,704,556			£59,203	£10,537
£146,321		£4,042,330			£73,050	£12,752
£153,662		£4,433,699			£80,458	£11,968
£155,984		£4,631,472			£90,646	£10,774
£144,869		£4,242,651			£69,527	£11,453
£126,718		£4,279,376			£66,105	£11,330
£117,484		£4,458,338			£70,555	£11,230

Appendix 2: *continued*

	Dividend	Capital Paid	Debentures	Reserve	Reserve Investment	Interest Income
1920	19.00%	£1,500,000	£2,277,635	£825,000		£297,668
1921	20.00%	£1,500,000	£2,140,072	£862,500		£309,404
1922	21.00%	£1,700,000	£2,567,345	£1,000,000		£334,107
1923	21.00%	£1,700,000	£2,717,175	£1,040,000		£355,006
1924	22.00%	£1,800,000	£2,776,095	£1,171,250		£387,145
1925	23.00%	£1,951,504	£2,872,020	£1,440,000		£416,753
1926	24.00%	£2,000,000	£3,151,738	£1,440,000		£454,326
1927	25.00%	£2,250,000	£3,513,535	£1,765,000		£487,553
1928	25.00%	£2,572,500	£4,127,305	£2,000,000		£563,026
1929	25.00%	£2,572,500	£4,236,495	£2,000,000		£618,143
1930	25.00%	£3,000,000	£4,518,705	£2,200,000		£675,934
1931	25.00%	£3,100,000	£5,168,760	£2,100,000		£692,152
1932	25.00%	£3,150,000	£5,316,740	£2,100,000		n/a
1933	25.00%	£3,150,000	£5,563,075	£2,100,000		£631,656
1934	25.00%	£3,250,000	£5,638,820	£2,100,000		£638,115
1935	22.00%	£3,250,000	£5,450,055	£2,100,000		£596,631
1936	22.00%	£3,250,000	£5,417,840	£2,100,000		£603,314
1937	23.00%	£3,250,000	£5,533,030	£2,100,000		n/a
1938	25.00%	£3,250,000	£5,769,665	£2,100,000		£706,856
1939	25.00%	£3,250,000	£5,880,975	£2,100,000		£676,343
1940	25.00%	£3,250,000	£5,777,245	£2,100,000		£668,168
1941	25.00%	£3,250,000	£5,693,230	£2,100,000		£648,397
1942	25.00%	£3,250,000	£5,624,875	£2,100,000		£649,495
1943	25.00%	£3,250,000	£5,552,704	£2,100,000		£641,559
1944	25.00%	£3,250,000	£5,467,525	£2,100,000		£667,832
1945	25.00%	£3,250,000	£5,449,950	£2,100,000		£699,620
1946	26.00%	£3,250,000	£5,489,865	£2,100,000		£716,660
1947	28.00%	£3,250,000	£5,442,940	£2,100,000		£795,239
1948	30.00%	£3,250,000	£5,565,455	£2,100,000		£880,174
1949	30.00%	£3,250,000	£5,634,905	£2,145,000		£870,689
1950	33.00%	£3,250,000	£5,799,485	£2,295,000		£895,482
1951	40.00%	£3,250,000	£5,701,565	£2,445,000		£988,314
1952	50.00%	£3,250,000	£5,421,740	£2,645,000		£1,116,595
1953	27.50%	£4,300,000	£5,516,660	£1,745,000		£1,179,662

Net Revenue	Mortgages	Investments	Investment Valuation	Property	Interest Paid	Management Expenses
£142,744		£4,617,191			£81,462	£12,758
£158,305		£4,535,262			£80,871	£14,140
£161,905		£5,356,994			£86,979	£15,816
£188,017		£5,564,135			£96,502	£15,585
£209,663		£6,049,529			£104,291	£18,711
£241,129		£6,575,191			£110,869	£19,298
£256,945		£6,851,965			£129,934	£21,399
£286,938		£7,968,519			£134,837	£21,021
£281,024		£8,632,182			£156,356	
£359,373		£9,323,521			£168,009	£23,609
£404,733		£10,054,094			£166,962	£24,810
£410,755		£10,840,045			£178,787	£27,802
£356,942		£10,917,097			£187,595	
£383,168		£11,324,427			£189,258	£27,963
£410,731		£11,282,441			£183,860	£26,988
£353,000		£11,101,832			£175,778	£28,759
£351,247		£11,033,330			£165,271	£26,404
£363,341		£11,343,727			£160,214	
£424,372		£11,623,419			£158,055	£28,862
£404,436		£11,657,905			£156,902	£26,938
£387,326		£11,455,860			£140,560	£28,369
£353,848		£11,398,996			£122,679	£28,959
£322,736		£11,353,345			£106,811	£29,180
£313,872		£11,231,756			£106,108	£29,928
£321,641		£11,196,040			£105,959	£30,255
£319,425		£11,165,182			£104,352	£30,435
£332,929		£11,069,615			£103,996	£30,243
£369,844		£11,356,660			£115,197	£33,893
£346,134		£11,869,181			£210,342	£35,587
£339,944		£11,701,553			£207,537	£38,322
£365,142		£11,916,995			£193,566	£43,901
£435,846		£11,826,741			£203,683	£41,991
£518,773		£11,704,161			£203,188	£44,473
£490,147		£12,040,977			£212,756	£49,880

Appendix 2: *continued*

	Dividend	Capital Paid	Debentures	Reserve	Reserve Investment	Interest Income
1954	31.00%	£4,300,000	£5,532,805	£1,845,000		£1,254,956
1955	37.50%	£4,300,000	£5,684,720	£1,995,000		£1,377,500
1956	45.00%	£4,300,000	£5,660,190	£2,195,000		£1,585,990
1957	50.00%	£4,300,000	£5,648,330	£2,395,000		£1,672,977
1958	25.00%	£6,400,000	£5,904,535	£500,000		£1,764,993
1959	28.00%	£6,400,000	£5,844,140	£700,000		£1,799,743
1960	34.00%	£6,400,000	£6,391,900	£11,000,000		£2,032,544
1961	37.50%	£6,400,000	£8,635,560	£11,250,000		£2,324,651
1962	37.50%	£6,400,000	£8,561,355	£11,500,000		£2,855,226
1963	14.00%	£14,800,000	£8,945,300	£3,350,000		£3,005,029
1964	15.00%	£14,800,000	£9,899,705	£3,949,387		£3,281,326
1965	17.50%	£14,800,000	£10,184,180	£4,286,938		£3,635,772
1966	19.00%	£14,800,000	£9,366,855	£4,786,944		£4,154,309
1967	21.00%	£14,800,000	£8,214,310	£5,269,985		£4,065,149
1968	20.00%	£14,800,000	£8,002,060	£5,639,218		
1969	21.00%	£14,800,000	£7,931,340	£5,909,431		£3,773,624
1970	22.00%	£14,800,000	£7,823,600	£6,184,929		£4,169,649
1971	22.50%	£14,800,000	£7,823,600	£6,422,377		£4,536,113
1972	24.00%	£14,800,000	£7,823,600	£6,691,412		£4,568,258
1973	25.20%	£14,800,000	£7,823,600	£6,626,996		£4,242,803
1974	27.36%	£14,800,000	£7,823,600	£6,917,053		£4,833,053
1975	21.00%	£14,800,000	£7,823,600	£7,179,283		£5,633,418
1976	21.40%	£14,800,000	£7,823,600	£7,286,293		£5,489,158
1977	25.40%	£14,800,000	£7,323,600	£7,441,210		£6,458,745
1978	28.40%	£14,800,000	£7,323,600	£7,705,716		£6,871,549

Net Revenue	Mortgages	Investments	Investment Valuation	Property	Interest Paid	Management Expenses
£562,302		£12,303,872			£221,204	£54,639
£648,535		£12,493,750			£226,512	£56,132
£796,585		£12,326,585			£237,931	£58,136
£830,142		£12,716,594			£254,047	£62,429
£876,183		£12,525,102			£265,642	£76,060
£961,424		£13,119,336			£280,312	£79,306
£1,217,113		£26,069,158			£268,988	£79,695
£1,280,941		£26,426,314			£438,131	£85,647
£1,341,906		£26,759,539			£432,951	£92,284
£1,424,646		£29,078,822			£427,336	£93,327
£1,544,957		£28,669,885			£498,149	£94,457
£1,713,389		£28,254,683			£507,343	£95,909
£2,111,665		£29,135,957			£500,807	£105,145
£3,214,255		£30,471,664			£469,603	£105,290
		£30,532,902			£451,221	£102,574
£3,198,445		£31,602,600			£457,983	£117,196
£3,599,235		£31,254,315	£110,886,125		£449,060	£121,354
£3,972,286		£30,922,900	£107,085,210		£426,503	£137,324
£4,017,785		£32,227,452	£139,954,152		£413,693	£136,780
£3,668,634		£32,106,015	£140,395,797		£430,079	£144,090
£2,714,526		£32,866,478	£112,804,345		£474,094	£153,886
£2,976,315		£35,628,774	£98,534,523		£457,799	£192,553
£2,871,475		£32,402,455	£137,754,614		£425,378	£220,108
£3,423,392		£33,196,769	£130,669,259		£390,905	£229,349
£3,910,974		£32,130,270	£142,612,991		£378,342	£252,427

Appendix 2: *continued*

Figures in £000s

	Dividend	Capital Paid	Debentures	Capital Reserve
1979	32.00%	£14,800	£7,323	£68,579
1980	40.00%	£14,800	£7,323	£75,008
1981	42.00%	£14,800	£7,323	£88,312
1982	45.00%	£14,800	£7,323	£106,553
1983	49.20%	£14,800	£7,323	£129,626
1984	54.00%	£14,800	£7,323	£158,236
1985	69.00%	£14,800	£1,648	£191,614
1986	83.00%	£14,800	£1,648	£234,664
1987	100.00%	£14,800	£1,648	£295,375
1988	110.00%	£14,800	£1,648	£325,808
1989	115.50%	£14,800	£1,648	£346,819
1990	140.00%	£14,800	£1,648	£386,114
1991	160.00%	£14,800	£1,648	£411,956
1992	172.00%	£14,800	£1,648	£443,018
1993	180.00%	£14,800	£1,648	£475,818
1994	188.00%	£14,800	£1,648	£516,038
1995	200.00%	£14,800	£1,648	£552,791
1996	53.00	£14,800		£583,607
1997	55.50	£14,800		£605,313
1998	59.00	£14,800		£747,215
1999	62.50	£14,800		£748,440
2000	64.50	£14,800		£848,050
2001	66.50	£14,800		£996,395
2002	68.50	£14,800		£1,017,555
2003	69.50	£14,800		£995,784 £
2004	70.50	£14,800		£995,296
2005	71.75	£14,800		£1,066,922
2006	73.50	£12,600		£1,952,056
2007	7.575	£16,798		£2,096,078

Unrealised Appreciation on Investments	Revenue Reserve	Investments at market value	Total Revenue	Interest Paid	Management Expenses
£60,463	£6,247	£161,746	£7,676	£373	£256
£46,946	£6,413	£154,892	£9,148	£465	£301
£57,455	£6,786	£178,030	£10,043	£636	£399
£75,739	£6,975	£200,762	£10,450	£489	£403
£132,867	£7,177	£269,922	£11,732	£587	£459
£167,315	£7,294	£337,521	£13,016	£471	£700
£228,972	£7,496	£413,663	£15,547	£543	£591
£199,242	£7,577	£414,463	£17,532	£425	£629
£256,565	£7,975	£537,125	£20,457	£245	£782
£167,817	£8,153	£471,172	£21,703	£94	£986
£221,782	£8,288	£576,726	£23,658	£80	£936
£282,255	£8,660	£687,868	£26,659	£102	£1,088
£191,154	£8,992	£598,317	£30,275	£81	£1,211
£310,884	£9,244	£755,539	£32,080	£89	£1,347
£398,745	£9,595	£862,787	£33,444	£78	£1,391
£536,718	£9,737	£1,042,252	£34,173	£77	£1,616
£370,409	£10,128	£898,303	£35,543	£76	£1,602
£612,690	£29,327	£1,194,560	£43,314	£92	£2,797
£720,624	£31,519	£1,310,324	£44,405	£88	£3,060
£944,231	£21,991	£1,650,957	£48,121		£3,653
£928,336	£36,661	£1,650,660	£48,607		£4,182
£984,615	£38,861	£1,863,560	£46,684		£4,974
£932,272	£39,459	£1,949,332	£45,754		£5,420
£597,550	£42,414	£1,614,994	£49,917		£6,142
150,597	£43,080	£1,155,412	£48,326		£6,381
£418,838	£445,689	£1,446,843	£51,050		£7,297
£493,481	£48,091	£1,592,236	£54,952		£9,669
	£66,361	£2,004,743	£61,478		£13,947
	£73,454	£2,538,385	£81,032		£25,180

Appendix 2: *continued*

	Dividend	Capital Paid	Debentures	Capital Reserve
2008	7.900	£16,798		£1,966,300
2009	8.000	£16,798		£1,378,674
2010	8.150	£16,527		£2,131,651
2011	8.395	£16,527		£2,158,630

from 1996 = pence per share

Unrealised Appreciation on Investments	Revenue Reserve	Investments at market value	Total Revenue	Interest Paid	Management Expenses
	£73,550	£2,729,397	£102,199		£38,114
	£78,806	£1,820,763	£117,283		£40,069
	£98,520	£3,172,639	£93,652		£36,819
	£71,541	£3,237,614	£101,943		£38,138

Index